John F. Kennedy and the Second Reconstruction

Contemporary American History Series

Contemporary American History Series
WILLIAM E. LEUCHTENBURG, GENERAL EDITOR

Lawrence S. Wittner, *Rebels against War: The American Peace Movement, 1941–1960,* 1969.

Davis R. B. Ross, *Preparing for Ulysses: Politics and Veterans during World War II,* 1969.

John Lewis Gaddis, *The United States and the Origins of the Cold War, 1941–1947,* 1972.

George C. Herring, Jr., *Aid to Russia, 1941–1946: Strategy, Diplomacy, the Origins of the Cold War,* 1973.

Alonzo L. Hamby, *Beyond the New Deal: Harry S. Truman and American Liberalism,* 1973.

Richard M. Fried, *Men against McCarthy,* 1976.

Steven F. Lawson, *Black Ballots: Voting Rights in the South, 1944–1969,* 1976.

Carl M. Brauer, *John F. Kennedy and the Second Reconstruction,* 1977.

Maeva Marcus, *Truman and the Steel Seizure Case: The Limits of Presidential Power,* 1977.

Morton Sosna, *In Search of the Silent South: Southern Liberals and the Race Issue,* 1977.

John F. Kennedy and the Second Reconstruction

Carl M. Brauer

New York

Columbia University Press

Carl M. Brauer is assistant professor in the
Corcoran Department of History,
University of Virginia

The Andrew W. Mellon Foundation,
through a special grant, has assisted the Press
in publishing this volume

Columbia University Press · New York · Guildford, Surrey
Copyright © 1977 by Columbia University Press
All Rights Reserved
Printed in the United States of America

LIBRARY OF CONGRESS CATALOGING IN PUBLICATION DATA
Brauer, Carl M. 1946–
John F. Kennedy and the second reconstruction.
(Contemporary American history series)
Bibliography: p.
Includes index.
1. Afro-Americans—Civil rights.
2. United States—Politics and government—1961–1963.
3. Kennedy, John Fitzgerald, Pres. U.S., 1917–1963.
I. Title.
E185.61.B7917   973.922   76–57686
ISBN 0-231-03862-3 (cloth)
ISBN 0-231-08367-x (paperback)
10 9 8 7 6 5 4 3 2

TO MY PARENTS

Preface

THE title of this book bears an ironic connotation. Writing as an amateur historian in 1956, John F. Kennedy denigrated Northern Radical Republicans of the 1860s for imposing Reconstruction on the defeated Southern states. Kennedy viewed that first effort to remake the South as harsh, punitive, and tragic. Yet twenty years later a somewhat more professional historian can identify Kennedy, a Northern liberal Democrat, as the key political figure in the development of a Second Reconstruction.

The two epochs differ from one another markedly. A century of industrialization and intellectual change has eliminated the possibility of any neat historical duplication. Moreover, the first Reconstruction followed a bloody civil war, fought between two dissimilar, antagonistic sections of the country. In the 1960s militant rebel yells again reverberated across the South, but none of its political or business leaders remotely desired a return to armed hostilities. Defiance of federal authority might occasionally serve expedient political interests or respond to enticing myths, but that defiance would have to remain symbolic. Likewise, few neoabolitionists of the civil rights movement and fewer still of their sympathizers in Congress clamored for a renewed military occupation of the South. Indeed, the eschewal of large-scale physical force by the nation's leaders, South and North, delineated one of the most consequential differences from the earlier period.

The two Reconstructions diverged in other important ways as well. For example, in the 1860s the Radical Republicans actively sought to prevent the return of the Democratic Party or the Southern ruling elite to their antebellum positions of power. Through most of the 1960s, by contrast, the Democratic Party controlled both the Congress and the Presidency. Some Northern Democrats did hope to alter the social basis of their Southern party, but that motive played a minor role. In addition, whereas the principal proponents of the far-reaching first Reconstruction were white Northerners, the vanguard of the Second Reconstruction consisted largely of Southern blacks.

In one fundamental way, however, the two Reconstructions converged: Both sought to guarantee black Americans their rights as citizens and as people. More precisely, both involved ambitious efforts by the federal government to remove racial barriers and create equal opportunities for all in the political and economic life of the nation. Although neither achieved that difficult goal, the later attempt approached it in several respects and may ultimately be regarded as a qualified success.

The first Reconstruction ended in failure, but very slowly and almost imperceptibly the fortunes of black people improved in the twentieth century. To a considerable degree the improvement derived from industrialization, which attracted Negroes to better economic opportunities in the nation's cities than they had in the impoverished and oppressive Southern countryside. Also contributing to progress were the franchise, a damaged legacy of Reconstruction which permitted some Negroes, mainly in the North, to participate in the political process; the growth of black institutions and organizations; the undermining of the intellectual bases of racism; the model of anticolonial movements of colored people around the world; the gradual rediscovery of citizenship rights by the nation's courts. Moreover, as in the mid-nineteenth century, blacks continued to receive the material and philosophical support of relatively small numbers of sympathetic whites who, though sometimes patronizing, provided valuable assistance. Hence, by the early 1960s blacks had achieved just enough progress to place in sight the possibility of actually achieving equality with their white fellow citizens.

The awareness of that possibility coincided with the coming to the Presidency of John F. Kennedy, a man who held an expansive view of the office and who stirred the nation's idealism. Indeed, in the course of winning America's highest political office, he contributed to the raising of Negro expectations. After becoming President, he initiated a far-reaching program of executive action to combat discrimination. One aspect of this, the Southern law enforcement effort by the Justice Department, under the direction of his brother Robert, marked an especially significant departure from the usual indifference of the past. Later, when social protest erupted in the spring of 1963, President Kennedy launched a drive for what was eventually to become the nation's most comprehensive piece of civil rights legislation. Taken together, the various initiatives of the Kennedy administration constituted the critical first stage of a Second Reconstruction.

This book describes and evaluates Kennedy's role in promoting this modern attempt to remove racial barriers to equal opportunity in American life. It analyzes Kennedy's motives and assesses his accomplishments and shortcomings. Although I focus on just one, albeit very important, aspect of his life, I hope to show my readers the kind of politician and President John F. Kennedy was. I hope also to shed new light on the roles of Robert F. Kennedy and Martin Luther King, Jr., the history of the civil rights movement and the South, the workings of the American political system, and the life of this country in a time of significant stress and change.

The research for this book began in January 1971, at the Kennedy Library, temporarily located in Waltham, Massachusetts, which has gradually been making its holdings available to the public. As each new group of papers opened there, I hastened to sift through them. Each time I discovered valuable new information, but rewarded the Library's staff only with imprecations to open the next set of papers. At last, I am reasonably satisfied that I have seen the preponderance of material relevant to my subject in its possession, including John Kennedy's personal, pre-Presidential, and White House files, the papers of key members of his administration— among them, Theodore Sorensen, Lee White, Burke Marshall, and Harris Wofford—as well as a significant part of Robert Kennedy's papers as campaign manager and Attorney General.

As time went by, however, I realized that though the papers of the administration would be central to my work, they would by no means provide a total picture. Therefore, I have traveled widely, examining as many other collections of relevant papers as I was permitted to see, including the following: Southern Regional Council, Voter Education Project, Southern Christian Leadership Conference, Charles Sherrod (Atlanta); Congress of Racial Equality, Americans for Democratic Action, Slater King (Madison, Wisconsin); National Association for the Advancement of Colored People, Stern Family Fund (New York City); Martin Luther King, Jr., John McCormack (Boston); Lyndon Johnson, George Reedy (Austin); Harry Byrd, Howard W. Smith, James J. Kilpatrick, Virginius Dabney, G. Fred Switzer, Francis Pickens Miller (Charlottesville, Virginia); Chester Bowles (New Haven, Connecticut); Emanuel Celler (Washington, D.C.); Paul Douglas (Chicago); Charles A. Halleck (Bloomington, Indiana); Thomas B. Curtis (Columbia, Missouri). I have also profited a great deal from oral histories, especially those conducted by the Kennedy Library, as well as from my own interviewing. In addition, I have made extensive use of printed sources including newspapers (national, Southern, and black) and periodicals, of memoirs, reportage, and polemics, of scholarly writings, and of government documents.

It is a pleasure to acknowledge the assistance given to me by numerous individuals and institutions. Frank Freidel first suggested that I explore the research possibilities at the newly opened Kennedy Library, then directed my doctoral dissertation out of which this book has grown. William E. Leuchtenburg provided extensive, highly perceptive editorial comments, teaching me many things about writing history. Nancy J. Schieffelin, my wife, and William W. Abbot and Joseph F. Kett, my colleagues, each read the manuscript painstakingly and made extremely valuable stylistic and substantive suggestions. Over the years a number of friends read my work in progress; Lewis Erenberg, Robert Fishman, Larry Hackman, Nell Painter, Edward Purcell, Barry Salkin and Daniel Yergin have all given me valued criticisms. August Meier and Allen Matusow supplied helpful research leads. Numerous participants in this history generously shared their experiences with me and in several cases opened their files to me. The Mark DeWolfe Howe Fund at Harvard, the University of Missouri Research Council, the Lyndon Baines Johnson Foundation, and the University of Virginia helped defray the costs of research, travel, and typing. Leslie Bialler and Bernard Gronert of Columbia University Press gave excellent editorial assistance and Barbara McCauley did a first-rate job of typing. In the many libraries, archives, and offices where I have done research, employees regularly went out of their way to help me. I owe a special debt to the staff members of the Kennedy Library who have worked faithfully under often trying circumstances. To all of the above, I give my heartfelt thanks.

CARL M. BRAUER
Charlottesville, Virginia
March 1977

Contents

John F. Kennedy and the
Second Reconstruction

ONE

A Moderate in
a Moderate Time

Relatively little in the national experience or in Senator John F. Kennedy's career in the 1950s foretold the imminence of the Second Reconstruction or his central role in it. The Supreme Court decreed school segregation unconstitutional, but the white South typically responded with resistance rather than compliance. President Dwight D. Eisenhower withheld his potentially significant leadership from the whole area of race relations, though in one dramatic instance he demonstrated the superiority of federal law to state defiance. An inspiring young black leader emerged in Montgomery, Alabama, while the largest racial organization struggled for survival in the South. Predominant in Congress, the Democratic Party embraced sharply conflicting views which, failing to be reconciled, produced rhetoric favorable to civil rights, but rhetoric unaccompanied by action. Moreover, the Democratic Party's stance epitomized the national experience. And the careers of few Northern politicians more accurately reflected that experience than that of Kennedy of Massachusetts.

THE Supreme Court in 1954 took a bold step by ruling that the practice of "separate but equal" in public education violated the Constitution, but the *Brown* decision remained essentially a statement of principle rather than a mandate for desegregation. Border states, the District of Columbia, and scattered Southern cities carried out the Court's intent, yet across the Old Confederacy many whites, deeply hostile to racial mixing, actively resisted school desegregation. Southern white opposition assumed many forms. Citizens' Councils, sometimes called White Citizens' Councils, became potent lobbying groups in many Southern states. In some localities, political life virtually required Council membership. State legislatures, meanwhile, explored various means for circumventing the federal ruling, and one state, Virginia, under Senator Harry Byrd, Sr.'s guidance, brought them all together under the rubric "massive resistance." Virginia went so far as to prefer closing its schools to desegregating them. Outrage at the Court's decision reached into Congress where nineteen Senators and eighty-two House members signed the "Southern Manifesto" in March 1956. They decried the Court's decision while pledging to use all lawful means to reverse it "and to prevent the use of force in its implementation." Two out of the three North Carolina Representatives who refused to sign it were quickly defeated at the polls.[1]

In one of the only salutary reactions to the Court's decision, some Southern states hurriedly upgraded Negro educational facilities. By spending money on Negro education they hoped to mollify their states' black residents. For example, Governor Luther Hodges of North Carolina appealed to the Negroes of his state to be satisfied with their new facilities and not be stampeded into "refusal to go along" by "any militant and selfish organization," a reference to the National Association for the Advancement of Colored People (NAACP).[2]

Resistance to school desegregation did not stop with resolutions, legislative enactments, and electoral politics. Several times it successfully employed violence. In February 1956, Autherine Lucy, a young black woman, entered the University of Alabama under a court order. When rioting broke out, state authorities did not quell it, and university officials suspended Lucy for her own protection. When she criticized the officials for doing so, they expelled her and the federal judge who sat on the case upheld her expulsion. Six months after this violent incident, Governor Allan Shivers of Texas used it to rationalize the deployment of state police to prevent the court-ordered integration of Mansfield High School. He instructed the Texas Rangers to arrest anyone who represented a threat to peace, meaning the Negro students attempting to comply with the federal court order. The tactic worked. Mansfield's Negroes relented and the federal judge did not press the issue.[3]

The Eisenhower administration, meanwhile, did little to discourage resistance to desegregation. In fact the Justice Department even declined the request of University of Alabama officials for assistance, and after the Mansfield incident the President declared that it was a local problem.[4] Eisenhower's policy followed electoral logic, as few Negroes but growing numbers of Southern whites voted Republican, and was also in accord with a conservative philosophy which looked favorably upon states' rights and askance at social engineering. After leaving office, Eisenhower wrote that he had personally agreed with the Court on desegregation but felt that it was improper for a President to state his opinion on a court ruling. One of the President's aides, however, recalled a contrary explanation for his silence. Eisenhower had told him that the *Brown* decision *"set back* progress in the South" and that it was wrong "to demand *perfection* in these moral questions." In either case, Eisenhower manifested little interest in the problems of Negroes. On one of the rare occasions when he agreed to meet with a black delegation, he counselled them to have patience.[5]

Ironically, in September 1957, six months after Eisenhower had told a press conference that he could not imagine ever using troops to enforce a court order, he found himself doing exactly that in Little Rock, Arkansas. The key individual in bringing this about was Federal Judge Roland N. Davies, a native of North Dakota, who was temporarily sitting in Little Rock. Unlike the Southern judges in the Lucy and Mansfield cases, Davies would not allow his decisions to be rendered meaningless by mob rule or political interference. Governor Orval Faubus, directly interfering with the local school board which was prepared to desegregate, attempted to thwart Davies's order by stationing National Guard troops around the affected high school, much as Shivers had used state police not long before. Undoubtedly, Faubus's confidence in this ploy was bolstered by Justice Department assurances that the government was not a party to the litigation and that disturbances in the city did not warrant federal intervention. The Justice Department also privately pressed the plaintiffs' lawyer to accept a postponement in the case, which he refused to do.

Judge Davies would not tolerate Faubus's interference and asked the Justice Department to enter the case as *amicus curiae* to uphold the integrity of his orders. The Justice Department could not refuse and soon state and federal governments moved onto a collision course. Faubus asked for and received a personal meeting with Eisenhower. But the summit conference failed to resolve the dilemma, and Davies again ordered the removal of the National Guard. At last Faubus capitulated. However, by this time Little Rock had become a rallying point for extreme segregationists. Although no threat to public safety had existed when the governor first sent the Guard, he had helped to create one by the time he removed it. Beleaguered city officials requested federal marshals to assist them in maintaining order when the Negro children entered a white high school, but Washington turned them down. Then, after a day of rioting by a white mob against Negroes, police, and reporters, Eisenhower completely reversed himself. He sent in paratroopers and National Guardsmen to establish order and uphold the integrity of the federal courts. A small detachment of troops remained through the school year. The following year, however, acting under authorization from the state legislature, Faubus closed the city's high schools.[6]

In a time when Washington was avoiding situations of racial conflict, the Little Rock crisis at least demonstrated the final legal authority of the federal government. Though some segregationists still clung to anachronistic states' rights theories, the incident showed where power ultimately resided. However, it also raised doubts about how that power should be applied. The white South recoiled at the appearance of troops, for they evoked bad memories of Reconstruction. Meanwhile it afforded the Democratic Party a rare opportunity for unity in a sphere where it normally suffered discord. A *Republican* administration had sent troops, and though Northern Democrats did not challenge Eisenhower's legal authority, many questioned his judgment. Thus the Democratic National Committee mounted a partisan attack on Eisenhower, holding him responsible for the crisis. And a prominent liberal Congressman, Stewart Udall, argued that the President should have taken a number of intermediate steps before calling in "massive retaliation" in the form of army troops.[7]

The Little Rock crisis did not initiate a change of policy. On the contrary, the administration still sought to avoid involvement in the racial issue. Although Congress in 1957 and in 1960 had given the Justice Department new authority to investigate voting rights infractions, the Department responded lethargically and brought few cases. It soon even retreated from certain advances in the handling of police brutality cases, which often had racial overtones. Moreover, given the opportunity in 1957 to appoint members to the new Civil Rights Commission, an independent advisory body, Eisenhower selected a panel which reflected his overall conservatism. Finally, the crisis brought no change in other aspects of administration civil rights policy, no manifestations of moral leadership by the President.[8]

Ordinarily, civil rights lawyers, mainly from the Legal Defense Fund of the NAACP, fought alone to make the Supreme Court's decree a reality in the 1950s. Eisenhower stayed aloof from the problem and Congress refused to grant explicit au-

thority to the Justice Department to initiate suits on behalf of
the victims of discrimination. Furthermore, in a follow-up decision to *Brown,* the Supreme Court placed the judicial onus
of enforcement on the district courts. This left matters in the
hands of Southern judges who often responded to white community pressures in this controversial area. Consequently,
very little desegregation occurred in the Old Confederacy in
the six years after the basic ruling.

Not only did civil rights lawyers fight a lonely, losing battle
for enforcement, but they also frequently had to divert their
precious resources to protect their sponsor's very existence.
Many Southern states mounted a full-scale legislative attack
on the NAACP, some even outlawing it entirely. Valuable
time and money were spent in proving the unconstitu-
tionality of these statutes to federal courts. Nevertheless,
these lawyers continued to press for school desegregation and
managed to demonstrate to the courts several other areas of
unconstitutional state behavior, such as the enforcement of
segregation in public transportation.[9]

Litigation remained one of the most fruitful means by
which blacks sought to obtain their rights, but they also em-
barked on other, more direct methods. In 1956, Martin Luther
King, Jr., a young, eloquent Baptist minister, led a successful
Negro boycott to desegregate Montgomery, Alabama's,
buses. This extraordinary effort in the heart of Dixie
catapulted King into international prominence and into a position of leadership among America's blacks. Then, in February 1960, black students at Greensboro, North Carolina,
quietly sat down at a racially restricted lunch counter and
waited for service. They were not served, but their attempt
touched off a wave of sit-ins across the country. Infrequent in
the 1950s, the direct action tactic of the sit-in, coming at the
dawn of the new decade, foreshadowed the social ferment of
the 1960s.

Civil rights proponents also revitalized a more traditional

method of achieving progress: political pressure. Blacks had moved en masse into the Democratic Party in the 1930s, largely for economic reasons. Most blacks who could vote were working class and middle class city dwellers. For them the New Deal meant economic relief from the Depression, something the Republicans had failed to produce. Furthermore, in 1948 the national Democratic Party added an explicit civil rights pledge to its economic program. In the 1952 Presidential election, Adlai Stevenson, enjoying what amounted to an endorsement from the NAACP, received approximately 75 percent of the Negroes' votes despite his selection of John Sparkman of Alabama as his running mate. After this, however, Negro enthusiasm for the Democratic Party waned, consequently increasing black political power.

Black loyalty to the Democratic Party declined for several reasons. In 1948 the Democrats experienced a sharp division over race, which ended in a forthright civil rights plank and a walkout by some segregationists. At the 1952 convention and again in 1956, the party failed to go much beyond the 1948 plank and seemed mainly interested in healing its old wounds. Both times civil rights advocates failed to extract meaningful loyalty pledges from Southern delegates. Simultaneously, the power of Southern Democrats in Congress grew visibly during these years. This made all convention promises of civil rights legislation seem empty. Finally, the Democrats suffered from guilt by association. The hostile reactions to the *Brown* decision by Southern Democrats carried with it the stigma of Negrophobia for all Democrats, especially when the party failed to repudiate its Southern members in Congress or in national conventions and campaigns.[10]

Unfortunately for the Democrats, their preference for moderation over advocacy coincided with an increased civil rights susceptibility on the part of black voters, particularly after 1954. Generally, Negroes still cast their ballots on the basis of economic interest, but many also gave high priority to civil rights. Reinforcing this tendency, national civil rights organizations and leaders moved away from their formerly close association with the national Democratic Party. The NAACP, for example, refrained from issuing evaluations of the Presidential candidates in 1956. Four years earlier its evaluation of Stevenson had been construed as an endorsement. In 1956, too, Adam Clayton Powell, Jr., a Democratic Congressman from Harlem who had long been the most outspoken civil rights advocate among black politicians, supported Eisenhower for reelection. Although Eisenhower may have privately regretted the *Brown* decision, he received political credit for appointing Chief Justice Earl Warren whom many blacks viewed as a champion of their rights.

Hence, as a consequence of the civil rights issue, black voters began to move back into the Republican Party, their political home from Reconstruction until the Depression, or at the very least, blacks refrained from voting Democratic. Thus, in 1956, a combination of switches to the GOP and a low turnout resulted in Eisenhower's doubling his proportion of the black vote in some areas. Eisenhower did particularly well in the South and in those border areas where the Democrats were hostile or unsympathetic to civil rights. Moreover, in several subsequent elections blacks continued their movement back to the GOP, even where liberal Democrats were running.[11]

This electoral trend placed the Democratic Party on notice that black votes could not be taken for granted. Simultaneously it held out the promise to Republicans of even greater gains in the future. It was no coincidence, therefore, that civil rights legislation was enacted only after this trend had been established. In the landslide election of 1956, the behavior of Negro voters made little difference in the outcome. But the Constitution prevented Eisenhower, a man of enormous personal popularity, from holding a third term, and everyone expected the 1960 Presidential contest to be much more narrowly decided. In a close race, Negro voters loomed as very significant.

No politically astute civil rights supporter, however, could become elated over this trend for it directly conflicted with another, even longer electoral pattern. The South was simply becoming more Republican. Resentment of the Northern wing of the Democratic Party, with its Negroes and civil rights sympathizers, its ties to labor and economic liberalism, contributed to this development. But it rested more on demography, for the South was changing politically primarily because of the immigration of Northern Republicans. Hence, Republican fortunes improved most markedly not in the rural regions, but in the burgeoning urban areas of the South. Indicative of GOP gains, Eisenhower carried Texas, Virginia and Florida in 1952. To these Southern prizes he added Louisiana in 1956. Naturally Republicans in these states did not want the GOP to become closely identified with civil rights because that would seriously endanger their progress to date: Southern Democrats would exploit any such identification unmercifully. [12]

At the same time, regular Southern Democrats could remind their Northern colleagues that if *their* party became an aggressive proponent of civil rights, Republican prospects in the South could only be further enhanced. Moreover, the national Democratic horizon had another dark cloud on it. In 1948, the splinter States' Rights Party took four normally Democratic states away from Truman. In the tense atmosphere of "massive resistance," a segregationist splinter movement could well recur. [13]

In this vortex of political pressures, Congress enacted its first piece of civil rights legislation in this century. The legislation bore the special brand of Senate Majority Leader Lyndon B. Johnson. As a Texan who harbored Presidential ambitions, Johnson may have wanted to demonstrate that he was not a parochial Southerner. But he also thrived in his role as a legislative conciliator and craftsman, in which he had had few peers. Johnson convinced his Southern colleagues to allow a watered-down version of a House-approved bill to pass the Senate without engaging in filibuster. Southerners accepted this arrangement because the amended bill seemed harmless enough and because they wanted to preserve the sanctity of their ultimate legislative weapon. The filibuster allowed them to ward off any measures which smacked of Reconstruction. In fact, they viewed Title III of the bill in exactly that way. It would have authorized the Attorney General to seek injunctive relief in the federal courts whenever an individual's rights were violated. Usually understood as a mandate for the national government to sue for school desegregation, its broad language implied a sweeping new scope to the Attorney General's activities. With Eisenhower's assistance, Johnson persuaded enough Northern Senators of both parties to join Southern Democrats in eliminating this provision. Appealing to feelings of moderation and practicality, Johnson also convinced a somewhat different majority to attach a jury trial amendment to the bill. It required trials by jury in cases of criminal contempt which might arise out of the bill's voting rights section. Southern Democrats believed that juries comprising indigenous whites would be even less threatening to the status quo than would federal judges. In its final form, the bill authorized Justice Department investigations of voting rights violations, and created a bipartisan Civil Rights Commission and a Civil Rights Division in the Justice Department. With good reason many viewed the outcome as a victory for the white South. The ability "to confine the Federal invasion of the South to the field of voting and keep the withering hand of the Federal Government out of our schools" was to Georgia's Richard Russell, the leader of the Southern forces, his "sweetest victory" in twenty-five years as a Senator.[14]

The 1958 Congressional elections increased Northern liberal

representation and emboldened civil rights supporters to seek the kind of strong measure that had been rejected in 1957. Delaying tactics in the House, the longest filibuster in Senate history, adminstration efforts to limit the scope of the bill, and the liberals' rather disorganized counter-efforts combined to produce a law in 1960 which made slight changes in the voting rights provisions but did nothing significant about school desegregation or about the apartheid practices that sit-ins protested while the filibuster droned on. "Like the mountain that labored and brought forth a mouse," Senator Paul H. Douglas of Illinois, a leader of the liberals, ruefully observed, "the United States Congress, after eight weeks of Senate debate and weeks of House debate, passed what can only by courtesy be called a civil rights rights bill." [15]

Thus, both the Republican President and the Democratic Congress demonstrated a distinct aversion to bringing about racial change in the South. Although civil rights advocates possessed greater legal, ideological, and political resources than in the past, they could not overcome the more considerable power of their opponents. If one word characterized the national experience on the racial issue in the 1950s, that word was "moderate." It denoted a favorable attitude toward the concept of civil rights, but a reluctance to act on it, particularly if it involved forcing it on the white South.

———————

Senator John F. Kennedy embodied the spirit of racial moderation as fully as any Northern politician. Although he represented Massachusetts, which had once been a center of abolitionism and which would have easily tolerated a spokesman for neoabolitionism, Kennedy consistently maintained a temperate position on the racial issue. His close aide, Theodore Sorensen, has pointed out that as a Senator, Kennedy "simply did not give much thought" to the subject of race relations, a field in which "he had no background of association or activity." He opposed discrimination but voted for civil rights "more as a matter of course than of deep concern." Moreover, he found "the approach of many single-minded civil rights advocates uncomfortable and unreasonable." [16]

Irish immigrants to the United States had been the victims of discrimination too, but if Kennedy's ancestors had ever felt the cruel sting of prejudice, it had not prevented them from getting ahead in their new land. His great-grandparents had fled their famine-stricken homeland in the 1840s for Massachusetts. John F. Fitzgerald, his maternal grandfather, rose to prominence in politics, winning election to Congress in 1894 and to the Boston's mayor's office in 1905. His paternal grandfather, Patrick Joseph Kennedy, achieved moderate success in both politics and business. Joseph P. Kennedy, his father, graduated from Harvard and made a great fortune through banking, investing, and motion pictures. In 1932 he broke with many Irish-Americans and backed the Presidential candidacy of Franklin D. Roosevelt rather than that of Al Smith. Roosevelt later rewarded Joseph Kennedy by naming him chairman of the Securities and Exchange Commission and then Ambassador to Great Britain. The latter post, which carried great social prestige, symbolized the arrival of Irish-Americans into the highest circles of American society. [17]

John Fitzgerald Kennedy's family of wealth and prominence was also one with singular characteristics. He was born in 1917, the second of nine children who were brought up to strive for excellence, to practice Catholicism, to be highly competitive and at the same time extremely loyal to each other, and to think for themselves. The Kennedy household was a whirlwind of high-spirited activity where laziness was rarely in evidence. John's parents sent him to private schools with few Catholics because they wanted him to escape parochialism and be able to move comfortably among America's Protestant elite. At Harvard his senior thesis on the background to British appeasement at Munich, which owing to his father's position he was able to research first-hand, earned him a bachelor's degree *cum laude* in 1940. With his father's assistance it was quickly published under the title *Why England Slept.* It was well received and enjoyed good sales.

Though brought up in a world of privilege, Kennedy acquired some appreciation for his ancestors' harder lives. On a trip to Ireland in 1947, he visited relatives who had stayed behind. After leaving their modest, thatched cottage with bare dirt floor, his female companion commented that the scene resembled "Tobacco Road." Her remark infuriated Kennedy. "I felt like kicking her out of the car. For me, the visit to that cottage was filled with magic sentiment," he reminisced privately when he returned to Ireland in 1963. Although documentation on this point is thin, Kennedy, it would appear, had primarily a sentimental attachment to his ancestors' history. He was not imbued with angry feelings about their mistreatment either in Ireland or in America. Yet Kennedy well knew that discrimination existed. No Catholic had ever been elected President of the United States, and Al Smith's nomination by the Democrats in 1928 had set off a hateful reaction. As a youngster, Kennedy himself had evidently been the victim of discrimination at least once, though in that instance the material consequence had been slight. In the mid-1950s he remarked to Belford Lawson, a Negro attorney and political supporter, that Groton, the famous preparatory school which Franklin D. Roosevelt had attended, had once rejected him because he was Irish. Kennedy told Lawson that he had had to attend Choate instead. Quite naturally Kennedy saw parallels between religious and racial prejudice and was philosophically opposed to both. But neither he nor his family had, after all, suffered very greatly from prejudice.

Moreover, no evidence has come to light that Kennedy knew blacks intimately enough to have learned how awful the effects of prejudice could be. Kennedy came to oppose discrimination of all kinds intellectually but there was little in his experience to create a passion about the subject. Indeed, he could look back on his family's own history and see proof that prejudice could be surmounted. Accordingly, when he wrote a letter of reference to Groton for Lawson's son (who was admitted), he remarked on the Negroes' progress.[18]

Kennedy formed detached and dispassionate views not only toward bias but also toward other social issues, though his feelings about foreign affairs ran deeper. Here his experiences were richer and more immediate. His father served as Ambassador to Great Britain during an epochal period and held passionate and controversial views on America's role in the world. Kennedy often disagreed with his father, but the subject of international relations aroused him as no other. He traveled through Europe on the eve of war and became far more involved in the research for his senior thesis than in any previous scholastic endeavor. (Until then he had been a rather indifferent student; afterward he began to consider a career in higher education or journalism.) Finally, the war itself profoundly and personally affected him. It took the lives of his older brother, to whom he was very close, and other relatives and friends. And it nearly cost him his own life. In 1943 a Japanese destroyer ripped in half the patrol boat he commanded, but Kennedy managed to save the lives of his crew. In addition to rallying his men, he towed one injured sailor several miles by gripping the man's life-belt in his teeth. After depositing his men on shore, Kennedy swam alone to another island seeking help. Thanks to his efforts and to the alertness of a native and Australian lookout team, Kennedy and his crew were rescued. The experience aggravated an old back injury, which developed into a chronic health problem, and it made him a war hero. Naturally the war only intensified Kennedy's interest in issues of war and peace. Eight years after its end, he asked Sorensen what Cabinet posts would interest him most if he ever had a choice. "Justice, Labor and Health-Education-Welfare," Sorensen replied. "I wouldn't have any interest in any of those," Kennedy said emphatically, "only Secretary of State or Defense." By the time of his death Kennedy had learned a great deal about domestic issues, but his interest in international matters remained uppermost.[19]

After leaving the service Kennedy worked as a journalist, covering international conferences, but by 1946 he had decided to enter politics. Joseph P. Kennedy, Jr., his older brother, had long aspired to a political career; however until the war John Kennedy had not. He lacked Joseph's facility for meeting and winning over strangers. But his brother's death, the war, and his work as a journalist impelled him to consider politics, for through that profession he might be able to prevent a future war. He successfully ran for Congress from an area in Boston and Cambridge which his grandfather had once represented. Although boyish in appearance, hampered by illness, and inexperienced in politics, Kennedy had a prominent name, a heroic war record, a well-financed campaign, and a large family and circle of friends who enthusiastically volunteered their assistance. Only six years later, with many of the same assets and liabilities, he pulled a major political upset by taking away the Senate seat of Republican Henry Cabot Lodge, Jr., at a time when Massachusetts and the country were favoring the GOP.

In his early years in politics, Kennedy proved a deft, tireless, and articulate campaigner, but his accomplishments in office paled beside his performance on the election trail. He looked after his constituents' needs, but established a reputation neither as a legislator nor reformer. To be sure, the times were not propitious for social reform. It was the age of the investigator, of Joseph McCarthy and his probes of communists in government and of Estes Kefauver and his examinations of organized crime. Moreover, Kennedy lacked seniority and continued to be plagued by ill health. Yet, he also sometimes seemed bored or impatient with the slow legislative process and he shied away from unpopular or crusading positions on the issues of the day. Moving with the tide of public opinion, he adhered to strict anticommunism in foreign affairs. Domestically, he voted with the liberals but did not seek or acquire a leadership role among them. In sum, Kennedy achieved far more success and fame in advancing his own career than in promoting any social or political cause.[20]

It is ironic that while convalescing from serious surgery in 1955, Kennedy researched and wrote a book on the theme of political courage. He explored eight instances in which Senators had acted on conscience rather than expedience. *Profiles in Courage* became a best-seller, won a Pultizer Prize for biography, and brought its author considerable attention. In addition, it certainly did not alienate Southern whites from Kennedy, for he adhered closely to the traditional view of Reconstruction which they favored. Thaddeus Stevens he portrayed as "the crippled, fanatical personification of the extremes of the Radical Republican movement." Lucius Q. C. Lamar, one of his "profiles," performed a courageous act by eulogizing Charles Sumner, "the South's most implacable enemy, the Radical Republican who had helped make the Reconstruction Period a black nightmare the South never could forget." In similar fashion, he wrote:

No state suffered more from carpetbag rule than Mississippi. . . . [Adelbert Ames] was chosen Governor by a majority composed of free slaves and radical Republicans, sustained and nourished by Federal bayonets. . . . two former slaves held the offices of Lieutenant Governor and Secretary of State. . . . Taxes increased to a level fourteen times as high as normal in order to support the extravagances of the reconstruction government and heavy state and national war debts.

Judging by his bibliography, Kennedy had not read any of the dissenting studies, written by black and white scholars, which had begun to challenge the widely held view of Reconstruction as a feast of vindictiveness and corruption. In the mid-1950s, it should be added hastily, most professional historians shared Kennedy's negative views of Reconstruction as well as his failure to consider the welfare of blacks while single-mindedly condemning Reconstruction.[21]

The book's success helped make Kennedy a candidate for national office in 1956. In the weeks before the opening of the Democratic convention, he was frequently mentioned as a possible running mate for Adlai Stevenson, who was expected to be the party's Presidential nominee for a second time. Kennedy was interested in this position, and took some of the limited measures open to Vice Presidential aspirants who did not want to appear foolish by seeming too ambitious. He sought to publicize his political attributes without actually conducting a campaign for the job. The choice of running mate, after all, customarily belonged to the Presidential nominee alone, not to the Democratic Party at large. Of course, Stevenson would want someone who would add strength to the ticket. Kennedy's assets included his Catholicism, youth, war record, and popularity in New England.

Kennedy also lacked a liability carried by Senators Estes Kefauver and Hubert Humphrey, two of his principal competitors, who were detested by Southern Democrats. In quest of the Presidential nomination in 1952 and again in 1956, Kefauver had supported the unsuccessful efforts to impose a stringent loyalty test on Southern Democrats and he had actively campaigned for Negro votes in primary elections. Moreover, he had refused to sign the Southern Manifesto. His fellow Senator from Tennessee, Albert Gore, also had refused to sign the Southern protest, and Lyndon Johnson, as Majority Leader, had been excused from participating. But Kefauver's independence, coming on top of other wayward behavior, convinced many Southern Democrats that he was a traitor to their region. Humphrey, on the other hand, had led the successful fight for a progressive civil rights plank at the 1948 convention. In the following years, as a Senator from Minnesota, he continued to be in the forefront of liberal forces in the racial area. Consequently, many Southern Democrats regarded him as a latter-day Charles Sumner. In Congress Kennedy voted for civil rights, but he never spoke out forcefully on the subject. As Governor Luther Hodges of North Carolina said, Kennedy was acceptable to the South.

Subsequently, on June 29, Kennedy wrote his father in France that he was considering having Senator George Smathers of Florida, a close personal friend, talk to Southern governors about his candidacy. Two days later Kennedy expressed his views on school desegregation on a national television broadcast. Little in them would cause him political difficulty in the South. The Supreme Court, he declared, had used the expression "deliberate speed" and had "left it to the judgment of the lower Federal Courts as to when it should be carried out," which he believed to be "a satisfactory arrangement." In the opinion of Michigan Governor G. Mennen Williams, a reporter then pointed out, "deliberate speed" were "weasel words." Kennedy responded that the South would go through a "tremendous change" as a result of the decision, but he did not think that the Supreme Court needed "assistance from any of us." [22]

Soon after the convention began in August, however, Stevenson requested that Kennedy nominate him for President, which made it seem highly unlikely that he would also ask him to take the second spot on the ticket. Despite his disappointment, Kennedy delivered an eloquent speech on behalf of the Illinois Governor. Then, after easily winning the nomination, Stevenson startled the convention by handing it the choice of his running mate. The balloting commenced less than twelve hours after this unexpected announcement, and so a frantic competition for delegates by a host of aspirants ensued. On the first ballot, the leading vote-getters were Kefauver, Kennedy, and Gore. The latter two divided the South's votes. Although Kennedy's reputation as a moderate may have helped him there, his major appeal rested on expedience. The South wanted to stop Kefauver. When journalist Ralph McGill asked a Mississippi delegate why he supported Kennedy, he replied, "Well, we'd be for anybody against that nigger-loving Kefauver of Tennessee." Ironically, while many Southern Baptists were backing the Catholic Kennedy against a fellow Southern Baptist, many Catholics were voting for Kefauver against their co-religionist. The memory of the religious conflict surrounding the Al Smith nomination in 1928 endured; they did not want to relive that experience. On the second ballot the field narrowed down to Kennedy and Kefauver. This time, boosted by a nearly unanimous South, Kennedy almost captured the nomination. However, Speaker of the House Sam Rayburn, permanent chairman of the convention, then took command and recognized a series of delegations who announced switches to Kefauver. That turned the tide and gave Kefauver the nomination. Because of his votes on agricultural legislation, Kennedy had been able to win few delegates in the Midwest and West. Kefauver, despite his unpopularity in the South, had twice waged primary campaigns for the Presidential nomination, was better known nationally, and, at a critical moment, enjoyed the assistance of a friendly chairman.[23]

In the long run, however, Kennedy benefited from this setback. His nomination would have done little to stem the Eisenhower tide, but many in the party would have attributed Stevenson's loss to Kennedy's Catholicism. Moreover, the Southern Democrats' enmity toward Kefauver allowed Kennedy to establish friendly working relations with them. "[H]ad you received the nomination," Governor J. P. Coleman of Mississippi wrote him the day before the election, "it would not have been necessary to have campaigned at all in Mississippi this Fall." "While I regret you lost the nomination for Vice President," Governor Marvin Griffin of Georgia reassured Kennedy, "you won respect from party leaders all over the country and can look forward to greater things in the future." [24]

Judging from the large number of speeches he made that fall, one might have guessed that Kennedy had won the Vice Presidential nomination; in fact he was beginning his quest for the top spot on the ticket four years hence. Elected to Congress before he was thirty, Kennedy decided, ambitiously and perhaps audaciously, before he was forty to seek the nation's highest office. "With only about four hours of work and a handful of supporters, I came within thirty-three and a half votes of winning the Vice Presidential nomination," Kennedy told David Powers, his friend and aide, soon after the election. "If I work hard for four years, I ought to be able to pick up all the marbles." His 1956 bid had suffered from a too-narrow base and a haphazard organization, and so he methodically set out to build his Presidential hopes upon the broadest foundation. He would appeal to all sections and viewpoints and disregard none, for each would command some delegates. [25]

In the area where his party was most polarized, however—race relations—it would be hard to satisfy both sides. At the least, Kennedy might hope to alienate neither. In the 1957 Congressional debate on civil rights Kennedy faced an early challenge to his political dexterity. The first test came in June over the procedural question of whether the civil rights bill should be sent to the Judiciary Committee. The Southerners wanted the bill forwarded to Judiciary because they expected to kill it there. A small group of liberals, led by Wayne Morse and including Kennedy, also wanted the bill sent there, but for a different reason. They feared setting a precedent of by-passing a committee with a major bill, and announced their intention to vote for a discharge motion if Judiciary did not report a bill after a reasonable amount of time. This odd Southern-liberal coalition lost. Nevertheless, two of Kennedy's Boston friends, officers of the NAACP, immediately wrote him of their dismay at his vote. He quickly reassured them of his loyalty on civil rights and sent them copies of Morse's explanation for the seeming deviation.[26]

Kennedy loyally supported the ill-fated Title III, but on the closer issue of the jury trial amendment, he again voted with the Southerners, who this time prevailed. Three things seemed to influence Kennedy's vote. "My observation of the debate during the last several days led me to believe," he explained to Ruth Batson, a Boston NAACP official, "that the Southerners would have filibustered the civil rights bill if a jury trial amendment were not adopted and it would have been impossible to obtain cloture." In later years, Lyndon Johnson offered confirmation. He told a civil rights audience that he had implored a group of Senators to vote for the amendment, without which the bill was doomed. Kennedy, he insisted, had demonstrated considerable courage in breaking with the liberal bloc to support the amendment. Secondly, Kennedy, not a lawyer, depended on advice from Mark DeWolfe Howe and Paul Freund, two eminent Harvard Law School experts on constitutional matters and friends of civil rights. They assured him that the jury trial amendment involved no abridgment of principle, and even cited its constitutional advantages. Finally, some of Kennedy's new Southern friends greatly desired the amendment. Several days before the vote, Kennedy received a not too subtle wire from Luther Hodges: "Hope very much you will support jury trial amendments civil rights bill consider principle honest fair still hearing good things about you and your future." On the same day that Kennedy wrote Ruth Batson to explain his vote, he also wrote Hodges, J. P. Coleman, and Marvin Griffin, to thank them for their advice on the amendment and to remind them how he had voted. Two and a half years later, Robert Kennedy, the Senator's brother and unofficial campaign manager, again recalled to Southerners this vote, as well as earlier opposition to bypassing the Judiciary Committee. In both instances, Kennedy was aligned with Lyndon Johnson against both Hubert Humphrey and Stuart Symington, two of the leading non-Southern contenders for the Presidential nomination.[27]

In courting Southern Democrats, Kennedy supplemented his Congressional record with frequent visits and speeches. Typically he talked about the economy, labor reform, or public service, though he often alluded to bright chapters of Southern history, especially to one he had written about in *Profiles,* the story of L. Q. C. Lamar. Consistent with his political ambition and his view of history, the Senator refrained from endorsing measures redolent of Reconstruction. During the Little Rock crisis he issued a statement against mob violence and the defiance of a court order. He assigned the responsibility for upholding the law solely to the President, but, along with many Democrats, maintained that there could be "disagreement over the President's leadership on this issue." Two days later a South Carolina legislator informed Kennedy that until he approved the use of troops, people in his state were prepared to back him in 1960. Now, however, "we really hope you do make an effort to obtain the nomination," the irate segregationist admonished, "so that we will have the pleasure of voting and working for your defeat." Calmly Kennedy replied that Adam Clayton Powell and Negro newspapers had attacked him for his Senate votes on civil rights. "I tell you this not to seek your sympathy or support," Kennedy assured him, "but to illustrate the difficulties which face any man in public life who tries to follow his conscience and considers each issue to the best of his ability on its own merits. No doubt you have encountered similar difficulties in your service in the Legislature." In a similar fashion, Kennedy proceeded with a planned visit to Mississippi during the Little Rock crisis. Informed that the state Republican chairman had challenged him to give his position on school desegregation, Kennedy told a silent audience of Democrats that he accepted it as the law of the land. Then he dared the Republican chairman to state his position on Eisenhower and Nixon and won his listeners' cheers. Thus, in approaching the white South, Kennedy did not hide his views on desegregation, nor did he call attention to them. Instead he focused on the common ground of respect for the Southern heritage, economic philosophy, the challenge of public service, and opposition to the Republican administration, which he did not have to remind anyone had sent troops to Little Rock.[28]

Kennedy's Southern efforts yielded tangible political results. After his landslide reelection to the Senate in 1958, a Georgia newspaper run by James Gray, a segregationist and state Democratic chairman, who happened to be a native New Englander, editorialized:

> Even today, the Kennedy magnetism is widely felt throughout Dixie, although the man from Massachusetts is on record as favoring obedience to the Supreme Court ruling on school integration, a legal dictum which five Deep Southern States, at least, will never accept willingly. Yet the fact remains that Southern sentiment generally agrees with Mississippi's Governor J. P. Coleman who said recently of Senator Kennedy that he is "sober and temperate on civil rights. He's no hell raiser or Barnburner."

To be sure, Kennedy's moderate stand on civil rights allowed and even encouraged Southern politicians to embrace him. But Southerners were attracted to him by the same qualities that appealed to politicians and the public elsewhere: his dynamism, his eloquence, his interest in them, as well as his good prospects of becoming President. For example, Alabama's Attorney General, John Patterson, heard Kennedy speak on organized crime before the Alabama League of Municipalities in 1957. Patterson's father had been killed while trying to rid a city of gangsters. Kennedy's speech impressed him. After winning his state's governorship in 1958, he sought out Kennedy in Washington and soon became a committed supporter. In addition to thinking that the Senator was highly qualified, Patterson believed he was going to win.[29]

Patterson was one of the few major Southern politicians to declare for Kennedy, but many others looked favorably upon his candidacy. Governors, in particular, liked Kennedy and they would be important in 1960 because they usually had a powerful voice in their state delegations. But Kennedy also enjoyed the tacit support of a number of Southern Senators, at least until 1959 when Lyndon Johnson's candidacy became quietly active. John Stennis of Mississippi, for one, transferred his allegiance from Kennedy in 1958 to Johnson in 1959. But even in November 1959, Robert Kennedy found Senator Herman Talmadge, whom he regarded as the most influential Democrat in Georgia, to be "extremely friendly" though likely to vote for Johnson on the first ballot. Talmadge's attitude typified the success of Kennedy's Southern efforts. As a Northerner who usually voted with the civil rights bloc in Congress, Kennedy could not hope to win many first ballot votes against the South's favorite son. However, as a moderate who had actively solicited delegates in the South, Kennedy had made himself acceptable there and had become a second- or third-ballot choice of many. Above all, he avoided being stigmatized as a Reconstruction Democrat.[30]

Inevitably Kennedy's moderation and his positive reception by Southern Democrats raised questions about his suitability in the minds of civil rights advocates. Clarence Mitchell, the NAACP's Washington lobbyist, criticized Kennedy after he voted with the Southerners on the procedural question in 1957. Although Kennedy defended his action to Mitchell, this influential lobbyist became an unrelenting critic in succeeding years. More important, Roy Wilkins, the NAACP's chief operating officer, added his voice to Mitchell's in 1958. Wilkins traveled to Massachusetts in the spring and sharply rebuked the Senator for his 1957 votes and for having his picture taken with his arm around Governor Marvin Griffin of Georgia. Kennedy immediately wrote to Wilkins that he could not remember that particular picture being taken. But even if it had, he failed to see anything inherently wrong with it. He also reminded Wilkins that he had voted for Title III. Wilkins answered that the "picture" was only "a figure of speech" and that Negro anxieties about Kennedy's good reception in Dixie were legitimate. Again Kennedy responded. He defended his votes on the civil rights bill and minimized his support in the South. "I am somewhat saddened," Kennedy added in a postscript, "that, when speaking of pictures, you emphasized one which does not exist instead of the picture of you and me which does exist, taken at the NAACP Banquet last fall." [31]

Criticism of Kennedy from the NAACP continued and he assiduously tried to halt it. After Kennedy heard from a friend that he had been the object of barbed comments at the NAACP's convention in July, he wrote Wilkins his strongest protest to date. Considering the fact that they were all going to be around Washington for some time to come, Kennedy maintained, it would be unfortunate "if an 'iron curtain' of misunderstanding were to be erected between our two offices." Kennedy set forth his grievances and made a request:

It seems to me that it would be important to you and your organization to lay to rest the suspicion current among many liberal Senators that I have been singled out for political reasons. Certainly the evidence supports this. You came to Pittsfield in the middle of my campaign for re-election to say that my record (a solid civil rights record for twelve years, as contained in the memo I earlier sent you) did not deserve the support of Negro

voters—while, according to the local press, treating compara-
tively lightly my Republican colleague who voted against Title
III. More recently, Mr. Mitchell, whose close association with Mr.
Nixon is well known in Washington, "was quite outspoken
against" me at the NAACP Convention in Cleveland, in the
words of a letter to me from one of our most responsible Massachusetts delegates.

I cannot believe that the NAACP, with whom I have had a long
and friendly association, would want to be involved by two of its
leaders in a partisan candidate-picking gamble at this time; and
that is why I think it is urgent that you and I have a discussion,
perhaps with Mr. Mitchell also, on your next visit to Washington.

Friends of the Senator also lobbied with NAACP Board members.[32]

Apparently Kennedy's arguments, his willingness privately
to admit error on the jury-trial amendment, and pressure
from the board convinced Wilkins to reverse himself. In October, Herbert Tucker, President of the Boston NAACP and a
supporter of the Senator, released a letter from Wilkins which
constituted a virtual endorsement of Kennedy's reelection. It
attested that "Senator Kennedy has one of the best voting
records on civil rights and related issues of any Senator in
Congress." Kennedy's campaigners in Boston's Negro wards
made ample use of the letter in the days before the election.
"I am glad our evaluation of your civil rights voting record
was useful," Wilkins cordially wrote Kennedy in December.
By the time of the NAACP's next annual convention, a Kennedy representative reported back that he now seemed "to be
in high regard with Roy Wilkins, both from his public and
private statements." Wilkins, the friend informed, had even
advised Vel Phillips, a black Democratic National Commit-
teewoman from Milwaukee, "to declare for the Senator in
Wisconsin." Although the convention itself became a show of
support for Hubert Humphrey, many of the rank and file
believed that the Minnesotan's chances were poor. Further-

more, Wilkins privately told Phillips that Kennedy was just as liberal as Humphrey.[33]

Much as he persevered with Wilkins, Kennedy pursued other avenues of winning civil rights advocates, primarily Negroes, to his side. After the 1956 convention, Kennedy asked Belford Lawson of Washington, D.C., one of the few Negro delegates to support him for Vice President, to help him become better known in the black community. Lawson and his wife, attorneys with good connections in Negro fraternal and professional organizations, agreed to introduce him to these groups. Belford Lawson declined to leave his law practice to work full time for the candidate, but Marjorie MacKenzie Lawson found political life somewhat more enticing and devoted a considerable amount of time in the following years to Kennedy's cause. She attended important national conventions as his representative and reporter, oversaw his 1958 reelection efforts in Boston's black community, sought the friendship of prospective delegates, and courted the Negro press.[34]

In a sense Marjorie Lawson had little to work with. Kennedy himself knew few Negroes and had no reputation as a civil rights advocate. On the contrary, his 1957 votes and his friendly receptions in the South posed difficulties. She therefore accentuated the positive. The black press, for example, was informed that he had been the first New England Senator to hire a Negro for his personal staff. The employee, a secretary in his Boston office, described her duties in detail for the editor of the Pittsburgh *Courier*, the largest circulating Negro newspaper. Similarly, Kennedy's appointment as Chairman of the Senate Foreign Relations Subcommittee on Africa delighted Mrs. Lawson because it could help Kennedy establish a record in a field close to the heart of civil rights supporters. Today, small gestures like these might seem trivial, but many middle class Negroes in the 1950s perceived them as symbols of progress and sympathy.[35]

Personal appearances at meetings also demonstrated Kennedy's interest in Negroes and simultaneously revealed an important dimension of his thought. When the Lawsons suggested that Kennedy attend an NAACP dinner in 1957, he agreed only reluctantly because it seemed a "little obvious." Kennedy had met few of the liberal Negro leaders before but he was impressed by this encounter. Yet, as Theodore Sorensen has pointed out, when Kennedy met with Negro groups he "was more likely to talk about the general problems of education, unemployment and slum housing than to focus directly on the race issue." In one such talk, which he undertook enthusiastically, Kennedy told a meeting of Negro college educators in 1959 that their schools shared the general crisis of American education. Everyone, he declared, should "raise their sights beyond the difficulties of racial integration at home to see the challenge of our contracting universe. Integration is itself a world-wide process." He urged Negro colleges to train people to meet their global responsibilities. Thus, Kennedy both magnified and reduced the racial issue. In its international context, he understood integration to be profoundly important. But he omitted discussing the tangible ways integration could be achieved domestically. No doubt, in dealing with the controversial issue in this way he reduced the risk of offending those Southern Democrats whose favor he also sought.[36]

Kennedy's efforts to improve his image among civil rights advocates produced mixed results by 1960. The organized Negro middle class became better acquainted with him. That served to cool their hostility to him, though generally not to transform it into admiration. Liberal whites, it should be noted, had evidently never been so much of a problem. Paul Douglas, for example, readily agreed to endorse Kennedy's civil rights performance in a Boston speech during the 1958 campaign. He simply overlooked aspects of Kennedy's voting record and his suspicions that Kennedy was courting Southern politicians. On the other hand, when James MacGregor Burns, a liberal political scientist, wrote a biography of Kennedy in 1959, he raised the question of whether the Senator's civil rights stand amounted to a profile in cowardice.[37]

Public opinion surveys repeatedly manifested doubts about Kennedy's civil rights record. A statement that accompanied the release of a 1958 Gallup poll comparing the preferences of Democratic voters between Kennedy and Kefauver observed that Kennedy has "voted with the Southern bloc in the Senate on several civil rights issues, and Kefauver . . . tended to side with Northern liberals." Kennedy pointed out the glib inaccuracy of this statement to George Gallup—Kefauver, for example, had voted to eliminate Title III altogether—and the pollster admitted error. Nevertheless, Kennedy could not easily refute the findings of his own private polls which demonstrated his relative political weakness with blacks. In June 1958, Louis Harris reported that 74 percent of Massachusetts Negroes planned to vote for Kennedy against the Republican nominee, who they felt was certain to lose, but compared to other groups, Negro support for Kennedy had declined. More portentously, two weeks before the 1960 Presidential primary in Wisconsin, Harris found Humphrey holding a four-to-one lead over Kennedy among Negro voters.[38]

In sum, Kennedy, a moderate by conviction and design, had effectively neutralized the racial issue by 1960. Southern Democrats and Negroes alike generally regarded him as an acceptable, though not preferred, candidate. This dual achievement attested both to Kennedy's political acumen and the prevalence of the attitude of racial moderation in the 1950s. In harmony with the national mood and experience, Kennedy favored civil rights but refrained from translating beliefs into action. The 1960 Presidential campaign would shortly put this attitude and Kennedy's representation of it to a rigorous test.

TWO

The 1960 Campaign: Promises and Compromises

As the 1960 campaign began in earnest, Kennedy had managed to avoid alienating Southern Democrats and blacks and had even acquired some popularity among both groups. Whether Kennedy could maintain and enhance his position with these conflicting entities in the months ahead would hold a key to his political success. Moreover, how he did it would carry significant implications for his conduct of the Presidency.

BECAUSE neither of the two major primary elections were to take place in the South, or in states with large black populations, the rivals, Kennedy and Humphrey, devoted little time to the civil rights issue. Rather they concentrated on the economy and on establishing their respective Presidential abilities. By defeating Humphrey in Wisconsin and West Virginia, Kennedy demonstrated his greater popularity and considerably reduced his party's fears about the political liability of his religion. Humphrey apparently took a majority of Negro votes in Wisconsin and Kennedy in West Virginia. But in both states, Negro voters constituted a small fraction of the total electorate and the candidates' showing among them received negligible attention.[1]

Kennedy's triumphs over Humphrey, his only important primary opponent, coincided with another significant development in the spring: Lyndon Johnson's capture of the South. Johnson's candidacy did not come out into the open until just before the Democratic convention in July. Well before that, however, his Southern friends in the Senate and

House worked quietly and effectively to guarantee him most of their first-ballot votes. Some Southern Democrats dissented, believing that the South could only regain its former power through the selection of independent electors who would throw the Presidential election into the House of Representatives. Harry Byrd, one of the South's most powerful conservatives, reassured one such dissenter, noting that Johnson possessed great honesty and ability. Though he did not agree with all of Johnson's votes, Byrd credited the Majority Leader with eliminating the "most iniquitous" parts of the recent civil rights bill. Byrd did not attend the Democratic convention, but he saw to it that the Virginia delegation was instructed to vote for Johnson and was firmly under control. Similarly, in other states, most Southern Democrats united behind Johnson's candidacy.[2]

Johnson undoubtedly realized that a strictly Southern candidacy stood little chance of success but, having failed to compete in primaries, he would find it difficult to establish himself as a truly national figure. Civil rights leaders Martin Luther King and Roy Wilkins had declared Johnson unacceptable. King suggested that if the Democrats chose Johnson, blacks might well turn to Nixon who "has made a real impression on the Negro." To be sure, Johnson's record on civil rights contained some encouraging signs. He had, after all, guided the 1957 bill to passage, even if it fell far short of ideal. Privately Johnson also favorably impressed some Negro leaders with his sincerity. In January 1960, he told a civil rights legislative conference that he shared the philosophy and objectives of Walter Reuther, the liberal labor leader. Wilkins, for one, personally believed that Johnson would make an excellent President in the race relations area, but as long as Johnson kept his similarity to Reuther "off the record," the NAACP leader would certainly reciprocate by keeping his favorable evaluation of Johnson to himself. Although Johnson's list of supporters did include several blacks, principally fellow Texans, the Majority Leader depended heavily on white Southern conservatives. For instance, in March, Johnson adopted Richard Russell's recommendations on how to respond to an influential Negro editor's telegram about the ill treatment of blacks in the South. The kind of public statement that Richard Russell would suggest was clearly unlikely to win over civil rights advocates. Nevertheless, Johnson did receive Adam Clayton Powell's endorsement in late June. But the Congressman's simultaneous denunciation of Kennedy's alliance with John Patterson probably won over few Negro delegates, for Powell displayed peculiar vision, which allowed him to observe Patterson behind Kennedy, but not Russell, Talmadge, and Byrd behind Johnson.[3]

Johnson's candidacy posited a threat and created an opportunity for Kennedy. It increased the danger that his opponents would coalesce long enough to prevent him from obtaining the majority needed for nomination. But it also allowed Kennedy to present himself as the liberals' best hope. He had opposed Humphrey, a favorite of many liberals, in the spring. Now his closest opponent represented the most conservative element in the party. Despite Kennedy's relative shift leftward, however, he stopped short of severing his ties with the South.

Kennedy's emergence as the liberal candidate received a boost in mid-June when sixteen prominent Stevenson backers issued a broadside on his behalf. They pointed out that until recently liberals had divided their loyalties among Humphrey, Kennedy, and Stevenson. But Humphrey had withdrawn and Stevenson insisted that he was not a candidate. Therefore, the "real struggle" at the Democratic convention would be between liberals and conservatives, idealists and professionals. They professed the greatest confidence in Kennedy's devotion to liberal idealism. "In particular some of us have discussed the question of a strong Civil Rights plank with him," they declared, "and he assured us that he favors pledging the Democratic Party to Congressional and Executive Action in support of the Supreme Court's segregation decisions and to whatever measures may prove necessary to make voting a reality for all citizens." [4]

Kennedy enhanced his liberal reputation by his own public statements. He told New York's Liberal Party that he expected to win the Democratic nomination for President without a single Southern vote in the convention. In addition, he said that he regarded the civil rights issue as a moral question. "Moral persuasion by the President," Kennedy asserted, "can be more effective than force in ending discrimination against Negroes." When a black newspaper interviewer asked Kennedy about making concessions to the white South, he repeated Hubert Humphrey's primary campaign pledge that if anyone expected him to betray the cause of civil rights for political expediency they could look for another candidate. Kennedy was even prepared to go a step further: "if anyone expects the Democratic administration to betray that same cause they can look elsewhere for a party." At a luncheon of African ambassadors, Kennedy gave a ringing endorsement to the sit-in demonstrations. He saw them as an encouraging sign that "the American spirit is coming alive again." Calling for individual and government support of the demonstrators' goals, he averred that "it is in the American tradition to stand up for one's rights—even if the new way is to sit down." [5]

Nevertheless, though most Southern delegates were planning to cast their first ballots for Johnson, Kennedy hoped to pick up some Southern defectors if a second or third ballot were held. In late May, South Carolina's Governor Ernest Hollings informed Robert Kennedy that perhaps a third of his state's delegates then favored the Massachusetts Senator. Hollings, however, was also a realist, who felt that "South Carolina being with Kennedy at this juncture could be very harmful to Jack." Apparently, Kennedy believed that he could win the nomination on the first ballot with minimal Southern assistance, because Stephen Smith, his brother-in-law and campaign aide, asked John Patterson to withhold nine out of the fourteen votes he could have delivered on the first ballot. Kennedy must have shared Hollings's perception of the dangerous implications of declared Southern backing—indeed, Patterson's endorsement had proved to be a continuing liability—but if additional ballots were required he would have to run the risk of tapping his Southern friends.[6]

In assuming an explicit liberal image, Kennedy endangered his standing with Southern Democrats. After Kennedy spoke to the Liberal Party in New York, Robert Kennedy warned him that he had better clarify what he said about being nominated without Southern votes. To say that he was not interested in them was "going to look like a gratuitous insult to the Southern political leaders who have been interested in you over the last few months. . . . You might not get votes from them but there is no sense in turning on them at this moment." Accordingly, the candidate informed Southern Democrats that he would be "happy and proud to receive support from delegates from any part of the United States." Moreover, several days later, one of Kennedy's top Southern campaign assistants, William C. Battle of Virginia, assured G. Fred Switzer, a Harry Byrd ally, that he had Kennedy's word that no deal had been made whereby Hubert Humphrey would be his running mate. Another Virginian, Senator A. Willis Robertson, a Johnson backer, had astutely observed to Switzer that Kennedy's remarks to the Liberal Party indicated that he did not expect Southern help for the nomination but that he wanted it in November. Kennedy told that audience that he did not expect Southern delegates to vote for him but he also said that he considered moral persuasion by the President more effective than force. Concurring with Robertson's evaluation, Switzer wrote: "This is the smartest thing Kennedy has done yet toward getting support in the South."[7]

As the convention got underway in early July, Kennedy continued to send friendly signals to both Southern delegates and Negroes. Kennedy received polite applause from an NAACP rally at the start of the convention, compared to cheers for Hubert Humphrey and boos for Lyndon Johnson's representative. The next President would have to use his full legal and moral authority, Kennedy declared, to bolster voting rights, as well as to achieve a nondiscriminatory public education system and an end to bias in federal housing. He praised the sit-ins, reminded his audience that vicious prejudice also existed in the North, and stressed the foreign implications of America's racial problem, noting that the white American was very much a minority person in the world. At about the same time, Robert Kennedy was telling Southerners that his brother only endorsed sit-ins if they were "peaceful and legal." The Supreme Court had not yet ruled on any sit-in cases, and many white Southerners assumed that the sit-ins were illegal and their perpetrators' arrests proper. To the press, Robert Kennedy denied that this interpretation represented a shift in his brother's position, but Southerners appeared pleased.[8]

In the most important business of the convention other than the selection of nominees, Kennedy, partly by design and partly through inadvertence, helped civil rights advocates secure a major victory. Kennedy was much more interested in counting delegates than in carefully dictating the content of the platform. Chester Bowles, a liberal, a former Stevensonian, and a Kennedy ally, chaired the committee and was generally sympathetic to leftward notions. With assistance from Harris Wofford, a former Civil Rights Commission attorney who had joined Kennedy's campaign team in May, Bowles drew up a strongly worded civil rights plank, though one which he fully expected to be watered down. At a critical juncture in the committee's deliberations, Robert Kennedy, unaware of his ally's expectations or the specific wording of the plank, instructed his brother's delegates to uphold the Bowles position. Wofford quickly apprised Robert Kennedy of what had happened, but it was too late. The Democrats had adopted the boldest civil rights plank in their history. It pledged vigorous enforcement of the voting laws, passage of fair employment practices legislation, and federal action to end discrimination in education and housing. To obtain the needed legislation, it cited the necessity for improved Congressional procedures, implying a reform of the filibuster and of the House Rules Committee. Above all, it stressed the need for "strong, active, persuasive and inventive leadership" by the President. Not skimping on rhetoric, the plank called "the peaceful demonstrations for first-class citizenship," which had recently been taking place, "a signal to all of us to make good at long last the guarantees of our Constitution." Naturally, Negro delegates and civil rights proponents were delighted with this document. But Kennedy evidently was less enthralled. As Sorensen later described Kennedy's reaction to the platform in general, it promised "too many antagonistic specifics that could not be fulfilled, raising too many unwarranted hopes and unnecessary fears." [9]

Disgruntled Southern delegates futilely submitted a minority report, but in contrast to 1948, they did not stage a walkout; Lyndon Johnson's candidacy probably acted as a safety valve. A rebellion on their part over the platform could only damage Johnson's chances. "I think the platform is a stench in the nostrils of all self-respecting Southerners," a conservative Virginia politician privately reflected several weeks later. But, despite his disappointment in Lyndon Johnson's acceptance of second place on the ticket, he could see no other course "than to vote for the Democratic nominees." [10]

Kennedy, of course, narrowly won the nomination on the first ballot. His closest opponent, Johnson, unable to overcome his conservative and regional identification, received few votes outside the South. Kennedy, on the other hand, had considerable strength in all regions except the South, though if a second ballot had been necessary, he almost certainly would have increased his total there. Significant, too, Kennedy's victory did not terrify Southern party members. As Arkansas Governor Orval Faubus told Sorensen before the vote, his state would back Johnson but it would not abandon the party if Kennedy were nominated. In the meantime, of the 52 Negro delegates and alternates, Marjorie Lawson estimated that Kennedy was favored by 42 or 43. These pieces of information suggest that through his nomination, Kennedy continued to enjoy relatively high acceptance by both Southern Democrats and blacks. In his first important decision as a nominee, however, Kennedy endangered this record.[11]

Kennedy's reasons for choosing Lyndon Johnson as his running mate have long been debated. His top aides have offered detailed but contradictory explanations. Sorensen has emphasized Kennedy's desire for a balanced ticket, in terms of region and religion, and his confidence in Johnson's ability to assume the Presidency if that were to become necessary. Kenneth O'Donnell, on the other hand, has recalled Kennedy's explanation that he had only wanted to assure the Majority Leader's assistance in the upcoming session of Congress and had not really expected Johnson to accept his offer. Furthermore, Kennedy told O'Donnell, if Johnson were to accept and the ticket won by a small margin—which was the only way it would win—Kennedy would prefer to work with Mike Mansfield as Majority Leader. After Kennedy became President, he offered no explanation when Myer Feldman, one of his assistants, broached the subject.

Whatever Kennedy's motives (and they most likely were complex though not necessarily well thought out) certainly among them was Johnson's popularity in the South. Conscious of history, Kennedy also surely recalled that Democratic nominees had frequently chosen Southerners. Al Smith had taken Joseph Robinson, Franklin Roosevelt had picked his earlier opponent, John Nance Garner, and Adlai Stevenson had selected John Sparkman. Johnson seemed to offer help in an area where Kennedy would most need it. Louis Harris had conducted a poll in South Carolina in June which demonstrated the obvious: Johnson's popularity and the liberal Humphrey's unpopularity. Moreover, a meeting with Southern governors, apparently held after he made his choice but before the announcement, confirmed the wisdom of Kennedy's decision. Governor J. Lindsay Almond of Virginia bluntly told Kennedy that without Johnson he could not carry Virginia or Texas; that with him, he could.[12]

Time would eventually tell whether Kennedy had made the right decision, but many liberals, labor leaders, and Negroes immediately expressed their grave reservations. To many of them, Kennedy's choice of Johnson seemed a betrayal and some planned to present their own Vice Presidential candidate in protest. In an attempt to dampen the incipient rebellion, Kennedy and Johnson appeared together before a group of Negro delegates. Johnson reminded them that he had come to the convention as a candidate for President, not Vice-President. But the majority had spoken decisively. "I'm not a cry-baby and I don't want to pout," Johnson declared. "I want to campaign from one coast to the other on the platform of this convention." Johnson reported that Kennedy told him that he could help unite the party and thereby bring victory. "I thought I had no choice except to do my duty and I'm going to do it and I don't believe you folks will be sorry," Johnson said, "I think you will be glad." In his remarks, Kennedy stressed the importance of the platform and asked for the delegates' advice and counsel in the fall. This and other reassurances staved off a floor fight over the nomination. Nevertheless, it was an ominous way to embark on a Presidential campaign in which the votes of Negroes loomed so significant.[13]

Developments at the Republican convention several weeks later did not reverse the signs. Following a bitter struggle between its Northern and Southern wings, the GOP adopted the most liberal civil rights plank in its history. The party of Lincoln pledged itself to the eradication of racial discrimination. It praised Eisenhower's record in this area, but it also did something he had not dared to do: endorse the Supreme Court decision on school desegregation. Yielding somewhat to the wishes of Southerners, it rejected the notion of requiring a fixed date for the filing of school desegregation plans. Nor did it mention the words "fair employment practices" or "sit-ins." It also refrained from promising bold Presidential action, but more explicitly than the Democrats, the Republicans called for reform of Congressional procedures. Justifiably, Joseph Rauh of Americans for Democratic Action (ADA) congratulated Roy Wilkins "on getting as much as you did out of the Republican convention," for though the civil rights plank did not equal the Democrats', it went much further than any in the past. Southern Republicans, meanwhile, were depressed. "I tell you," lamented one Southerner to political reporter Theodore White, "we've lost Louisiana. Lyndon Johnson's going to come across the border now and talk 'magnolia' to them and they'll vote Democratic and we could have had Louisiana, we could have had it." [14]

The liberal platform victory at the Republican convention was related to Richard Nixon's quest for the Presidential nomination, and it also carried implications for the fall campaign. Nixon reportedly made ideological concessions to New York's liberal Governor Nelson Rockefeller in order to keep him from becoming a last minute candidate and spoiling his own bid. After winning the nomination, Nixon asked Rockefeller to be his running mate. The New Yorker declined, but United Nations Ambassador Henry Cabot Lodge accepted. Nixon later revealed in a memoir that he expected Lodge to bolster the ticket in the area of foreign policy. But he must have also realized that, unlike Lyndon Johnson, Lodge would be no impediment to Negro support. Indeed, with the combination of the civil rights plank, Lodge, recent electoral trends, and his own good reputation among Negroes, one might have expected Nixon to mount a powerful campaign for black votes in the fall.[15]

At the brief special session of Congress held after the conventions, Republicans introduced civil rights legislation, discomforting their Democratic adversaries. It was obvious that such legislation had no chance of passage in the limited time available and, if debated, would wreck Democratic unity. Kennedy and other Northern Democrats were placed in the embarrassing position of joining with Southerners in tabling the bills. Promising to take up civil rights at the next session of Congress, Kennedy and the Democrats sought instead, and in vain, to pass other social welfare legislation they had also promised. The Democratic inaction on civil rights naturally provoked considerable criticism by Republican racial spokesmen publicly, but also by Roy Wilkins and other organizational leaders privately. Moreover, as Arthur Schlesinger, Jr. reported to Archibald Cox, his Harvard colleague and fellow Kennedy supporter, it immediately "revived the fears of those who opposed Lyndon's nomination" and it "greatly complicated the task of bringing liberals of the New York-California school (not to speak of Negroes) into the Kennedy camp." Several weeks later things had not improved. Schlesinger then wrote Kennedy that the ADA had endorsed him after considerable debate and with little enthusiasm. As one liberal explained, "we don't trust Kennedy and we don't like Johnson; but Nixon is so terrible that we have to endorse the Democrats." Schlesinger attributed the liberals' tepidity largely to the fact that in many localities regular politicians were tightly controlling the campaign. But he also believed that the selection of Johnson and the disappointments arising out of the special session had contributed significantly to the liberals' lack of enthusiasm.[16]

Fortunately for Kennedy, Nixon did not adopt and expand the tactic of the special session during his campaign. Instead of continuing to exploit the Democratic division on civil rights, Nixon concentrated on capturing the electoral votes of the South. As Dewey and Eisenhower had done before him, Nixon placed a higher priority on the white South than on the votes of blacks. However, he diluted his Southern strategy. While campaigning extensively in the South, he attacked the Democrats' platform as radical, expressed his devotion to Jeffersonian principles of local government, and favored the course of voluntary desegregation, but at the same time endorsed civil rights generally and praised the Eisenhower administration's record. Southern Republicans urged him to emphasize the former parts of his message and eschew the latter. Senator Barry Goldwater of Arizona, who proved to be the GOP's most popular 1960 performer in the South, followed that course. But Nixon never went so far as would have been necessary to negate the effects of Little Rock, the Warren Court, Kennedy's running mate, or popular suspicions about his own devotion to civil rights.[17]

On the other hand, the Republicans conducted a feeble campaign for the votes of Negroes. E. Frederic Morrow, the only black professional on Eisenhower's staff, took a leave of absence to work for Nixon. Although he had been promised a significant role, he was disillusioned to find that his advice was not heeded and that Negro voters were neglected. During his entire two months with the campaign, Morrow later explained, "I never had a secretary or anyone to answer my considerable campaign mail; I never had a dime to spend for anything other than personal expenses. No literature, no workers, no assistants." Negro leaders from around the country who called him for assistance were dismayed to be turned down flat. Jackie Robinson, the baseball hero, was the "only national speaker of any importance" to be used in the Nixon campaign and "he, too, had a heavy heart from the ignorance with which the campaign was being conducted." Nixon's bid for Negro votes was damaged further by a public relations debacle in mid-October. Campaigning in Harlem, Henry Cabot Lodge pledged that there would be a Negro in the Cabinet. Almost immediately, a Nixon aide announced that Cabinet members would be appointed without regard to race. The next day, in Winston-Salem, North Carolina, Lodge denied that he had made the pledge, but as Nixon later pointed out, the incident plagued them through the rest of the campaign. Undoubtedly, it endeared Nixon neither to Negroes nor to Southern whites.[18]

Kennedy, on the other hand, recovered from the setbacks of August and mounted an effective drive for the votes of Negroes. In doing so, Kennedy employed certain traditional Democratic methods but also initiated new approaches. He directed a large, though rather discordant, group of experts to mobilize black public opinion in many of the proven ways— through newspaper advertising, voter registration, and organizational politics. Yet, he also waged a campaign in which the elimination of racial discrimination became an integral part of his general appeal for a revitalized America. By combining the traditional with the new, he created a powerful magnet for black votes and simultaneously raised expectations of what a President might accomplish in the civil rights area.

The theme of Kennedy's overall campaign was explicitly laid out to his speechwriters in late July and never significantly altered: "to summon every segment of our society . . . to restore America's relative strength as a free nation . . . to regain our security and leadership in a fast changing world menaced by communism." Civil rights was one of the issues to which this theme was applied. Kennedy repeatedly talked of the importance of racial discrimination in the broad context of America's destiny. In his opening statement of the critical first televised debate with Nixon, Kennedy declared that the Negro baby, and also the Puerto Rican and Mexican baby, at birth had "about one-half as much chance to get through high school as a white baby . . . about one-third as much chance to get through college . . . four times as much chance that he'll be out of work in his life." Kennedy insisted that America "can do better." In preparation for the debate, Harris Wofford had urged him to include these facts in order to demonstrate to Negroes "a feeling about the existence of discrimination, and understanding of the need for action." Although it is impossible to measure the exact effects of Kennedy's remarks upon black people in general, Roy Wilkins, for one, later recalled that they made a profound impression on him. No Presidential candidate had ever before given such prominence to the cruel human consequences of discrimination.[19]

In the course of the campaign, Kennedy pledged to take a number of specific civil rights actions as President. During the special session of Congress, Kennedy, partly in compensation for Democratic inaction, signed a statement in conjunction with the Leadership Conference on Civil Rights which urged Eisenhower to issue an executive order on housing, as the moderate Civil Rights Commission had suggested eleven months before. Declaring that federally assisted housing could be "desegregated by the stroke of a presidential pen," Kennedy broadly implied that if elected he would wield the required pen. In speeches devoted to civil rights in Los Angeles and New York, he ventured beyond this specific promise. He outlined three areas in which he would move as President. A great deal, he explained, could be accomplished through leadership in the executive branch to make sure that the government itself did not practice or nurture discrimination. Secondly, he promised Presidential leadership in

Congress and asked Representative Emanuel Celler and Senator Joseph Clark to draft legislative proposals that would fulfill the commitments made in the platform. And, he maintained, the President could exercise enormous moral and
educational authority:

> [O]nly the President, not the Senate and not the House, and not
> the Supreme Court, in a real sense only the President can create
> the understanding and tolerance necessary as the spokesman for
> all the American people, as the symbol [applause] as the symbol
> of the moral imperative upon which any free society is based.
> This is a great issue which transcends in many ways many of the
> issues which we debate in the Congress and through the States.
> It is the question of whether we believe the precepts upon which
> this democracy was founded.

Moreover, Kennedy often related the domestic racial situation
to America's image in the nonwhite world.* In the second
debate, he described the United States as a "goldfish bowl
before the world." "How many members of the Foreign Service are of African descent?" he asked a Harlem audience.
Then he promptly told them: "There are over 6,000 people in
the whole Foreign Service—23 out of 6,000. That is not very
many, when Africa will poll one-fourth of all the votes in the
General Assembly by 1962." [20]

To supplement his personal campaigning, Kennedy employed a group of individuals to serve as assistants and surro-
gates in seeking the votes of black people. The group's organization was sometimes chaotic and it was wracked by
internal conflicts over status and power. Nevertheless, it far
outpaced the comparable Nixon operation. Playing significant roles in it were Marjorie Lawson, who had worked for

---

* Of course, Kennedy was not the first to emphasize the foreign implications of
America's racial situation. Civil rights spokesmen and politicians had been using
this argument since World War II. In the second debate, Richard Nixon said it was
necessary to solve the problem of discrimination in order to deprive Khrushchev of a
propaganda point. Kennedy, however, did bring a consciousness of Africa to this
argument that was new for politicians.

Kennedy in a similar capacity since 1957; Harris Wofford, a white lawyer with close connections to Martin Luther King, Jr. and other civil rights leaders; R. Sargent Shriver, Kennedy's brother-in-law, who had been involved in a Catholic race relations committee in Chicago; Louis Martin, a black newspaperman who had once worked for the Democratic National Committee; William Dawson, a Chicago Congressman and leading practitioner of traditional Negro politics; Frank Reeves, a black lawyer and Democratic National Committeeman from Washington, D.C. who had earlier worked for Hubert Humphrey.[21]

This operation departed in several interesting respects from comparable Democratic efforts in the past. Larger and more influential, it enjoyed relatively easy access to the candidate. Moreover, a most significant difference was connoted in the title it carried. Marjorie Lawson, public opinion polls, and Negro delegates to the Democratic convention all agreed that black voters were attaching heavier weight than ever to the civil rights issue when they entered the polling booth. Therefore, the old campaign designation of "Minorities Section" gave way to the more trenchant "Civil Rights Section." [22]

Negro newspapers and magazines amply manifested the work of the Civil Rights Section. Advertisements for Kennedy were plentiful and often poignant. One widely used advertisement depicted a little black girl handing a carnation to the candidate and his wife, Jacqueline. Some placed pictures of Kennedy and Roosevelt side by side; others quoted Kennedy's tribute to the sit-ins. Nixon's advertising, by contrast, generally was not specially geared to the black audience. Kennedy also received widely publicized endorsements from black celebrities, including entertainers Harry Belafonte and Lena Horne, and Jersey Joe Walcott, a former heavyweight champion. Although many of these publications followed the practice of nonpartisanship set by civil rights leaders and refrained from editorially endorsing either candidate, Kennedy received favorable notice in news and social columns much more frequently than Nixon.[23]

The Kennedy campaign became identified with racial progress in a number of other ways. Early it banned participation in segregated meetings. Therefore Lyndon Johnson actually campaigned through the South from the back of a train in order to avoid meeting halls where segregation was practiced. Moreover, several blacks, including Andrew Hatcher, who worked under Pierre Salinger in press relations, traveled with the Kennedy party and impressed black newsmen with the importance of the role they played. In addition, the Civil Rights Section sponsored a conference in October to which it invited the nation's leading civil rights activists ostensibly to discuss the future direction of the movement. The NAACP Board of Directors voted against participation because they suspected partisan motives. They perceived correctly; the conference became a virtual Kennedy rally.[24]

However, one initiative stands out from the rest, not because it singlehandedly won him the election, as some have claimed, but because it dramatized Kennedy's personal sensitivity to civil rights. This, of course, was his phone call to Martin Luther King's wife at the time of her husband's imprisonment. The unfolding of this event provides interesting insights into Kennedy and his campaign. At the same time it illuminates the mood of many blacks in 1960.

In mid-October, Martin Luther King was supposed to have been in Miami at a special board meeting of the Southern Christian Leadership Conference to which Kennedy had been invited to speak. Three Southern governors had warned Kennedy that if he allied himself with King they would throw their states to Nixon. Kennedy planned to attend the meeting anyway; but then he learned that Nixon was also going to address the board, and that neither candidate could expect an endorsement. Deeming the risks of the meeting too great and the possible gains too slight, Kennedy withdrew. Subsequently, the meeting was cancelled altogether. Instead of being in Miami, King returned to his home in Atlanta just about the time that a sit-in began at Rich's, a leading department store. King had earlier cautioned against undertaking demonstrations during the election campaign. Nevertheless, now that students had begun one, King, present in the city, felt morally bound to join it. He was soon arrested for trespassing.[25]

Within a short time, however, William Hartsfield, Atlanta's racially moderate mayor, had King released from jail. Without authorization from Kennedy, Hartsfield announced to the press that he had released King in response to Kennedy's personal intervention. Hartsfield believed that his action had benefited Kennedy enormously. Soon after he made the announcement Hartsfield learned that the local Negro Republican leader had contacted GOP headquarters in Washington to get them to do something, but the Mayor had acted first and thought he had won over the black vote for the Democrats. Wofford, meanwhile, nervously informed Kennedy's staff of what had transpired. Worried that the Mayor's announcement would cost the Senator the election in the South, they released a statement contradicting Hartsfield's account. The press release merely said that a Kennedy campaign aide had inquired about King's constitutional rights.

Almost immediately, though, Kennedy was given a further opportunity to identify himself with King's plight. The previous May, King had been placed on probation by a DeKalb County court for driving without a valid license. Judge Oscar Mitchell, hearing of King's arrest for trespassing in Atlanta, sentenced King to four months of hard labor for violating probation. Learning of this development, the civil rights specialists in Kennedy's campaign drafted a protest statement for him to issue. Georgia's Governor Ernest Vandiver meanwhile urged Kennedy to keep his silence, promising to secure King's release himself.

When Coretta King heard that her husband had been taken to a rural prison farm to serve his sentence, she, in near hysteria, called Harris Wofford, an old friend. After trying to reassure her of her husband's safety, Wofford discussed with Louis Martin what Kennedy might do. They concluded that it would be both decent and politically useful for the Senator to call Mrs. King to express his concern. After some delay, Wofford reached Sargent Shriver in Chicago and outlined their idea. Concurring in it, Shriver drove to the airport hotel where the Kennedy entourage was staying for the night. Fearing the opposition of Kennedy's politically cautious inner circle, he waited as they gradually departed. Finally, the last one, Kenneth O'Donnell, entered an adjacent lavatory. With his foot lodged against the door, Shriver broached the subject with his brother-in-law. He acknowledged the reasons for not issuing a statement, but urged him at least to call the frightened lady. Responding that he thought it was a wonderful idea, Kennedy asked Shriver to dial her number. He then spoke briefly but comfortingly to her.

The call evoked strong reactions. Morris Abram, an Atlanta ally of both Kennedy and King, telephoned Wofford that King's father, an important figure in his own right among black Baptist laymen and ministers, had informed him that he was now switching his well-publicized support from Nixon to Kennedy, despite the Democrat's Catholicism. "I'll vote for him, even thought I don't want a Catholic," the elder King declared. "But I'll take a Catholic or the Devil himself if he'll wipe the tears from my daughter-in-law's eyes. I've got a suitcase full of votes—my whole church—for you to give to Senator Kennedy." * But, weighing the losses against the

---

* At the end of the campaign, Kennedy talked to Wofford about King's father's political conversion. "He said that he was going to vote against me because I was a Catholic. Now he's going to vote for me just because I called his daughter-in-law. That's a helluva bigoted thing to say, wasn't it?" Wofford agreed. A few minutes later, Kennedy turned "and with his best grin said, 'Well, we all have fathers, don't we?' " In: Harris Wofford, interviewed by Berl Bernard, Nov. 29, 1965, Kennedy Library Oral History Program, 27–28.

gains, campaign manager Robert Kennedy instantly concluded that the call had been a grave political error. He angrily reprimanded Wofford and Martin for the probable loss
of three Southern states. Defending the call, Martin fabricated
a story to the effect that Nixon was planning to call a press
conference to blame King's arrest on the South and the Democrats. Soon Robert Kennedy himself telephoned Judge Oscar
Mitchell to complain about his severe treatment of King. Most
likely, the younger Kennedy was largely motivated by fear of
a Nixon counterattack, though he was entirely capable of
moral outrage at the unfairness of the judge's sentence.

Actually neither call became a major story in the white
media or an issue in the campaign. As Sorensen later related,
John Kennedy was "sufficiently uncertain of its impact to
make no speech or press release" on his call. He restricted his
public comment on it to one sentence: "She is a friend of
mine and I was concerned about the situation." Initially, the
American Broadcasting Company was the only major network
to report the call. Two days later, when King left the Reids-
ville prison as a result of his lawyer's appeal, the Columbia
Broadcasting System recorded the event on its evening news
show. The report also covered the elder King's endorsement
of Kennedy. Shortly afterward, Governor Vandiver of Georgia
criticized the Kennedys' actions, but contrary to Robert Kennedy's worst fears, no great damage was done in the South.
His fears might have been realized had this incident occurred
early in the campaign, but by this time most Southern Democrats were firmly in the Kennedy camp and without major attention from the media a public-opinion revolt did not develop.[26]

In the black community, however, John Kennedy's call received considerable publicity. Negro newspapers widely reported it. But more important, Kennedy's Civil Rights Section
worked feverishly to distribute two million copies of a pamphlet about the incident outside black churches and throughout black communities in the days before the election. " 'No

Comment' Nixon versus a Candidate With a Heart, Senator Kennedy: The Case of Martin Luther King," read the pamphlet's cover. Inside were several effective quotations.
Coretta King told of how much better she had felt after Kennedy called and conveyed concern for their welfare. She also
noted that she had heard nothing from Nixon or anyone on
his staff. King's father admitted that he had intended to vote
against Kennedy because of his religion, but was now going to
give him that "suitcase full of votes." Ralph Abernathy,
King's long-time associate in his civil rights work, was
quoted to the effect that it was "time for all of us to take off
our Nixon buttons." "Senator Kennedy did something great
and wonderful when he personally called Mrs. Coretta King
and helped free Dr. Martin Luther King. This was the kind of
act I was waiting for." King himself did not explicitly endorse
Kennedy but he did express his gratitude to him for helping
secure his release. "It took a lot of courage for Senator Kennedy to do this," extolled King. "For him to be that courageous shows that he is really acting upon principle and not
expediency." If not an endorsement in itself, King's statement, taken together with those closest to him, amounted to
the same thing. It represented a significant shift from June
when King led Harris Wofford to believe that he might support Nixon.[27]

The comments of the King group broadly implied a hunger
for compassion and recognition from the nation's political
leadership. Although Presidents had rarely afforded much of
either in the past, the renascence of a civil rights movement
coincidental with Eisenhower's steady indifference to blacks
probably worked to build up appetites for them by 1960.
Merely through a symbolic act, a personal gesture, Kennedy
had apparently fulfilled an important need. Indicatively, that
gesture alone carried enough weight to convince King's circle
to endorse Kennedy.

The inclusion of several statements, by King and others,

against religious bigotry in the widely distributed pamphlet further implied that in one important respect, black Americans, predominantly Protestant, shared a prejudice with their white coreligionists. Although some blacks probably sympathized with Kennedy because they viewed him as a fellow victim of prejudice, some others indulged in anti-Catholic prejudice themselves. For example, King's father had based his initial objections to Kennedy on religious grounds. Hence, the pamphlet gave considerable space to a refutation of religious bigotry.[28]

In an election post-mortem, John Kennedy looked back on this series of events which many commentators and President Eisenhower had regarded as decisive in winning him critical Negro votes in the extremely close contest. "The finest strategies are usually the result of accidents," Kennedy reflected to John Kenneth Galbraith. Indeed, fate had intervened; but Kennedy had a staff alert to the symbolic value of a simple phone call and able to translate the call into votes, and Kennedy himself had been willing to make the call, all of which demonstrated a sensitivity to the black political temper that was missing in the Nixon campaign. Nixon's black campaign aide had urged that a statement be issued in support of King at the same time the Kennedy campaign was acting, and apparently Deputy Attorney General Lawrence Walsh had prepared some kind of a statement; but none was issued. Several Negro Republicans in Washington feebly attempted to criticize King's kind words for Kennedy, but they went largely unnoticed. The Nixon campaign, by this point, had already evinced considerably more concern for capturing the white South than Negro votes.[29]

Kennedy, of course, also worried about the South. The initial contradiction of Mayor Hartsfield, Shriver's cautious approach to the candidate, Robert Kennedy's display of temper, and public relations restraint all pointed to a desire to avoid alienating white voters and politicians in the South. Moreover, the cautiousness that marked the handling of the Martin Luther King incident permeated the entire civil rights operation in the campaign. Two of the people who served as Kennedy's liaison to Southern Democrats, Robert Troutman, Jr. of Georgia and William C. Battle of Virginia, were given a voice on civil rights strategy. Similarly, Kennedy's statement on an executive order against discrimination in housing was delayed and modified as a result of pressure from Senators Richard Russell and John Sparkman. And the conference sponsored by the Civil Rights Section was called the "National Conference on Constitutional Rights and American Freedom." "Constitutional" was substituted for "Civil Rights" out of deference to white Southern sensibilities.[30]

Finally, Kennedy's handling of the civil rights issue in the televised debates, though impressing Roy Wilkins, subtly promised the South no repetition of Little Rock. His opening remarks in the first debate, about the poor economic and educational prospects of the nonwhite baby, posed little threat to white Southerners. His remarks on the Little Rock situation in the second debate might well have even gratified Southern whites. He criticized Eisenhower for lacking leadership. Though he never completely spelled out where he thought the President had erred, he hinted that if Eisenhower had made it clearly understood that the Supreme Court ruling was to be carried out, the Little Rock crisis could have been avoided. Moreover, if it had been necessary to use force, it should have been in the form of federal marshals, not troops. Thus, Kennedy deftly offered something to both black and white Southerners, moral leadership, which could sustain the rights of Negroes without a reinstitution of Reconstruction-like measures that would trammel the rights of whites. Indicatively, all the Southern governors except one immediately wired Kennedy, from a conference they had been holding, their congratulations on his overall performance.[31]

As Kennedy's selection of Johnson implied, he hoped to

win the South's electoral votes, but during the summer his prospects of doing so dimmed. Many Southern Democrats despised the platform and were insufficiently mollified by Johnson's presence on the ticket. Indeed, a more ominous message than anything that came out of the convention was passed among several influential Democrats in August. "Dick Russell told me today that Kennedy will implement the Democratic platform and advocate Civil Rights legislation beyond what is contained in the platform," Harry Byrd wrote to James F. Byrnes. The precariousness of Kennedy's situation in the South derived also from his religion and his liberal economic views. The South and Southwest, both heavily Protestant, were expected to react most strongly against his Catholicism. It was for this reason that Kennedy chose a convention of ministers in Houston to deliver his most important defense of his ability to serve as President without interference from his church. Generally conservative economically, the South also distrusted Kennedy's attitude toward business. "We are having a great deal of difficulty in the Southern states such as South Carolina, Mississippi, Texas, " Robert Kennedy informed Sargent Shriver in early August, "on the grounds that Jack's views are socialistic and he wants the state to control both man and business." In order to correct that misimpression, Kennedy created a National Committee of Business and Professional Men and Women for Kennedy and Johnson, chaired by a Southerner, Luther Hodges, Governor of North Carolina and a former businessman.[32]

Gradually, however, Johnson's presence on the ticket helped considerably in the South. Even though Richard Russell believed that Kennedy posed a serious threat on civil rights, he still maintained a close friendship with Johnson. He and Herman Talmadge, his Georgia colleague, early loaned Johnson several of their staff assistants to help out in the campaign. Both Georgia Senators issued tepid endorsements of Kennedy in late September, but when Johnson spoke in their state they embraced the Texan enthusiastically. Russell described Johnson as "the ablest legislator who has served in the Congress in the past half century." "Lyndon Johnson is capable of filling with notable distinction any position in the gift of the American people," he concluded. Introducing Johnson in Macon, Talmadge compared the Majority Leader to Henry Clay. Like Clay, Johnson had "thwarted extreme legislation" and "kept our region from dividing." In November Russell even briefly joined Johnson on the campaign trail, which for the Georgian was highly unusual. Russell's decision to do so grew out of an incident in Dallas in which a rowdy group of right-wing demonstrators had denounced Johnson as a Judas, spit at him, and knocked off the hat of his wife, Lady Bird. Johnson later claimed that rather than try to avoid the confrontation, he had purposely waded into it, apparently because he recognized its potential value. In any case, the ugly incident did offend Russell's sense of civility. He told reporters that right-wing demonstrations would only help the Democrats. He also credited Johnson with having lessened Southern unhappiness over the platform. Disenchantment still existed and would reduce the Democratic majority, but Russell felt confident that the South would back the ticket.[33]

In his most publicized campaign trip, Johnson whistle-stopped through the South in mid-October. "What has Dick Nixon ever done for Culpeper?" he asked his first group of listeners along the tracks in Virginia. Reporters quickly dubbed the train the "Cornpone Special," but the public liked the drawl and the style, and the twelve hundred local politicians who joined Johnson for short rides on the train understood perfectly the meaning of the question. The Democratic Congress treated the South generously whereas the Republicans kept the purse strings tight. Reportedly, many politicians were also reminded by this master of the quid pro quo that if he and Kennedy were elected they would be in a position to continue Democratic largesse—if the South voted for them.[34]

Johnson did not repudiate the liberal Democratic platform, though he chose his words of endorsement carefully. He often called for "full constitutional guarantees to all citizens regardless of race or color," but he also appealed to the South's regional pride and alluded favorably to the South's "civil rights." In the economic sphere, too, such as in his position on the oil depletion allowance and "right to work" laws, Johnson placed distance between himself and the platform. Although liberals had initially been angered by Johnson's nomination, in the heat of the campaign between Kennedy and Nixon, they repressed it. "I am establishing a club called 'Johnsons Anonymous,' the members of which, every time they feel like attacking Johnson, take a drink instead," an apparently inebriated Joseph Rauh wrote to one of Kennedy's more liberal aides. Similarly, Senators Hubert Humphrey and Joseph Clark refrained from pressing the issue of filibuster revision on the candidates in the fall. And when Roy Wilkins polled all Congressional candidates for their views on rules reform, Johnson, standing for reelection to the Senate while simultaneously running for Vice President, failed to fill out the NAACP's questionnaire. "I stand upon the platform," Johnson responded, without mentioning the platform's lack of specificity on this particular point.[35]

Kennedy and Johnson would not have agreed with the sentiments expressed by some of their conservative Southern supporters, but they did not disown them. For example, in Mississippi, where a slate of unpledged electors was on the ballot, James Eastland and John Stennis, the state's two powerful Senators, endorsed the national ticket but rejected the platform. "National conventions can freely frame platforms, but only Congress can enact them into law. . . . We are now in an era of power politics, and we know from experience that the strongest and most effective way to protect or preserve the interests of our State and country at this time is with national party affiliation." Eastland later appeared on local television and credited Johnson with taking "everything relating to integration out of those civil rights bills." Southern Democrats loyal to the national ticket also attacked the Republicans for meddling in local affairs, as in Little Rock and investigations into voting infractions. "The Republican Presidential candidate knows of and condones this modern Reconstructionism," charged South Carolina Senator Olin Johnston in referring to a federal investigation into the voting records of three of his state's counties. He blasted Attorney General William P. Rogers, whom he described as Nixon's "chief adviser," for turning the Justice Department into a "political gestapo." "Rogers' agents," decried the Senator, "are busily engaged in the filthy business of crucifying the people of the South for minority group votes in big cities." [36]

These arguments did not persuade all Southern Democrats to embrace the national ticket. In Virginia, especially, powerful conservative office-holders refused publicly to take sides in the election. Senator Harry Byrd, Chairman of the Senate Finance Committee, and Congressman Howard Smith, Chairman of the House Rules Committee, resisted all requests to join other Southern Democrats in endorsing Kennedy-Johnson. In part, their resistance derived from their greater devotion to conservatism generally, not just from their opposition to desegregation. In addition Byrd was struggling to maintain control over the state's political organization. Governor J. Lindsay Almond, who had broken with Byrd over the extent to which "massive resistance" was to be applied, worked hard for the ticket. As a Byrd ally observed to two fence-straddling Congressmen, were Kennedy to carry the state, Almond would receive the credit. He then pointed out, "Almond is dead politically unless this state votes for Kennedy." Although Byrd endorsed neither party's candidates in 1960, he privately advised a high Republican official on ways to help that party's Presidential candidate in the South.[37]

Generally, however, Kennedy enjoyed a high degree of loyalty from Southern Democrats. Even though he became progressively more liberal through the year, he succeeded in evading the despised label of Reconstruction Democrat. He promised bold new civil rights actions to win over doubtful black voters and as part of his overall theme of revitalizing the nation, but he never suggested that they would entail full-scale federal intervention in the South. Indeed, by choosing the South's favorite son as his running mate, and then assigning him a major portion of the campaigning there, he reaffirmed his long-standing reputation as a racial moderate.

Viewing the party's handling of the racial issue in mid-October, Harry Byrd wrote James Byrnes that it was "trying to play both ends against the middle"—an accurate enough description and it had long been the case. Moreover, the same could have been said for Nixon and the Republicans. In 1960, however, Kennedy demonstrated a superior facility in this delicate aspect of modern American politics. Winning the closest Presidential election in recent times, Kennedy outpolled Nixon in all Southern states except for Virginia, Florida, and Tennessee. And, equally important, he ran up substantial black pluralities nationally, completely reversing the Republican gains of four years before.[38]

A closer look at some of the returns is revealing. Nixon actually did better in the South than his relatively paltry 45.98 percent of the popular vote there would indicate, for that figure is distorted by several states' idiosyncracies. Where the Democratic Party was virtually the only party, in Georgia, Louisiana, and Alabama, Kennedy received disproportionately large pluralities. However, when the electoral votes were actually cast, all eight of Mississippi's electors, and six of Alabama's eleven, defied the national ticket and voted for

Harry Byrd. In Texas and South Carolina, Kennedy barely squeaked by Nixon. Undoubtedly, without Johnson on the ticket, Kennedy would have fared much worse in the South, almost certainly losing Texas, and probably the election. Moreover, Nixon carried the South's cities, continuing the growing Republican trend there.[39]

Although the evidence on the effects of the racial issue on Presidential voting by Southern whites is not conclusive, it tends to suggest that the issue did not sway many votes one way or the other. Louis Harris reported to Kennedy in September on places where segregationists backed him, and others where they preferred Nixon. A Gallup Poll completed several days before the election found that Southerners believed Nixon could better handle integration problems by 35 to 17 percent. Unfortunately, Gallup did not break down this statistic by race. Significantly, however, nearly a majority of those polled felt there was "no difference" or expressed "no opinion." One can infer that Nixon generally failed to benefit from his more conservative position on race and states' rights or from his extensive personal campaigning in the South. Indeed, an intensive survey of white public opinion in one Southern city found that whites failed to distinguish between the candidates on civil rights. Moreover, a post-election computer-assisted study concluded, in part, that extreme segregationists were more likely to stay at home than vote for Nixon. Inevitably, most of the psephologists' attention has been drawn to the influence of religion on voting behavior. The University of Michigan's voter analysts, probably the nation's most informed and cautious, concluded that religion hurt Kennedy in the South, but admitted that they did not know the effect of the racial issue.[40]

The impact of the civil rights issue on black voters is somewhat clearer. Kennedy won back many of the Negro voters who had deserted the Democrats in 1956. Gallup estimated that Kennedy garnered 68 percent of the Negro vote, a 7 percent improvement over Stevenson's last showing. But studies of particular wards in Northern cities indicated that Kennedy picked up 80 percent and more of this vote and, equally important, the turnout was high. In numerous states where the election was close (especially Illinois, Michigan, New Jersey, Pennsylvania, Missouri, Texas, and South Carolina), Kennedy's pluralities among Negroes exceeded his margin of victory. Of course, the same might be said of several other blocs of votes since the contest was so close.[41]

Certainly, all black voters did not cast their ballots strictly on the basis of the civil rights issue. Undoubtedly, many were influenced by Kennedy's stand on other matters relevant to their lives such as the economy and social welfare measures. Yet Kennedy did recover many of the lost votes of recent years and he did do better than his early public opinion polls indicated he would, which implies that his campaign made a positive impact. Many observers assumed that his phone call to Coretta King accounted for his success. But Atlanta's Negroes, who could have been expected to be most influenced by it, actually preferred Nixon to Kennedy. Obviously, it is not possible to pinpoint one thing that made the difference. Rather, one must look at the total picture—Kennedy's advanced rhetoric, his organization, his sensitivity to the black temper. Moreover, in none of these respects did Nixon offer much competition. This stood in contrast to the white South where Nixon presented a strong challenge.[42]

Thus, in 1960 Kennedy managed to maintain and build upon his reputation as a racial moderate sympathetic to civil rights. However, during the long campaign he made commitments that would be difficult for him to live up to as President. He had reassured white Southerners that he would not favor a reinstitution of Reconstruction, yet he had promised Negroes a wide range of Presidential action on their behalf. There was an important difference in the nature of these two promises besides their obvious contradiction. His promises to whites implied a continuation of the status quo; his promises to blacks implied significant change. And the overriding theme of Kennedy's campaign was that the President should promote progress in all aspects of American life. One might have guessed that if Kennedy ultimately had to decide between continuity and change, he would choose change.

Moreover, Kennedy's campaign helped to heighten black expectations. He had pointed out numerous ways in which nonwhites suffered in American society as a result of discrimination and proposed that something be done about them. He had spoken more frequently and acted more sensitively on civil rights than any previous major party nominee. And because of the closeness of the election Negroes could feel that they had contributed significantly to his victory. Therefore they looked expectantly toward his administration. As the NAACP publication editorialized in December:

> The bright spot in the recent presidential election is the important part played by the Negro voter. . . . Therefore, in light both of the Democratic platform and the heavy Negro democratic [sic] vote, Negro citizens are expecting the new administration in Washington to do something effective about civil rights and race relations. Don't forget that the Democrats promised to stand on their platform. . . .
>
> Negro citizens, as a result of the elections, are in no mood to consent to a "cease-fire" in the field for full civil rights. They are tired of the daily humiliations of racial segregation and discrimination.

Kennedy soon had to decide how to fulfill his commitment to fight discrimination.[43]

THREE

Leadership and Caution in the White House

In his campaign for President, Kennedy promised executive, moral, and legislative leadership to combat racial discrimination. In his first year in the White House he provided substantial executive, a kind of moral, and virtually no legislative leadership in the civil rights area. Although Negroes and white Southerners had contributed roughly equally to his election, only the latter constituency continued to exercise considerable power. Nevertheless, his executive program, even though compromised in many ways, represented a significant departure from the normal Presidential indifference.

THROUGHOUT his drive for the Presidency, Kennedy implored his countrymen to revitalize America, to "get America moving again." Although he won the election, the voters chose him by one of the narrowest margins in history, placing Kennedy in a dilemma. He had promised a broad array of changes, but nearly half the electorate had supported his opponent, who had generally voiced satisfaction with the way things were.

The historic sectional and ideological division of his party further complicated Kennedy's difficulty. He enjoyed healthy Democratic majorities in both houses of Congress, though they had been reduced in size from 1958. More important, the power of Southerners in Congress exceeded their considerable numbers. As a result primarily of the senority system, and secondarily of their legislative acumen, Southerners dominated the upper levels of Congress. Although some Southern Democrats, such as Byrd, were so conservative that

they could not be expected to accede to any of the liberal programs promised in the campaign, others were much more
amenable to the kind of domestic legislation Kennedy had
called for. However, their friendliness could be endangered
by a struggle over civil rights legislation. "If we drive [John]
Sparkman, [Lister] Hill and other moderate Southerners to
the wall with a lot of civil rights demands that can't pass anyway," Kennedy asked Theodore Sorensen, "then what hap-
pens to the Negro on minimum wages, housing and the
rest?" [1]

Kennedy did not announce his decision to forego civil
rights legislation for some time, but it was foreshadowed by
his reaction to two struggles within Congress over rules. He
abstained from participating in a Senate fight over revision of
Rule XXII which pertained to limiting debate. Some liberals
had hoped that with a Democratic President's assistance, they
could modify the rule so as to make it easier to stop filibus-
ters. But without help from either Kennedy or Mike Mansfield, the new Majority Leader, rule reform went down to
defeat. Kennedy did become heavily involved in a narrowly
successful battle to increase the size of the House Rules Committee. His motive here was to make it easier for economic
and social welfare, not civil rights, legislation to reach the
floor. The selection of Southerners to fill newly created places
on the Rules Committee publicly confirmed that this reform
had not been aimed at smoothing the way for civil rights legislation. [2]

The new President recognized certain advantages in not
quickly revealing his decision to defer civil rights legislation.
It increased his bargaining power with Southern Democrats.
A month after taking office he asked one of his assistants to
talk to Congressman Emanuel Celler and Senator Joseph
Clark. During the campaign he had asked them to draft civil
rights bills and now he wanted to maintain "close liaison
with them." "It may be proper for them to hold hearings this

year . . . and then have the fight next year," the President instructed, "but I don't want statements to be issued that we have withdrawn our support of this matter." In late December, Harris Wofford had counselled Kennedy on another reason for not tipping his hand. Negro and civil rights groups, Wofford advised, had not yet "adjusted to the idea of the primacy of executive action." They were used to a dearth of Presidential action which caused them to concentrate their attention on Congress, and "they would greet a decision to forego legislation as a sell-out." "After they have tasted the fruits of executive action," Wofford continued, "they will know the barrenness of their legislative lobbying, and see that the logic of such executive action will lead to complementary legislation—and lead there sooner than a party-splitting legislative battle at the beginning of your Administration." [3]

Accordingly, Kennedy refrained from revealing his decision on legislation. He failed to inform Roy Wilkins of it when they met in early January. "When I feel that there is a necessity for a congressional action, with a chance of getting that congressional action, then I will recommend it to the Congress," he explained to a reporter in March. Several weeks later Wofford clarified the administration's position somewhat. Addressing a civil rights audience, he observed that "during the last years of racial crisis the Government . . . was flying on only one engine in civil rights—the Federal Judiciary." "But now," he declared, "the Executive Branch is beginning to turn. This is a tremendous new source of power. Have you really focussed on the possibilities?" Wofford cautioned against the ill effects of defeatism that could carry over from their long years in opposition to the government: "Are we on guard to avoid a tendency to prefer to lose a long, loud fight for a Congressional civil rights bill rather than to win a quiet, steady campaign for effective executive action?" Wofford also reminded his audience that Kennedy's victory resulted from an incongruous alliance of the new South of Lyndon Johnson and an appeal for civil rights. In the future, Wofford maintained, that combination would sometimes seem uneasy and even impossible, but it would work.[4]

As Kennedy's decision became clear, civil rights leaders publicly rebuked him for abrogating his pledge. The New Frontier looked to Clarence Mitchell "suspiciously like a dude ranch with Senator James O. Eastland as the general manager and Howard Smith as the foreman." Privately Roy Wilkins adopted a much more conciliatory tone. After Wofford's March speech Wilkins wrote to him that it would have been shrewder for the administration to have won the Senate rules fight, and that little was gained by completely abandoning the legislative approach. Wilkins also complained that organizations such as his had not been adequately informed in advance of the decision. Wilkins had praised Kennedy publicly and before an NAACP convention in January and so he evidently had been taken by surprise. He asked if people like himself could "tell their boards or their membership that they had switched their emphasis without being able to say what dividends the switch might produce." Yet, the NAACP's chief operating officer characterized his criticisms not as "a quarrel," but as a "difference with the Kennedy administration."[5]

The mildness of NAACP comments had to do in part with the weakness of its position in Congress. Of the four black House members, only two had acquired enough senority to possess substantive power and neither of them chose to exercise it in retaliation for Kennedy's inaction. William Dawson, Chairman of the Government Operations Committee, had never demonstrated a predilection for civil rights activism. He always preferred to work loyally within the establishments of Congress and the Democratic Party. By contrast, Adam Clayton Powell, Jr., Chairman of the Labor and Education Committee, had repeatedly shown a willingness to crusade against racial discrimination, though rarely in concert with civil rights organizations. In early 1961, Powell too bowed to party regularity. He announced that he was desisting from attaching the so-called Powell Amendments to social legislation which had to pass through his committee. These amendments required that federal funds not be spent in any discriminatory program. They had effectively doomed several pieces of legislation in the past, such as aid to education, because few Southern Democrats would vote for a bill with this kind of stipulation.[6]

In addition, white Democratic liberals, principal advocates of civil rights legislation in the past, evinced little concern over Kennedy's abandonment of such legislation now. Celler and Clark, for example, had drafted a series of bills at Kennedy's request, but did not introduce them until May. Kennedy consented to their introduction but refused to issue a statement endorsing them. On the contrary, the very next day White House Press Secretary Pierre Salinger specifically disassociated the administration from the bills. Harris Wofford and Louis Martin privately questioned the wisdom of Salinger's disavowal but it was not qualified. Wilkins criticized it publicly and privately expressed his annoyance that Salinger had also said that there had been "very little pressure" for new civil rights legislation. But no Democrat in Congress made an issue of it. After eight years of Republican control of the White House, they were not disposed to rebuke a generally liberal Democrat in his first months in office. They took Kennedy's decision in stride.[7]

Republican liberals twitted their Demcratic counterparts for their silence, but they constituted a distinct minority in their party. In fact Senate Minority Leader Everett Dirksen, normally a sharp critic of Kennedy, refused even to characterize the President's behavior as a broken pledge. Indicatively, at the start of the new session of Congress, Republican liberals had openly criticized the standard Republican strategy of coalition with Southern Democrats, but their party leaders immediately and clearly rejected their advice by helping to quash filibuster reform and opposing expansion of the House Rules Committee. In succeeding months the conservative coalition would again work together. Moreover, conservative Republicans were becoming bolder in their bid for white Southern votes. In November, Barry Goldwater made an unambiguous appeal for segregationist support. He told an Atlanta audience that he favored watering down the Republicans' 1960 civil rights plank. He also endorsed a constitutional amendment which would strengthen state authority over public education.[8]

Kennedy's inauguration meanwhile had generated considerable excitement and fostered the belief that a new day had dawned for America. In particular, it furthered the promise of Presidential leadership that Kennedy had contributed to so significantly in his campaign. Indeed, that promise had captivated many people, especially liberals. Benjamin Muse, a liberal Virginian and experienced observer of the Southern scene, traveled widely in the days following Kennedy's election. The predominantly white Southern liberals and moderates with whom he spoke believed that "the moral force of positive and often expressed administration support of the school desegregation rulings and civil rights in general would be immensely helpful." Few favored new civil rights legislation, but all desired the vigorous application of existing laws. Muse also found the editors of the Washington *Post* sanguine about the possibilities of executive action without the need for new legislation. Several months later, the Southern Regional Council, the liberal racial and economic council with which Muse was affiliated, submitted a forty-eight-page report to the President. It was entitled "The Federal Executive and Civil Rights." "The presidency is the center of American energy," the report declared. It emphasized heavily the actions that could be taken without new legislation. Many influential newspapers, including several in the South, gave the report extensive treatment.[9]

The prospects of executive action also charmed civil rights leaders and experts. Setting forth in *The Nation* a series of proposals for change, Martin Luther King stressed measures the executive branch of government could take. When John Hannah, Chairman of the Civil Rights Commission, met with Kennedy in early February he made a number of suggestions, each of which relied exclusively on the executive authority of the President. Even the NAACP, generally legislatively oriented, succumbed to the trend. It sent delegates to visit many executive departments in July, and the following month Roy Wilkins submitted a detailed report to the President of administrative actions that could be taken to defeat racial discrimination.[10]

Of course, if the administration had only talked about executive action, enthusiasm for a nonlegislative approach would have vanished rapidly. But from its inception, the new command offered encouraging signs that it meant business. And within its first several months of life, it followed up with concrete programs and actions. These were often diluted by compromise, but not enough to turn civil rights leaders against Kennedy.

The earliest signs that Kennedy would bring about genuine change appeared in the employment of Negroes in government. Before his inauguration, Kennedy designated Robert C. Weaver to be Administrator of the Housing and Home Finance Agency, an important bureau which had excellent chances of being elevated to Cabinet status in the near future. Weaver, who had long experience in the housing field, was chairman of the board of the NAACP, which pridefully commended Kennedy on his choice. The appointment signalled "unmistakably the mood of President-elect John F. Kennedy on civil rights," Roy Wilkins told that organization's annual meeting. In Negro newspapers, the Weaver story received prominent attention.[11]

Events at the inauguration itself also intimated a bright future. Roy Wilkins learned that the new President had noticed that no Negroes were marching in one of the military units and that he had immediately ordered an inquiry. That Kennedy should have been so sensitive to that kind of detail on the most important day of his life greatly impressed Wilkins. Simeon Booker, national reporter for *Ebony*, was also affected when he was assigned to the news pool to accompany the President-elect, a breakthrough for the Negro press. Moreover, in its coverage of the inauguration's social celebrations, that magazine offered pictorial proof that black people were gaining a new recognition on the New Frontier—a large number of blacks participated in the festivities.[12]

These occurrences accurately foretold what was coming. In its first year, the Kennedy administration fundamentally altered past patterns of official indifference, neglect, and insensitivity. Through employment policy, rhetoric, and general awareness of black aspirations, it changed the tone of governmental behavior toward racial discrimination. In retrospect, some of the specific changes may appear cosmetic, token, and wrongly motivated, but certainly at the time many black people perceived them as positive improvements over the practices and attitudes of the past.

Kennedy chose a dramatically large number of Negroes for high-level appointment. During his first two months in office he selected, in addition to Weaver, forty Negroes for important posts. Among these were Frank D. Reeves as Special Assistant to the President; Carl Rowan, Deputy Assistant Secretary of State for Public Affairs; Andrew Hatcher, Associate White House Press Secretary; George L. P. Weaver, Special Assistant to the Secretary of Labor; and Clifton R. Wharton, Ambassador to Norway. Louis Martin became Deputy Chairman of the Democratic National Committee, and generally stayed out of the limelight though he probably had greater access to and influence in the White House than any other black appointee. However, from a public relations standpoint the most significant designation came in September when the President placed Thurgood Marshall on the Second Circuit Court of Appeals in New York. To many black Americans, Marshall was a hero, having argued their constitutional rights with repeated success before the Supreme Court, most notably in *Brown v. Board of Education*. Although Robert Kennedy assured Marshall that he had been chosen solely for his legal abilities, not as an expression of support for the civil rights movement, the delaying tactics of the Senate Judiciary Committee, which held up confirmation for a year, served as a continual reminder to blacks that it was President Kennedy who had honored "Mr. Civil Rights." [13]

The Negro press paid particular attention to several appointments in the District of Columbia where rule by a white Southern-dominated Congressional committee had long frustrated the aspirations of its black residents, now a majority of the population. The President supported home rule to no avail. He did succeed in naming the District's first black Commissioner. He early designated Frank Reeves of his own staff, but Reeves was forced to withdraw his nomination after the Congressional committee revealed that he had once had tax liens on him. There were intimations of even more serious financial indiscretions as well. Clarence Mitchell and Chuck Stone, a black journalist, charged the administration with treating Reeves too harshly, but that aspect of the story never captured the headlines as another black, John B. Duncan, soon was named to the administrative position in the District. The following spring, Marjorie Lawson, after turning down several offers and not receiving others that she wanted—quite possibly because of sex discrimination —agreed to serve as a judge in the District's juvenile court. Several months earlier she had accepted membership on

the President's Committee on Equal Employment Opportunity.[14]

The Negro press reported these appointments because of
their news value, but the Kennedy administration also took
pains to make sure that they knew of them as well as of other
manifestations of progress in race relations. Much as in the
campaign, Kennedy cultivated the friendship of the black
media. By desegregating the White House press pool and
shortly later its photographers association, the administration
earned the gratitude of the Negro press. The administration
also hired a number of black reporters to work as public information officers in various government agencies and departments. The reporters provided the nation's black press
with a steady stream of encouraging news, which also enhanced the image of the administration. The country's 142
black newspapers, which had a combined circulation of one
and a half million, regularly brought many blacks news and
information the white media did not report.[15]

The accession of blacks to high government positions
raised the issue of social relations, in which the Kennedy administration also demonstrated its sympathies for racial
equality. In the spring, Secretary of Labor Arthur Goldberg
attacked racial bias in private clubs, specifically citing the
prestigious Metropolitan Club. A number of the administration's members and friends were soon resigning from it, including Attorney General Robert Kennedy, who quit in September after having tried for six months to get its board of
governors to change its policy. In addition, the President's
own membership to the Cosmos Club was withdrawn after
his sponsor, John Kenneth Galbraith, resigned because Carl
Rowan had been refused membership. Some of these liberal
members and friends of the administration banded together
to form a new nondiscriminatory club, the Federal City Club.
Equally important, the Kennedys also set an example with
regard to entertaining in their homes. They regularly invited

Negroes to social gatherings both at the White House and at Robert Kennedy's Virginia home. By contrast, the society editors of the Washington *Post* could not, in November 1960, recall Eisenhower's ever entertaining Negroes, with the exception of foreign officials and possibly Ralph Bunche of the United Nations.[16]

In defiance of common practice, Kennedy's black appointees did not work exclusively in race related assignments. Indeed, several took pride in their conviction that race had been irrelevant to their being hired. They refrained from becoming civil rights activists within the government, preferring instead to demonstrate that Negroes could perform well and loyally in regular jobs, and not turn into special pleaders for their people's cause. In several instances black officials seemed so loyal to the administration's interests that civil rights leaders thought they had forgotten their own origins. Andrew Hatcher, for example, received a stinging rebuke from Roy Wilkins after he advised a local NAACP chapter to drop civil rights activism and devote itself to fighting juvenile delinquency, crime, and other social problems. Wilkins acidly reminded Hatcher that leading Southern segregationists had long been urging the same course.[17]

Actually, whites held most of the administration's key positions in the race relations area. Without question Robert Kennedy manned the government's most critical and sensitive post in this regard. As Attorney General he headed a team of lawyers who were deeply involved in enforcing civil rights laws and managing Southern crises. It is obvious that merely by giving his brother these responsibilities, the President was implicitly recognizing the importance of civil rights.

A number of Presidential assistants also carried civil rights responsibilites. Harris Wofford found himself in the difficult position of urging the President to speak out more forcefully while simultaneously serving as a buffer between him and civil rights leaders. When several student activists asked for a

meeting with Kennedy, Wofford recommended to his appointments secretary that the President agree rather than
"wait until they launch fasts in jail or encampments outside
the White House asking to see him." At the same time, Wofford advised that "the way to avoid 'summit meetings' with
big delegations and great expectations and possible disappointments is to hold occasional informal meetings." Frederick Dutton, who held a rather anomalous position as "Cabinet Assistant" also devoted considerable time to coordinating
civil rights activities in the executive branch. Within a year
both of these men had moved into foreign service jobs, Wofford at the Peace Corps and Dutton at the State Department.
Even before the end of 1961, Lee White, a Deputy Special
Counsel and Sorensen subordinate, had moved into the role
of principal White House staff man on civil rights.[18]

Changes in personnel and shifts in organizational lines
proved to be less important than the new concern for civil
rights, which was permeating the executive branch of government. The President himself set the tone by taking up the
issue of employment discrimination at an early Cabinet meeting and following up on it several months later. Similarly, he
created a subcabinet group to coordinate interdepartmental
efforts to thwart discrimination. This group scored an early
success by marshalling the resources of several agencies and
departments to aid Negro victims of economic reprisals in
Fayette and Haywood Counties in Tennessee. White landlords had evicted black tenants from their farms after the
tenants had participated in a voter registration drive. The
subcabinet group was short-lived, but with its creation each
department and agency had appointed a senior officer to deal
with the problem of racial discrimination. In general that responsibility endured in most bureaus after the group itself
faded from existence.[19]

The new President also altered an established government
body in a significant way. Through his appointments, Ken-

nedy consciously set out to liberalize the Civil Rights Commission. In theory, Erwin Griswold (a white Republican and Dean of the Harvard Law School) and Spottswood Robinson (a Virginia Negro, a Democrat and Dean of Howard Law School) preserved the Commission's balances of Democrats and Republicans, Northerners and Southerners. But in fact their addition to the investigative and reporting panel changed its outlook. Gone from the Commission were the Southern governors who had taken the sting out of its reports and sometimes dissented from its recommendations. In addition, its new staff director, Berl Bernhard, was much more progressive than his predecessor. Hence, the Commission's voice would soon become united, outspoken, and eventually an annoyance to the administration.[20]

The new government made another important innovation—it became much more accessible to civil rights leaders than the Eisenhower or any past administration had been. Although civil rights leaders rarely expressed complete satisfaction with the government's performance, they received from Kennedy and his subordinates recognition and a hearing. For example, the President met at the White House with a sixty-five-member NAACP delegation in July. Their spokesman, Bishop Stephen G. Spottswood, thanked Kennedy for establishing a "moral tone," but urged him to reconsider his decision to forego legislation. "The President listened intently and then, in a firm but gracious speech reiterated his belief that enforcement of existing laws plus action on the executive level would be most effective at this time," Roy Wilkins later reported to his board. Kennedy charmed this group, as he got chairs for the women and led a select few on a tour of the mansion. In 1967, Clarence Mitchell, who rarely had a kind public word for Kennedy, observed that no other President he had seen would have been treated so sympathetically, considering that he had yielded no ground. With anyone else, Mitchell stated, the delegation "would have been denouncing the President. But this group instead came back in a very good mood." [21]

Indeed, the President's relaxed manner and directness could disarm potential critics. Once a delegation of Negro publishers began reading a rehearsed statement during their fifteen-minute meeting. Kennedy reached for their text, insisting that he could read it faster himself, and asked them to speak freely. Afterward one of the publishers described his reaction: "My mind froze. I kept saying to myself, 'This is what we fought for—recognition.' I just couldn't think." On another occasion, at about the time the Freedom Rides occurred, Kennedy met with the Peace Corps Advisory Council, some of whose members—including Harry Belafonte, Benjamin Mays, Morris Abram, and Eugene Rostow—had an abiding interest in civil rights. Harris Wofford expected that several of these men would reproach the President for not acting more decisively, but only Rostow did so. After the group departed, the President angrily asked Wofford to identify his critic. He wondered how someone could call into question his unprecedented initiatives on behalf of civil rights. Wofford informed the President that his critic was the brother of Walt Rostow, one of Kennedy's foreign affairs advisers, and that he only wanted a stronger Presidential statement in support of the Freedom Riders. Possibly Kennedy took civil rights criticism with greater ease from blacks than from whites, because he had become similarly upset with Joseph Rauh when the ADA leader questioned his basic approach. [22]

The Kennedy administration also extended a new degree of rhetorical support to the civil rights cause. Evidently fearing an adverse reaction from Southern Democrats, Kennedy avoided the "bully pulpit." He did not devote a major address to the racial issue. Kennedy's "moral leadership," promised in the campaign, took the form of exemplary conduct rather than ethical preachments. Still, the administration, led by the President, substantially raised the level of rhetorical support for civil rights. During the first year, the President, among other things, endorsed school desegregation, congratulated several cities on their successful implementation of school desegregation, and participated in ceremonies marking the signing of corporate pledges to end job discrimination through voluntary action. In addition, numerous members of the administration spoke out, most notably the Attorney General. To an audience at the University of Georgia, Robert Kennedy praised the two black students who had recently desegregated it. In a Voice of America broadcast he predicted the election of a Negro to the Presidency in the foreseeable future. And, referring to racial discrimination, he told a group of clergymen that he could not "see how anyone can wear a collar and not speak out against this evil." [23]

Repeatedly, the Kennedys and members of the administration placed their comments in an international context. "The denial of constitutional rights to some of our fellow Americans on account of race—at the ballot box and elsewhere—disturbs the national conscience, and subjects us to the charge of world opinion that our democracy is not equal to the high promise of our heritage," the President stated in his only reference to civil rights in his first State of the Union message. The following month he expressed the nation's debt to the educators, school children, and parents who had cooperated in the difficult transition to school desegregation. America's "survival as a free nation," he maintained, depended on its school system. Therefore it was "no time for schools to close for any reason, and certainly no time for schools to be closed in the name of racial discrimination." If we are to give the leadership the world requires of us," he observed, "we must be true to the great principles of our Constitution—the very principles which distinguish us from our adversaries in the world." "In the worldwide struggle," Robert Kennedy told an audience made up preponderantly of white students and faculty at Georgia, "the graduation at this

University of Charlayne Hunter and Hamilton Holmes [its first black students] will without question aid and assist the fight against communist political infiltration and guerrilla warfare." [24]

The foreign implications of America's racial problems had been worrying many Americans since the 1940s, but to the new administration in Washington they seemed especially significant. From the time he entered politics Kennedy had been most concerned with issues of war and peace. After winning the Presidential election in November, he directed his speech writers to focus his inaugural address on foreign policy. When drafts of the speech including domestic issues sounded too partisan, Kennedy omitted virutally all references to domestic matters. "At the last moment," Sorensen recalled, "concerned that his emphasis on foreign affairs would be interpreted as an evasion on civil rights, he added to his commitment on human rights the words 'at home and around the world.' " Kennedy's State of the Union message reflected a similar ordering of priorities. After enumerating America's domestic ills, he observed that "all these problems pale when placed beside those which confront us around the world." Likewise, the new President gave foreign affairs highest priority in his schedule. [25]

Quite likely, those who invoked the foreign implications of America's racial problems saw in this theme something beside its intrinsic merits. Connecting antidiscrimination with anticommunism provided them with a clever rhetorical wedge into the minds of patriotic but racially conservative audiences. But it would be wrong to assume that the foreign theme was merely a ruse on the part of Kennedy or others, for it also appeared when the audience was known to be sympathetic to civil rights. "The Vice President has just come back from Sengal [sic]," the President told the first meeting of his new committee to provide equal job opportunity, "and in conversation with him about it, he indicated the importance of our establishing our image in accordance with our constitutional promise." Johnson reiterated this point in his comments. Similarly, Robert Kennedy told a group of Negro publishers that "if there is a racial incident in any corner of the United States, within hours it is flashed around the world. The Communists seize upon it for their propaganda mill." [26]

Internal racial considerations and foreign policy also melded in other tangible ways, as in the selection of a Secretary of State. Kennedy came very close to naming Senator J. William Fulbright to that post. However, he dropped the scholarly Arkansan largely because Fulbright's signing of the Southern Manifesto against the *Brown* decision would, as many liberals hastened to point out, cause serious difficulties in the Third World, particularly Africa. Subsequently, powerful Southern Democrats, angry at Fulbright's rejection, retaliated by opposing Chester Bowles for the same job. Bowles, they complained, had written the civil rights plank. Although in both cases, in Bowles's especially, there were other considerations, either man's chances to become Secretary of State would certainly have been enhanced had no racial element been involved. Instead of these men, Kennedy chose Dean Rusk, a native Georgian though not a segregationist. As both Fulbright and Bowles ultimately became leading critics of Rusk and of America's involvement in the civil war in Vietnam, one can only speculate how the course of history might have been altered had either man become Secretary in 1961. [27]

In the late 1950s and early 1960s, as African colonies acquired independence, the number of black diplomats living in the United States increased steadily and so did incidents of discrimination against them, particularly in housing and public accommodations. Because he wanted to improve America's image in the Third World and because he had served as chairman of a Senate subcommittee on Africa, Kennedy came to office disposed to be especially sensitive to this problem. Upon presenting his credentials to Kennedy, Adam

Malick Sow, Ambassador from Chad, told the President in blunt language that he had been ingloriously ejected from a Maryland restaurant on his way to Washington from New York. "I was thrown on my rear end as a result of entering the Bonnie Brae restaurant over on Route 40," Pedro Sanjuan, the interpreter and protocol officer, translated. Kennedy immediately ordered Sanjuan to take measures to prevent a recurrence of this kind of incident. The State Department's Office of Protocol lobbied successfully with the Maryland legislature for a public accommodations law, persuaded its governor to apologize publicly to offended Africans, and even convinced officials in one city to give a testimonial dinner on behalf of an ill-treated diplomat. In late August, a poignant test of the desegregation efforts was made when three black newsmen from Baltimore's *Afro-American*, dressed in top hats and tails and posing as diplomats from the mythical African country of "Goban," entered five restaurants along Route 40. In two, they were seated in segregated areas; in three, in white areas. To the extent that the restaurants were desegregated, the test demonstrated that white Americans could sometimes be persuaded to abandon apartheid practices at home in order to win a nonwhite constituency abroad.[28]

The restaurant problem proved the most tractable in this area. Gradually Maryland restaurants began to treat all customers alike. The Office of Protocol meanwhile frequently settled for more expedient, less general solutions. For example, when African ambassadors took trips in the South, the office did all it could to shelter the diplomats from racial insults. Once when the Ambassador of Ghana insisted on staying at the Shamrock Hilton in Houston, a protocol officer acquired Lyndon Johnson's assistance in making the necessary, though temporary, arrangements. Diplomats rarely were fooled by sanitized trips, but even if they had been they were bound to encounter discrimination sometime during their stay in the United States. In fact, they were most likely to suffer it when they were looking for housing in Washington it-self. In 1963, the protocol office reported that "every non-white diplomat looking for housing in Washington since April 1962 has found at one time or another that he or she was undesirable because of the color of his or her skin." Ironically, Pedro Sanjuan, who regularly dealt with these problems, found few African diplomats who expressed much concern for the plight of black Americans. Nevertheless, the President as well as other white Americans apparently as-sumed that race relations in the United States mattered a great deal to the Africans.[29]

For reasons of discretion and diplomacy, the administra-tion often soft-pedalled its attempts to lower racial barriers to foreign visitors, but it trumpeted its efforts to eliminate dis-crimination in direct and federally contracted employment. Although the improvement of America's foreign image was one of the motivations for this endeavor, the primary incen-tives were probably ethical and political. Kennedy wanted to end job discrimination because it was the right thing to do. Having deferred civil rights legislation, he also hoped to show that as chief executive he could deal effectively with a major problem confronting black people. Indeed, his govern-ment-wide employment effort carried much of the burden for testing his ability to carry out his promise of meaningful ex-ecutive action. It also embodied certain inherent limitations.

In early March, Kennedy established by executive order the President's Committee on Equal Employment Opportunity (PCEEO) by combining two existing but largely ineffectual committees. He directed the new panel to "ensure that Amer-icans of all colors and beliefs will have equal access to em-ployment within the government." In addition, he ordered the committee to conduct a racial survey of the government's employment practices in order to provide a "yardstick by which to ensure future progress." Kennedy designated Lyn-don Johnson to be chairman of the committee. The Vice President initially was reluctant to accept the position, but Kennedy pointed out that Nixon had served in a similar capacity and that Johnson, as a Southerner, would be roundly criticized if he failed to follow suit. Although Johnson presided at its meetings and took an active role in some of its functions, much of its work was supervised by the Secretary of Labor, first Arthur Goldberg, later W. Willard Wirtz, who was named vice-chairman. The reason for this was simply that the Secretary of Labor had at his command the resources of a large department whereas the Vice President had only a small staff. The committee's other members included the Attorney General, the Chairman of the Civil Service Commission, as well as other government officials and private citizens.[30]

The important role assigned to the Secretary of Labor connoted one of PCEEO's difficulties. Kennedy had created the committee without Congressional authorization. It drew its operating budget from departmental contributions. In funding the committee in this manner, Kennedy continued a practice established by Eisenhower, who had adopted it in order to get around the disabling rider that Richard Russell had attached to an appropriations bill to stop the operations of Truman's employment panel. Unmistakably, it was a device to circumvent Congress. The committee had a relatively small budget, usually around a half million dollars, but no one knew how much money was actually spent in its activities since most of them were carried out by other agencies. Although PCEEO reported the same amount of spending as its predecessor, in reality its programs required much higher spending on its behalf.[31]

Southern congressmen occasionally criticized the committee, but Richard Russell had agreed to allow it to operate with the same budget as Eisenhower's panel, and the kind of publicity that PCEEO generated was unlikely to provoke a full-scale attack on its existence. Lyndon Johnson's prominent role alone tended to calm Southern Democrats. Moreover, the committee's most publicized program, the Plans for Progress, stirred up no memories of Reconstruction. It was promoted by Robert Troutman, a college classmate of the President, a public member of the committee, and a white Georgian with high political connections. Troutman so firmly believed in the Plans that he advanced a considerable amount of his own money to its establishment. Under it, government contractors voluntarily signed agreements in which they promised to survey their employment practices and make specific improvements over time. With considerable fanfare, including the President's participation, Lockheed Aircraft in Marietta, Georgia, signed the first Plan in late May. Within the next year, dozens of defense contractors as well as labor unions followed suit. In late May 1961, Lyndon Johnson explained to representatives of the nation's largest defense contractors that the discrimination problem could not "be solved by a police agency waving a nightstick at Americans." At the same time he emphatically insisted that though there were many self-interested reasons for combatting discrimination, such as improving the nation's image abroad, the overriding reason was that it was "the right thing to do." Similarly, George Reedy, Johnson's full.time assistant on racial matters, privately attributed two great virtues to Plans for Progress. It was "more likely than any other approach to really do something for Negroes" who need jobs and were victimized by discrimination, and it so involved PCEEO "in constructive activities that the temptation to the Committee staff to become a cop with a night stick chasing down individual cases would be held to the minimum." Thus, honorable motives lay behind this program, but time would tell whether its focus on voluntary action would produce substantive progress.[32]

The President, it should be noted, did vest in the committee new powers to initiate investigations rather than wait for complaints, and to terminate contracts where employers persisted in discriminating. Very quickly the committee established a record for hearing and correcting complaints of discrimination, particularly within the government itself, which was far superior to its predecessor's. After a year of operations, Arthur Goldberg reported to Kennedy that it had processed more complaints in one year than its predecessor had in six, and that corrective action was twice as likely as before. However, because PCEEO was not, in Lyndon Johnson's words, "a persecuting or prosecuting committee," it seldom used its authority to terminate or hold up contracts with private employers. As Michael Sovern, a legal expert on employment discrimination, later pointed out, if the committee had regularly exercised this authority, it would have been the only such agency in the country to do so, even though Northern states had statutory antidiscrimination panels. Sovern also reported that the committee feared an adverse court decision on its authority had it pursued this course. Undoubtedly, Kennedy and Johnson were also concerned with an adverse Congressional reaction should the committee wave a nightstick.[33]

Before PCEEO began to function, reports came to the White House of the employment situation in several departments. At the prompting of the President, Under Secretary Chester Bowles reported in January that the State Department's Personnel Office could only make "rough estimates" on the racial distribution of its employees. Nevertheless, those estimates told a significant story. For example, they indicated that there were fifteen Negroes out of 3,674 Foreign Service Officers. Few members of other racial minorities could be identified either. At the Justice Department, Robert Kennedy uncovered an equally bad record. He ordered an employment survey soon after he took over. Completed in April, it revealed that all of the Department's 56 messengers were black, but that only 10 out of the 995 attorneys located in Washington were. (Robert Kennedy's own figures were 10 out of 950. See chapter 4.) At the same time, among the 742 lawyers in U.S.

Attorneys' offices only 9 were black. The one black U.S. Marshal worked in the Virgin Islands. Among the 552 Deputy Marshals, 17 blacks were counted. Meanwhile, at the Federal Bureau of Investigation, which employed 13,649 persons, 48 were black. "This record of the Department of Justice," John Seigenthaler, Robert Kennedy's assistant and complier of the survey, somberly wrote, "should be a matter of considerable embarrassment to the Department charged with responsibility for enforcing the Nation's civil rights laws and with a large concern for protecting the Constitutional rights of all citizens." [34]

To paint a more complete picture, Kennedy charged PCEEO with surveying the record of the entire federal government. Partial surveys of government employees had been done before and had indicated that although Negroes were employed in considerable numbers, they tended to be heavily concentrated in the lower-paying, nonsupervisory jobs. The committee's extensive new studies dramatically confirmed the existence of this pattern. By July 1961, the committee had learned that though Negroes constituted 12.6 percent of the government's employees, "there was but one Negro reported in GS–18 and one in GS–17 [the highest civil service ranks] throughout the entire Federal Government." Although Negroes constituted nearly 20 percent of the White House staff, only one was a Presidential appointee. Accounting for the rest were 2 secretaries, 19 clerical workers, 37 messengers, and 9 in miscellaneous jobs. Out of 10,227 employees in the Treasury Department who were GS–12 or above, 37 were Negroes; out of 6,900 in Agriculture, 15 were Negroes; out of 69,955 in Defense, 444; out of 4,556 in State, 26. Even where the ratio was most favorable, in HEW, there were only 72 out of 4,098. In the highest ranking jobs, those above GS–18, there were approximately 5 Negroes in the entire government. [35]

These statistics were not released to the press in 1961, although several newsmen did obtain and disclose some of them before their general publication in 1963 when the administration was able to demonstrate a sharp improvement. Progress resulted principally from heightened consciousness at the upper levels of government. The President himself maintained such pressure on his subordinates that Roy Wilkins later recalled that "it got to be kind of a sub rosa joke around Washington even among the Negroes that Kennedy was so hot on the Department heads, the Cabinet officers, and agency heads that everyone was scrambling around trying to find himself a Negro in order to keep the President off his neck." Wilkins may, in fact, have exaggerated the amount of Presidential pressure. Kennedy never, for example, fired a subordinate for failing to bring blacks into responsible positions; and although he continued to select blacks for high posts after his early wave of appointments, he never added another Negro to his own staff beyond the one, Andrew Hatcher, he had in the summer of 1961. Nevertheless, Wilkins's recollection had a basis in fact. Many important officials did concern themselves with this matter. The Civil Service Commission began a special recruiting program at Negro colleges and universities. It also organized field conferences around the same theme. At the Justice Department Robert Kennedy actively sought Negro attorneys, told Division heads and U.S. Attorneys and Marshals that he expected them to take personal responsibility in hiring Negroes, and notified Howard Law School and other law schools of openings, encouraging black applicants.[36]

Although Kennedy's decision to forego legislation disappointed many civil rights advocates, the alternative of executive action held great promise. However, just as fears of adverse Congressional reaction prompted Kennedy to drop his promise of legislation, they also circumscribed his use of executive powers. The equal employment effort was somewhat restricted by such concerns. Other possible actions, such as the housing order, were postponed altogether. Still, Kennedy and his aides sincerely hoped to achieve racial progress and worried about the damage discrimination inflicted upon America's foreign image. "The dynamics both here and abroad compelling desegregation in this country are accelerating," Frederick Dutton wrote to Harris Wofford, Andrew Hatcher, and Louis Martin in July. "How to provide leadership for those forces and moderate Southern difficulties without destroying the Congressional coalition at mid-term is the nub of the problem." [37]

Congressional considerations directly affected Kennedy's decision to postpone the housing order. First, he delayed its issuance because he did not want to offend Senator John Sparkman and Congressman Albert Rains, both of Alabama and each the chairman of his chamber's housing committee. Sparkman had objected to Robert Weaver's appointment as Housing Administrator and Kennedy decided not to push him or Rains any further until a housing bill was enacted. Even after Congress passed Kennedy's housing bill in June, he still did not issue the order. Both Robert Weaver and Harris Wofford urged him to do so, arguing that the time was appropriate—that delay could be politically damaging in the black community and that it could possibly lead to increased white resistance. Kennedy's political counsellors, Lawrence O'Brien and Kenneth O'Donnell, urged delay. They realized that Kennedy still needed the Alabamans to win Congressional approval of a new Department of Urban Affairs. Meanwhile, Sparkman and Rains communicated their objections to Kennedy directly and even Atlanta's mayor, William Hartsfield, complained about its timing. The President heeded the voice of delay.[38]

Kennedy became personally involved with one aspect of discrimination in the armed forces. At his inaugural parade he had noticed the absence of Negroes from the Coast Guard contingent. He initiated action that eventually led to the un-

covering and elimination of a "whites only" policy at the
Coast Guard Academy. Similarly, while reviewing an honor
guard on the occasion of a state visit by an African dignitary,
he took note of the small number of blacks. Concerned about
the impression these ceremonial units were making, he apprised Robert McNamara, Secretary of Defense, of the situation. McNamara investigated, discovered that Kennedy was
correct about the paucity of blacks in these units, and quickly
increased their numbers.[39]

Although Kennedy improved Negro representation in the
Coast Guard and ceremonial units in Washington, he approached the problem of segregation in the National Guard
much more cautiously. Early White House inquiries to the
Department of Defense about persistent discrimination in these
units brought inadequate responses. Later Ralph Horton, Assistant Secretary of the Army and a friend of the President,
warned the White House about trouble that was sure to come
from Senator Richard Russell, Chairman of the Senate Armed
Services Committee, and the Southern Congressional delegation should this matter be pursued. Carlisle P. Runge, Assistant
Secretary of Defense, made similar remonstrations, and also
advised that Southern states might completely deactivate their
units rather than desegregate them, thereby threatening national security. He did point out that the Department "was
making considerable progress in the integration of Guard units
in ways which do not involve the direct confrontation of state
officials," for example by assigning Negroes to activated units.
In November, Lee White confirmed the necessity for a cautious
approach. He informed the President that a committee to study
the problem would be acceptable to Defense, but that it should
have "no enforcement function." In July 1962, Kennedy appointed a committee to look into discrimination in the military
and named Gerhard A. Gesell, a Washington attorney, as chairman.[40]

Kennedy heeded Southern Democrats by not promulgating

certain executive actions, but he also pleased them by appointing Southerners to high office. Two enjoyed Cabinet status. Dean Rusk, born and educated in Georgia, had lived most of his adult life in the North; but Secretary of Commerce Luther Hodges, former Governor of North Carolina, bore the reputation of a moderate segregationist. After joining the administration, he favored a slow, quiet, and cautious approach to desegregation. Not surprisingly, Kennedy also rewarded some of his most loyal Southern supporters with jobs. He named Charles Meriwether, John Patterson's associate and finance director of Alabama, to the Export-Import Bank over the protests of the NAACP which believed that Meriwether's ties with Patterson and the Citizens' Council disqualified him. Kennedy offered Frank Ellis, who had helped deliver Louisiana's electoral votes in a close contest with an independent electors' slate, the directorship of the Office of Civil Defense Management. Eventually Kennedy, displeased with Ellis's zealous advocacy of fallout shelters, named him to the district court in Louisiana to remove him from Washington. Louisiana Senator Allen Ellender deferred to Kennedy on this appointment, but normally the President bowed to Democratic members of the Senate on judgeships. The passage of a court expansion bill early in his administration necessitated an unusually large number of appointments. Largely because of his deference to the Senate, a number of his Southern judges turned out to be men who placed maintenance of segregation above the requirements of law.[41]

By not pressing civil rights legislation or filibuster reform, by emphasizing voluntarism instead of coercion, and by his appointments, Kennedy clearly aimed to win Southern Democratic support for his legislative program. Although some Southerners helped tie up in committee certain of his proposals (such as medicare and aid-to-education) and forced the weakening of others (such as minimum wage legislation) Southern Democrats generally cast their votes with Kennedy during 1961. On a large number of issues where a party division occurred (including agriculture, expansion of the House Rules Committee, area redevelopment, minimum wage, welfare revision) a sufficient majority of Southern Democrats backed the administration position to bring victory. Congress's performance fell short of liberal hopes, but it is erroneous to assume, as it has been, that Kennedy was at loggerheads with Congress or with Southern Democrats. Of course, it was true that in his first year in office he did not seek the most controversial legislation he might have: civil rights.[42]

At the outset, then, Kennedy succeeded in preserving and extending the kind of record that had allowed him to win the votes of both Southern Democrats and blacks in 1960. He produced enough dramatic though largely symbolic changes to hold the friendship of blacks—in appointing Negroes to high office, by lending the Presidential imprimatur to desegregation, through the equal employment programs, and in giving black people a fuller degree of recognition than at any time in the past. Civil rights leaders voiced some disappointment in him but little antagonism. To Southern Democrats, meanwhile, he demonstrated restraint, respect, and circumspection. He stirred up none of the embers of Reconstruction. Undoubtedly, Kennedy's civil rights approach implied a central ambiguity for it promised change and stability simultaneously. How long it might continue this way was unclear and generally unaddressed. To Robert Kennedy, however, the President entrusted the immediate responsibility for its survival in the most difficult area of all, law enforcement in the South.

FOUR

Southern Law Enforcement Policy

Under Robert Kennedy the Justice Department stepped up civil rights enforcement but eschewed the role of a federal police force. It established close liaison with racial activists but at the same time enjoyed friendly relations with Southern politicians. For both political and philosophical reasons, Robert Kennedy and his principal subordinates endeavored to advance the civil rights of Negroes while trying to avoid any large-scale or systematic intervention in the states and localities. Thus, civil rights enforcement assumed a new place of importance in the Justice Department but traditional balances between local and federal legal authorities were maintained.

A T thirty-five, Robert Kennedy was the youngest Attorney General in history; he was, however, by no means the least experienced in politics or government. After graduating from the University of Virginia Law School in 1951, he worked briefly as a Justice Department attorney. In 1953 he served on the staff of Senator Joseph McCarthy's Permanent Subcommittee on Investigations for six months. After sharp clashes with chief counsel Roy Cohn, he resigned and soon began to work for the Democratic minority though he remained loyal to McCarthy and his objective of rooting communists out of government. In the late 1950s he acquired considerable fame, not for pursuing communists, but for exposing gangsterism and corruption in the labor–management field, particularly within the trucking industry and the Teamsters union. As chief counsel to the Senate Select Committee on Improper Activities in the Labor or Management Field, popularly known as the Rackets Committee or the McClellan Committee, after its chairman, John L. McClellan of Arkansas, he headed the largest team of investigators to be sponsored by a Congressional committee up to that time. When not working as an investigator, Robert Kennedy was helping to advance his older brother's political career. He managed John Kennedy's uphill but successful campaign for the Senate in 1952. In the months preceding the Democratic convention in 1960, he played a major role in rounding up delegates and in running the primary campaigns. After the nomination was won, he supervised John Kennedy's general election drive.

Because his career had been limited largely to investigations and campaign management before 1961, Robert Kennedy seldom articulated his political views. He shared with his brother a belief in the influence of valorous individuals upon the nation's history. "The great events of our nation's past were forged by men of toughness, men who risked their security and their futures for freedom and for an ideal," he wrote in *The Enemy Within*, his report on the work of the McClellan Committee. Anticipating his brother's campaign theme, he asserted:

> It seems to me imperative that we reinstill in ourselves the toughness and idealism that guided the nation in the past. The paramount interest in self, in material wealth, in security must be replaced by an actual, not just a vocal, interest in our country, by a spirit of adventure, a will to fight what is evil, and a desire to serve. It is up to us as citizens to take the initiative as it has been taken before in our history, to reach out boldly but with honesty to do the things that need to be done.

Other than some recommendations on crime, however, he did not spell out precisely what he thought needed to be done or how to do it, quite probably because he had not decided. Years later he remarked that when he became Attorney General "I didn't lose much sleep about Negroes, I didn't think about them much, I didn't know about all the injustice." [1]

Like his older brother, Robert Kennedy was brought up to

strive for excellence, to compete fiercely, to practice his religion, and to be unwavering in his loyalty to family. Perhaps in
compensation for his younger age and smaller stature, however, he pushed himself even harder than his brother. To those
who liked him he seemed persistent, aggressive, and determined, but his detractors regarded him as vindictive, ruthless,
and even fanatical. Probably because of his unusually strong
religious convictions, he was apt to see things clearly in terms of
good and evil. He tended to be less intellectual and rational
than his older brother, and more passionate, intuitive, and tem-
peramental. He viewed himself as a tough character and reveled in mixing socially with people from the lower levels of society. Again, perhaps owing to his family position and stature, he
was inclined to identify with the underdog in society.[2]

Robert Kennedy's nomination as Attorney General sparked
considerable criticism, but from the President's standpoint it
carried several clear advantages. Republicans raised the issue of
nepotism and questioned the younger Kennedy's maturity and
experience. Some liberals and independents, too, worried
about these things, but also wondered about his respect for civil
liberties and doubted the propriety of having a campaign manager serve as the nation's chief law enforcement officer. Nevertheless, the appointment provided the President with an absolute loyalist and a seasoned politician in what promised to be
the most sensitive Cabinet post. Both loyalty and political wisdom would be needed to fulfill the administration's commitment to advance civil rights without alienating the powerful
and vital Southern wing of the Democratic Party. Moreover,
had he named him to a subordinate position in the State or
Defense Departments, as Robert had apparently preferred, it
would have created obvious difficulties for his superior. Robert
Kennedy did not have any experience in the national security
fields so it would have been imprudent and impolitic to have
him head a department. However, it is interesting to note that
the President actively involved him in foreign affairs soon after

his inauguration. In 1962 he played an absolutely essential role during the Cuban missile crisis. It is quite possible that in a second Kennedy administration, he would have become Secretary of State.[3]

Although some Republicans and liberals criticized the appointment, Southern Democrats accepted it with equanimity. Indeed, John McClellan, an influential Southerner who was also a former employer and a personal friend of Robert Kennedy, encouraged him to accept his brother's offer. At his confirmation hearing, Southern Democrats treated him gently. In the face of rigorous questioning from Republican Kenneth Keating, Robert Kennedy refrained from endorsing outright the Democrats' liberal civil rights plank. "We have to move strongly and vigorously," he asserted; but he quickly added that he did "not think that this is a subject or matter that can be solved overnight." Those were undoubtedly reassuring words to Southern Senators Eastland, Ervin, and McClellan, who were present at the hearing.[4]

In time, an unusual number of the generally young attorneys whom Robert Kennedy assembled to help him run the Justice Department attained high office and national prominence though in 1961 none was well known. The one whose name was most familiar was Byron White of Colorado, a former Rhodes Scholar, who had been a college and professional football star. White had headed John Kennedy's drive for independent voters in 1960. He became Deputy Attorney General in 1961, and became President Kennedy's first Supreme Court appointee in 1962. Nicholas Katzenbach, also a Rhodes Scholar, headed the Office of Legal Counsel, which advised the President, and succeeded White as Deputy Attorney General. In 1964, he followed Robert Kennedy as Attorney General and later served as Under Secretary of State. Another of Robert Kennedy's young attorneys, Ramsey Clark, replaced Katzenbach as Attorney General. The son of Supreme Court Justice Tom Clark, he headed the Justice Department's Lands Division in 1961. At forty-nine one of the older Justice Department appointees, Archibald Cox, professor at Harvard Law School and an important academic ally of John Kennedy, established a distinguished record as Solicitor General. And in 1973, he achieved considerable fame as the first Special Prosecutor in the Watergate case, hired and then fired by President Richard Nixon. A late appointee of the Eisenhower administration, John Doar, a Wisconsin Republican, stayed on as First Assistant in the Civil Rights Division in 1961. In 1964 he became Assistant Attorney General for Civil Rights, but his name became a household word in 1973 and 1974 when he served as chief counsel to the House Judiciary Committee's inquiry into the impeachment of President Nixon. Clearly, no other department of government in 1961 possessed as many individuals who would achieve the future prominence of these men from Justice. Quite possibly, few departments have ever had the concentration of young legal and executive talent that the Kennedy Justice Department had.[5]

To be his Assistant Attorney General for Civil Rights, Robert Kennedy chose Burke Marshall. Harris Wofford who might have seemed a logical contender for this job, was not selected for a number of reasons. Wofford was a known civil rights advocate. He had worked for the Civil Rights Commission, had advised Martin Luther King, and would probably have had trouble winning confirmation from the Senate Judiciary Committee. Furthermore, he had clashed with Robert Kennedy and Byron White during the campaign. Burke Marshall, on the other hand, had not worked in the campaign, nor had he ever worked publicly for civil rights. A 1951 graduate of Yale Law School, he had risen to a partnership in the prestigious Washington firm of Covington and Burling, specializing in antitrust work. Personally he was very interested in civil rights problems and had contributed, behind the scenes, to the development of the voting referee plan that Congress had approved in the 1960 Civil Rights Act. "Perhaps the most enigmatic move of the new

administration was the appointment of Burke Marshall, a
Washington lawyer, as Assistant Attorney General," Clarence
Mitchell reported to the NAACP Board. Although Mitchell had
heard that Marshall favored protecting civil rights, there was
"nothing in his public record to show" that he had "any first
hand knowledge of the problem." Of course, from the administration's perspective, that was one of his assets. Southern
members of the Judiciary Committee in the past had been slow
to confirm the designee for this office, but Marshall encountered relatively little difficulty, especially after Robert Kennedy
appeared personally at his hearing. Interestingly, the new Attorney General himself had nearly rejected Marshall. The soft-
spoken, taciturn corporate lawyer had failed to make a favorable impression on the equally reticent Kennedy. Nevertheless,
after receiving many reassurances of Marshall's legal ability, he
proceeded with the appointment. Soon, Marshall became a
close friend and valued associate. Fairly quickly too, Marshall
had earned the respect of civil rights activists and experts,
including Clarence Mitchell.[6]

The Attorney General administers a large and diverse department, but from the beginning Robert Kennedy devoted a
disproportionately large amount of his time to civil rights. It
was the most politically sensitive responsibility that the Department had, and he naturally wanted to see that it was
handled carefully. Accordingly, he established a rule that voluntary compliance should always be sought from local officials before a federal court order was requested. In line with
this, he personally called Louisiana officials to warn them
that the government was prepared to seek contempt-of-court
sentences if they continued to withhold state money from the
recently desegregated schools of New Orleans. As a result of
his warning, state funds were released. According to Don
Oberdorfer, who in early March reported on Kennedy's administration of the Justice Department for the Washington
Post, this kind of quiet informal approach was adopted with

the hope of lessening bitterness and the long delays which typically accompanied court contests between local and federal authorities. Early in his tenure the new Attorney General elaborated on his views of civil rights enforcement to Peter Maas for an article in *Look*. He firmly asserted his belief in the equality of all people, but observed that some individuals, by whom he clearly meant white Southerners, "have grown up with totally different backgrounds and mores, which we can't change overnight." He pointed out that discrimination was not confined to the South, even though many Northerners believed that it was. And he told Maas that he could not imagine this administration "ever sending troops to any part of the country" as Eisenhower had to Little Rock. He could not, he said, "conceive of this administration's letting such a situation deteriorate to that level." [7]

In private discussions Robert Kennedy reassured Southern officials of his department's reasonableness, but he also decided to make its policies public so he accepted a student-initiated invitation to speak at Law Day exercises at the University of Georgia in early May. No Attorney General in memory had spoken on civil rights in the South, but Kennedy evidently believed that the time had come for a clear statement of intent. Such a clarification might ease the task of law enforcement while simultaneously reducing the possibility of extreme political reactions when the Justice Department sought changes in the South. By this time, there had already been one outcry from Southern politicians and segregationists after the government went to court to prevent the closing of public schools in Prince Edward County, Virginia. A school closing there would not only have effectively thwarted desegregation but also would have denied black children an education altogether. [8]

The particular occasion Kennedy chose was tension-filled. Five months before, the university had suspended its first two Negro students, Charlayne Hunter and Hamilton Holmes, after protesting whites rioted. However, in contrast to the situation at the University of Alabama in 1956, a federal judge had ordered their reinstatement, and the university had complied and had restored order to the campus. Hunter and Holmes courageously endured ostracism and verbal abuse from many white students, but at least they were enrolled as students. In the week before the Attorney General's speech, Justice Department spokesmen tipped off Georgia newsmen that his acceptance of the invitation represented a conscious acknowledgment of the state's successful handling of desegregation. They also let it be known that he intended to speak of civil rights as a national, not exclusively Southern, problem. Meanwhile, Kennedy took great pains in preparing his address. It went through many drafts, and he consulted Southern allies and moderates about it. Still, he appeared nervous before delivering it to the white audience. Apparently the only black person present was Hunter, who was reporting on it for a Negro newspaper. Many of the state's leading politicians, however, cautiously absented themselves from the occasion.[9]

A little self-derogatory humor lessened tension a bit, as did some flattering remarks about Georgia—including words of praise for its orderly handling of desegregation. Kennedy remarked that he had been advised that it was wise, when speaking in Georgia, to claim that one had relatives there. He could not make that claim, but acknowledged his brother's political debt. "This state," observed the former campaign manager, "gave my brother the biggest percentage majority of any state in the union and in this last election that was even better than kinfolk." Turning more serious, the Attorney General attributed to law a vital role in the fight against international communism. Organized crime and illegal business and labor practices, he charged, damaged America's international position. Civil rights difficulties did too, according to Kennedy, who depicted Hamilton Holmes and Charlayne Hunter as freedom fighters.

The Attorney General next addressed the issue of school desegregation. He defended his department's intervention in Prince Edward County. And he endorsed the correctness of the *Brown* decision, although he declared that what mattered most was not his opinion of it but the fact that it was law. After stressing the importance of granting the ballot to all citizens, he remarked that a lot of hypocrisy about discrimination existed in the North, pointing out that he had found only 10 Negroes among the 950 attorneys employed in the Justice Department. Meanwhile Northern financial leaders, and union and government officials, he complained, decried discrimination when it occurred in the South but practiced it in their own lives.

Robert Kennedy then spelled out Justice Department policy. It would always try to win voluntary compliance with the law, but if the effort failed it would not hesitate to bring legal action. Reiterating an earlier theme, he asserted that segregationist mobs not only damaged the lives of the children involved and undermined respect for law and order, but hurt the United States in the eyes of the world. He promised that the Justice Department would uphold all laws, civil rights among them. Quoting Henry W. Grady, Georgia's leading proponent of the New South creed in the nineteenth century, Kennedy identified himself with the need to place nationalism before sectionalism. In conclusion, he vowed to expend all he had materially, physically, and spiritually "to see that freedom shall advance and that our children will grow old under the rule of law." [10]

Kennedy's forthrightness, nationalism, and criticism of Northern hypocrisy evidently touched his listeners for they gave him a lengthy standing ovation. Southern newspapers afforded the speech prominent attention and moderates like

Ralph McGill and Reg Murphy of the Atlanta *Constitution* hailed it. "Never before, in all its travail of by-gone years, has the South heard so honest and understandable a speech from any Cabinet member," McGill observed, without mentioning that he had been consulted on its content. Southern conservatives, meanwhile, did not react vocally against it. Civil rights organizations and spokesmen endorsed it enthusiastically, the NAACP expressing its "profound appreciation." "Your speech in Georgia was a peach," Louis Martin wrote Robert Kennedy. "Congratulations are pouring in from brothers everywhere, here and abroad. If you keep this up, one of these days I might be able to go back home," Martin quipped. For an Attorney General merely to tell the South directly and unambiguously that he intended to uphold the law was, to civil rights advocates, a great step forward.[11]

Within several weeks, however, Robert Kennedy's seeming ability to satisfy and even please both opponents and proponents of desegregation faced a serious challenge when Alabama officials stood idly by and allowed white mobs to beat the Freedom Riders, an integrated group of civil rights activists. A Supreme Court decision in December, 1960, precipitated the Freedom Rides. In *Boynton v. Virginia*, the Court extended its earlier prohibition of segregation on interstate buses and trains to terminal facilities. The Congress of Racial Equality (CORE), a relatively obscure and small pacifist organization but one which had just chosen a dynamic new leader in James Farmer, seized the opportunity created by the judicial ruling to dramatize the continuing practice of segregation in Southern terminals. Under its sponsorship in the spring of 1961, numbers of interracial bus riders began to test the effectiveness of the court's decision. Several of them were arrested and assaulted in the Carolinas, but the most serious violence occurred in Alabama. On May 14, outside Anniston, a white mob stopped one of the Freedom Riders' buses, assaulted its passengers, and destroyed the vehicle. When a second bus arrived, the mob roughed up its passengers and accompanied them to Birmingham. Upon their arrival in the city, the Freedom Riders were attacked by their uninvited companions and by a large gang of segregationists who lay in waiting. Birmingham Police Chief Eugene "Bull" Connor unconvincingly explained that the police had failed to prevent the violence because it was Mother's Day and they were undermanned. Governor John Patterson responded to the incidents by issuing a statement that it was impossible to protect racial agitators and suggested that they leave the state. Meanwhile, the badly mauled CORE Freedom Riders flew on to New Orleans. At first they had encountered difficulty merely getting out of Birmingham, but John Seigenthaler, Robert Kennedy's administrative assistant and a native of Tennessee, arrived and facilitated their safe departure. The Freedom Rides were far from over, however. In the next several days John Lewis and other student activists from Nashville gathered in Birmingham, determined to proceed.[12]

The mounting violence attracted national publicity and the close attention of the Attorney General who worked behind the scenes to ensure order and to make it possible for the Freedom Rides to continue. He immediately ordered the FBI to investigate the violent incidents; a week later the federal government arrested four men and charged them with the fire bombing of the bus in Anniston. Kennedy also tried to persuade the Greyhound bus company and its union to supply another bus and driver. And he and Seigenthaler tried to convince Alabama officialdom to preserve law and order. Some officials, such as Floyd Mann, the head of the state police, required no persuasion. Mann consistently did his best under very trying circumstances.[13]

Governor Patterson, on the other hand, was proving unreceptive. For the better part of a week, Patterson refused to take phone calls from the Attorney General or even from the President, whose political ally he had long been. Patterson

did, however, call a press conference at which he announced
that "Alabama isn't the Congo." He declared his utter lack of
sympathy for the Freedom Riders. "When you go somewhere
seeking trouble you usually find it," Patterson said. "The
state of Alabama can't guarantee safety of fools, and that's
what they are." Even the segregationist Montgomery *Advertiser*, which called the Freedom Riders "slobbering trash,"
believed the Governor had gone too far. It ran a critical editorial under the title, "The Governor of Alabama a Mob
Leader?" Like most newspapers in the state, the *Advertiser*
opposed integration, but opposed violence too. Riotous conditions hurt "profits and payrolls" and damaged the South
politically in the nation, the newspaper argued. Evidently
Patterson worried more about his political standing with Alabama's most extreme segregationists than about the region's
reputation in the country. Moreover, his own dedication to
segregation transcended politics and reason. Two months
after the Freedom Rides crisis, Milton Cummings, one of the
state's leading industrialists, commented to Benjamin Muse
that when it came to race relations, Patterson was a "patho-
logical case." [14]

On Friday, May 19, Patterson finally returned a phone call
to the Attorney General and agreed to meet with John
Seigenthaler, Kennedy's representative. Later that day Patterson assured Seigenthaler that he had "the will, the men, the
equipment and the force to protect all people in Alabama,
visitors and others, whether on the highways or elsewhere."
Ominously, however, Patterson's office did not even acknowledge the meeting with Seigenthaler. The following
morning, under state police protection, the Freedom Riders'
bus made a rapid trip from Birmingham to Montgomery. Unfortunately the Montgomery police who were supposed to
protect the Freedom Riders at the bus terminal did not show
up. An ugly mob did, and set upon the integrationists and
assembled newsmen. Seigenthaler himself tried to rescue a

young, white woman passenger who was being assaulted. As she urged him to leave her alone lest he get hurt, he was clubbed from behind and fell bloodied and unconscious to the pavement. He came to thirty minutes later in a police cruiser and was taken to a hospital where he again passed out. John Doar, who was in Alabama working on voting rights cases when the crisis erupted, witnessed the scene at the terminal and immediately called Washington. "It's the most horrible thing I've ever seen" he reported. "It's terrible, terrible." A number of the pacifistic integrationists took serious beatings; ambulances run by whites refused to come to their aid; the city's police were completely ineffectual. "We respond to calls here just like any place. But we have no intention of standing guard for a bunch of trouble makers," explained L. B. Sullivan, the chief of police. Were it not for the courageous leadership of Floyd Mann, who personally went to the aid of the victims, several of the assaults might have become murders.[15]

With the new outbreak of violence, Robert Kennedy set into motion contingency plans that had been drawn up the preceding week. The plans called for the Justice Department to seek a federal court injunction to stop Ku Klux Klansmen from interfering with interstate travel and another injunction requiring Montgomery police to protect travelers. The plans also envisioned sending several hundred U.S. Marshals and deputized federal enforcement agency personnel, such as Border Patrolmen, to Alabama to ensure order in the event of a continued local failure. Two hours after the Attorney General tried to reach Alabama's Governor to apprise him of his plans, Patterson returned the call. According to Robert Kennedy's memorandum of the conversation, Patterson related that his assistant had spoken to Seigenthaler and that he was going to be fine. (He did recover quickly from his concussion and bruises and returned to Washington within two days.) Informed by the Attorney General of what he was about to do, Patterson protested only about the use of marshals, who he claimed were not needed. Kennedy inquired as to how, if outside assistance were unnecessary, he could explain the beatings that had just taken place. Apparently Patterson could not answer satisfactorily and Kennedy suggested that instead of his sending in marshals, the Governor call out the National Guard. That would be an "embarrassment" to him, Patterson demurred. Kennedy then pointed out that he had actuated his crisis plans most reluctantly and only after he had been unable to reach Patterson by phone. He complained about the Governor's elusiveness and about Seigenthaler's beating. Nevertheless, after the Governor expressed the fervent hope that no one in the Justice Department would criticize him publicly, Kennedy so assured him. After several similar exchanges, the conversation ended, as it began, "on a relative note of good cheer." [16]

The next day, Sunday, Federal District Judge Frank Johnson in Montgomery issued the injunctions sought by the Justice Department, and the marshals gathered at nearby Maxwell Air Force Base. Byron White personally commanded the force, which he assured the press was there simply to supplement local law-enforcement officials. Except for a few marshals who kept watch at the terminals, including the airport where they protected Martin Luther King when he arrived, they stayed at the base throughout the day. At the same time, Robert Kennedy (*Business Week* later reported) called Southern Congressmen "urging them to keep their statements moderate, and promising not to back the freedom riders himself except by providing the protection of the law." [17]

On Sunday evening, however, a dire emergency necessitated the deployment of the marshals for police duty. Martin Luther King had come to Montgomery to speak before a gathering in support of the Freedom Rides at the church of his close colleague, Ralph Abernathy. Unhappily, the meeting also attracted a large crowd of hostile whites who congregated outside the church taunting its inhabitants, throwing rocks and bottles, and burning a car. When local and state officials failed to protect the church, marshals came to the rescue and for several hours held the mob at bay with tear gas and billy clubs. Finally, around 2:00 A.M. Patterson called up the National Guard, but it was dawn before the church's inhabitants could safely return home. The Montgomery *Advertiser* reported that Negroes were disappointed that the Guard, rather than federal troops, had been summoned, but also related that there had been close cooperation between King and Washington. "President Kennedy is on our side. He's giving us his full backing," one Negro youth said. "Bless God! We now have a President who's going to make sure we can go anywhere we want like the white folks in this country," declared a black woman.[18]

Ardent segregationists reacted far less favorably to the federal involvement. Patterson invited the press to sit in on a conference he was to have with Byron White, who had expected the meeting to be private. The Governor scolded White and threatened to arrest federal officials who violated local law. (Patterson's threats were almost certainly just for effect. Most marshals were already back at the base, and he knew that the federal government was only interested in preserving order, not in intervening directly to prevent segregation.) The *Advertiser* soon denounced everyone connected with the affair—the Governor, the Freedom Riders, the white mob, and the Kennedys. If the disorder had been caused by a labor dispute, it editorialized, the President would be silent "and his little brother wouldn't be sitting at that big desk barking orders over the phone and looking like Mickey Rooney just in from a game of touch football." This was, the paper declared, "Little Rock without defiance of a federal court order and with the bayonets tipped with a rose." It then went on to observe that the officers would be better employed "protecting the women of Washington from the current rape orgy." The Alabama Congressional delegation meanwhile wired Robert Kennedy demanding that the marshals be withdrawn.[19]

Many white Southerners, however, understood and even supported the federal intervention. James Folsom, Patterson's moderate predecessor as governor, phoned the Justice Department to assure it that there was ample precedent for using marshals and that they should stay as long as necessary. Editorial opinion in the state also generally agreed that the breakdown of order had necessitated the use of marshals. "I don't sympathize a bit with that busload of agitators that came in here with the sole purpose of causing trouble," Winton Blount, a prominent Montgomery contractor, told the *Wall Street Journal.* "But neither do I sympathize with that bunch of rag-tailed hoods and no-good bums who attacked them. I'm a strong segregationist, but mob violence is not the answer under any circumstances." Indeed the *Wall Street Journal* found that many businessmen across the South were concerned that racial violence was hurting the region's economy. In Congress, meanwhile, many Southerners blasted the Freedom Riders as agitators, but refrained from condemning the administration. One Southern Senator, Sam Ervin of North Carolina, even publicly praised the use of marshals.[20]

The relative lack of criticism could largely be explained by the simple fact that the administration was only maintaining public order and not trying to impose integration. Byron White told a press conference at the air base the day after the intervention that the marshals would not interfere with the arrest of Freedom Riders. "That would be a matter between the Freedom Riders and local officials. . . . I'm sure they [the Freedom Riders] would be represented by competent counsel," White elaborated. Responding to the protesting Alabama Congressmen, Robert Kennedy gave an unemotional summary of the facts, noting Patterson's unavailability, Seigenthaler's beating, and the repeated failures of local law enforcement, and assured them that the government had "no intention of permitting the marshals to remain in Alabama a minute longer than is necessary." The public statements of both the Attorney General and the President were terse, neutral calls for public order and a "return to reason." Finally, the marshals did not evoke many memories of an occupying army. They wore business suits, did not carry rifles, fought the mob without using firearms, and were actually on the scene in force only a matter of hours.[21]

The day after the marshals' intervention in Montgomery the limited nature of the administration's role was highlighted. The Freedom Riders were determined to proceed to Jackson, Mississippi, and the administration hoped they could do so without a recurrence of violence. On May 22, Burke Marshall called Attorney General Joe Patterson of Mississippi to ascertain the attitude of the state government. Patterson was ambivalent. He believed in maintaining order, but he also disliked the Freedom Riders intensely. "I think they ought to go home and quit their darned Communist conduct," the state attorney general declared. "We are not going to fool with them like that. They are not coming in for a good purpose. Why should we put guns around them and protect them when they are here to create trouble? They've got no business in Mississippi." Marshall emphasized that the federal government could not prevent the Freedom Riders from proceeding, asserted that the students had a right to travel, and urged a realistic attitude. His purpose in calling was "to find out what the law enforcement methods would be." "It is only because of the publicity and the difficulty of the situation that I am calling you in advance," Marshall explained.

Patterson appreciated Marshall's calling but resented the fact that the integrationists were "taking advantage" of the power of the federal government. Repeatedly Marshall pressed Patterson on whether the state would preserve order.

Tacitly conceding the right of Mississippi authorities to arrest the Freedom Riders, Marshall said "it's the difference between winding up in jail and winding up at the mercy of a mob." Nevertheless, at the end of the conversation it was not certain that Patterson would guarantee the safety of the travelers, but Marshall could safely assume that he would be happy to arrest them.[22]

The next day, however, the prospects for averting violence brightened. Governor Ross Barnett acknowledged his responsibility to uphold order. He obviously also knew that local authorities would have a free hand to arrest the Freedom Riders. He called up the National Guard and promised a police escort for the Freedom Riders from the Alabama line to Jackson. On the evening of May 23 he had a brief but amicable conversation with Robert Kennedy. He inquired whether there was any way to stop the integrationists from proceeding. After Kennedy ruled out that possibility, Barnett assured him that they would not "have any riots," that the highway patrol and guard would protect the Riders. Kennedy was pleased. The Justice Department received similar assurances from Allen Thompson, the Mayor of Jackson. Throughout this phase of the crisis, Kennedy was also in close contact with Senator James Eastland, but unfortunately these phone conversations were unrecorded.[23]

James Farmer and twenty-six other integrationists dined without incident in the white cafeteria at the Montgomery bus terminal on May 24 and boarded two buses bound for Jackson. Under police escort they traveled at high speed between Montgomery and Jackson. But when they got off the buses and tried to use the Jackson terminal's facilities, they were immediately arrested by local police and charged with a variety of minor crimes such as disturbing the peace. After the arrests, Robert Kennedy issued a public statement asking for a "cooling-off period" in the Freedom Rides. Observing that the President was about to leave for a summit conference with the leader of the Soviet Union, he asked that people refrain from any activity that might bring discredit on the United States, for it could harm the President's mission.[24]

That evening, in a phone conversation with Martin Luther King, who was now serving as a spokesman for the Freedom Rides, the Attorney General repeated his request. As Edwin Guthman, the Justice Department's press secretary, recalled the conversation, King argued that the police escort of the buses had made the demonstration meaningless. Kennedy wanted to see the Freedom Riders released from jail, but King insisted that they would stay there as a matter of conscience and philosophy. Their continued incarceration would not "have the slightest effect on what the government" or the Attorney General would do, Kennedy coldly responded. When King hinted that thousands of students might yet fill the jails of Jackson, Kennedy answered that King could do what he wanted, but warned him not to "make statements that sound like a threat. That's not the way to deal with us." King tried to explain that direct nonviolent action was the only course open to the oppressed and asserted that all past gains had come through some kind of pressure. Kennedy responded that this particular problem would not be settled in Jackson but by "strong federal action." He apparently did not indicate specifically what kind of action. King expressed his appreciation for what the administration was doing but averred that his generation could not wait for freedom. The conversation concluded with King saying that the demonstrators would stay in jail.[25]

Evidently some of the Attorney General's arguments had their effect on King, for he soon urged a "temporary lull" in the Rides. Under CORE sponsorship, however, three hundred more integrationists came to Jackson over the summer and were arrested. In addition, more than one hundred other Riders were jailed in a number of other Southern cities. Yet, in the absence of mob violence, these subsequent detentions received little attention from the press or the federal government. Civil rights attorneys, meanwhile, were unsuccessful in their attempts to get federal judges to enjoin these arrests, and it was not until April 1965 that the Supreme Court reversed the original Mississippi convictions. However, despite the slow pace of legal vindication, CORE leaders exulted in the project's success. That organization's historians have quoted James Farmer as saying that the Rides "catapulted CORE into fame." Certainly they established Farmer as a nationally important civil rights leader, increased CORE's membership, and attracted financial contributions. Undoubtedly, the Freedom Rides also generally stimulated racial activism throughout the country, perhaps most notably in the Deep South.[26]

Although Robert Kennedy did not attempt to intervene in any arrests, he did try to end discrimination in interstate transportation terminals. On May 29, he asked the Interstate Commerce Commission for more stringent regulations against discrimination than it had thus far promulgated. His request was supported by Dean Rusk, who submitted evidence showing how discrimination was damaging the American image abroad. In late September, the ICC ruled as Kennedy had asked. And soon after the new rules took effect in November, Robert Kennedy proudly announced that most Southern communities had accepted them. "Despite strong personal feelings and even antagonisms, these communities—to their great credit and the credit of the Nation—have peacefully accepted the regulations and respected the law," he happily reported. A number of communities were still holding out, but most had accepted desegregation of their terminals.[27]

During the following months the Justice Department worked quietly behind the scenes to win full compliance. The department desired results, not victories in court, and it often found local officials who also preferred to effect change silently and without legal conflict. In Mississippi, powerful politicians assisted the department's efforts. Burke Marshall reported in early 1962 to Robert Kennedy on his work:

On January 8, I discussed with Senator Stennis the segregation of bus terminals in Meridian, Mississippi. The Senator had discussed this previously with the Mayor and other city officials who want to avoid litigation. I informed the Senator that we would attempt to avoid litigation if that could be done without making Meridian a focal center, or leaving it as an isolated problem. Mr. Heilbron of this Division went to Mississippi and had discussion of similar problems with the Mayors of Vicksburg and Natchez. In addition, I discussed all of these problems with Governor Coleman [Barnett's predecessor] whose advice has been asked by some of the cities.

Soon Marshall informed Kennedy that, after considerable negotiations, segregation signs in bus stations in Meridian, Vicksburg, Natchez, and Laurel, Mississippi, had been taken down voluntarily. Negotiations also led to the removal of signs in Natchitoches, Louisiana. Marshall cautioned Kennedy that "neither the negotiations nor the removal of these signs have received any public notice, and I am under commitment not to draw public attention to them." Although the department tried to resolve the situation without going to court, in several instances, such as Jackson and McComb, Mississippi, an injunction had to be obtained to get the desired results. Nevertheless, by the end of 1962, CORE was satisfied that this particular struggle had been won.[28]

The administration was also pleased with its handling of the crisis. Soon after it ended, Robert Kennedy told a reporter that several critical goals had been achieved: the federal government had established its commitment to safe interstate travel; the protest against segregation had been channeled into the courts for resolution; law and order had triumphed over mob rule. The Freedom Rides episode demonstrated several important things. It showed that the Kennedy administration would respond in positive, tangible ways to a racial crisis in the South, would not tolerate mob rule, and had successfully brought about an end to segregation in terminals. But there were definite limitations to the administration's intervention. It had used force as a last resort, when King and his audience were seriously endangered, and then it had used civilian marshals rather than military troops. Most important, it had not interfered with local police authority. It had eschewed the role of policeman, and only exerted force when local authorities abdicated their responsibility to uphold order. It had countenanced the arrests of Freedom Riders but would not tolerate mob attacks on blacks or on King. As soon as Governor Patterson assumed responsibility for maintaining order by mobilizing the National Guard, the marshals had been withdrawn.

Burke Marshall later recalled that the Autherine Lucy case of 1956 had been very much on his and Kennedy's minds. They were determined to avoid a similar instance in which a mob's will would prevail over a judicial decree. Moreover, they were pleased that they had been able to accomplish this without altering the federal system of law, which granted the states and localities primary authority for maintaining order in the streets. In June 1961, Marshall explained to a Fisk University audience that the federal government had been powerless to prevent the arrests of Freedom Riders. It was, according to Marshall, "one of the frustrations" of a federal system of law.[29]

Lecturing three years later at Columbia University, Marshall elaborated on these "frustrations," but his views were essentially those he held in 1961. Although Marshall believed that constitutional authority might have been found for a federal court to enjoin these arrests, he was concerned that the practical effect of such an injunction would "have been chaotic and more destructive of the federal system than what happened in Mississippi." What would have been the practical consequences of a federal court order preventing local authorities from making certain kinds of arrests, he wondered. Who would assume police powers in the community? When the marshals first arrived in Montgomery, that city's police chief had pointedly asked whether they intended to take over traffic and other normal police duties. Once local police authority had been enjoined, a vacuum would be created which the federal administration did not wish to fill. A national police force did not exist (the deputy marshals were a makeshift force which could not be kept there indefinitely) and was not desirable. On the other hand, Marshall said, "the time spent under the federal system in protecting the rights of demonstrators under law performs a function of its own by creating a period in which to attack directly the substantive problem of discrimination . . . instead of attempting to prevent the police from interfering with demonstrations protesting the discrimination." That, said Marshall, was precisely what had happened in Mississippi. Ultimately, local authorities did stop enforcing segregation in bus terminals, under injunction or threat of injunction.[30]

There were other reasons for the administration's taking heart. On the eve of the President's summit meeting in Vienna the American government had demonstrated its commitment to equal rights. Perhaps most important of all, the administration had not permanently alienated its white allies in the South. Some more extreme segregationists, it is true, spread the word that the Kennedys had instigated the whole episode, and the Louisiana legislature overwhelmingly adopted a resolution accusing the Kennedys of mounting a "hate-the-South" campaign. Yet, many white Southerners did not see it that way. Southern Congressmen typically criticized the Freedom Riders, not the Kennedys. Even John Patterson told the press several days after the Montgomery crisis that although the administration had committed errors of judgment he still considered President Kennedy a friend.

Public opinion polls also contained relatively cheering news for the President. A Gallup Poll on June 18 asked: "Do you think President Kennedy did the right thing or the wrong thing in sending U.S. Marshals to Montgomery, Alabama?" In the South, 50 percent of those polled said it was right, 29 percent said it was wrong, and 21 percent had no opinion. The comparable percentages for Eisenhower's troop deployment in Little Rock had been 36 right, 53 wrong, 11 no opinion. Nationally, 70 percent approved Kennedy's action and only 13 percent disapproved. In the general survey of Presidential popularity, Gallup found an 8 percent decline in Kennedy's rating in the South between May and June (from 71 to 63 percent) but in August the figure was up to 66 and by January it stood at 70.[31]

Although the administration came through the Freedom Rides crisis without suffering a major political reversal, it had been a near miss. If state authorities had not finally agreed to contain mob violence, the deployment of federal troops would have been unavoidable and the political costs would have been high. Soon after the May crisis subsided, several key government officials, including Robert Kennedy, Burke Marshall, and Harris Wofford, encouraged civil rights leaders to launch a large-scale voter registration project. They would have been reluctant to admit it, but the channeling of civil rights activism into voter registration work offered a much lower risk of the kind of violence that had accompanied the Freedom Rides—violence that had almost necessitated federal military intervention. Furthermore, as Harris Wofford had pointed out to John Kennedy in December, an increase in Negro registrants would enhance his legislative program because it would bolster moderate and liberal Congressmen at the expense of conservatives. For the immediate future, Wofford argued, moderate and liberal Southerners would continue to oppose civil rights legislation and support other progressive legislation "while behind their back, with their open or tacit approval, the Executive will be increasing the Negro vote which can help re-elect them." "Most of the Congressional bitter-enders," he advised, "who oppose any form of Federal action on civil rights are against most of the social legislation of the new administration anyway." [32]

Clearly much remained to be done in this area when the new administration took office. From 1940 to 1954 the percentage of voting-age Negroes registered to vote in the South had risen from 5 to 20 percent. In 1956 the figure was 25 percent; it was unchanged in 1958. Despite the NAACP's announced goal, after the passage of the 1957 Civil Rights Act, of registering three million Negroes by 1960, and despite a voter registration drive by the national Democratic Party in the election year, the figure had risen only to 28 percent. By contrast close to 70 percent of white southerners were registered that year. Negro registration was much greater in cities than in rural areas, but even in the urban South there was vast room for improvement. In the rural counties of the South's Black Belt one would hardly know that the Fifteenth Amendment to the Constitution had been adopted ninety years before. The Civil Rights Commission in 1959 and 1961 merely verified what had been obvious all along—that in many counties of the South Negroes were effectively deprived of the most basic political right. Its 1961 report on voting showed that in twenty-two Alabama counties less than 10 percent of the voting-age Negroes were registered. In two of these counties, no blacks were enrolled at all, even though they constituted 80 percent of the population in each. In only four of the state's counties were more than 50 percent of the Negroes registered. In four Louisiana parishes where blacks made up substantial majorities of the population, no black was registered to vote. In the sixty-nine (out of eighty-two) Mississippi counties where the Commission was able to acquire data, blacks constituted 37.7 percent of the voting-age population, but only 6.2 percent of them were able to vote.

Most shocking of all, the Commission uncovered twenty-three counties in five states where blacks made up a substantial proportion of the population and yet not a single black was registered to vote.[33]

Because of this situation, several philanthropic foundations interested in social change had by 1961 begun to consider funding a large-scale voter registration project in the South. Their leader was Stephen R. Currier, president of the Taconic Foundation and founder and president of the Potomac Institute. Currier, it should be noted, did not view himself as an agent of the Kennedy administration. He had been a staunch Stevenson supporter, and in 1961 he regarded the Kennedys with a certain mistrust. In February he held a long meeting with Martin Luther King and in the summer and fall representatives of Taconic, the Southern Regional Council, and civil rights groups held additional meetings. Burke Marshall and Harris Wofford attended these meetings, offering their encouragement and full government cooperation.[34]

The idea of the project encountered some resistance from civil rights groups. Several of the youthful idealists of the Student Non-Violent Coordinating Committee (SNCC), which had been formed in 1960 in the wake of the sit-ins, suspected that it was a ploy adopted by the Kennedy administration and possibly Martin Luther King aimed at cooling off their militancy. Others in SNCC, however, saw it as an excellent opportunity to do grass-roots organizing. It would at least provide SNCC with something they needed but chronically lacked—money. To demonstrate that their commitment to social change had not wavered—or been purchased—SNCC chose to do its voter registration work in the most reactionary and dangerous areas of the South—in Mississippi and southwest Georgia in particular. The more important resistance to the project came from the NAACP—the oldest, largest, and best-established civil rights organization. It had long conducted voter registration efforts and was worried that some other organizations might impinge on its existing operations. It also preferred to maintain close control over its programs and distrusted the newer, publicity-conscious racial organizations. Already it had undergone several distasteful experiences in which another organization reaped publicity while the NAACP picked up the expensive legal tab.[35]

After some bickering and negotiation, the NAACP's fears were allayed and in January 1962 the Voter Education Project (VEP) was announced. The press release proclaiming its birth invoked the most memorable part of President Kennedy's inaugural address, in which he had urged Americans to ask what they could do for their country. Significantly, too, it placed its own creation within the context of national security. "The times are too serious, the threat of Communist power and ideology too vicious, for America not to be true to itself, to its Constitution, to its old faith in the free and responsible individual," it declared. Although the Project did not formally begin until April 1, shortly after it received a favorable tax ruling from the Internal Revenue Service, by November 1961 small grants had already begun to flow into established registration projects. The VEP was administered by the Southern Regional Council in Atlanta, directed by Wiley A. Branton, a black lawyer from Arkansas, and funded principally by grants from the Taconic Foundation, the Field Foundation, and the Stern Family Fund. By January 1964 the VEP had dispensed over $580,000 to five national civil rights organizations and thirty-eight independent local groups.[36]

During its first twenty-one months of operations, VEP claimed to have registered over 327,000 new voters, 287,000 of whom were black. Most of these gains occurred quietly in cities and counties where Negro registration met no official opposition. As early as the 1962 elections, racial moderates saw signs that the new registrants were having a salutary effect on the South's politics. Although Negro registration encountered stiff opposition in many counties of the South's Black Belt, the voter drives hastened the awakening of black activism even if they did not yield significant increases in registrants. Before long, some of these less successful efforts would help to produce serious strains between their leaders and the Kennedy administration. But in 1961, though some younger civil rights activists questioned the administration's motives, many felt that they were its working allies. Indeed, Jesse Morris, a SNCC worker, told an interviewer that he considered his organization "an arm of the Justice Department." [37]

The nascent identification of the civil rights movement with the administration sprang from several related factors. In sharp contrast with past governmental indifference, this administration evinced a deep interest in the welfare and direction of the civil rights movement. In June Robert Kennedy met personally with a group of student activists, most of whom had participated in the Freedom Rides. He urged them to direct their energies to voter registration. Similarly, Wofford and Marshall attended organizational meetings of VEP and promised full government cooperation. Secondly, many civil rights activists were affected by the general spirit of the New Frontier. President Kennedy's calls for selflessness and vigor, his invocations of the national heritage and destiny, and his youthfulness and receptivity to new ideas all nurtured the idealism, patriotism, and daring of those who might challenge the status quo in America's racial practices and beliefs. In working for social change, many could feel themselves pioneers along the New Frontier. Finally, Robert Kennedy's address at Georgia, the government's involvement in the Freedom Ride episode, and the Justice Department's revitalization in 1961 all suggested that the administration meant business. [38]

Significant changes at the Justice Department became clear soon after the administration took office. With the encouragement of Robert Kennedy, Burke Marshall brought the minus-

cule Civil Rights Division to life. (Its Congressional authorization, it should be pointed out, was for a mere forty
attorneys compared to the Antitrust Division's three hundred.) Marshall quickly made two important procedural
changes. Whereas in the past most suits had been handled by
the U.S. Attorneys, Marshall gave his attorneys full authority
to argue their own cases in court. He also pulled them away
from desks in Washington and sent them out into the field to
take part in investigations, to negotiate with local officials,
and if necessary to take them to court. The Division's morale
improved at the same time the number of cases steadily increased. Its lawyers were litigators, investigators, and agents
for change, not Washington bureaucrats.[39]

In addition, Robert Kennedy in March instructed representatives of the Division to make extensive use of the FBI and
told the investigative bureau to be prepared for a large work
load. "Within the next three months," according to John
Doar, Marshall's first assistant, and Dorothy Landsberg, a
Division attorney, "The Civil Rights Division requested, and
the FBI completed, voting investigations in 34 Southern counties." These early investigative efforts were hampered by the
Divisions's ignorance about the various devices that Southern
registrars employed to deny Negroes the franchise. For example, where literacy tests were used, a registrar would
supply white applicants with the answers to recondite questions about the state's constitution, and give blacks no help at
all. But Division attorneys soon learned how to conduct an
investigation and how to gain the maximum value from the
FBI. By April 1962 the text of its request for an FBI investigation into Choctaw County, Alabama, Doar and Lansberg have
recalled, "went on in the most minute detail for 174 pages,
explaining, anticipating, cautioning, and coaching the Bureau
agents." [40]

The Civil Rights Division received an early challenge when
Judge Frank Johnson of the Middle District of Alabama set

February 20 as the trial date for a pending voter suit in Macon
County. John Doar and other attorneys from the Division
went into the field themselves. With the help of a voluntary
staff from Tuskegee Institute, which was located in Macon
County, they began to organize and analyze the registration
records that the FBI had photographed the previous December. They also interviewed Negroes who had been failed on
their literacy tests even though in many cases they taught or
had been educated at Tuskegee. FBI agents, meanwhile, interviewed whites, and their reports soon confirmed what the
records analysis indicated—that scores of barely literate
whites had "passed" the literacy test. Armed with all of this
evidence, the Justice Department made a convincing case before Judge Johnson. He ordered the registration of sixty-four
Negroes immediately, established future standards for the
enrollment of others, and saw to it that the registrar complied.[41]

Voting rights suits often required a tremendous amount of
preparation by the Division. Hundreds of witnesses had to be
examined, thousands of pages of registration records and literacy tests photographed and analyzed to compile proof that
Negroes had systematically been denied the franchise on account of their race. Doar and Landsberg described their attitudes upon going to trial:

> We were litigators, insisting that the proof be there when we
> entered the courtroom, stubborn and competitive enough to
> prove our cases ourselves. We were not "gee whiz" lawyers.
> The Division was not prepared to take the terrible risk of los-
> ing a single case because of lack of proof. We faced tough judges.
> We wanted the proof to be so overwhelming so as to lock up the
> trial judge; if necessary to persuade the Appellate Court to re-
> verse; and to convince the whole country as well.

Accordingly, in some cases the government introduced a
staggering amount of evidence. In the suit involving Montgomery County, Alabama, it introduced sixty-nine exhibits,

one of which consisted of 10,000 documents in five filing cabinets. In that particular case, local officials offered an evidentiary defense. Sometimes, however, they would not even bother. After Doar presented a massive amount of evidence in the government's case against Louisiana, the defense attorney rose and said, "The burden is on the government to prove that we're discriminating," and sat down.[42]

Defendants in these cases enjoyed one great advantage over the government and the victims of discrimination. The federal district judges who tried the cases often had little sympathy with the cause of racial justice. Consequently many would be slow even to authorize the government to photograph records, the first step in the long road to Negro enfranchisement. Even after the government had won a case, judges often enforced the decisions languidly. They failed to appoint voting referees to serve as officers of the court, which the 1960 Civil Rights Act had authorized. Frequently, too, they issued incorrect or inadequate rulings, procrastinated unreasonably, and even dismissed cases, all of which the government had to challenge in higher courts. Invariably the Justice Department prevailed, but the process took a great deal of time and energy. Contrary to Robert Kennedy's claim before the American Bar Association, the department rarely succeeded in winning pre-trial settlements from local officials. Indeed, the principal reasons for even trying to obtain them were political. According to Marshall, the department hoped to blunt two frequent charges against it: that federal interference was unwarranted because the states had "the will and the power to correct wrongs themselves"; and that suits were "brought in the South in order to gain political advantage in the North."[43]

Despite the considerable efforts that the Justice Department put into voter suits, they had little immediate impact on Negro registration. "We have moved from no registration to token registration," John Doar lamented to a reporter after

two years' experience. Over a year later Marshall publicly acknowledged that in county after county, in Louisiana, Alabama, and Mississippi, the actual gains in Negro registration
had been negligible, often just a fraction of a percentage
point or only a few percentage points.[44]

Where large gains occurred special circumstances obtained.
In Fayette County, Tennessee, the chief obstacle to registration was economic reprisal, not official obstruction. White
landlords were forcing black sharecroppers off their land for
trying to register. A government lawsuit against this kind of
intimidation along with delivery of Agriculture Department
food to the victims broke the back of this resistance to the
registration of blacks. The other major successes, specifically
in three Louisiana parishes and three Alabama counties, were
largely attributable to two unusual Southern district judges,
J. Skelly Wright and Frank Johnson respectively. In the Alabama cases, Macon County's registered Negroes increased
from 13 to 42 percent, Bullock County's from .1124 to 27.6
percent, and Montgomery County's from 11.3 to 19 percent.
Judge Johnson simply demanded results, threatening to appoint a voting referee, and insisted on substantial proof of
compliance with his ruling.[45]

For the most part the district courts moved slowly and President Kennedy himself appointed one of the more dilatory
judges as well as other judges who proved unfriendly to the
civil rights cause. William Harold Cox in Mississippi caused
numerous delays in voting rights cases and clashed bitterly
with civil rights advocates from the bench. J. Robert Elliott
presided over numerous hearings pertaining to the Albany,
Georgia, protest movement and earned its enmity. Clarence
W. Allgood handed down rulings unfavorable to the Birmingham protests of 1963. E. Gordon West of Louisiana made
pro-segregationist remarks from the bench. Even as early as
1962 civil rights lawyers were privately criticizing Kennedy's
Southern judicial appointees. In December 1962, their criti-

cism received wider circulation when Yale law professor
Alexander Bickel assessed Kennedy's civil rights record for
the *New Republic*. Since then civil rights proponents have
generally evaluated Kennedy's Southern judicial appointments unfavorably.[46]

Although he was President less than three years, Kennedy
made an unusually large number of judicial appointments as
a result of the enactment of the Omnibus Judgeship Bill in the
spring of 1961, which increased the number of judges. In
theory, the President made district court appointments with
the advice and consent of the Senate. In reality, the Democratic Senators made them for their own states "with the advice and consent of the President," according to Joseph
Dolan, Deputy Assistant Attorney General, the administration's liaison with the Senate on this matter. Kennedy was
merely following tradition in deferring to his party's Senators. He had not challenged the Senate's prerogatives on the
filibuster, and he certainly did not want trouble over judgeships in which Senators usually took a proprietary interest.[47]

Because of their seniority, Southern Senators commanded
especially powerful positions from which to protect their judicial patronage. James Eastland chaired the Judiciary Committee and had guided the Judgeship Bill through his committee. He hardly expected to be excluded from naming the
judge in Mississippi. If he were antagonized, he could ob-
struct other legislation the administration sought from his
committee, including antitrust and immigration; and he
could delay judicial appointments from other districts, as he
and other Southerners did in the case of Thurgood Marshall's
confirmation for the southern New York district.[48]

Kennedy in 1961 planned to elevate J. Skelly Wright from
the Louisiana district court to the Southern regional appeals
court. Wright had a distinguished record, which included his
courageous order to desegregate the New Orleans public
schools. Senator Russell Long objected to the promotion, fear-

ing that a segregationist opponent might use it against him in an upcoming election. Bowing to Long, the President instead placed Wright on the appeals court which sat in Washington. Burke Marshall would have preferred to have Wright's talents available in the South, but according to him the President viewed the situation more practically. "Russell Long was an important Senator," Marshall has reflected, "and what was the point of doing something he [Kennedy] was going to lose on and make Russell Long mad at him." Similarly, in Virginia Harry Byrd opposed J. Lindsay Almond's appointment to the district bench but not to the Court of Customs and Patent Appeals, which sat in Washington. Governor Almond, once a loyal member of the Byrd organization, had broken with the powerful Senator over "massive resistance." Almond had also worked for the national Democratic ticket in 1960 and the Kennedys therefore wanted to reward him. Even so, the administration proceeded with the less important appointment only after triple-checking it with Byrd.[49]

Normally the Senate's judicial candidates were lawyers who had high political connections, a record of public service, a prestigious law practice, or all three of these things. In most Southern states few blacks had these qualifications, through no fault of their own. On the other hand, white lawyers who possessed them rarely had a record of support for civil rights. If they had aligned themselves with the cause of racial justice, either at the bar or in their communities, they would have thereby eliminated themselves from lists of prospective judges. Moreover, once on the bench, an individual was subject to considerable community pressure on the question of civil rights, especially in the Deep South. Several judges who went against the grain on civil rights were ostracized by the white community or attacked by local politicians.[50]

The Justice Department made some effort to gauge future judicial behavior by investigation and even personal interview, but to little effect. In Alabama, Clarence Allgood's appointment was quietly endorsed by that state's civil rights groups. Although the American Bar Association's committee on the judiciary initially found him "unqualified," the President nominated him. He turned out to be a segregationist. Similarly in Georgia, Austin T. Walden, Atlanta's Negro Democratic leader, approved J. Robert Elliott, the candidate of Senator Herman Talmadge. Chief Judge Elbert Tuttle of the Fifth Circuit Court of Appeals, after consulting with a Georgian on his court, told Robert Kennedy that he thought Elliott would be fair. From the perspective of many civil rights activists in Georgia, those proved to be wrong estimates. Upon the nomination of William Harold Cox, a close friend of James Eastland, Roy Wilkins protested vehemently. But Robert Kennedy and Burke Marshall interviewed Cox, who assured them that he would uphold the Constitution as interpreted by the Supreme Court. Before long, it was apparent that Wilkins's objections had been well founded.[51]

To be sure, many of Kennedy's judges did try their best to uphold civil rights laws and the mandate of higher courts. In fact, a quantitative comparative analysis of Eisenhower and Kennedy appointees indicated that Kennedy actually appointed more integrationists in the South than Eisenhower, whose record of judicial appointment of civil rights advocates has been held in higher regard. It should be pointed out, however, that Kennedy's integrationists were concentrated outside the troubled Deep South states and that several of Eisenhower's judges issued courageous rulings from precarious locations. In addition, other Eisenhower appointees were highly respected liberal members of the Fifth Circuit Court of Appeals.[52]

Privately, Robert Kennedy and other members of the administration later admitted having erred in some of these appointments; but they also were inclined to defend themselves by pointing out how segregationist some of Roosevelt's, Truman's, and Eisenhower's selections were. To an administration intent on rigorous enforcement of existing civil rights laws and the channeling of protest into legal proceedings, however, there must have been small comfort in either admission or defense. "It is inevitable that most district judges want to do as little as possible to disturb the patterns of life and politics in their state and community," Burke Marshall observed after three years' experience.[53]

From a practical political standpoint, the administration had very little room in which to maneuver on judicial appointments. It was simply not feasible or even possible to name avowed integrationists to the district bench in the Deep South. "Now how are you going to find a lawyer in Mississippi who has a substantial amount of practice of the nature and character that would warrant his consideration by the President . . . for judicial appointment who had views on civil rights that are in accord with the view of the NAACP?" Joseph Dolan later asked. And he realistically answered his own question: "Well, if his views on civil rights were in accord with the NAACP he wouldn't have any clients in Mississippi." The administration only hoped that its appointees would be fair and reasonable. Yet, time would show that some judges completely lacked these qualities when they ruled on civil rights.[54]

Behind the failures of its district court appointees lay a central paradox of the administration's Southern law enforcement policy. The Kennedys hoped to prod the South into voluntary acceptance of the civil rights of black people. But it refrained from doing anything which smacked of federal coercion. Rather, it went along with the traditional methods of judicial selection, deferring to the Senate. At the same time, however, the administration encouraged the civil rights movement to entrust its aspirations to the federal judicial process, in particular by promoting voter registration. During the next several years, the federal judicial system would prove inadequate. And the civil rights movement—in part inspired by the actions and promises of the Kennedy administration, in part frustrated by manifestations of its traditionalism—would place pressure on the federal government to bring about changes much more quickly and far-reaching than practically anyone had anticipated in 1961.

FIVE

A Harder Road

Through the first eight months of 1962, Kennedy adhered to the civil rights approach he had set in 1961 but its application became more problematic. Race played a role in two Congressional defeats: creation of a Department of Urban Affairs and abolition of literacy tests in voting. Several elections in the South yielded conflicting signs of emerging moderation and extremism. The administration explored new avenues of executive action, related to the economy and school desegregation, but its showcase program for eliminating job discrimination, Plans for Progress, came under attack from representatives of those it was supposed to be benefitting. Although it was still possible for the administration to travel down the middle road, that road became noticeably harder.

ON January 2, 1962, columnist William S. White, a centrist, praised the Kennedys for their "moderation" on civil rights, for their adherence to the middle path despite "pressure from screaming ultra-liberals in the North and howling ultra-conservatives in the South." He predicted that the Kennedys would maintain the same direction in the future. Testifying before an appropriations subcommittee several weeks later, Robert Kennedy substantially confirmed White's prediction. With regard to race relations, the Attorney General said, "I feel very strongly that this problem is not going to be solved by just passing some laws. It will require some understanding." He explained how violence in newly integrated schools had been averted the previous fall by behind-the-scenes discussions between Justice Department representatives and local officials. Although he suggested that some new legislation might be useful, he maintained that much progress could be achieved through "good will" and the government's continued unpublicized efforts.[1]

In his first year in office, President Kennedy had done little that regular Southern Democrats could not tolerate. Shortly after Kennedy took office, Benjamin Muse spoke to a number of Southern governors and editors and found that "each emphasized the danger in 'stirring things up,' the importance of making 'quiet progress,' or 'unnoticed progress,' and keeping the thing out of politics and out of the papers as far as possible." Although the administration's racial policies became highly visible at times—during the Freedom Rides, on the numerous occasions it examined voting records or went to court, and through its employment program—on the whole they remained uncontroversial enough for most Southern Democrats. In August 1961, no less a Southern patriarch than John McClellan defended the administration's record against the criticisms of liberal Republican Senator Jacob Javits. Although he had not always agreed with Kennedy's decisions, McClellan told the Senate, the President's efforts and methods redounded to his credit. The administration, he admonished Javits, "should be praised and not condemned by those who adovcate so-called civil rights."[2]

When the new session of Congress convened in January, the racial issue began to play a much greater role in Congressional deliberations than it had in 1961. This was logical, for 1962 was an election year. Politicians on all sides of the racial issue thus began to regard their constituents' sensibilities particularly closely. In quick succession two of Kennedy's legislative requests, for the creation of a Department of Urban Affairs and for the abolition of literacy tests in voter registration, became enmeshed in racial controversy on Capitol Hill.

In 1961 the President had deferred issuing the executive order against discrimination in housing until he could win

Congressional approval of a new Department of Urban Affairs. Because he planned to name Robert Weaver its first Secretary, he had not wanted to risk the defection of Alabamans Albert Rains and John Sparkman, chairmen of the House and Senate housing committees, whose support would be essential. Lee White reported to Kennedy in August 1961 that the Urban Affairs bill had excellent prospects. McClellan, it was true, had voted against the bill in committee, but a phone call from the President might win his acquiescence. Sparkman, meanwhile "indicated strong approval and will probably allay the fears of many Southern Senators." In the House, Rains was the key, but assuming there was no trouble, there would be little difficulty with him or his colleagues, according to White. "The only other possible source of trouble," he cautioned, "would be a question about Weaver being your choice for the Secretaryship and at present it appears that this will not erupt." [3]

When the new session of Congress began, however, rumblings of Southern opposition were heard. On January 22, the New York *Times* reported that the racial issue threatened the Department's creation and that John Sparkman had told a Southern radio audience that the Kennedy plan "subordinated housing too much" and that he had not decided how he would vote. Two days later the House Rules Committee refused, by a nine to six margin, to grant the enabling legislation a rule for floor action. Joining together to form the majority were all five Republicans, who normally voted against the administration, and four Southern Democrats. In the latter group, Howard Smith of Virginia and William Colmer of Mississippi had consistently opposed the administration, but two regular Kennedy allies, James Trimble of Arkansas and Carl Elliott of Alabama, lined up against the administration this time. According to the leading Congressional reporting service, Trimble had been prepared to back the bill if his vote had been pivotal, which it was not. Along with the rest of

Alabama's Congressional delegation, Elliott faced a statewide at-large primary in the spring, as a result of that state's failure to redistrict. He reportedly feared the political ramifications of supporting the bill. It could have been construed in Alabama as an endorsement of the first black Cabinet member.[4]

Several hours after this setback, Kennedy told a press conference that he planned to appoint Weaver Secretary of the new department, which he would now try to create through submission of a government reorganization plan. Under the terms of the Reorganization Act of 1949, the President could establish a department if within sixty days it was not disapproved by a majority in either Congressional chamber. At a later news conference, Kennedy reiterated his intention to appoint Weaver. "Obviously, if the legislation had been passed, Mr. Weaver would have been appointed," the President declared. "It was well known on the Hill. The American people might as well know it." [5]

Assuming the loss of Southern Democrat support, Kennedy was hoping to use Weaver's color to cow the Republicans into backing the bill. He reasoned that Republicans would be reluctant to vote, in effect, against Weaver. Conveniently, Roy Wilkins and Clarence Mitchell of the NAACP enlisted in the cause. They pointed out to Republican Congressman Thomas Curtis, for example, that President Eisenhower had won Republican support for the creation of the Department of Health, Education and Welfare by announcing in advance the appointment of Oveta Culp Hobby, a conservative publisher and a woman, as its first secretary. They also urged that the department be established in order to meet the nation's pressing urban needs.[6]

Kennedy's tactic failed to convert Republicans. Everett Dirksen and Charles Halleck took pains to remind the public that their party had opposed the department before the President announced Weaver's selection. Thomas Curtis, an influential House member and civil rights sympathizer from suburban St. Louis, asked Clarence Mitchell: "Is the NAACP for a Department of Urban Affairs or is it helping the Democratic party develop a campaign issue for 1962 as many of the Kennedy supporters in the Press claim was the real purpose behind the President's move?" To some extent, racial politics figured in the GOP position. During the House debate on the reorganization plan, Republican William Ayres of Ohio observed that "very few Members of Congress need fear the adverse votes of Negroes on this issue. Outside of 12 Southern States there are very few congressional districts—only 57 out of 437—where Negroes equal 10 per cent or more of the total population." In support of his contention, he submitted a statistical table, based on the census, which detailed the racial makeup of Congressional districts outside the South. Yet, most Republicans probably opposed the department for nonracial reasons; many regarded it as an undesirable accretion to an already oversized federal bureaucracy and many of them did not represent major urban areas. However, as Ayres candidly attested, relatively few of them had to worry about antagonizing a large black constituency.[7]

Meanwhile, with the Weaver appointment on public display, most Southern Democrats hastened to follow Carl Elliot's path. Like him they recoiled at what amounted to voting for the first black Cabinet member. To make matters even worse for the administration, the Democratic leadership mishandled the reorganization plan. Three days before the House vote, Speaker John McCormack virtually surrendered by predicting the plan would lose, which sent waverers scurrying from the administration position. In the Senate, Majority Leader Mike Mansfield, aching to get a favorable vote there before the more dubious House vote occurred, hastily endorsed the use of a discharge motion to extract the plan from McClellan's Government Operations Committee. The discharge motion alienated the Senate's more senior members, including non-Southerners. In the end, the administration suffered a decisive 58 to 42 defeat. On the losing side were four liberal, Northeastern Republicans (Clifford Case of New Jersey, Jacob Javits and Kenneth Keating of New York, and Hugh Scott of Pennsylvania) and 38 Democrats, including only the three most liberal Southerners (Ralph Yarborough of Texas, and Albert Gore and Estes Kefauver of Tennessee). In the majority were all the other Southerners, Sparkman included, eight quite senior Northern and Western Democrats, and the remainder of the Republicans. The next day the House laid the plan to rest by a 264–150 vote. The roll call reflected the sectional and party divisions of the Senate vote.[8]

It is impossible to infer the outcome had the President not tipped his hand on Weaver. Apparently most Republicans were determined to oppose the plan anyway. It is at least possible, however, that the Southern Democratic drift away from the administration might have been stemmed, but only if the vote had been postponed until after the 1962 elections. One obvious lesson could be drawn from the defeat. When Southern Democrats abandoned the administration en masse, Kennedy needed to retain the loyalty of all other Democrats as well as to win a sizeable number of Republicans to his side. Two other legislative matters, the poll tax and the literacy test, would require similar arithmetic.

The abolition of the poll tax had by 1962 become a fairly uncontroversial matter. Only five states—Alabama, Arkansas, Mississippi, Virginia, and Texas—still levied poll taxes on voters in federal elections, and many Southerners favored their proscription. Indeed, the abolition of this tax through constitutional amendment enjoyed the principal sponsorship of Senator Spessard Holland of Florida, a conservative. In 1960 the Senate had approved his amendment by a lopsided 72–16 margin, but in the rush to pass a constitutional amendment granting District of Columbia residents the right to vote in Presidential elections, it had been shelved. In 1962, when it was again under consideration, the NAACP and some of its liberal friends expressed a strong preference for abolishing the poll tax through statutory enactment. Holland and other Southerners would not be a party to any statutory tampering with voting because it might undercut their usual grounds for opposing voting rights legislation: that the constitution had substantially reserved to the state legislatures the authority to set voting qualifications. Acting on the advice of the Justice Department and Emanuel Celler, Chairman of the House Judiciary Committee, who had promised Holland the amendment and who felt confident of victory only if the constitutional route were followed, the President went along with Holland. In the Senate, Jacob Javits's attempt to outlaw the poll tax by statute was tabled on a motion by Mike Mansfield. Congress quickly approved the measure, and in January 1964 the Twenty-Fourth Amendment was approved by the states. By cooperating with Southern Democrats, Kennedy had attained a victory, though he had to concede a debating point about constitutional authority. In this particular instance, the concession did not cause him pain because, according to Theodore Sorensen, Kennedy estimated that "the number of Negroes and less affluent whites enabled to vote" by this measure "could make a difference in his 1964 re-election race in Texas and Virginia." [9]

In early 1962, the administration also asked Congress to outlaw the use of literacy tests in the registration of voters for federal elections. To qualify to vote, in effect to demonstrate literacy, a person would only have to complete the sixth grade; all other literacy tests would be abolished. The bill was aimed directly at eliminating one of the most blatant methods of preventing blacks from voting. Local registrars would no longer be able to prevent Negroes from voting in federal elections because they did not comprehend an obscure section of the state constitution. Burke Marshall frankly admitted to a civil rights audience that the administration's bill "did not accomplish everything" in the area of voting rights. It would "not automatically make voters out of all Negro citizens of the proper age"; but "its passage would be a tremendous stride forward. It would not only make what litigation we find necessary much easier," Marshall said, "but it should also encourage many citizens to register to vote who now—whatever the attitude of the current registration officials—are too discouraged by past inequities to attempt to register." [10]

Actually the Justice Department, not the White House, initiated and promoted this legislation. Robert Kennedy and Burke Marshall wanted it enacted to buttress their voting rights efforts in the South. Moreover, Mike Mansfield thought it a good bill, agreed to sponsor it himself, and apparently convinced Everett Dirksen to cosponsor it. The President went along with his brother because he hoped the legislation would deflate criticism from civil rights spokesmen and liberal Republicans that he had reneged on his campaign promises. Furthermore, this particular piece of legislation, narrowly drafted to exclude state elections from its coverage, fell in the area where Congress had acted twice before in recent years. It was also the area which Southern Democrats were likely to resent the least. Throughout the life of the bill, the White House maintained a low profile. The Justice Department conducted whatever lobbying the bill enjoyed. But from the day the legislation was introduced, it had rough sledding. [11] •

On January 30, Lyndon Johnson, presiding over the Senate and clearly deferring to the wishes of the bill's prominent sponsors, referred S. 2370 to the Judiciary Committee. Several liberals, Jacob Javits most vociferously, protested. They wanted the bill sent to the Rules Committee because the Judiciary Committee had been a graveyard for civil rights legislation. Mansfield accordingly promised that he would attach the bill as an amendment to another bill if the Judiciary Committee should fail to report it within ninety days. Mansfield then assured Georgia's Richard Russell of his intention to give the Senate forty-eight hours' notice before he moved the amendment so that Southern forces could be ready. By a 61 to 25 vote, with many liberals of both parties dissenting, the Senate now concurred in Johnson's referral of the bill. Although the leadership prevailed in this opening skirmish, the discontent of Southerners on one side and liberals on the other had been made clear. [12]

When Robert Kennedy testified on behalf of the literacy test bill before a Senate Judiciary subcommittee in March and April, he had to contend not only with North Carolinian Sam Ervin's critical cross examination on the constitutionality of the measure but also with New Yorker Kenneth Keating's complaints that the legislation did not go far enough. Keating preferred legislation that he was sponsoring with Javits which included coverage of state elections. Kennedy explained that state elections had not been included because that would have made passage more difficult. But numerous liberal spokesmen before the committee expressed dissatisfaction with the administration's limited approach. Representatives of the NAACP, AFL–CIO, and ADA all favored broader coverage. Roy Wilkins was happy that the administration had recognized that its civil rights program needed a "legislative base," but called the bill "a token offering on the full civil rights program pledged by the administration's party platform of 1960." Without minimizing the need for voting legislation, Wilkins stressed the neglected areas of fair employment practices and school desegregation. Like the Attorney General, who had testified several days before him, Wilkins employed the old chestnut of American's image abroad. He urged that this country's domestic practices be made consistent with its international objectives:

> In preaching against the sins of disfranchisement, why must our Government's target be always the Babylons overseas in a far land? Why do we not bring our moral outrage, our love of de-

mocracy, and the majesty and power of our undoubted constitutional authority to bear upon the sin spots within our own borders? Why not decree—through the enactment of this and other legislation—free elections for all the people in every section of the United States? Is Albania's soul more precious than that of Alabama? If not, if Louisiana is as important as Lithuania, then the Congress should act favorably and speedily upon the pending bills.[13]

Congress did not heed Wilkins's message. When the Judiciary Committee showed no signs of releasing his legislation, Mansfield attached it to a private bill on April 25. Immediately a well-organized Southern filibuster began. In 1960 liberals had forced the Senate into round-the-clock sessions to wear down the Southerners but the filibuster had not been broken then and the debate ended only when a compromise was adopted leaving the legislation weak. However, no one seemed interested in such a fight in 1962. The proposal's limited scope had dampened the enthusiasm of liberals, and neither Mansfield nor the White House was disposed to conduct a divisive intraparty struggle anyway. "The debate has been somewhat desultory, with two or three speeches a day and a very limited exchange of ideas," the Majority Leader declared on May 1 when he announced that he would seek a cloture motion the following week.[14]

As the vote neared, the Justice Department and Senator Dirksen, the Minority Leader, lobbied for cloture, but it soon became obvious that neither had been very persuasive. Former President Eisenhower announced at a press conference that he thought the bill would be unconstitutional. On the Senate floor, Republican John Sherman Cooper of Kentucky, a highly respected and influential proponent of civil rights, said he could not vote for cloture because the debate had been too brief and because he was inclined to believe that the legislation was unconstitutional. Before the roll was called, Robert Kennedy conceded that his side would not get the requisite two-thirds majority for cloture, but he expected at least to muster a simple majority. He did not even do that well. The Senate defeated cloture 53 to 43. In the majority were 23 Republicans, 23 Southern Democrats, including Gore and Kefauver, and 7 Northern Democrats, most of them from Western states of low population who traditionally sided with the South on procedural motions as a way of protecting their own small-state interests. Thirteen Republicans and thirty Northern Democrats supported cloture.[15]

Immediately after this setback, Mansfield offered a motion to table the literacy bill in order to test sentiment for concluding the debate. By a margin of 64 to 33—precisely what would have been needed to invoke cloture—the Senate rejected tabling. In the majority were many Republicans and non-Southern Democrats who had been on the other side in the cloture vote. Looking on this as a favorable omen, the President told a press conference: "if that vote indicates that the members are for it, that could be very encouraging." But Kennedy evidently misread the sign. Indeed, Mansfield might well have erred in giving moderate members the chance to record a vote against tabling which appeared to balance their vote against invoking cloture. However, tactical error did not cause the failure of the literacy bill. The votes needed to pass it were simply not available, or close to being available. When the leadership tried to obtain cloture a second time on May 14, the outcome virtually duplicated the first tally. One of the original members of the majority did not participate, but no Senator switched sides. With that, the leadership gave the bill up for lost and supported its own motion to table so that the Senate could move on to other business.[16]

Friends of civil rights placed the blame for the defeat in different quarters. The small vocal band of liberal Republicans blasted the administration's acquiescence. Joseph Clark, a leading Democratic liberal, agreed that "the leadership gave up," that Mansfield did not have his heart in the fight after the demoralizing first cloture vote, but he conceded that Mansfield's decision to quit after the second attempt may well have been wise. The bill's principal difficulty, Clark maintained, had been the "lack of any deep conviction behind it." Civil rights groups, he said, were mainly interested in securing the passage of the old Title III Bill and in obtaining legislation to promote school integration, and therefore "they did not strongly support the effort to have the pending legislation brought forward for a vote on the merits and passed." Chuck Stone, a black political journalist, observed that the administration had failed but attributed the failure ultimately to the inability of blacks to exercise their own collective power to obtain what they wanted.[17]

"The discouraging results of the battle for the literacy test bill," Joseph L. Rauh, Jr. wrote Paul Douglas, "do not obscure the fact that there were a few valiant souls who really care about minority rights and who carried this fight with courage, dedication and skill." The basic problem had undoubtedly been that there were so few "valiant souls," for what the failure most clearly demonstrated was the absence of any Congressional willingness to enact new civil rights legislation. In particular, it showed the conservative sentiments, on this issue, of a substantial majority of Senate Republicans. Reflecting on this central fact, Mike Mansfield pessimistically forecast to the President and the Justice Department that Kennedy would not be able to win approval of any civil rights bill. He believed that the Republicans would simply never give him the 25 votes needed for cloture.[18]

In fact Kennedy could expect scant Republican support for legislative requests of any kind, although more often than is generally assumed he did receive the backing of Southern Democrats, particularly on matters relating to the economy. On the eve of the desegregation of the University of Mississippi, in September 1962, many Southern House members did vote to recommit the administration's college aid legislation, but the National Education Association also favored recommittal because it was dissatisfied with the bill's disposition of the church–state issue. When the administration lost a showdown in the Senate on medical care for the aged, the most important Democratic dissidents came from border or western states, not the South. In the House Ways and Means Committee, several Southern Democrats sided with the administration on its medical care legislation, but Chairman Wilbur Mills of Arkansas and two other Democrats, one from Florida and one from Kentucky, opposed it and the legislation was stalled in committee.[19]

Often Kennedy enjoyed the loyalty of his Southern party members. Henry H. Wilson, Jr., who worked on Kennedy's Congressional liaison staff, analyzed four important administration victories in the House in 1962—recommittal of the tax bill, final passage of debt limit increase, farm bill recommittal, and trade bill recommittal. He found that forty-two Southern Democrats voted with the administration 100 percent of the time; twenty-two, 75 percent; three, 66.7 percent; eleven, 50 percent; six, 25 percent; and thirteen, none of the time. Among the last group, five were from Mississippi and four from Texas. Meanwhile the Republican picture contrasted sharply. "Of the 174 Republicans none voted with us on more than two of the four roll calls, eight voted with us on two, forty-six with us on one, and 122 did not vote with us once." He also pointed out that if the President did not have his Southern votes, he would "have to pick up between sixty and seventy seats just to stay where we are." Furthermore, Southerners, with very few exceptions, according to Wilson, remained loyal to the administration although they:

1. Can look for little or no help in their districts either financially or organizationally either to organized labor or to the party structure;

2. Must encounter their critical tests not in the general election, but in the primaries, where they get no help from having the President at the head of the ticket;

3. Have established through the years entrenched habits of voting with the Republicans;

4. Must look for their financial and community support to local business leaders who are totally responsive to the national pressure groups which oppose all our programs, and

5. Can gain little from us but a kind smile and a pat on the head.[20]

The relatively high degree of Southern loyalty can be explained in several ways. Many Southern Democrats undoubtedly took their party allegiance to heart, and especially respected their party's Congressional leaders who in turn sympathized with the President's objectives. In addition, many shared Kennedy's general economic and governmental philosophy. Moreover, they could afford to side with him politically because he continued to be popular in the South at large. In mid-September, 1962, the Gallup poll found the President receiving nearly the same general approval rating below the Mason-Dixon line (65 percent) as above it (68 percent). And his popularity in the South was probably secure as long as he did not advocate extreme measures on civil rights. There were, however, some places in the South where association with Kennedy or with the federal administration he headed proved to be a serious political liability in the spring and summer of 1962.[21]

In Mississippi in 1962, Congressional redistricting brought about a contest between two incumbents, Frank E. Smith and Jamie Whitten. Smith had a liberal record on everything but race. He later confessed that he only swam with the anti-civil-rights tide so that he could win election and support liberal economic and foreign policies in Congress. Whitten, on the other hand, was liberal neither in his voting record nor his beliefs. At every turn in the campaign, Whitten identified

Smith with the Kennedys, integration and the "socialistic"
New Frontier. A campaign song that preceded his speeches
began with this verse:

> *Skunks in the stump holes*
> *monkeys in the trees,*
> *Frank's crawled in bed with*
> *the Kennedys.*

Smith countered that it was advantageous for the district to
have a representative who was a friend of the President, that
he, a real Democrat, could get more done for his constituents.
He also tried to convince segregationists that in his quiet
ways he could be more effective in preventing integration
than Whitten. The President meanwhile kept his distance,
though he privately contributed $2,000 to Smith's costly cam-
paign. The Justice Department, too, quietly deferred inspect-
ing voting records in Smith's home county until after the
primary.[22]

In light of recent Mississippi politics and Smith's identification as the liberal candidate, he did not fare badly in the
June 5 primary. He received 21,000 votes to Whitten's 34,000.
A Negro minister received 2,000. Whitten had several advantages besides Smith's relationship to the national administration. Most important, the state's political machine backed
him. In addition, Whitten held a powerful position as chairman of the Agriculture Appropriations Subcommittee which
made him more attractive to the state's farmers. Indeed, his
powerful committee position evidently even brought Whitten
some assistance from the Washington bureaucracy. For example, although Smith had been the only Mississippian to
support the housing bill in 1961, and had assisted the state
university in making an application for federal housing assistance, Whitten was given the prestige of announcing the application's success in 1962. Soon after the election, the Presi-

dent rewarded Smith for his loyalty by appointing him to the Board of Directors of the Tennessee Valley Authority.[23]

Neighboring Alabama also had a choice between moderate and extremist candidates. In the past, Alabama had often rejected extremism and a poll in early 1962 indicated that former Governor James E. Folsom, a flamboyant, hard-drinking racial moderate, held a comfortable lead. The runner-up in the poll, George C. Wallace, had finished second to John Patterson in the 1958 election. Apparently Wallace was convinced that he had lost then because he had been identified as the racial moderate. He would expunge that stigma in 1962. Benjamin Muse happened to observe Wallace campaigning in a hotel lobby during the primary campaign. He heard Wallace state his preference for closing parks to integrating them, and speak at length on the "mistake" of "appeasing niggers" at home and abroad. "Asked for his opinion of Bobby Kennedy, his reply was too revoltingly obscene" for Muse to repeat. Two years later Muse encountered Louis Eckl, an old personal friend of Wallace, a Florence newspaper editor, who had asked Wallace why he could not talk about something other than race. "I started off talking about schools and highways and prisons and taxes—and I couldn't make them listen," Wallace reportedly replied. "Then I began talking about niggers—and they stomped the floor." [24]

Wallace captured the most extreme segregationist position in his race against several more moderate opponents. Ominously he campaigned not so much against them but against a noncandidate, Federal District Judge Frank Johnson, who had issued a number of decisions supporting civil rights for Negroes. Wallace attacked Johnson repeatedly, calling him, in a state-wide television address, "an integrating, scalawaging, carpetbagging liar." Wallace swore that as governor he would refuse to abide by any federal court order forcing racial integration which he considered illegal, "even to the point of standing in the schoolhouse door in person" to block it. In the first primary Wallace finished first but Folsom, who insisted throughout the campaign that the "Civil War is over," and that "we gotta have law and order in this state," fell by the wayside, a victim both of his views and his personal habits. In the runoff, Wallace handily defeated the lesser known Ryan DeGraffenreid, a state senator who favored orderly legal resistance to desegregation, not open defiance.[25]

The Alabama outcome undoubtedly caused some consternation in the Kennedy administration, because Wallace's campaign suggested that he might try to defy federal authority in the manner of Orval Faubus. Burke Marshall publicly expressed his dismay that Wallace, a lawyer and former state judge, could attack the federal judiciary the way he had. Even more worrisome to Marshall was "that not one voice from the Bar of the State of Alabama—or for that matter from the bar anywhere—was raised to protest an attack on a federal judge which was based upon nothing but his acceptance of his responsibility to give effect to federal law." [26]

The administration could take heart from the gubernatorial primary results in neighboring Georgia, however. In it former state senator Carl Sanders, a racial moderate, defeated the outspoken racist, former governor Marvin Griffin. It was the first Georgia primary since 1908 to be decided by a straight popular vote instead of by the county unit system. A three-judge district court panel had just overturned the old system which gave rural voters much more weight than urban voters. (The following year, in his first and only argument before the Supreme Court, Attorney General Kennedy successfully defended that ruling in an appearance as *amicus curiae*.) Endorsed by Wallace, Griffin took a hard prosegregationist position. Sanders, too, favored segregation but by contrast rarely mentioned the issue. Sanders was very much the spokesman of Georgia's business leaders who felt that racial discord and defiance of federal law were bad for business. He declared that his victory marked an end to an era when race was the paramount issue in Georgia politics. Georgians "may not like all that goes on," Ralph McGill optimistically forecast, "but they will not support any candidates, now or in the future, who seem to be willing to discredit education, to close the schools of cities and, perhaps, of the state." [27]

Extremism might have had a greater popular appeal in the South in 1962 had the President crusaded for civil rights. However, no more than in 1961 did Kennedy exhort the nation to purge itself of racial discrimination. During racial crises in Georgia and Mississippi, to be discussed in succeeding chapters, the President spoke out on behalf of preserving order, not of securing justice. To news conference queries about race relations Kennedy typically gave terse answers. For example, a reporter on May 17 reminded Kennedy that it was the eighth anniversary of the *Brown* decision and asked him if he felt progress had been rapid enough. "While progress has been made," Kennedy answered, "I think we can always improve equality of opportunity in the United States." In late July a reporter asked him to comment on Martin Luther King's opinion that the President could do much more in the area of moral persuasion. "I made it very clear that I'm for every American citizen having his Constitutional rights," he rather defensively replied, "and the United States Government under this administration has taken a whole variety of very effective steps to improve the equal opportunities for all Americans and will continue to do so." [28]

Following the defeat of the literacy test bill and Mansfield's pessimistic forecast about the President's chances of winning civil rights legislation in the future, the administration began to lay greater emphasis upon an economic approach to the problems of black people. In addressing a Negro insurancemen's group, Robert Kennedy spoke optimistically about the administration's accomplishments, and urged his audience to help young Negro school dropouts who might otherwise become "malcontents, criminals and persons who have little faith in freedom and democratic ways" to return to school or enter training programs. In June Burke Marshall argued in a memorandum to the Attorney General "that the basic national long-range problem with the Negro is economic." Moreover, dealing with that problem through legislation rather than with the more controversial issue of discrimination had several advantages. A job training program, for example, would allow the administration to skirt deep-seated white Southern hostility to Fair Employment Practices legislation. Unlike the old FEPC, Marshall's contemplated programs were neither punitive nor aimed principally at the South. Meanwhile Robert Kennedy had taken a deep personal interest in juvenile delinquency. A commission he headed to study that problem was soon recommending measures which paralleled Marshall's. Within a year, the administration, at the President's direction, was drawing up an antipoverty legislative program to set before Congress. Interestingly, much of the rationale for it came from the Justice Department.[29]

As in 1961 the administration eschewed civil rights measures which smacked of retribution. Accordingly Marshall testified before a House subcommittee in April against legislation that would have withheld federal funds from local school districts which maintained segregation. Though denial of funds might in some cases lead to desegregation, Marshall argued, in others the school district might well decide to do without the funds. Withdrawing funds might be preferable to doing nothing, but it was "essentially negative and punitive in character." The administration preferred "the positive, direct, approach of a desegregation suit to a withdrawal of funds." Furthermore, he announced the Justice Department was studying the feasibility of bringing suit in school cases.[30]

Both the NAACP and Adam Clayton Powell, Chairman of

the House Committee on Education and Labor, pressed the government to take administrative action on the education front. In December 1961, the Office of Education had notified colleges and universities which had been selected for language institutes under the National Defense Education Act that a nondiscrimination clause was being included in all new contracts. In response only six Southern institutions had withdrawn from the program while twenty-two others remained. Then in March, Abraham Ribicoff, Secretary of Health, Education and Welfare, announced that effective September 1963, federal funds would be withheld from school districts serving children of parents living on military bases if the districts practiced segregation. Ribicoff did not go nearly so far as the NAACP wished, but as Clarence Mitchell reported to his board, it represented a reversal of the "unfair policy established by former Secretary Arthur S. Flemming." [31]

The Justice Department, however, acted more daringly in September, when it filed its first impacted-area suit in the case of Prince George County, Virginia. Impacted areas were those in which military installations were located and which received federal funds to assist the local districts in educating the children of military personnel. Many Southern Congressmen resented the Justice Department's initiative. As Senator Herman Talmadge quickly protested, the Congress had three times denied the Attorney General authority to file school suits. The Department proceeded anyway, and by the following January had filed four additional suits, in Alabama, Louisiana, and Mississippi. As Marshall explained the legal bases of the suits to Robert Kennedy, each of the recipient school boards had given written assurance to the federal government that the grant would be in accordance with the laws of the state. The Supreme Court had ruled that state laws requiring segregation were unconstitutional. Therefore the government could assume that the money was being used in a constitutional way, that is, without racial segregation. Marshall also pointed out that Congress had denied the Attorney General the authority to bring suit to vindicate individual rights, but the purpose of these suits was "to enforce the government's own interest in the morale and efficiency of its servicemen and employees; its interest that the laws of the United States (including the impact-area [*sic*] legislation) be carried out in a constitutional manner; and its direct interest that the statutory assurance be complied with in a constitutional manner." [32]

Before bringing suit in impacted-area cases, the Justice Department, as usual, tried to arrive at a satisfactory nonjudicial settlement. In a memorandum to Robert Kennedy, Burke Marshall described one such attempt in Huntsville, Alabama, location of the Redstone Arsenal. On July 30, 1962, Marshall met with a group of five leading white citizens in Huntsville: the president of the local bank, a businessman and director of the bank, the owner of a large grocery business, the editor of the newspaper, and the superintendent of schools. Owing to the efforts of the first four of these men, the city had already accomplished a degree of desegregation. Two of the men served on a biracial committee along with two black leaders, although the community at large did not know of the committee's existence. All five believed that school desegregation had to begin, but thought there was not sufficient time to prepare for it by the coming September and all expected that Governor Patterson would interfere to prevent it. They expressed willingness to make a personal commitment to begin desegregation in the fall of 1963, however. Marshall was satisfied with that commitment but expressed doubt that George Wallace would permit desegregation voluntarily, although a court order could give "him a retreat, as in the cases of Vandiver in Georgia, Davis in Louisiana, and Almond in Virginia." The Huntsville people recognized the Wallace danger, and the school superintendent questioned whether the school board would take any steps without a court order. The newspaper editor, Marshall reported, "who has been sought out by George Wallace and has been told by him that he did not really mean his campaign speeches, said he would feel out Mr. Wallace on the question of what his attitude would be. He will not involve us at all." Marshall doubted whether the editor would get any kind of firm reassurance from Wallace and advised the Attorney General that it would be necessary to file suit. The earliest effective date they could hope for on a court order, he added, would be the fall of 1963. Finally, the Huntsville leaders had suggested that it would be wise to desegregate several cities at once because Wallace would then be less apt to try to close all the schools. On Marshall's recommendation the Justice Department subsequently filed two suits in Alabama.[33]

Discussions like this one in Huntsville greatly heartened the administration. Although a demagogic governor might yet interfere with the city's prerogatives, powerful leaders of the local community, at least, were cooperating to bring about desegregation. The Justice Department naturally kept specific negotiations discreet, but Robert Kennedy, the administration's most vocal spokesman on civil rights through 1962, publicly lauded the great gains that were being made through voluntary action. "Solid, plugging [biracial] committee work may not have the headline appeal of an incident of violence, but it is far more important," he told a convention of black newspaper publishers whom he urged to give full coverage to voluntary efforts in the South.[34]

Ironically in the summer of 1962 black newspapers gave considerable coverage not to a triumph of voluntarism but to what many of them perceived as its great failure—the President's Committee on Equal Employment Opportunity. C. Sumner (Chuck) Stone, editor of the Washington *Afro-American*, wrote Lyndon Johnson in March complaining about the Committee's dismal record to date, calling the Plans for Progress "a publicity sham," and sarcastically deriding its Executive Director "whose sole claim to fame seems to lie in the fact that he has never insulted a Negro and was able to administer a state FEPC program without having it explode in his face." Shortly thereafter, the Committee's chief operating officer (Executive Vice Chairman), Assistant Secretary of Labor Jerry Holleman, resigned his government posts after acknowledging that he had accepted a $1,000 gift from the exposed criminal, Billie Sol Estes. Then to shake public confidence in the committee further, its Executive Director John Feild leaked to the press his own dissatisfaction with the influence of Robert Troutman of Georgia on the Committee's work. On June 18 the New York *Times* reported that the committee was torn between the compulsory compliance favored by Feild and the voluntary approach espoused by Troutman. Lyndon Johnson immediately wrote the *Times* to deny the existence of an internal dispute. There was need both for contract compliance and voluntarism, he insisted, and promised that the Committee would continue to pursue both. Furthermore, he pointed out that participation in a voluntary Plan did not relieve an employer of his federal contractual obligations. "Justice has been too long delayed by abstract procedural arguments. People are entitled to fair play and equal treatment now—while they can still enjoy its benefits—and it is my intention to sponsor any and every legitimate form of action that will produce results," he asserted.[35]

The controversy continued to swirl, and Troutman stood at its center. Some civil rights advocates, both within and outside the government, had distrusted him from the beginning. Troutman fervently believed in the voluntary approach of the Plans for Progress and never hesitated to tell anyone, in his Southern drawl, precisely how he felt. Evidently he even convinced some people that the Plans took up most of the Committee's time, which was not true; they only took up most of his own time. His critics also suspected Troutman because of his association with some of Georgia's leading politicians. When he sponsored a dinner in a segregated hotel to honor Congressman Carl Vinson, their suspicions of his wickedness were confirmed. At this point, Herbert Hill, the NAACP's labor secretary who happened to be on very friendly terms with liberal Republicans, publicly denounced Troutman as "an avowed segregationist" and the Plans for Progress as "one of the great phonies of the Kennedy administration's civil rights program." [36]

At the end of June Troutman resigned from the Committee. As he explained privately to the President and Vice President, he had advanced $50,000 of his own money to the Plans project, had devoted enormous amounts of his time, and had achieved "amazing" results. "While the venture became immediately impressive to those (the nation's key employers) who could help achieve great nationwide success," he wrote Kennedy, "it became equally unimpressive to those who speak for the people whom Plans for Progress sought to aid (the nation's large Negro population). Incredible but true!" A month later, Troutman, still believing in his program, met with Roy Wilkins. He impressed Wilkins with numerous charts on employment figures, "both those showing the paucity of Negro employment in certain categories, and those indicating improvement," as the NAACP official later reported to his board. Wilkins was apparently less impressed with Troutman's trumpeting of a "moderate approach" and his disdain for a "hard" approach, which could "arouse resentment and lessen cooperation." [37]

Although he accepted Troutman's resignation, the President maintained confidence in both him and the project. After he read a final report from Troutman in August, he wrote Lyndon Johnson that the results had been "most impressive" and indicative of "one approach to the problem of improving the role of the Negro in our economy that should be pursued." Indeed, he was convinced "that a great deal of the criticism directed at the Plans for Progress resulted from completely irrelevant factors quite unrelated to the merits of the program." Furthermore, he hoped the Committee would continue to pay careful attention to the program, especially now that Troutman's report had established a measuring stick for the future. Kennedy was concerned about the administration's being "embarrassed if the companies that have already participated pull out or if we do not continue the dynamic approach to these companies that Bobby [Troutman] carried out so effectively." "It seems to me that from a practical point of view," he concluded, "the test in the years to come is going to be whether we have made any real progress in aiding the Negroes—every potential approach should therefore be pursued." [38]

Although correct in part, the President's analysis of the situation failed to take account of several critical facts. Troutman's figures did show substantial percentage increases in the number of Negro employees. For example, the first six employers to report, in December 1961, showed a 24.9 percent increase in the number of black professional and administrative personnel and a 16.0 percent increase in the number of black craftsmen. But reports also indicated that even with these percentage increments, Negroes still made up only 1 and 3.5 percent of all employees in these respective categories. To white politicians, the percentage increases meant success, but from the standpoint of Negroes there was still a long way to go. The Plans for Progress were worthwhile. They did, as Kennedy pointed out, establish a valuable yardstick. They resulted in greater numbers of Negroes being hired. In addition, unnoted in 1962, they also softened the attitude of big business toward giving the federal government a statutory role in the area of hiring. In 1964 large government contractors readily acceded to equal employment legislation, but if they had not had the Plans experience, they might well have constituted a powerful opposition to this concept. Nevertheless, the Plans had been oversold and Troutman had contributed in no small measure to the sale.[39]

Its reputation damaged, the committee moved to recover the confidence of civil rights leaders. It commissioned Theodore Kheel, a New York labor lawyer and mediator and Urban League officer, to study its operations. Reporting in early August, he endorsed the Plans for Progress but called for greater follow-up work. He made a number of suggestions for reorganizing the staff and improving its efficiency, urging that its "primary attention" be devoted to "complaints where a significant adjustment in work patterns appears possible." Kheel also recommended that the committee secure a "more aggressive public relations program." Following Kheel's recommendation, Lyndon Johnson named a new full-time administrative officer: Hobart Taylor, Jr., a black lawyer and son of a prominent Houston ally of Johnson, who had formerly served the committee as a special counsel. Adam Clayton Powell, Jr., and Roy Wilkins enthusiastically endorsed his appointment. The combination of Kheel's involvement, Troutman's resignation, and Taylor's appointment succeeded in quieting the committee's critics, at least temporarily.[40]

The controversy over the President's Committee on Equal Employment Opportunities revealed the administration's vulnerability to criticism from the civil rights movement. Civil rights proponents had voiced skepticism about the workings of a central part of the government's executive action program and the President's Committee had hastened to defend itself and to make personnel changes. Yet, this was just the beginning of the administration's difficulties. In late 1962 it faced criticisms from the civil rights movement for failing to protect persons from physical violence in the South. And it also encountered the most direct and serious challenge to its efforts to bring about orderly change by white Southerners in Mississippi. Thus, the problematic developments of the first part of 1962 foreshadowed even greater trouble ahead.

SIX

The Problem of
Federal Protection

Civil rights proponents initially found much to commend in the Kennedy Justice Department. They appreciated Robert Kennedy's personal involvement and commitment and the Department's burst of activity and innovation, all of which represented a sharp break with the past. But by mid-1962 some civil rights activists had begun to criticize the Department for failing to protect them from violence and from the vagaries of local criminal enforcement in the South. The problem of federal protection was one of the knottiest the Department faced and one for which it never developed a completely satisfactory answer.

ROBERT KENNEDY had at the outset defined his department's civil rights role: it would promote racial progress through mediation and, when necessary, through legal enforcement of existing statutes, particularly those relating to voting rights. This definition comported not only with the Attorney General's perceptions of his moral and legal obligations but also with his brother's political welfare. John Kennedy had successfully campaigned for the votes of both blacks and white Southern Democrats. It would have been bad politics to have kept civil rights enforcement in a subordinate position and would perhaps have been ruinous to have used large-scale force in the South. In addition, Robert Kennedy and Burke Marshall believed that Negro rights had in the long run failed to survive after the Civil War because they had been established by an alien federal force; when that force was removed, the Negroes' rights rapidly withered and died. They hoped to see civil rights take root this time and were therefore determined to make the absolute minimal use of federal force. Moreover, they viewed the franchise as a fertile soil for cultivating all other rights—free speech, free assembly, and due process most especially. They expected that the flowering of voting rights would put an end to the need for federal sustenance of Southern Negroes' other rights.[1]

The President, of course, also held a traditional view of Reconstruction. In February 1962, David Donald, the eminent American historian, was invited to lead an after-dinner discussion at the White House on Reconstruction. (The discussion was one of the "Hickory Hill seminars," named for Robert Kennedy's home, where they were usually held. Because he was visiting Indonesia, the Attorney General missed this session.) Several weeks later, Donald described his evening in a letter to Mrs. J. G. Randall, widow of his mentor. The discussion had been lively and the President took active part, Donald reported. The professor did not find Kennedy's "mastery of American history particularly impressive," reflecting "a sort of general textbook knowledge of about twenty-five years ago and not much familiarity with recent literature or findings." Whether Kennedy learned anything from Donald that night is unclear. Events subsequently prompted Kennedy to modify his thinking about Reconstruction, and it is at least possible that Donald helped prepare Kennedy to change. Donald also observed that Kennedy viewed history "largely in personal terms—great men and their influence." (In private discussion the historian found the President "determined to go down in our history books as a great President" and curious about the ways to do so.) [2]

From the Justice Department's standpoint the Freedom Rides episode marked a successful implementation of its policy. It had worked effectively behind the scenes to win local cooperation in preventing mob rule. When Governor Patterson proved intransigent, it dispatched a plain-clothes federal force to demonstrate federal purpose, and it withdrew the marshals after Patterson assumed his legal obligations. The Department then did nothing to dissuade the Jackson officials from arresting the Freedom Riders. After the crisis subsided, it requested new, more stringent regulations from the Interstate Commerce Commission (ICC) and gradually won Southern compliance with them. Simultaneously, Robert Kennedy, Burke Marshall, and Harris Wofford encouraged equal rights activists to channel their energies into voter-registration work.

The Freedom Rides through Alabama and Mississippi had generated enormous publicity and raised several clear-cut issues, but a situation developing in Albany, Georgia, in December 1961, attracted much less attention and touched on somewhat more ambiguous questions. Albany, in southwest Georgia, had a population of over 50,000 persons, approximately 20,000 of whom were black. In 1961, few Negroes were registered to vote and all public facilities, including the bus terminal, were strictly segregated. In October several members of the Student Nonviolent Coordinating Committee (SNCC) arrived in the city to establish a voter registration program. After the ICC issued its new regulations in November, the SNCC members spearheaded several tests of the city's compliance. At the time of these tests, the city's police made a number of arrests which precipitated protest marches by hundreds of Albany's Negroes and the creation of the Albany Movement, a coalition of Negro adult and youth groups. Its goals included the release of those arrested, desegregation of terminal facilities, and the opening of biracial talks. City officials turned a deaf ear and had Chief of Police Laurie Pritchett arrest the marchers, which he did in an orderly and nonviolent fashion.

When the black community's spirits flagged, Movement leaders invited Martin Luther King in, and he led a demonstration which ended in his own arrest together with those of the President of the Movement and over 250 others, which brought the total behind bars to over 700. King refused bond and vowed to stay in jail through Christmas and invited thousands of people from around the country, especially clergymen, to join him. Meanwhile, Burke Marshall worked behind the scenes to bring the conflicting parties together and to reduce tensions. Within several days of King's arrest, the city had released all local demonstrators on property bonds and reduced the pecuniary bonds on nonresidents. It also consented to comply with the ICC regulation and to discuss the grievances of the Negro community at an early meeting of its new city commission. The Albany Movement reciprocated by calling a halt to demonstrations. Before leaving Albany, King hailed the agreement at a press conference, praised the nonviolence of Albany's police, and stated that the city's racial problems were well on their way to a local solution. For his part, Robert Kennedy telephoned the city's mayor and congratulated him on the orderly solution to the crisis.

Through the winter and spring, however, conflict returned to Albany as city officials refused to desegregate public facilities and the black community began to boycott the municipal bus line. The situation was exacerbated by further demonstrations, sporadic arrests and trials, and the slaying of a Negro man by an Albany policeman who claimed self-defense. SNCC, meanwhile, expanded its voter registration activity to the rural counties surrounding the city. In these they encountered even greater resistance from local officials and a much higher risk of physical violence. The experience in these counties, moreover, was repeated in other rural areas of the Deep South where members of SNCC and CORE, in particular, were attempting to register voters and kindle black hopes.[3]

In the face of violence, harassment, and frustration in Albany and elsewhere, civil rights activists began to criticize the Justice Department for not correcting the situation. Although the Southern Regional Council in March praised President Kennedy's use of executive power as a "genuine turning-point in American racial relations" comparable in importance to the *Brown* decision, it simultaneously criticized Robert Kennedy for giving a virtual endorsement to Albany's record of mass arrests. (The Council failed to recall that King had praised Chief Pritchett at the same optimistic juncture at which the Attorney General had congratulated the Mayor.) Several times in the spring, SNCC members and sympathizers demonstrated at the Justice Department where they received friendly receptions. Stokely Carmichael, who in later years achieved notoriety as a proponent of "black power," led one of these protests, a small sit-in at Robert Kennedy's office. In 1961, however, Carmichael consented to his group's removal by wheelchairs. These demonstrations, moreover, received little publicity.[4]

The Congress of Racial Equality (CORE) undertook the most elaborate exposure of the developing problems of harassment and violence. It sponsored a Commission of Inquiry into the Administration of Justice in the Freedom Struggle. Chaired by Eleanor Roosevelt, the Commission included such liberal luminaries as Norman Thomas, Roger Baldwin, Kenneth Clark, Joseph Rauh, and Telford Taylor. The Commission convened in Washington on May 25 and 26, 1962, and took over 300 pages of testimony from civil rights activists who described their experiences and frequently criticized the Justice Department and the Federal Bureau of Investigation for failing to be of assistance. The press and the electronic media gave the Commission scant coverage, and numerous congressmen, liberals and conservatives alike, declined Eleanor Roosevelt's invitation to attend the hearings.[5]

Burke Marshall expressed mild interest in the Commission and asked to have any information it developed which related specifically to a violation of federal law. Frequently, he and other Justice Department officials denied any basis for federal jurisdiction. For example, when SNCC demonstrated at the Department in March, it complained about the jailing in Louisiana of three of its members, including its chairman, who had been charged with serious criminal offenses. Marshall explained both to the demonstrators and the Attorney General that the federal government lacked legal authority to intervene in the state prosecution. Yet, as the Commission of Inquiry later reported, and as numerous critics of the Justice Department often pointed out, existing federal laws did provide jurisdiction in some local law enforcement situations. Federal laws allowed for intervention in two areas in particular: police brutality and voter intimidation. But in both there were substantial barriers to effective enforcement.[6]

The principal federal police brutality statute, 18 U.S.C. 242, dated from Reconstruction and had lain dormant until the 1940s, when the Justice Department brought a prosecution under it. The Supreme Court upheld its constitutionality in 1945, but stipulated that the prosecution must prove that the defendant had the specific intent of depriving his victim of a constitutional right. In other words, the defendant would have to have been motivated by something more than mere malice. This stiff legal requirement contributed significantly to the difficulty of investigating, prosecuting, and convicting. From January 1, 1958, to June 30, 1960, the Department received 1,328 complaints of police brutality. After investigation, the Department authorized 52 prosecutions, and eventually obtained six convictions. Indeed, from 1959 through 1964, the federal government was able to get only thirteen police brutality convictions nationally (under Section 242 and its companion 241). Moreover, convictions carried relatively light penalties. The offense was a misdemeanor not a felony; the maximum penalty was a fine of $1,000 and one year's imprisonment for each violation of Section 242. Its companion statute, Section 241, carried a much heavier penalty but was aimed at private, not official, violence. Court rulings had rendered it virtually inapplicable to police brutality cases. Federal civil law also provided some remedy for victims of police brutality, and even though less exacting standards of proof were required, few victims of police brutality possessed the means to press a private suit through the courts.[7]

The Justice Department did attempt to strengthen the government's hand through legislative enactment. In March 1962, it sent a draft of a bill to Capitol Hill which would have made it a federal crime for police to inflict summary punishment on a prisoner or to use force to obtain a confession. It would have lessened the burden of proof for the government and would have increased the penalty for conviction. But the bill succeeded only in precipitating a flood of letters from the nation's police chiefs who vehemently opposed it. Moreover, no powerful faction or even an individual member of Congress actively promoted the bill and it never even received the benefit of hearings.[8]

The problem of criminal enforcement went beyond the restriction imposed by the law and courts, however, for in the rural Deep South it was impossible to obtain convictions of white police for beating or even killing Negroes; juries were entirely white. Although the federal courts had overturned convictions of blacks because members of their race had been systematically kept off juries, the law seemed to offer no remedy whatsoever for an all-white jury system which consistently acquitted white police officers of violence against blacks. Convictions could be appealed but acquittals obviously could not. There was a federal law against racial exclusion from juries, but there had been no prosecutions under it in the twentieth century. "It is reasonable to conclude," the Civil Rights Commission dryly reported in 1961, "that in communities where strong racial prejudice prevails the Government is likely to find it very hard to persuade a jury to convict a white official for discrimination against the excluded minority race." Thus, blacks were often caught in a vicious cycle of exclusion and repression in the criminal justice system. In Mississippi, for example, jury lists were made up from voter lists, but blacks were generally denied the vote. A Negro who was deprived of the franchise could be attacked by a sheriff for trying to register, and the sheriff would be exonerated by an all-white jury which approved every effort to maintain all-white hegemony. In several documented cases precisely this series of frightening events occurred.[9]

The Civil Rights Division's forty attorneys were devoting most of their time to voting rights cases, which they expected to win, not to police brutality cases, which they were likely to lose. Because Marshall believed that the franchise would eventually provide Negroes with relief from capricious and wanton police behavior, he understandably continued to concentrate his limited manpower in the most promising area. He kept in charge of his small criminal section a man who would authorize prosecutions only in the strongest cases. Perhaps for this reason too Marshall rarely allowed prosecutions to proceed on the basis of criminal informations rather than indictments. Informations were sufficient to prosecute under section 242 because the offense was a misdemeanor, not a felony.[10]

Under the recently enacted civil rights laws, the federal government also had a responsibility to protect voters or potential voters from intimidation, threats, and coercion. Through a case begun in 1959 and successfully completed during the Kennedy administration, the courts defined intimidation to include acts of private economic coercion. Private acts occurred frequently, but the most formidable obstacle to registration efforts was official intimidation and harassment. However, like the police brutality statutes, this law presented enforcement difficulties. It provided only for civil, not criminal action. This meant that the government could seek injunctive relief on behalf of aggrieved parties. The Justice Department had no reluctance about doing so, but federal judges were extremely hesitant about enjoining criminal prosecutions even though local officials frequently used their own legal machinery to repress Negroes and thwart registration drives. Under rules of comity, federal courts were traditionally reluctant to interfere in pending or future state criminal proceedings. Only once, in a blatant case in Tylertown, Mississippi, in 1961—when a voter registration worker was pistol-whipped by the county clerk and then arrested by the sheriff—did the Justice Department prevail upon a federal judge to enjoin the victim's prosecution on trumped-up charges.[11]

In addition to these narrow bases for federal intervention, the President possessed broad authority to suppress domestic violence and insurrection. He had partially based his deployment of marshals in Montgomery on it. However, in that instance there had been a risk of mob rule, followed by international disgrace. More often violence came in the form of sporadic and isolated acts of terror and intimidation outside the spotlight of publicity: a shotgun fired at the home of a Negro leader in the dead of night, a black teacher's contract not renewed because of her participation in local activism, a voter registration worker roughed up by a deputy sheriff in a jail cell. The President could have sent marshals or troops to areas where sporadic violence was endemic; he could have replaced local police with some kind of federal police. That would have evoked memories of Reconstruction in him and the country; it would have angered the diplaced local and state authorities; it would have led to court battles and perhaps even physical confrontation; and it would have alienated his Democratic constituents in the South and their powerful representatives in Congress. The need for a re-establishment of federal policing of the South had not been clearly demonstrated to the public at large. Moreover, no influential individuals or groups pressured Kennedy to move in this direction. Critics of the administration in the civil rights movement, and, to a much lesser extent, in Congress, generally urged only that the government enforce the narrower statutes in a more vigorous way. [12]

Although many factors, including the requirements and traditions of the law, the operation of the jury system, and the size and administration of the Civil Rights Division, impeded enforcement, the FBI made the situation even more problematic: It was undermanned in the rural South; its agents frequently were natives of the areas where they served and often shared the racial attitudes of their fellow whites. Apparently the only black FBI agents in 1961 were chauffeurs. As an agency with a carefully groomed public image of success (the FBI always "got its man") it worried about the consequences for its reputation of investigating cases where the criminal would most likely not be indicted at all or would be acquitted if he were. As a crime-fighting force, it disliked having to do investigations for civil suits, which was all the voter intimidation law provided for. Moreover the FBI had traditionally eschewed the role of a federal police force. Effectiveness in its other work often depended on harmonious relations with local police departments, which it was reluctant to endanger by probing their possible criminality. [13]

Though in name a division of the Justice Department, the FBI had by 1961 become a powerful bureaucracy whose independence and reputation were jealously guarded by its legendary chief, J. Edgar Hoover. An extraordinary bureaucrat and master of public relations, Hoover had been the Bureau's first and only Director. Attorney Generals came and went, but Hoover stayed on, often reporting directly to the President, whoever he might be, and enjoying harmonious relations with an indulgent Congress. The House Appropriations Subcommittee, which oversaw his budget, approved it year after year without challenging a line in it. After his death in 1972, the press began to report that Hoover's power in Washington

had derived in considerable part from his possession and use
of confidential files which detailed indiscretions and impro-
prieties in the personal lives of politicians and public figures.
In February, 1975, Attorney General Edward Levi confirmed
the existence of such files. However, to date not enough evidence has become available for historians to determine
with reasonable certainty how politicians, including the Kennedys, were affected in their conduct of office by knowledge
of, or fears about, these files.[14]

Several things about the Kennedys' relations with Hoover
and the FBI can be established with a reasonable degree of
certainty however. Richard Neustadt, a prominent political
scientist who counselled John Kennedy on staffing the Presidency in the fall of 1960, recommended Hoover's retention.
"His reappointment seems a matter of course," Neustadt advised; "you might as well make the most of it by an early announcement, particularly since you may well find some
things you would like him to do for you, quite confidentially,
before Inauguration." (By this Neustadt probably meant personnel checks.) Evidently Kennedy agreed, for he called
Hoover the day after his election was confirmed. "I received
your call this morning with a deep feeling of humility and
pride," Hoover immediately wrote the President-elect.
"Quite naturally, I was very greatly honored to learn of your
desire that I continue as Director of the FBI." Seemingly,
Hoover was initially well disposed toward both Kennedys; he
encouraged Robert to accept the Attorney Generalship when
his brother offered it to him.[15]

Two facts, however, soon placed a strain on the new Attorney General's official relations with the Director. Because he
was the President's brother and his most trusted adviser,
Robert Kennedy held greater power, relative to Hoover's,
than any of his recent predecessors. The new Attorney General indulged Hoover by arranging private meetings for him
with the President, but *he* arranged the meetings. Although it

cannot be shown that the Director resented the marked decline in his status, it is revealing that Hoover reverted to his old form of bypassing the Attorney General immediately after President Kennedy's assassination. Second, Robert Kennedy was determined to take complete charge of the Justice Department and to initiate new policies and programs. Hoover unhappily discovered that Kennedy's Public Information Office had taken the unusual step of editing his speeches along with those of other Department officials. Apparently, Hoover chafed the most at the Attorney General's concerted effort to root out organized crime, which Hoover did not regard as a serious problem. The Department's new degree of involvement in civil rights must have also irritated Hoover, who held very conservative racial views. [16]

The administration, though, sought accommodation with Hoover. Gradually certain compromises were worked out. The Attorney General did not gain complete control over the Bureau or Hoover, but he did win some concessions. The FBI actively participated in the Department's vigorous voting rights effort. It photographed records and interrogated witnesses. The Civil Rights Division soon discovered that its own attorneys had greater success in obtaining testimony from black people, who tended to distrust white Southern lawmen, FBI agents not excepted. Conversely, the FBI had greater luck questioning white witnesses. Hoover also consented to have the Bureau conduct preliminary investigations of police brutality violations immediately upon receipt of complaints. William P. Rogers, Robert Kennedy's predecessor, had previously gone along with Hoover's desire that the FBI not investigate at all until specifically requested to do so by the Civil Rights Division, which consumed precious time and further vitiated enforcement. Robert Kennedy tolerated the Bureau's independence in several respects. He did not insist that the FBI increase the size of its force in the South or that it operate more as a policeman with regard to possible infractions of federal law. He did not require the FBI to undertake the onerous job of analyzing voting records, but left this task to the small Civil Rights Division.[17]

The Kennedys and Hoover treated each other diplomatically, probably in part out of mutual respect, in part out of mutual wariness. At Robert Kennedy's recommendation, a sentence praising the investigative agencies was included in his brother's 1962 State of the Union Message. When Theodore Sorensen told him that the President might omit the encomium, the Attorney General implored his brother not to. "We made a lot of progress over the past year and a note of recognition by you . . . would be a tremendous help to us," he explained. "I hope that for the 'second most powerful man in the Western World' [an epithet journalists had given Robert] you will leave it as it is." The sentence remained. For his part, Hoover carefully cultivated his personal relations with the Kennedys. For example, he sent congratulatory notes to Robert Kennedy on his birthday and on the arrival of a new son and he thanked him for attending graduation exercises at the FBI Academy. Similarly, Hoover congratulated the President for his success in the Cuban missile crisis in October which prompted an effusive response. "As you know, I have long had the highest admiration for you and the members of the FBI and your common dedication to our country," the President wrote Hoover. "This strong feeling is a family matter which came to us first from our father and which has since been confirmed by our own experience." [18]

The Kennedys thus dealt circumspectly with Hoover and the FBI, but with regard to civil rights enforcement they had little reason to act otherwise. They had secured the FBI's assistance in preparing voting rights suits in which they placed great hope. The relevant criminal law, meanwhile, presented many obstacles to effective enforcement in addition to the FBI's apathy. Although some civil rights advocates began to call for a more vigorous federal role in the spring of 1962, they neither attracted much national publicity nor acquired backing on Capitol Hill for their cause.

Short of providing police protection and bringing multiple prosecutions, the Justice Department did provide a service which somewhat ameliorated the civil rights activist's dangerous situation in the Deep South. Very simply, Civil Rights Division attorneys were often on the scene and always accessible by telephone. Visits to voting rights workers and collect phone calls to the Justice Department from small Southern police stations undoubtedly saved a few lives and served to deter some brutality. Local officials would think twice before mistreating people with a direct line of communication to the Justice Department. Endangered activists naturally availed themselves of this service often. [19]

Civil rights workers in the South were frequently disappointed that the federal government did not investigate and prosecute cases of brutality and intimidation more vigorously, however. Robert Moses, who headed the Mississippi voter registration project, wrote to his Atlanta headquarters in December 1962, that the federal government *"must* [file a] broad suit to stop economic reprisals and physical violence to prospective registrants and those who work to get others registered," and should also file suits to abolish the poll tax for local elections and to eliminate the literacy test. The Justice Department, he observed, was reluctant to file intimidation suits. "There will probably have to occur more evictions and widespread publicity before they will file a suit to stop economic reprisals in Sunflower County," Moses wrote. Moreover, when the government did ocasionally bring a violent white to trial, civil rights activists were often disappointed by the results and by the prosecution's performance. For example, the government brought a deputy from Sasser, Georgia, to trial under the police brutality statute in January 1963. After his acquittal, several SNCC workers who had been the policeman's victims recorded their dismay. The attorneys from the Civil Rights Division who prosecuted the case, they indicated, had asked that the witnesses refrain from interracial gatherings during the trial and had then failed to question the defendant aggressively enough. One of the SNCC workers also noted that the verdict had come as no surprise because the all white jury "entered the court with their decisions ready-made." He attributed the jury's verdict to three factors: "1. One of their boys was being persecuted [*sic*]; 2. They have no sense of justice; 3. They detest the Federal Government." [20]

Although many civil rights activists hoped that the federal government would do more to prevent violence, they also believed that the problem would persist as long as racial prejudice twisted people's minds. Activists wanted greater federal involvement, but also realized that even Washington, with all its powers, could not easily reverse the tragic conditions which had been created over a long period of time and which they longed to remedy. Jack Chatfield, a SNCC worker in southwest Georgia observed in December 1962:

What we need right now in Terrell County is the passage of the "B" suit, now pending, which will prohibit intimidation *of any form* in the affairs of voter registration. I have spoken of the great fear that Negroes have of losing their jobs. If only they could be assured that participation in the movement or association with us (the latter is important) would not jeopardize their jobs, I think there might be a greater movement.

I have found, though, that talk of Washington and "federal power" sometimes falls on dead ears [*sic*]. There is at the most a nebulous conception of government, or perhaps what I take to be that is really a disbelief in the government's real power [*sic*]. And the important thing is that no federal action can negate the solid wall of Mr. Charlies, or the steady gait of two centuries.

I don't think the answer lies entirely in federal action; on the other hand, we must have it. But we must have many things, including a renovation of minds, an ultimate defiance, and ringing laughter (now concealed, if at all existent) at the thought that there is any such thing as a "nigger."

It must be born in mind that when you ask a man to "join" you, you are at the same time demanding a confession that his life up until now has been lived upside down; you are demanding that a man disrupt his universe—smash his windows, walls and staircases; you are demanding that he spurn what he has come to be able to endure, though he mocks it; and what he has been compelled to enjoy, though with spasms of shame and humiliation.

You are asking a great deal of the average mind—and after the entrance of Washington, you will be asking the very same things. And it is healthy to consider that the average American is either ignorant of or doesn't give a damn about anything anyway.[21]

At times, civil rights activists raged against the failure of the federal government to protect them. "I speak to the President of the United States and to his brother, the Attorney General," Charles Sherrod of SNCC fumed after the acquittal of the Sasser policeman. "Your failure to throw the full weight of your offices behind our attempts, black and white together, to make real the tenets of democracy . . . is a black mark for your administration. If we are murdered in our attempts, our blood will be on your hands; you stand in the judgement of God and our people." But in another moment, Sherrod reveled in martyrdom. "We have a choice to make; we can suffer under the brutality of unjust men in the South or we can suffocate in the North—we *must* suffer," he wrote. "It seems good sense, then, to suffer one last time, that all may not have to suffer in the same way that all of us have. Millions in the South feel that they have no choice to make. We are the last Negroes and liberals; if we are victorious over this system, human beings will be our posterity." [22]

It would seem then that civil rights activists in the Deep South had rather mixed emotions about the lack of adequate federal protection. At times they judged Washington culpable; at others they believed it was impotent just like they were. They perceived the Justice Department occasionally as an antagonist, but more frequently as an ally. Likewise, they viewed themselves as betrayed victims of the Kennedys' empty promises and the nation's ugly history, or as idealists willing to accept martyrdom for the sake of humanity.

For the most part, Southern injustices remained sporadic and isolated enough to evade the public spotlight, but events in Albany, Georgia, in the summer of 1962 showed the reality for a short time. In July, the situation there again reached crisis proportions when the city's court, after months of delay, sentenced Martin Luther King and Ralph Abernathy, his top aide, to pay a fine of $178 or spend forty-five days in jail. They had been convicted in February of disorderly conduct and parading without a permit. Possibly politics motivated the sentencing, for Georgia was in the midst of its gubernatorial primary campaign. James Gray, who controlled the city's newspaper and television station and was chairman of the State Democratic Executive Committee, backed the extreme segregationist candidacy of Marvin Griffin. Perhaps Gray and his allies in the city's court hoped to boost Griffin's prospects by bringing King and Abernathy back from Atlanta for sentencing, which they might have expected would rekindle enthusiasm for mass marches and thereby fan the flames of white extremism.[23]

At their sentencing on July 10, King and Abernathy, evidently hoping to inspire new determination in the flagging Albany Movement, chose to go to jail. In the next two days, Albany's black people reacted in two distinctly different ways: some angrily threw bricks and bottles at police; others marched nonviolently in protest and were arrested. Administration spokesmen in Washington meanwhile divulged that the President had asked the Attorney General for a report and that Robert Kennedy was in touch with Georgia officials. In a gesture that was reminiscent of one two years before, Burke Marshall called Coretta King and informed her that the Department was trying to secure her husband's release.[24]

Indeed, the day after that call, King and Abernathy were

released from jail after an unidentified black man paid the combined $356 in fines. In fact they were practically expelled from jail. "I've been thrown out of lots of places in my day, but never before have I been thrown out of jail," Abernathy told a mass meeting that night. The identity of the man who paid the fines remains a mystery. It is possible that he acted completely independently for reasons of his own. More likely, he was an agent for an interested group, possibly local whites who supported Carl Sanders, Griffin's moderate opponent, who hoped that King's release would dampen the excitement that was beginning to mount. Perhaps the Justice Department had a hand in their release. The Department acknowledged that it had called people in the city, and that payment of the fines might have resulted from the calls, but it denied having advance knowledge that they would be paid. The Department's basic objectives in Albany had not changed from the winter—to mediate differences insofar as possible, but to avoid direct involvement. Obviously any mediator would recommend against the jailing of key figures in the dispute; prison terms did not foster the good will necessary for a settlement. But the Department had an added incentive to promote an amicable resolution, for Sanders' election was clearly preferable to Griffin's.[25]

An amicable settlement did not follow however. King was now fully committed to lead a campaign of massive civil disobedience. He called for nonviolent protest which would "turn Albany upside down." In the next week Negro groups tried to integrate the city's public facilities—including the library, parks, and swimming pool—but the police either turned them back or arrested them. Laurie Pritchett, Albany's police chief, continued to win King's praise for his nonviolent handling of the situation, but the city's white establishment would not open negotiations or yield to the protestors' demands. Indeed, James Gray appeared on his television station to denounce King and Abernathy. The leading gubernatorial candidates, meanwhile, accused each other of being in league with King. Griffin charged that King supported Sanders; Sanders countered that Griffin and King had joined hands in causing discord.[26]

In the face of mounting turmoil, the Justice Department increased its contingent of attorneys and FBI agents on the scene; but the lawyers, in particular, only seemed to antagonize the city's white leadership. Mayor Asa Kelley charged that one of the attorneys was fomenting disorder; the Department immediately denied it. Civil rights activists, on the other hand, were less disturbed over the government's role. King was sanguine about the effectiveness of massive nonviolent demonstrations. In his speech before the National Press Club—he was the first Negro ever to address this influential group of journalists—he did not criticize the Justice Department, though in answer to a question he did propose that the federal government "take a definite stand" on Albany.[27]

Two days after King's Washington appearance, Albany activists had stronger grounds for criticizing the Kennedy administration, for they then learned that District Judge J. Robert Elliott, a Kennedy appointee, had temporarily enjoined further demonstrations in the embattled city. King called the injunction "unjust and unconstitutional," but he obeyed it because he felt that the federal courts had given the civil rights movement its greatest victories; moreover, his attorneys assured him that a higher court would overrule Elliott. Three days later, Chief Judge Elbert Tuttle of the Fifth Circuit Court of Appeals vacated the order. He held that Elliott had no jurisdiction over the matter and that Elliott's decision had been based on two Reconstruction statutes intended to control state, not individual, action. (Tuttle was probably chagrined by Elliott's order because he had personally vouched for Elliott's objectivity before the appointment was made.) [28]

The situation in and around Albany rapidly became uglier. Hours after Tuttle had overruled Elliott, approximately two thousand Negro youths rampaged, throwing rocks at police, injuring two of them. "Did you see them nonviolent rocks?" Pritchett sardonically asked the members of the press. King immediately cancelled a scheduled march and declared a day of penance for the violence. Some police officials soon showed that they did not share Pritchett's preference for treating demonstrators nonviolently. A deputy kicked the pregnant wife of one of the Movement's leaders when she visited incarcerated demonstrators in a town 35 miles from Albany. (Albany's jail was filled to capacity.) The local sheriff reportedly explained to the FBI that the woman had scratched and cursed the officer and had then fallen. Several days later the sheriff of Daugherty County (where Albany is located) caned this woman's husband, a lawyer, when he inquired about the health of a white SNCC worker who had been beaten by fellow prisoners in one of the outlying jails. In addition, a sheriff and his deputies stormed into a voter registration meeting in one town and verbally threatened those in attendance. The Justice Department investigated the incidents of violence by officials, but only in the latter case did it bring suit, under the voter intimidation statute. It tried to obtain an indictment in the caning incident without success.[29]

The Justice Department also urged Albany's officials to negotiate with the city's protesting black populace. Mayor Asa Kelley reported that Robert Kennedy had told him that the situation was beginning to have international implications. Kelley, a moderate by comparison with the members of the city commission, replied that King and other outsiders would have to leave the city before a dialogue could be opened. But King stayed, the demonstrations continued, and on July 27 King was again arrested and jailed.[30]

Before King went to jail, the Albany Movement was

beginning to lose steam. Its leaders were having a hard time getting people to volunteer for jail duty. Consequently they looked to Washington for help. "Bobby Kennedy?" Dr. William G. Anderson, President of the Movement, asked a St. Louis reporter, "What's he done for us?" When he was equally critical of the President, the reporter asked how the Chief Executive could intervene in this local situation. Anderson replied: "He could use the moral influence of his office. He could declare his support for our efforts. He could urge that the whites negotiate with us. But he hasn't done it." He repeated his criticism on *Meet the Press*, a televised press conference show on July 29. There he urged the President to appoint a personal representative to investigate the situation in Albany. King, too, though more restrained in his criticisms than Anderson, told a reporter before going to jail that "if the President would counsel the people, it would mean a great deal." [31]

The President responded quickly. At his news conference on August 1, he spoke out on Albany. He said he was in constant touch with the Attorney General, who was following the situation closely. After vaguely referring to the legal issues involved, Kennedy urged Albany officials to negotiate with its Negro citizens just as the United States was negotiating with the Soviet Union:

> Let me say that I find it wholly inexplicable why the City Council of Albany will not sit down with the citizens of Albany, who may be Negroes, and attempt to secure them, in a peaceful way, their rights. The United States Government is involved in sitting down at Geneva with the Soviet Union. I can't understand why the government of Albany, City Council of Albany, cannot do the same for American citizens.
>
> We are going to attempt, as we have in the past, to try to provide a satisfactory solution and protection of the constitutional rights of the people of Albany, and will continue to do so. And the situation today is completely unsatisfactory from that point of view. [32]

Civil rights supporters were pleased by Kennedy's statement. King wired him that he was "gratified by directness of your statement to Albany crisis." Even Jacob Javits commended Kennedy. But Mayor Kelley said the remarks were "inappropriate," that it was purely a local matter, and he refused to negotiate with King. Georgia's Senators also took exception to the President's remarks. "This stamp of approval upon the constant violations of the city laws from the highest source in our land," Richard Russell observed, "is certain to encourage the importation of many other professionals and notoriety seekers and worsen an already bad situation." He imputed Kennedy's remarks to politics, saying that the President hoped his comments would help his brother Edward win election to the Senate from Massachusetts. Herman Talmadge was even less kind to the demonstrators, who he said were playing into the hands of the Communists. Less explicit in his criticism of the President, he merely urged high officials to encourage the "departure of outsiders." [33]

By early August, the Albany situation had attracted a good deal of publicity and the concern of numerous people sympathetic to civil rights. In Washington, a group of ten liberal Senators, five from each party, held meetings to discuss the crisis and conferred with the Justice Department on the course of action it should take. Congressman William Fitts Ryan, a liberal Democrat from New York City, went to Albany as an observer. On August 2, a delegation from civil rights organizations met with Robert Kennedy and Burke Marshall. Clarence Mitchell of the NAACP urged a broad program of federal intervention, including the use of criminal informations, joining private suits by Albany citizens, and pressuring the city's officials by threatening to withdrew military installations and other federal assistance from the area. He also suggested that the Justice Department bring suits to desegregate schools and public facilities, to stop state prosecutions, and to prevent police from arresting people who sought public services. In the event that these suits failed, the President should seek additional law. The Attorney General flatly rejected bringing broad suits, but he was sympathetic to joining the private ones in Albany. Marshall offered some encouragement on using criminal informations, pointing out that the Department had done so in a Louisiana case. Four days later, more than one hundred ministers met with Marshall, Lee White, and Berl Bernhard, staff director of the Civil Rights Commission. They wanted the President to make a nationwide television address in which he would take a strong stand on the ethical issues at stake in Albany. They also asked that King's arrest be investigated, that the President invite leaders of both sides to come to Washington, and that the President issue a second Emancipation Proclamation.[34]

The disagreement over federal policy naturally created the possibility that Albany would become a partisan issue in Washington; but the liberal Republicans, who were most likely to attack the President, resisted the temptation. In turning down an invitation to visit Albany, Jacob Javits wired Wyatt Walker that "President Kennedy's declaration of support for your efforts to negotiate with the City Commission is a most encouraging development and I believe his position is fully supported by the nation." Undoubtedly reasons of conscience played a part in liberal Republican neutrality—partisan politics might have only exacerbated the situation. Yet politics may also have underpinned their statesmanship. When an NAACP official wrote to Republican Congressman Thomas B. Curtis, a liberal on civil rights, to complain about an apparent lack of concern by the administration and Congress, the Missouri representative sharply responded that Negroes would be wise first to abandon the Democratic Party. "If the Negro voter is going to continue to vote where he gets pleasing words and government handouts and have his leaders play sneaky politics with the enemies of his people, it leaves little opportunity for people who want to befriend him," Curtis explained. As far as Albany, Curtis agreed to watch and study it and perhaps make "a beneficial suggestion here and there." But, he warned, "until the Negro leaders abandon the Democratic party and give the friends they have in the Republican party a helping hand there isn't too much of a practical nature I can do." [35]

As Robert Kennedy had indicated on August 2, the government was favorably disposed toward participating in some of the pending litigation on Albany. Accordingly, on August 8, the Justice Department entered an injunction hearing before Judge Elliott as *amicus curiae.* The city was now seeking a permanent injunction, the temporary one having been thrown out by Tuttle. In its brief, the department argued against the city. It declared that the court should not consider the injunction because the city did not have "clean hands," since it continued to enforce segregation in public facilities. The department did not expect its intervention to have much effect on the outcome but did hope it would have symbolic significance. It had such significance for Albany's disputants on both sides. Mayor Kelley called it "an affront to those of us in the South who are prepared to stand fast for law and order." From his jail cell, King said he was encouraged, for the department's brief vindicated the position of the Albany Movement. "While I consider this no solution to the problems," stated King, "it is an expression on the part of the administration of their legal and moral support [which is] of inestimable value for the ultimate solution of the problem." [36]

Two days after the Justice Department's legal intervention, there seemed to be forward motion in the dispute. King received a suspended sentence and was released from jail. He announced that he was leaving Albany temporarily and that marches were being suspended to give negotiations a chance. He took heart from the fact that the Recorders Court, which had just released him, had been integrated for the first time. A few days later, on August 15, the City Commission did for the first time meet with a Negro committee, but the commission would not yield to the committee's demands. After this disappointing event, King returned to Albany several times and there were sporadic demonstrations. The black community's enthusiasm for marching and for imprisonment had waned. The Albany Movement continued to hold weekly mass meetings, but attendance declined, and the Movement shifted to less demanding tactics such as law suits. With Albany's Negroes quiescent, Judge Elliott apparently no longer felt the need to enjoin demonstrations. He never issued the permanent injunction, which a higher court in any case would surely have reversed. He did, however, refuse to issue the restraining order sought by the Justice Department that would have prevented intimidation of voting rights workers in Terrell County. And in February he turned down the Movement's request for court-ordered desegregation of public facilities and its petition for noninterference with peaceful protests.[37]

For all the suffering of its participants the Albany Movement achieved few tangible results. The library was integrated after the seats were removed; but the city closed its parks and sold its swimming pool, and schools remained strictly segregated. Ironically, one of the only things the Movement could take credit for hardly required the great turmoil which had taken place. As a result of a voter drive which increased black registration by a third, Daugherty County went for Sanders in the September primary.[38]

In the following months, the Movement's participants and sympathizers surveyed the wreckage and concurred on one point: the federal government had failed miserably. With the exception of Howard Zinn, who called for the government to protect individual rights by legal and police action and for more Presidential statements and federal mediation, these commentators were vague in prescribing an alternative federal course. This first citywide campaign of massive civil disobedience in American civil rights history had failed to achieve its objectives. Pritchett's jails had proven to be stronger than the endurance of Albany's black people. King's conviction that "unearned suffering is redemptive" had failed to maintain the black community's participation in seemingly hopeless demonstrations and futile deprivations. Perhaps recoiling from these harsh realities, civil rights adherents blamed Washington.[39]

It is not clear how the federal government might have averted the Albany setback. Its statements and legal intervention pleased one side and antagonized the other, but did not bring them together in a meaningful way. The city reluctantly desegregated its interstate terminal facilities, and Negroes could register to vote in Albany; and so the federal government could not intervene on those two bases. No existing federal law required a city to desegregate its parks, swimming pools, or libraries; and none required elected officials to meet with a delegation of aggrieved citizens. The most serious incident of white violence had involved a beating of a prisoner by other prisoners, which was not a violation of federal law. In the caning incident, a grand jury had refused to indict. Judge Elliott took care not to upset traditional rules of comity in the Terrell County case; most federal judges would have acted similarly. In these and other violent incidents, the Justice Department and FBI files are not available so it is impossible to form a conclusive opinion on the federal government's performance, but on the face of the evidence it does not appear that the federal government could have acted much differently than it did.

In mid-August, three Washington-based civil rights experts—William Taylor and Berl Bernhard of the Civil Rights Commission, and Harold Fleming of the Potomac Institute—privately suggested to Lee White a new course of federal action in Albany. Their proposal, which reflected similar thinking among some Congressional liberals, was that the President send a personal representative to the beleaguered city. Lyndon Johnson was their first choice for this job; Lucius Clay, the soldier-diplomat and a native Georgian, was their second. They admitted that the mission might not succeed, but it might possibly provide the necessary "face-saving device" that both sides needed. They speculated that the Albany situation was bound to be duplicated. The mission could test a new technique for dealing with such crises; and it could also be of political benefit to the administration:

> The present state of affairs lends itself to political exploitation by critics of the administration. The Department of Justice is using its legal power diligently and well. The Attorney General and Assistant Attorney General Burke Marshall have also worked persistently and quietly to influence Albany leadership positively. These activities are, necessarily, discreet and unpublicized. They do not relieve the frustrations of the Negroes involved, or of their sympathizers throughout the country. This is evidenced by the dissatisfaction with the Administration in general and the Justice Department in particular, currently heard in Negro protest and civil rights quarters. Unfair though such criticism may be, it is a political fact of life that must be reckoned with. What is needed is a meaningful public move that symbolizes the concern of the President and the Administration—an action dramatic enough to nullify the carping of the critics and to provide tangible evidence of support for civil rights.[40]

The White House did not follow this recommendation in Albany, probably because King soon left the city, tension subsided, the Movement diminished, and public attention waned. Kennedy did however adopt the proposal the following year when an even more explosive situation of a similar nature developed in Birmingham. The President's personal representatives would not prove to be very successful there, and perhaps would not have been any more so in Albany, though such a mission might, as its originators imagined, have spared the administration the subsequent harsh criticism of civil rights supporters.

Albany marked an important turning point in the civil rights movement. King and the Albany Movement had forged a significant new tactic: a community-wide nonviolent assault on apartheid practices. Although the Albany campaign had led mainly to frustrations, it had created a new tool for social change which had great potential. When it was used next, in Birmingham the following spring, it would have enormous repercussions. Yet, interestingly, neither Albany, nor later Birmingham, fundamentally affected the federal police role, which remained within the bounds of tradition.

SEVEN

The Battle of Ole Miss

For political, personal and historical reasons John Kennedy always hoped to avoid a new Little Rock. A military intervention could cost him in popularity among white Southerners, in Congress, and ultimately at the polls. He believed that as an active President, in contrast to the passivity of Eisenhower, he would be able to prevent local—federal confrontations from reaching the point where troops were necessary. And he viewed the sectional conflict of the mid-nineteenth century as a tragedy whose passionate feelings should not be revived by the use of federal military might. Nevertheless, he found it necessary in October 1962 to send American soldiers against American citizens.

ON January 21, 1961, the day after Kennedy was inaugurated, James H. Meredith, a black twenty-eight-year-old Air Force veteran, impressed by the new President's commitments to encourage civil rights at home and to enhance the image of the United States abroad, wrote the University of Mississippi registrar for an application. Recognizing that he would need legal assistance, Meredith, a student at all-black Jackson State, went to Medgar Evers, Mississippi field secretary of the NAACP. Evers put Meredith in touch with the NAACP Legal Defense Fund which soon assigned one of its attorneys, Constance Baker Motley, to the case. In the meantime, William Higgs, a young, white Harvard Law graduate who had returned to his native Mississippi to work for racial integration, telephoned Burke Marshall in Meredith's presence. Marshall told Meredith that the Civil Rights Division was very interested in his effort and would do all that it could to assist him.

The next several months were consumed by Meredith's necessary though futile efforts to gain admission on the same basis as any white Mississippian similarly qualified. Finally, at the end of May, the university, affectionately known as Ole Miss, formally rejected his application. Meredith immediately brought suit in the federal district court of Judge Sidney C. Mize. Marshall, meanwhile, requested and received a copy of Meredith's complaint from Motley. During the next year, the case crept through the courts but began to attract publicity. Mize, a Roosevelt appointee, and Ben C. Cameron, named by Eisenhower to the appellate court, were evidently unsympathetic to Meredith and managed to slow the judicial process considerably. Nevertheless, the federal courts had by early September 1962 clearly established Meredith's legal right to enter the university.[1]

The exercise of that right, however, stood in serious jeopardy. For some time, extreme segregationist rhetoric had pervaded the political life of Mississippi. Ross Barnett, enjoying the support of the Citizens' Council, had won the governorship in 1959, brandishing especially strong language. As the day of Ole Miss's desegregation approached, a chorus of the state's politicians, segregationists, and communications media howled objections. Spurious criminal charges were lodged against Meredith and the state legislature made it illegal for a criminal to attend a state school. Governor Barnett himself took the lead. On September 13 he asked a statewide television audience to join him in opposing the federal government's policy of racial genocide (to him, integration meant the death of the white race). To establish a constitutional basis for his position, Barnett harked back to South Carolina's 1832 attempt to nullify federal law.[2]

In Washington administration officials closely observed the developing legal confrontation between federal courts and the state of Mississippi. They had two basic purposes in mind: to uphold the integrity of federal courts and laws and at the same time to win compliance from state officials without resorting to force. Every official involved in the matter hoped to avoid using federal troops in the manner of Little Rock. In late August the Justice Department entered the case officially for the first time. The clerk of the Supreme Court requested a memorandum on the power of Judge Cameron to issue stays and the power of Justice Hugo Black to set them aside. As *amicus* the Department argued that Cameron's stays were improper and that Black could set them aside. On September 10, Black, indicating that he had consulted other members of the Court, did precisely that. On September 13, Judge Mize issued the necessary order for Meredith's admission. That same night Barnett made his interposition speech. The following day, the Justice Department obtained permission from the Court of Appeals to enter the case. The Department realized that a legal crisis was impending and wanted to get a measure of control over the proceedings in order to support the courts and make sure that the court's orders would be clearly understood by university and state officials.[3]

The Justice Department also worked behind the scenes to secure compliance. It conferred with several Mississippi moderates, including university professors, journalists, and Barnett's predecessor, James P. Coleman, who publicly professed devotion to segregation but was known to express moderate sentiments in private. Hoping to place economic pressure on the university and the state, the Department suggested that the *Wall Street Journal* conduct a survey of business opinion in Mississippi on this matter. On September 26 that paper reported many Mississippi businessmen were worried about the economic consequences of a state–federal confrontation, but were afraid to admit this publicly because they also feared a boycott by the Citizens' Council. In addition, the Department organized administration officials, including

Cabinet Secretaries, to lobby key businesses to persuade individual members of the university's Board of Trustees to comply with court orders.[4]

Robert Kennedy also established a direct line of communications with Barnett on September 15, and initially there seemed to be cause for hope. Barnett at least assured him at that time that there would be no violence. Simultaneously he asked that Meredith register at the state capitol in Jackson rather than at the campus in Oxford. Meredith, however, preferred Oxford and the Attorney General supported him in his choice. Barnett informed Kennedy on September 18 that the Board of Trustees insisted that Meredith register at Jackson. Yet the following day, state Attorney General Joe Patterson and Colonel T. B. Birdsong, chief of the Highway Patrol, agreed to provide a safe escort for Meredith from where he was ensconced in Memphis to Oxford. The next morning, September 20, Patterson withdrew the offer to accompany Meredith to Oxford, explaining to Marshall that a warrant had been issued for Meredith's arrest. Several hours later Meredith was tried *in absentia* in Jackson and convicted on specious grounds of false voter registration. The Department and Meredith's attorney meanwhile had succeeded in persuading Judge Mize to issue injunctions barring Meredith's arrest. Having learned through the FBI that the Oxford sheriff was planning to arrest Meredith anyway, Marshall hurriedly called Tom Watkins, a prominent business attorney and representative of the Governor. Barnett agreed to have the arrest warrant rescinded, but he would not permit Meredith to be registered. Late that afternoon, Meredith was accompanied to Oxford by several U.S. Marshals and Justice Department attorneys. Mississippi state police provided an escort. Barnett himself, having been granted authority to act by the school's trustees, ceremoniously read Meredith a proclamation denying him admission and then presented the document to him. A Justice Department representative warned Barnett of his legal accountability. Highway Patrolmen then escorted Meredith from the campus and the state. As they sped from the campus, jeering students threw rocks.[5]

The controversy immediately moved back to the courts. That night, three university officials were ordered to appear the next day before Judge Mize on contempt of court charges. When they came before him, Mize exonerated them on the grounds that they had handed authority over to the Governor. On September 24, the school's trustees appeared before the entire Fifth Circuit Court of Appeals in New Orleans to face similar charges. After a six-hour hearing, the Court unanimously found the trustees in violation. The judges refused to accept the argument that the trustees had handed authority over to Barnett. The Court offered to purge the trustees of contempt if they agreed to register Meredith the next day. The trustees consented. That evening Robert Kennedy personally informed Barnett of their capitulation. The Governor expressed his shock and refused to commit himself to guaranteeing Meredith's safety. "I would rather have this [Meredith's protection] done by the local authorities, not by the federal government," Robert Kennedy implored. "The arrangements you made the other day were completely satisfactory. I would much rather have it in your hands. If I can get assurance we will stay out of it but we have to have assurances from you." But Barnett refused to commit himself.[6]

In fact Barnett seemed to be courting confrontation as he issued another proclamation repudiating federal authority and ordering the summary arrest of any federal officer who interfered with state law. The Appeals Court quickly responded by issuing a sweeping injunction against many Mississippi officials, including Barnett. It protected Meredith and federal officers from arrest, obstruction, and interference. That afternoon, September 25, Meredith was accompanied by John Doar and James McShane, Chief U.S. Marshal, to a state office building in Jackson where the university trustees were scheduled to meet. The registrar was prepared to fulfill his obligation, but Barnett, backed by a large contingent of state legislators and police, blocked Meredith's entrance to the trustees' room. Again the Governor read a proclamation to Meredith, and again Meredith and his companions were forced to leave to the accompaniment of taunts from a crowd gathered outside. Barnett waved to the same crowd and received an approving roar. That night the Appeals Court ordered Barnett to appear before it three days later to show cause why he should not be held in contempt.[7]

On the day Barnett blocked Meredith's entrance, Robert Kennedy spoke to him several times and tried to persuade him to relent. Barnett said he would treat Kennedy "with every courtesy but I won't agree to let that boy get to Ole Miss. I will never agree to that. I would rather spend the rest of my life in a penitentiary than do that." Robert Kennedy reminded Barnett that Mississippi was "part of the United States." Barnett conceded that "we have been a part of the United States but I don't know whether we are or not." "Are you getting out of the Union?" the Attorney General asked. Kennedy tried different tacks. At one point he urged Barnett to allow Meredith to attend Old Miss for just six months as a kind of trial, but Barnett would not yield. Kennedy also repeatedly explained his own position in terms of his responsibility to uphold federal law. Once he angrily asserted that if Barnett were in his position he "would do the same damn thing." He reminded Barnett that the Appeals Court, which had ruled unanimously, was made up of Southerners: "This is not a bunch of northerners telling you this." They also wrangled about why Meredith was being denied admission. Barnett charged that Meredith was a criminal, which Kennedy refuted. Meredith was being kept out, said Kennedy, for one simple reason—he was black. So it went; they could agree on nothing. The day's conversations ended with Kennedy warning Barnett that Meredith would attempt to register

the next day in Oxford. Barnett replied that he was not anticipating any violence on campus. That night Kennedy assured
Meredith that nothing would make him quit, that they would
keep the pressure on Barnett and eventually succeed.[8]

As promised, Meredith and his federal companions went to
Oxford the next day, September 26. They were repulsed by
Lieutenant Governor Paul Johnson and a small army of state
troopers at a roadblock well in front of the school gates. Before television and news cameras, Johnson read a proclamation denying Meredith admission. That morning Tom Watkins had suggested to Marshall that the state might yield
before a symbolic show of federal force, and so, James Mc-
Shane tried gently to move Johnson aside. There was also a
little pushing and jockeying for position, but if Johnson had
heard about the stratagem, he was now having no part in it.
Neither he nor the troopers and sheriff with him would yield,
and Meredith and his companions were forced to withdraw
once more.[9]

Tom Watkins, acting on behalf of Barnett, immediately initiated a new charade in discussions with the Justice Department. Barnett was apparently becoming nervous about his
impending day in court and about the possibility of a jail
sentence and a heavy fine. Furthermore, the threat of violence
loomed ever larger as militant segregationists and right-
wingers, emboldened by the Governor's acts of defiance,
openly prepared to stand at his side in future confrontations.
The Justice Department, intent on avoiding the use of troops
and wishing to keep local law enforcement responsibilities in
the hands of Mississippi authorities, showed itself willing to
go quite far in the elaborate charade that Watkins and Barnett
now devised. As finally worked out—this time with Paul
Johnson's full involvement—Meredith would be accompanied
by twenty-five to thirty marshals. After the usual ceremonies,
all the marshals would draw their guns on Barnett, Johnson,
and their state troopers, who would then yield to superior

federal force and allow Meredith to register. The state, moreover, agreed to assume full responsibility for preventing mob violence in Oxford. Robert Kennedy seemed satisfied: "Governor, that's all I wanted. That's the best thing in the long run." Interestingly, Mississippi's James Eastland, a leading segregationist spokesman in Washington, who had been acting as an intermediary, privately told the Attorney General that Barnett had overstepped himself and that this whole act was ludicrous. He also appreciated the necessity for using troops if all else failed. Publicly, Eastland condemned "judicial tyranny." [10]

As it turned out, the farce was never performed. Thousands of students and self-appointed vigilantes, many of them armed, were waiting for the federal convoy in Oxford on September 27. From all over the state, sheriffs and deputies were converging on the town prepared to stand with their governor. Barnett and Johnson made some feeble attempts to disperse the crowd, but the Governor, about a half hour before Meredith was due to arrive, implored the Attorney General to call off the operation in order to avert violence and protect Barnett's political career:

BARNETT: There are dozens of trucks loaded with people. We can't control people like that. A lot of people are going to get killed. It would be embarrassing to me.
RFK: I don't know if it would be embarrassing—that would not be the feeling. [11]

Robert Kennedy's doubts about the operation had been growing through the day, and he now ordered the convoy's return to Memphis. This had been done, he announced, because federal forces might not have been sufficient to accomplish their mission without major violence. During the day, the Justice Department also revealed that he had consulted with Major General Creighton W. Abrams, Assistant Deputy Army Chief of Staff for Military Operations. This rev-

elation indicated that the Justice Department was preparing
to use troops if necessary. Meanwhile, Jack Greenberg, head
of the NAACP Legal Defense Fund, told the press what he
had been telling the Department privately—that much greater
force was needed and that he was now advising Meredith not
to return to Oxford until the government was ready to use its
full powers. Perhaps in answer to that criticism, a Justice
Department spokesman explained the next day that the Department was prepared to receive all of Mississippi's rhetorical invective. The Department was determined that the law
be obeyed, but could accept a few days' delay, he said, for
"that time is worth losing in the hopes of avoiding the divi-
siveness, the damage to this country that would be caused by
using troops." [12]

On Friday, September 28, the Fifth Circuit Court of Appeals found Barnett guilty of contempt. Barnett did not appear in court, having successfully evaded the subpoena, but
five attorneys, representing the state, argued on his behalf.
Among them was John C. Satterfield of Yazoo City, immediate past president of the American Bar Association. Burke
Marshall presented the government's case against Barnett.
During the proceedings, Chief Judge Elbert Tuttle cautioned
Marshall that long delays ran the risk of effectively frustrating
the court's order that Meredith be registered. Marshall replied
that more time was necessary. The court gave Barnett until
the following Tuesday morning either to purge himself by re-
tracting his proclamation and removing all the impediments
he had placed before Meredith or to face arrest and a fine of
$10,000 for each day he remained in violation of the order. [13]

The following day the administration proceeded along two
avenues. It made preparations for large-scale civilian and military operations, including the drafting of the necessary Presidential proclamations authorizing their use. And it renewed
negotiations with Barnett. This time the President himself
participated in the talks. "Well now here's my problem Gov-

ernor," President Kennedy explained. "I don't know Mr. Meredith and I didn't put him in the University, but on the other hand under the Constitution I have to carry out the orders of the Court. Now I have to carry that order out. I don't want to do it in any way that causes difficulty to you or anyone else, but I've got to do it. Now I would like to get your help in doing it." Barnett described the pressures he was under, and expressed great confidence in Watkins whom he was sending to Washington to negotiate with the Attorney General. To the President's amusement, Barnett ended the conversation on this cordial and mundane note: "Appreciate your interest in our poultry program and all those things. Thank you so much." [14]

Barnett found himself in a very difficult position. He had to worry about his pending sentence. Meanwhile, his allies in the Citizens' Council and other militant groups were descending upon Oxford and Jackson ready to stand with him and armed to fight the federal forces. Although Barnett had done much to incite these people, he shrank from violence. If he yielded to the federal government, he would face the political wrath of his militant allies. If he did not yield, there would be civil insurrection in Mississippi. Jackson's two white newspapers, under the same ownership, continued to back him, but the Memphis *Commercial-Appeal,* the Mississippi edition of which was highly influential in the state, opposed Barnett's continued resistance. Like Tom Watkins at Barnett's side, it reflected the thinking of the state's most powerful business interests, which foresaw disastrous consequences from civil strife. Little Rock's economy had stagnated as a result of the 1957 crisis. Mississippi, by several indices the nation's poorest state, was trying to attract business, and could only expect an egregious setback from a violent confrontation. An insurrection might have made Mississippi a proud symbol to segregationists, but it was certain to discourage prospective businesses from locating there. [15]

On Saturday, September 29, Barnett capitulated—partially. He agreed to have Meredith registered in Jackson on Monday while he was diverting attention to Oxford. But the Kennedys still wanted to know: could he and would he maintain order in Jackson when Meredith registered and in Oxford when he arrived the next day to begin classes? They did not want Meredith admitted only to be immediately lynched or driven from the campus. On that issue Barnett was at first equivocal, but he eventually promised to maintain order. In Washington hopes were raised that the crisis had been satisfactorily resolved, but Barnett soon called back and began to vacillate on maintaining order. Ominously, the Governor received an hysterical welcome during the half-time of an Ole Miss football game in Jackson. He spoke only three sentences to the crowd of 46,000, and after each it roared its approval: "I love Mississippi. I love our people. I love our customs." He did not ask Mississippi's people to refrain from violence.[16]

The administration resumed its preparations for the worst contingencies. Shortly after midnight, Norbert Schlei, head of the Office of Legal Counsel, went to the White House to obtain the President's signature on documents federalizing units of Mississippi's National Guard, and ordering all persons obstructing justice in Mississippi to "cease and desist" and to disperse peaceably. Kennedy inquired if these were the same kind of documents that Eisenhower had signed for Little Rock. Schlei answered that they were except that the wording had been improved. After he signed the papers Kennedy rapped on the table with his hand. He told Schlei that the table had belonged to Ulysses S. Grant. Schlei started out of the President's quarters to tell the press about the new development when the President came sprinting after him. He instructed him not to mention Grant's table. The memories of the Civil War and Reconstruction were evidently on Kennedy's mind, but he wanted to contribute nothing to their revival in the nation. In Mississippi where Confederate flags were being unfurled everywhere, the memories, or more accurately, the myths, were in full ascendance.[17]

The next morning, Sunday, September 30, Barnett pleaded with Robert Kennedy to postpone Meredith's admission. Kennedy declined. He also rejected a new, more elaborate, and more dangerous drawn-guns act. Barnett suggested that the government had better have plenty of troops ready because they would be needed. Finally, in anger, Robert Kennedy told him that the President was going on television that night and would reveal Barnett's secret plan to allow Meredith to register in Jackson while he diverted attention to Oxford. Barnett immediately began to crumble: "That won't do at all. . . . Don't say that. Please don't mention it." The Governor, obviously afraid of what this revelation would do to his reputation among the diehards, suggested that they bring Meredith into Oxford that very afternoon. Kennedy told him to talk to Watkins and make the necessary arrangements, but the Attorney General made clear that he did not want to speak to the lawyer who he believed "broke his word to the President of the United States." Later Watkins complained to Marshall about the administration's violation of confidentiality, but Marshall refused to yield this bargaining chip:

> Last night you were talking to the President of the United States about a national problem of great dimensions. He was willing to suffer criticism, I am sure, to do everything he could to permit the Governor to get out of a situation he got himself and the State of Mississippi into, without violence. That's why he reached the agreement with the Governor that he did. That's why it is absurd to think you can reach an agreement with the President of the United States and then call it off.

Robert Kennedy agreed that the President would not reveal the secret deal if things proceeded in a satisfactory fashion that afternoon and if Barnett made a statement on maintaining law and order.[18]

For the next several hours state officials seemed to be co-

operating. Over five hundred marshals, actually many of
them specially deputized Border Patrolmen, began to move
onto a quiet Oxford campus in the late afternoon. They gathered around the Lyceum, the main administrative building,
where they expected Meredith to be registered on Monday.
Shortly after, Meredith himself arrived at his dormitory,
where he would spend the evening and night in relative
peace—and fortunate obscurity—guarded by twenty-four
marshals. For the first couple of hours the several hundred
spectators at the Lyceum were well behaved, more curious
than ominous. They expected to see Meredith register, not
realizing that he was already in a dormitory and would not be
enrolled until the next day.[19]

Toward dusk, however, the crowd, largely made up of students, grew steadily in size and ill-will. Organized cheers
began: "2–4–1–3, we hate Kennedy" and "Go to Cuba, nigger
lovers." Several newsmen were attacked, lighted cigarettes
were tossed onto the canvas tops of the military trucks that
had transported the marshals. Rocks, bottles and pipes were
thrown at the marshals themselves. For an hour they stoically
endured these attacks; and several were injured. Some of the
state police tried to maintain order; others merely observed
the scene. At 7:25 the FBI monitored a Highway Patrol radio
signal ordering a withdrawal. Inside the Lyceum, Deputy Attorney General Nicholas Katzenbach, field commander for the
night, argued with Barnett's political representative on the
scene, who may have been responsible for the withdrawal
order. From Jackson at 7:30 Barnett made a television address
to fulfill his earlier bargain with Kennedy. He reported that
Meredith had been placed on campus by "means of government helicopters" and "accompanied by federal officers."
Barnett then revealed his capitulation and urged nonviolence,
but framed both messages in defiant language:

I urge all Mississippians and instruct every state officer under
my command to do everything in their power to preserve peace

and to avoid violence in any form. Surrounded on all sides by the armed forces and oppressive power of the United States of America, my courage and my convictions do not waver. My heart still says, "Never," but my calm judgment abhors the bloodshed that would follow.[20]

From his office a short while later, the President made his own plea for peaceful compliance. It was the first time he had addressed a national television audience specifically on a civil rights matter, and his comments were geared to Southern, and particularly Mississippi, whites. Indeed most of the arguments that had been privately made with Barnett in the previous several weeks were now repeated and expanded. First, he said that court orders were being executed, so far without the use of National Guard or other troops. Kennedy explained that people were free "to disagree with the law but not to disobey it." The suit, he pointed out, had been brought privately by an individual; he did not mention why Meredith had been previously excluded from the university. He listed by their state of origin the appeals court judges, all Southerners, who had upheld Meredith's suit, and explained that it was his duty to implement their order. Expressing his regret that the executive branch had to enter the case at all, he indicated that all attempts at persuasion and conciliation had been tried and had failed. He praised other Southerners for complying with the law and enumerated other states whose universities had accepted "students regardless of race." Acknowledging that the South was going through a difficult period of transition, he averred that "neither Mississippi nor any other southern State deserves to be charged with all the accumulated wrongs of the last 100 years of race relations." On the contrary, he maintained that "to the extent that there has been failure, the responsibility for that failure must be shared by us all, by every State, by every citizen." He praised Mississippi for its long record of courage and patriotism: "This is the state of Lucius Lamar and many others who have placed the national good ahead of sectional interest." Kennedy then cited Mississippians' valorous record on the battlefield, and urged the university's students to abide by that tradition by complying with the law. In concluding, he reminded his countrymen of their destiny abroad. "Let us preserve both the law and the peace and then healing those wounds that are within we can turn to the greater crises that are without and stand united as one people in our pledge to man's freedom." [21]

It is impossible to estimate how many students heard Kennedy's conciliatory or Barnett's defiantly framed pleas for order, but neither succeeded in calming them. In fact, a minute or two before the President began his speech, the White House received word that the marshals had fired their first volley of tear gas. Shortly thereafter, the Highway Patrol, claiming that their masks were inadequate to protect them from the kind of gas being used, withdrew from the scene. That would not have been so bad had they only stationed themselves at the campus entrances and prevented outsiders from getting in, but the largely student rioters were soon augmented by thousands of outside militants, some of them armed with weapons more lethal than rocks. Within an hour of the first tear gas volley, marshals began to be felled by gunfire. One marshal, who was shot in the neck, appeared to be fatally wonded, though he later recovered. An hour after the gunfire began, Katzenbach told Robert Kennedy that troops were needed. The only troops that came soon were the approximately fifty-five members of the Oxford National Guard under the command of Captain Murry Falkner, a cousin of author William Faulkner. The large military forces billeted in Memphis would take somewhat longer to arrive. [22]

One high ranking though retired army officer, Major General Edwin A. Walker, was already on the scene. Walker had commanded the federal troops at Little Rock in 1957. Two years later he joined the ultra-right-wing John Birch Society.

After being admonished and transferred from his command
in Germany, in 1961, for trying to influence his men's voting
and for making derogatory speeches about former government officials, Walker retired, devoting himself fully to fighting the "international Communist conspiracy." In the days
leading to the Ole Miss confrontation, Walker had issued
numerous calls from his Dallas home for patriotic Americans
to join him in Mississippi to oppose the federal government.
Apparently Walker did not participate in the riot himself, but
his presence and exhortations only exacerbated the situation.
Walker was later arrested though he was never brought to
trial for his conduct. He did however undergo a psychiatric
examination. James J. Kilpatrick, a conservative journalist
personally sympathetic to the General, later informed Walker's attorney that some of Barnett's advisers had been
"shocked at Walker's demeanor," one of them observing that
"he seemed to be almost hypnotized." [23]

The President, Robert Kennedy, Burke Marshall, Theodore
Sorensen, and several staff members stayed up through the
night, trying to assist the besieged forces and reduce the
bloodshed. They called Barnett and Watkins repeatedly and
were told that the Highway Patrol was on the scene and was
assisting, but they knew otherwise. Barnett was at least
friendly, at one point even praising the President's speech.
The White House command also tried to expedite the arrival
of the military, but met with considerable frustration. The
Army's wheels turned excruciatingly slowly and communications were terrible. The White House did, however,
have an open telephone line to the beleaguered marshals,
whom it both encouraged and restrained. During the height
of the riot, Edwin Guthman reported from the Lyceum that
the situation was beginning to resemble the Alamo. From the
safety of Washington, Robert Kennedy wryly responded,
"Well, you know what happened to those guys, don't you?"
Naturally the marshals wanted to draw their pistols, but the

White House ordered them not to, which probably averted even worse violence. For five hours the marshals and the small contingent of Guardsmen fought off attacks with nothing more than tear gas and bravado. At 2:15 A.M., with the marshals' supply of gas nearly exhausted, the first troops from Memphis arrived on campus. By dawn thousands more had poured in. By means of tear gas and superior numbers, the troops secured the campus and the town where some rioters had continued their rampage.[24]

The riot took a heavy toll. Two persons were killed by gunfire, one a French newsman, the other an Oxford repairman. About a third of the marshals were injured, twenty-eight by gunfire. By late Monday about three hundred persons were taken into custody, roughly one-third of them Ole Miss students. (Some of those detained were students at other colleges.) Most were released by Tuesday; thirteen were criminally charged. Robert Kennedy and other key Washington officials soon conducted an internal review of their own handling of the situation. They concluded that they had inadvertently contributed to the outbreak of violence by such errors as deploying the marshals so hastily that they forgot their bullhorns and overestimating the assistance they could expect from the Mississippi Highway Patrol. What seems most notable in retrospect is how restrained the marshals were. In 1970, military and police forces on the campuses of Jackson State College in Mississippi and Kent State University in Ohio— under infinitely less provocation—opened fire on students. In 1962, at least, the highest officials in Washington maintained close and effective control over federal forces on the scene. The remarkable restraint exercised by the marshals almost certainly reduced the number of casualties.[25]

On Monday morning, October 1, Meredith was duly registered and the next day he attended his first classes. Marshals and military police accompanied him everywhere. Although they protected him from physical violence, they could not stop the racial taunts hurled at him. Most of the troops were soon withdrawn as a semblance of order was established. Under pressure from moderate faculty and the university's accreditation association, the university administration recovered its governing authority from Barnett and began to assume its responsibility to police itself and prevent disruptions. A substantial number of faculty and students approached Meredith humanely and decently in the next days and months, and some, particularly those who went first, suffered severe abuse from the state's white supremacists. But Meredith suffered the most. Generally ostracized, under constant threat and harassment, followed everywhere by his federal guard, Meredith somehow endured his ordeal and was graduated the following August. It would be several years before black students could matriculate at Ole Miss in a relatively uneventful way, but James Meredith will always have the satisfaction of knowing that he made it possible.[26]

The federal–state conflict continued to be fought out in the courts long after the riot had ended. The state tried to bring Chief Marshal McShane to Mississippi justice. In mid-October the Justice Department requested that Barnett be fined $100,000 for civil contempt. Because President Kennedy did not want to make more of a political martyr out of Barnett than he already was, the Department did not recommend a criminal contempt charge or a prison term. That did not satisfy either Constance Baker Motley of the Legal Defense Fund, or more important, the Fifth Circuit Court of Appeals which in November directed the Attorney General to prepare criminal contempt charges against Barnett and Paul Johnson. The case was still under adjudication when the Kennedy administration came to an abrupt end. Later the court dropped the matter.[27]

The confrontation reverberated through Mississippi politics. The State Senate passed a resolution expressing its "complete, entire and utter contempt for the Kennedy ad-

ministration and its puppet courts." James Eastland attacked
the marshals, on whose "amateurism" he blamed the violence. John Stennis echoed this charge. Paul Johnson, the victorious Citizens' Council gubernatorial candidate in 1963
(under the constitution Barnett could not succeed himself)
flaunted his image as a man who had been at the barricades
to stop the Kennedys, Meredith, and integration. But interestingly, he promised, upon taking office, that hate would
not motivate his administration and declared that the time for
reaction was over. His subsequent disengagement from the
Citizens' Council concluded a process that had actually
started during the Oxford crisis. Mississippi businessmen
had remained silent before the eruption at Oxford, but on
October 2, over two hundred of them met in Jackson to
discuss how to prevent violence in the future. Similarly, in
his final months as governor, Barnett's relations with the Citizens' Council cooled. Unfortunately, after the Council lost
some of its political power in the state, a number of its frustrated members turned to the Ku Klux Klan and to its terroris-
tic methods of preserving white supremacy. [28]

The state's belligerent behavior generated relatively little
support outside Mississippi. Conservative columnists David
Lawrence and Arthur Krock did criticize the courts and the
administration for acting hastily. Yet one of the most conservative, William F. Buckley, though adhering to state's rights
doctrine, could not overlook the fact that in Mississippi constitutional theory may have merely served as a cover for
white supremacist belief. Alabama's Congressional delegation sent the President a telegram deploring the use of force
and urging the immediate removal of marshals and troops;
but the governors of Georgia, North Carolina, Florida, and
Tennessee, when reached by a reporter for the Charlotte *Observer* on the eve of the riot, agreed that Barnett was leading
his state to a certain defeat. After the riot, Governor Ernest
Vandiver of Georgia took issue with Barnett's defiance, and

Governors Terry Sanford of North Carolina and Farris Bryant of Florida even praised the President for his handling of the situation. Senator Allen Ellender of Louisiana declared that the law must be obeyed whether good or bad. A survey of Southern editorial opinion conducted by the Montgomery *Advertiser* on October 2 indicated that outside Alabama few newspapers sympathized with Mississippi. Indeed several blamed Barnett for the violence while praising Kennedy. "President Kennedy has set the correct tone for all America . . . and particularly the townsmen and students at Oxford," the Jacksonville (Florida) *Journal* editorialized. "He has pointed out that tyranny is but a step away when respect for the law must be enforced with tear gas and bayonets. . . . We uphold every Southerner's right to use every peaceable means . . . [to] defend or maintain what he believes is right. Those who go beyond this point . . . do not have our sympathy" [*sic*].[29]

.Several things account for the temperate reaction of the white South. The administration had acted unambiguously but with restraint. It had asked to enter the case as *amicus*, had never wavered about the ultimate outcome, and at the same time had shown itself to be moderate through its willingness to accept short delays, its initial reliance on small numbers of marshals, and its oft-expressed desire to avoid confrontation and the use of troops. With Little Rock, the Eisenhower administration had at first seemed uninterested but later had abruptly sent troops. Kennedy consciously set out to avoid a repetition of that experience. "In contrast to your predecessor," Theodore Sorensen, suffering with an ulcer, reassured Kennedy from his hospital bed on September 28, "you are demonstrating how many graduated steps there are between inaction and troops." By the time the troops finally had to be called, Kennedy had shown himself to be a moderate, an unvengeful upholder of the majesty of the law and the nation. His televised speech on Sunday night was

carefully designed to reinforce that image of him. While the
national administration was demonstrating its purpose and
reasonableness, Mississippi's segregationists were depicting
themselves as irrational, uncompromising, and violence-
prone. Even so, these contrasting images might have had
quite opposite effects had the Oxford events occurred in 1957,
when "massive resistance" was at its peak. Southern politics
had grown more moderate since then. The deployment of
troops to Little Rock and the Kennedy administration's clear
commitment to law enforcement had made talk of active
physical resistance seem futile. School desegregation had become inevitable. "Most of us know the Southern cause is
doomed and it's ridiculous to keep spouting defiance," an
unnamed Alabama Congressman told Paul Duke of the *Wall
Street Journal*. An increase in black electoral participation also
nurtured the change in the Southern political climate. Some
white politicians continued to disregard the interests and
feelings of blacks, but in many areas, as blacks increasingly
exercised the franchise, office-seekers had no choice but to
consider them. Finally, many politicians had grown more en-
amored of the South's new economic growth than of fighting
for a lost cause. "South Carolina is not convinced that segregation is bad morals or bad law but there is an increasing
feeling here that it is bad business," James Reston reported
from that state in mid-October. Governor Ernest F. Hollings,
he wrote, was "not here in Columbia weeping for Gov. Ross
Barnett of Mississippi. He is in Milan, Italy, talking over the
Italian radio about the possibilities of trade between South
Carolina and the countries of the European Common Mar-
ket." In the view of many Southern politicians and businessmen, racial turmoil would discourage investments from the
North and abroad.[30]

Public opinion polls relayed a somewhat similar message.
According to the Gallup poll, the President's popularity in the
South suffered only a transitory setback following the Oxford

crisis. From a 65 percent approval rating in September, he dropped to 52 percent in early October and 51 percent in late October. Outside the South, Kennedy's popularity did not fall below the 65 percent mark in the same period. But he made a quick recovery in the South; by the November rating he had returned to the 65 percent level, which is about where he stayed until the spring. In November his popularity in the rest of the nation had risen sharply also, to 76 percent. No doubt both increments resulted from the successful conclusion to the Cuban missile crisis, but Kennedy's continued high rating in the South in ensuing months proved the November recovery to be no temporary aberration. It might also be observed, however, that though Kennedy's popularity in the South returned to its earlier level, it did not keep pace with his ratings elsewhere. Nevertheless, on the basis of polls and political and editorial opinion it seems certain that the Mississippi confrontation did not seriously hurt Kennedy's standing among white Southerners.[31]

The November elections tended to corroborate the existence of a moderate trend in the South, not by commission, but by omission. Kennedy did not become an important issue in most contests. An exception was the Alabama Senatorial race where James Martin nearly defeated incumbent Lister Hill. Martin, a conservative Republican, captured 49 percent of the vote, a remarkable showing at this time for a candidate of his party in the Deep South. He did especially well in those counties where segregationist sentiment was strongest. Martin charged his opponent with being the "number one Kennedy man" in the South and urged Alabamans to "show the Kennedys we will not be kicked around any longer." In several other Senatorial contests Republicans were equally belligerent, but the Democratic incumbents won easily. Meanwhile, five Republicans gained formerly Democratic House seats. "I think it is . . . heartening to know," William E. Miller, Republican National Committee chairman, wrote Charles Halleck, House Republican leader, "there is no longer such a thing as the one-party South." Louis Harris, who had been Kennedy's pollster in 1960, wrote the President: "The reason for the Republican pick-ups is that the entire Democratic Party of the South is changing rapidly into a far more moderate and liberal party." He predicted that Republicans would continue to make advances in the South in 1964 and 1966, but as ultra-right-wingers.[32]

Blacks and liberal whites, meanwhile, generally looked favorably upon Kennedy's handling of Ole Miss. On October 4, Louis Harris reported to Kennedy that his organization "happened to be checking New York state day by day in continuous polling over the Mississippi events and in two days' time, the Jewish vote (21% of the state) jumped 11 points from 61 to 73 [sic] percent Democratic." "The Negro vote," he reported, "went from 65 to 84 percent Democratic." To be sure, a number of civil rights activists and sympathizers, among them James Farmer and I. F. Stone, criticized Kennedy for not praising the valor of black Mississippians, including Meredith, in his television address. The editors of the leftist magazine *Liberation*, on the other hand, believed that Kennedy had erroneously implied that all white Mississippians were racists. The editors also suggested that instead of sending troops, the President should have personally escorted Meredith onto the campus and talked with students and officials. Yet, to most civil rights supporters the issue was clearcut. In their view, Barnett and Mississippi represented evil while Meredith was a courageous Negro whose life and rights Kennedy fully protected.[33]

The kind of upsurge that Harris discovered in New York in October evidently did not endure until the elections, for both Republican incumbents, Governor Nelson Rockefeller and Senator Jacob Javits, received slightly higher percentages of the black vote than they had gotten in their last previous races. (The New York *Times* reported that Rockefeller captured 35 percent compared to 33 in 1958, and Javits 42 compared to 38 in 1956.) This did not mean, however, that blacks had changed their minds about Kennedy's performance in the Meredith case. Ole Miss was simply not at issue in New York, and by election day black voters had returned to their normal political loyalties, approximately two-thirds Democratic, one-third Republican. Indeed, as Louis Harris reported to Kennedy on November 19, in the face of an overall decline in Democratic voting in the big cities, black slippage had been much smaller than that of urban voters generally or those of Jewish, Polish, Irish, and Italian voters specifically.[34]

Undoubtedly Kennedy was pleased that the Ole Miss crisis had not seriously injured him politically, but he could also take comfort in the fact that America's image abroad had not suffered very much as a result of it either. At his direction, the United States Information Agency compiled reports from its field posts evaluating "the impact of the Oxford crisis, including a comparison with Little Rock." On October 19, Donald M. Wilson, the agency's acting director, sent the President a summary of the findings:

> Reaction to the Oxford crisis was considerably more moderate in both quantity and intensity than to the Little Rock affair, and showed substantially more understanding of U.S. racial progress. News coverage was lighter in most places and almost without exception more objective. Racialism was deplored, but was generally put in perspective. Several posts suggested that the heavier coverage of Little Rock was because it was the first dramatic revelation of the problem, which by now has lost some of its news value.
>
> The coverage of the Little Rock case tended to emphasize violence and defiance of authority, while in the Mississippi case the determination of the U.S. government got early and heavy attention.

Kennedy was certainly also gratified to learn that the "best understood" aspect of the crisis was "the firmness and determination" of his administration "in enforcing law and justice."[35]

From the President's standpoint, the Oxford crisis had clearly not been a disaster. Indeed, in many ways he could call it a success. But he was not entirely satisfied with the government's performance or with his own. He was perturbed at the length of time the military took to arrive on the scene. He was annoyed with himself for having believed Barnett, and he regretted that he had not ordered the troops in earlier. If the troops had arrived when he expected them to, he believed, at least one of the deaths might have been averted. During the night of rioting, he discussed with his subordinates preparations for the coming crisis at the University of Alabama, whose racial exclusiveness was already being challenged in the courts. As that crisis approached, he would be quicker to call in the troops, although he would first attempt much the same process of negotiation and pressure that he had used in Mississippi.[36]

Oxford produced no great change in direction in Kennedy's racial policies. It did not cause him to backtrack, to accelerate his existing programs, or even to develop new ones. Nor did he regard it as an omen. But it led him to question some of his assumptions about Reconstruction. Sorensen recalled:

> What it did show to the President—on which he remarked on more than one occasion—was that history depends on who writes it. The Mississippi legislature prepared a carefully documented report of the affair which placed all of the blame on the marshals. A local court in Mississippi indicted the chief United States marshal and others as having caused all of the difficulty. These and other similar incidents convinced the President that historians who rely on local documents may not be getting a true history, and he specifically wondered aloud whether all that he had been taught and all that he had believed about the evils of reconstruction were really true.

Thus, if Oxford had not caused Kennedy to revise his policies, it did jar his thinking in an important way which brought closer the day when he would revise them.[37]

EIGHT

Winter of Discontent

In late 1962 and early 1963 the Kennedy administration adhered to established civil rights policies. It also finally fulfilled a campaign pledge for an executive order on housing discrimination and held out hope that it would provide further moral leadership, including a possible fight for new legislation. During this winter, however, civil rights sympathizers voiced misgivings about the administration's record and direction. They acknowledged gains that had been made under Kennedy, but were increasingly inclined to judge them inadequate. In Martin Luther King's opinion, for example, the administration, despite good intentions, had brought about only a national acceptance of "tokenism," which he regarded as a dangerous and insufficient palliative. Yet, Kennedy remained personally popular with the black masses and even with most civil rights spokesmen.

DURING the 1960 campaign Kennedy had criticized Eisenhower for not eliminating housing discrimination with a "stroke of the pen" and had promised that as President he would issue an executive order prohibiting racial discrimination in federally assisted housing. Several times since becoming President, Kennedy had contemplated issuing the order but had refrained because of his consideration for Southern Congressmen. As time went by, however, civil rights proponents, liberal Republicans, and newsmen asked Kennedy when he was going to make good on his promise. Once Jacob Javits joined picketers at the White House to protest Kennedy's inertia. Antidiscrimination enthusiasts sent pens and ink to the President as not very subtle reminders of his campaign statements. That gesture amused Kennedy, but there could be little doubt by the summer of 1962 that his failure to issue an order against housing discrimination had become a political embarrassment to him. He therefore directed his subordinates to begin again to prepare an order. Over the next several months, a complex political and bureaucratic process took place in which many parties offered conflicting advice to the President on the order's scope and timing. In each instance, he heeded the counsel of caution.[1]

Kennedy settled the question of timing before deciding the more intricate problem of scope. On strictly political grounds he decided to issue the order after the Congressional election rather than before it. Although Michigan Senator Philip Hart's office advised that the order would be helpful before the election, the office of Senator Pat McNamara, from the same state, favored a delay becuase "in Michigan the Negro community is already so strongly Democratic that it would not be very helpful." There were even stronger reasons for postponement. Kennedy worried about the order's possible effects on Albert Rains's chances for re-election in Alabama's at-large race. Meanwhile, several important Northern Democratic Representatives, Martha Griffiths of Michigan, Leonor Sullivan of Missouri, and Byron Rogers of Colorado, warned White House Congressional liaison chief, Lawrence O'Brien, that the order could have devastating political consequences. Griffiths even put her concern in writing. She described the tense situation in the white suburban neighborhoods of her district over the prospect that Negroes might buy property there. In her view, there was not enough time before the election for "the white areas to understand the full implications of this order," for them to "throw the rocks and settle down." If an order were to be issued at all, she hoped that it would not come before an election "because it will be interpreted as political and as an attempt to buy votes." She knew of no Democratic Congressman from suburbia who believed that he was in danger of "losing colored votes; but he does feel such an order could cost white votes." She sardonically concluded: "In case the counsel of those seated less close to the fire than I am prevails, however, and I lose this election, would you mind asking the President if I can have the next Supreme Court vacancy, where I can legislate far from the prejudices of the precincts." [2]

For several reasons, Kennedy was also persuaded to act cautiously on the question of scope. In July the National Association of Home Builders publicized a survey of its membership which purported to show that there would be a drastic decline in housing construction if the executive order were issued. From this opinion survey the organization extrapolated that the order could cause as much as a six billion dollar decline in the Gross National Product. The Housing and Home Finance Agency discounted the survey after having it analyzed by an independent research firm, which questioned its premises, methods, and conclusions. Yet, as the *Wall Street Journal* reported in early November, many builders still expected a housing order to hurt their industry. The extent of the damage, they believed, would depend on its scope. Kennedy could not be absolutely certain about the economic consequences of a broad order, but he could be sure that a narrow order would not set back this important segment of the economy. [3]

Concerned government officials agreed that the executive order should cover public housing and direct, guaranteed mortgages (through the Federal Housing Administration, the Veterans Administration and the Farmers' Home Agency), but were in dispute over whether the order should be retroactive and whether it should cover financial institutions (banks and savings and loan associations). The Justice Department's Office of Legal Counsel questioned the legality of making the order retroactive and of covering banks. It would not predict how the courts would ultimately decide these issues, which were certain to be adjudicated. Moreover, as Treasury Secretary C. Douglas Dillon pointed out, the President's authority to dictate loan policy to federal banking agencies was highly questionable. Robert Weaver, however, urged that Kennedy exercise his clear-cut authority to extend the order to the savings and loan associations. Yet, to include them while leaving the banks out would seem to give the banks a competitive advantage. In addition, the associations, which had historic ties to the Democrats as opposed to the banks' attachment to the Republicans, had recently received a costly tax ruling while the Federal Reserve Board had increased the limit on dividends banks could pay. Kennedy and his subordinates also were concerned about the political repercussions of a broad order. Because of Kennedy's explicit campaign promise, Southern Congressmen recognized that some order was inevitable, but wanted it kept minimal. Several Northern Democrats had also conveyed the emotional fears and prejudices of white homeowners.[4]

On the basis of these economic, legal, and political considerations, Kennedy decided to issue the most narrow order possible. It would not be retroactive and would cover only public housing and direct, guaranteed federal loans, not financial institutions. So narrow had the order finally become that the President dispatched his brother Robert and Burke Marshall to break the news to Robert Weaver who he feared might resign in protest; but Weaver acquiesced. Kennedy also announced the order's promulgation most cautiously—at a press conference on Thanksgiving eve, a time when the country's attention was normally diverted to feasts and football. Moreover, the announcement, as Sorensen later wrote, "was deliberately sandwiched in between a long, dramatic, and widely hailed statement on Soviet bombers leaving Cuba and another major statement on the Indian border conflict with China." The timing concerned Kennedy enough that he actually signed a blank sheet of paper for the publicity photographs before he left the White House for his Thanksgiving holiday—the order itself had not been completed in time.[5]

A week after the President issued the order, Robert Weaver reported to the White House that there had "been surprisingly little adverse reaction." He noted that Senator A. Willis Robertson of Virginia and columnist David Lawrence had made the strongest opposing statements and that neither had received much public support. His agency had not gotten much mail about the order, and most of what did arrive was favorable. Given the very limited nature of the order and its cautious dissemination, however, the relative silence of the opposition should not have been surprising. As *Business Week* soon pointed out, the order would have minimal immediate effect. It had "less scope and fewer teeth than some of its more ardent partisans had hoped." Moreover, the business magazine reported, according to government housing officials, in Northern states that already had similar antibias regulations in effect there had been no large-scale movement of blacks to the white suburbs. The blacks' fear of white hostility and their general inability to afford the high prices of suburban homes impeded their mobility.[6]

Supporters of housing desegregation gave the order a mixed reception. They were gratified by the symbolic gain that the executive action represented which, as one integrationist put it, was the "first use of federal power on a broad basis to endorse the principle of residential desegregation." The National Committee Against Discrimination in Housing, the NAACP, and the Urban League acknowledged the order as an important first step, but they were dissatisfied with its limitations and were waiting to see how vigorously it was enforced. Initially the Pittsburgh *Courier* had a similar appraisal, but after surveying Negro realtors who believed that the order would not have the slightest impact, its editors warned that "Negroes are getting very weary of tokenism hailed as victories." [7]

In January, the President announced the appointment of David L. Lawrence, former Governor of Pennsylvania (not to be confused with the conservative columnist), as chairman of a special interagency enforcement committee. However, in enforcement, as in the matters of timing and scope, Kennedy proceeded with extreme caution. Indeed, in late April, the NAACP, CORE, the Urban League, and the National Committee Against Discrimination in Housing, issued a joint statement criticizing the administration's lax implementation. After its release, members of the Washington chapter of CORE picketed the Housing and Home Finance Agency (HHFA). Not until several weeks later did Kennedy partially mollify these groups by announcing the appointment of the eight public members of Lawrence's committee. As an interagency committee, created without Congressional authorization, its funding was very limited. Most responsibilities for enforcement actually devolved on the affected agencies, particularly HHFA. It inserted nondiscrimination clauses in all new contracts for public housing and later for urban renewal projects. And it also occasionally took action against housing contractors who persisted in discrimination.[8]

In fact the order had little impact on racial patterns in housing. Whether a more comprehensive one would have had greater effect is, however, questionable. Low incomes were the most formidable barrier to blacks' upward or outward residential mobility, and the President hardly had the authority to raise incomes by executive fiat. The racial attitudes of whites also loomed as significant. Neither the office of the President nor any other government institution could work a rapid transformation in popular attitudes. Indeed, the Northern states which had tried to break down discrimination in this area could show little gains for their efforts. In contrast to most other racial issues in the early and mid-nineteen sixties, white hostility to black advancement in housing cut across regional lines. The loud warnings of Northern Congressmen in 1962 gave evidence of this. In 1966, after having passed two major civil rights laws in the preceding two years, Congress pointedly failed to act on Lyndon Johnson's request for an open housing law. It finally enacted one in 1968 in the wake of Martin Luther King's murder. In all probability, a more sweeping order in 1962 would have had neither the dire effects that Kennedy feared nor the salutary ones that its proponents desired. Like the order that he did issue, it would have been primarily a symbol, though perhaps a more significant one than the circumscribed order Kennedy offered in its place.[9]

Small symbolic gains made less of an impression on civil rights advocates in late 1962 than they had at the start of the administration. "It is my judgment that the record the administration has written in civil rights to date is unimpressive, shows no commitment to firm and steady progress and fails to live up to the excellent statements made by the President during the 1960 campaign," Roger W. Wilkins, State Department official and nephew of the NAACP leader, wrote Ralph Dungan, a White House aide, just before the President issued the housing order. In addition to the housing measure, Wilkins wanted the President to back school desegregation legislation, make stronger and more frequent statements, appoint blacks to the American mission at the United Nations and to ambassadorships in places other than Africa, broaden the powers and jurisdiction of the Committee on Equal Employment Opportunity, and pay greater heed to the recommendations of the Civil Rights Commission.[10]

Although civil rights proponents had never been completely satisfied with Kennedy's record, the dramatic change of atmosphere the administration had engendered had initially allured them. High-level appointments of blacks, a vigorous federal employment effort, the new activism of the Justice Department, access to the President and his subordinates, and the Kennedys' sensitivity to civil rights

constituted a significant break with the malaise and indifference of the Eisenhower years. However, by late 1962 the thrill
was gone. The Kennedy administration seemingly had nothing new to offer and the innovations of 1961 had come to
seem ordinary. Meanwhile most blacks still had a very long
way to go to attain justice and equality.

Simeon Booker, a reporter for *Ebony* and *Jet,* later recalled
the disconsolate mood of civil rights leaders after they met
with the President in mid-December of 1962. This particular
meeting grew out of a conference they had recently held on
American policy toward Africa. The parley with the President
went well, but afterward Booker found the delegates discouraged, not about foreign prospects but about domestic ones.
"We've gotten the best snow job in history. We've lost two
years because we admired him [President Kennedy] for what
should have been done years ago," one leader lamented, according to Booker. An aide to one of the leaders asserted:
"We're not going about this right. We shouldn't have been
here. We've got to quit begging the Kennedys for this and
that. We've got to start demanding our rights." [11]

Sensitive to this new mood, six liberal Democratic Senators
wrote the President in early January. They commended his
executive actions in the field of civil rights but declared their
conviction that "the time has now arrived for similar forthright action in the legislative field." The reason they advanced was purely political: "many Democratic members of
the Senate class of 1958 believe strongly that their re-election
in 1964 will be materially affected by the Democratic civil
rights record compiled by the 88th Congress." They urged
Kennedy to seek legislation that would strengthen the Civil
Rights Commission, deal with job discrimination and school
desegregation, and eliminate the literacy test as a voting
requirement. They also requested his assistance in the upcoming struggle to modify the Senate filibuster rule. [12]

Kennedy had to be concerned about the kind of political

difficulty these Senators described to him. Indeed, if Nelson Rockefeller won the Republican Presidential nomination, which Kennedy anticipated in late 1962, he also had to worry about his own standing among Northern blacks. However, his anxieties about Congress remained. The November elections had not appreciably allayed them. A major part of the President's legislative program still awaited passage. At best, a fight over civil rights would slow up its passage; at worst, it would kill it. Perhaps most important, it did not seem likely to the President that civil rights legislation could be enacted anyway. Mike Mansfield's gloomy prediction that no Democratic President could get civil rights legislation through Congress weighed on Kennedy's mind.[13]

In January Kennedy's decision against seeking civil rights legislation gradually became manifest. In his State of the Union message to Congress, on January 14, he proposed a bold new tax cut and reform. He also spoke fairly explicitly on pressing national needs in the areas of health, education, recreation, and mass transit. But his comments on civil rights were confined to a plea for free access to the franchise. A further indication of the administration's position came several weeks later when the President remained on the sidelines during the Senate contest over filibuster reform. At the same time Lyndon Johnson refused to make rulings from the chair that would have aided the reform cause. Without assistance from the Democratic leadership, in the White House or the Senate, reform was once again tabled.[14]

Liberal Republicans in the House quickly tried to fill the legislative void. Six Republican members of the House Judiciary Committee, including William McCulloch, its ranking GOP representative, joined together at the end of January to issue a press release criticizing the Kennedy administration and proposing a civil rights package similar to the one liberal Senate Democrats had urged on Kennedy privately. Without support from the White House, this legislation could go no-

where. Moreover, its proponents only appeared to speak for a
fraction of their party. Everett Dirksen had rebuffed Clarence
Mitchell when he asked for assistance on filibuster reform
and had also revealed that he did not feel any obligation to go
out of his way for blacks. He was annoyed at unfavorable
stories about him that had appeared in the Chicago Negro
press during his reelection campaign the previous fall.
Around this time, too, Jacob Javits was expressing his dismay
at the tendency of the Republican Party to add Southern segregationists to its ranks. Conservative writers like William F.
Buckley and James J. Kilpatrick, meanwhile, were delighted
at Barry Goldwater's popularity in the South which they
agreed rested on "something more than his laissez-faire position on the Negro problem," in Buckley's words. Thus, liberal Republicans could do little more than embarrass the administration, but, significantly, they were not alone in that
ability. [15]

The Southern Regional Council in January published its
own study of the results of Plans for Progress in the Atlanta
area. Of the twenty-four Plans for Progress firms surveyed,
only seven evidenced compliance with the objectives established in their pledges. Of these seven only three—
Lockheed, Western Electric, and Goodyear—appeared to have
cooperated vigorously. Moreover, the survey pointed out that
even before Kennedy's election, Lockheed was claiming more
than 1,300 Negroes (including some foremen) among its
20,000 employees in Marietta. The report attributed subsequent improvements not to the Plans for Progress, but to a
series of complaints filed by the NAACP and to a cooperative
company management. [16]

In a memorandum to Lyndon Johnson, Kennedy conveyed
his suspicion that both an article in *Newsweek* on the Council's report and the report itself were "somewhat less than objective," but they did "point up the need to keep after the
companies." He believed there should be constant review

and pressure from the staff of Johnson's committee. Kennedy could not "quite understand why so many are willing to assume that a voluntary program cannot be effective—especially since, as I understand it, the 'Plans for Progress' companies are still subject to all of the compulsory requirements and machinery established by your Committee." He requested a report from Johnson's staff on policing procedures, and continued to "regard the program as one with great potential." [17]

Johnson's staff procrastinated on the report, but by March 1 Burke Marshall had completed his own examination of the Plans, which substantially confirmed the Southern Regional Council's finding. He discovered that the Committee had made only a cursory review of the records of signers of the Plans. A company neither protected itself from normal compliance procedures by signing a Plan, nor did signing mean that the company would do anything out of the ordinary to eliminate job discrimination. The Committee's staff was just then beginning to conduct a systematic review of the employment records of all government contractors, and was also making spot-check plant visits. Plans companies would be included in this review, but would not receive special scrutiny. [18]

Less than a week later, a civil rights study group Johnson had convened discussed the future of the Plans for Progress. (Among its members were Marshall, W. Willard Wirtz, Louis Martin, Andrew Hatcher, Marjorie Lawson, and Lee White.) The group arrived at a consensus "that the Plans for Progress program should be brought along rather slowly, and that our recent gains be consolidated before new companies are taken in." They thought it "necessary to bring out the accomplishments which had already been achieved before pressing this program vigorously in the future." This became the policy. There were no more Presidentially-attended Plans-signing ceremonies until December, after Kennedy's death. The administration withdrew from public view one of its most highly vaunted civil rights programs. The withdrawal was not an admission that voluntarism would not work; indeed, Kennedy still maintained his faith in it. But it did, in effect, acknowledge that the voluntary Plans had served as a cosmetic and ineffectual substitute for meaningful enforcement. To reestablish the credibility of the Plans, the Committee would now have to devote itself to vigorous follow-up.[19]

Relations between the administration and the Civil Rights Commission also grew tense during the winter. In early December Robert Kennedy discouraged Chairman John Hannah from proceeding with a public hearing the Commission was planning to hold in Mississippi. The Attorney General wrote him that "public hearings now in the area of race relations by any federal agency" in Mississippi were bound to hinder the work of his department, particularly in its prosecution of criminal contempt cases against Ross Barnett and Paul Johnson. In the event of a jury trial, he feared that Barnett and Johnson would charge that the federal government was attempting to prejudice their cases through the hearings. Of course the charge would be baseless, but Robert Kennedy argued that in these controversial cases it was necessary to avoid "even the appearance of impropriety or questionable ethical conduct by the federal government." He suggested that the Commission's work could proceed without holding public hearings in the state. Furthermore, he observed that the Commission's hearings sometimes overlapped with the Justice Department's own work. As an example he pointed out that the Commission's counsel had submitted the names of three Mississippi counties in which the Commission planned to examine the voting situation. But, Kennedy asserted, the Justice Department was already investigating suffrage violations in all three and had legal action prepared in one. Although he acknowledged that this was not a "complete reason" for the Commission to refrain from making its own investigation, it did seem to him "relevant in balancing the needs of the federal government at the moment." [20]

Bowing to these arguments, Hannah wrote the Attorney General that "the Commission would be remiss not to yield to your request to forego, for the time being, its scheduled public hearing." He added, however, that the decision was "difficult" because preliminary investigations pointed to a situation which urgently demanded the "fact-finding activities the Commission" was "uniquely able to provide." The Commission soon found itself embarrassed by its acquiescence. In a series of telegrams, the Mississippi Council of Federated Organizations, a coalition of the state's civil rights groups, expressed its disappointment in the Commission's failure to come to Mississippi. The Commission's own State Advisory Committee issued a report which charged that the federal government had "not provided the citizens of Mississippi the protection due them as American citizens." Though conceding that the Department of Justice had "acted in good faith," the Advisory Committee asserted that "the present interpretation of the function of the Civil Rights Division was "unduly and unwisely narrow and limited." It urged the President to take corrective action and the Commission to hold formal hearings in Mississippi. The report also called on the Commission to submit legislation to Congress "designed to protect American citizens from being physically abused by persons acting under the color of governmental authority at any level." The bombing of the home of the Advisory Committee's Vice Chairman added an element of urgency to this recommendation. During the next several months there was growing sentiment on the Commission to hold hearings in Mississippi, but Robert Kennedy continued to oppose this. [21]

The Civil Rights Commission's turnabout on the Mississippi hearing in response to Robert Kennedy's urging reflected a certain ambivalence in its feeling about its own role. Initially it had served essentially as an investigatory body.

However, by mid-February 1963, when the Commission's members met with President Kennedy, they believed that they had already uncovered sufficient information about civil rights denials "to provide a basis for intelligent Federal action." Indeed, were investigation "to continue to be the only function of the Commission," they "would recommend that the agency be terminated." They proposed instead that the Commission be given "an operational role," perhaps including mediating local racial conflicts such as in Albany, Georgia, or serving as a guarantor of nondiscrimination in federal programs, and that its term be "extended to at least five years to permit long-range planning and avoid the waste and inefficiency resulting from a phaseout of operations every two years" (its legislated term of existence). Robert Kennedy shared the Commission's reservations about its role, and privately drew unfriendly comparisons between it and Congressional committees which probed subversive activities. Meanwhile Commission lawyers were voicing skepticism about the need for a new voting rights bill which the Civil Rights Division was again contemplating, preferring in its place legislation which would hasten school desegregation. Indicative of the hard feeling that had developed, Berl Bernhard, staff director of the Commission, privately sought a meeting with Lyndon Johnson to discuss the work of the President's Committee on Equal Employment Opportunity. Bernhard tipped off Harry McPherson, an aide to Johnson, that the Vice President was about to become the target of "terrific abuse" on the matter of the Committee's ineffectiveness. Bernhard, suspecting that the attack might have help from White House sources, regarded this as "wretched stuff" because it "hits somebody" who "responds a great deal more sincerely and basically to the underdog than the President does." Such were the relations between the Kennedy administration and the Civil Rights Commission in 1963.[22]

An issue that the Mississippi Advisory Committee had

made public, Washington's abstention from large-scale interference in Southern law enforcement, became the subject of a
law suit in early January. William Higgs, a civil rights attorney, and seven SNCC workers were plaintiffs in a civil suit
which asked the federal district court in Washington, D.C., to
order Robert Kennedy and J. Edgar Hoover to

> protect plaintiffs and their constitutional rights by investigation,
> arrest, and prosecution of offending law enforcement officers of
> the state of Mississippi and of its political subdivisions, and of-
> fending residents of the state of Mississippi acting individually
> or collectively and/or in concert and conspiracy with said law en-
> forcement officers.

The plaintiffs and their lawyers, Higgs and William Kunstler,
held a press conference at which they described brutality in
Mississippi. They also made clear that they bore no ill-will
toward Kennedy or Hoover. They expressed their appreciation for what the Justice Department was doing; they merely
wanted it to do more. Seven months later the district court
dismissed the case on the grounds that it did not have the
power to order the executive branch in the manner requested,
while also noting the thinness of evidence of neglect of duty
presented against the defendants. The appellate court later af-
firmed the dismissal.[23]

In several respects this episode typified the attitude of civil
rights activists toward the Kennedy administration. They appreciated what had been done but wanted more. Although
the President was not providing all they desired, he continued to hold their faith in his sincerity. Roy Wilkins told
the annual membership corporation meeting of the NAACP
in early January, President Kennedy "is aware and alert and
has a feeling on this great problem of race." To retain that
faith, Kennedy adopted Louis Martin's idea to hold a large
Lincoln's Birthday reception to commemorate the centennial
of the Emancipation Proclamation. At least 800, and possibly
as many as 1,400, black and white civil rights, community,

and government officials attended the White House dinner and reception. Clarence Mitchell absented himself in protest of the administration's failure to seek civil rights legislation, but other members of his politically active family, including his wife, could not resist the Presidential invitation. Kennedy, accompanied by Louis Martin and Andrew Hatcher, mingled with the guests, who *Ebony* proudly observed constituted the largest gathering of Negroes ever held in the White House. Indeed, this reception marked the culmination of an important trend established by Kennedy—the granting of full social recognition to blacks by the nation's President.[24]

Though it is difficult to measure precisely, Kennedy probably enjoyed even greater popularity among blacks at large than he did among civil rights leaders. After a disappointing meeting with Lyndon Johnson at which they unsuccessfully sought his assistance on filibuster reform, several activists reconvened in the office of Joseph Rauh of Americans for Democratic Action. He later recalled that "everybody was sitting there despondently." Someone suggested that they launch a public attack on Kennedy's inertia. Roy Wilkins warned that if they tried this they might discover that they did not have "many troops" behind them. He then described how he had been in North Carolina the week before speaking to a Negro group. "I went after Kennedy, hook, line and sinker. I said he hadn't done anything, and I blasted away. And they all sat on their hands. . . . Then I mentioned some little thing he did and the place went up in smoke with everybody cheering." Robert Kennedy shared fully in this popularity. When he spoke at predominantly black Howard University in early March, a thousand students reportedly treated him like a "conquering hero." In a question and answer period following his speech, the Attorney General parried critical questions about American foreign policy from foreign students. Meanwhile, the American Negroes, journalist Fletcher Knebel wrote, "roared with laughter and applause." Afterward hundreds of friendly students mobbed his limousine. Knebel attributed Kennedy's popularity not only to his actions as Attorney General but also to his efforts to desegregate restrictive Washington clubs and his entertainment of Negro celebrities like Harry Belafonte and Rafer Johnson at his home. Thus, despite his seeming loss of initiative, President Kennedy stood on political high ground. Civil rights leaders might want him to wage a battle for legislation, and liberal Republicans might snipe at him for his unwillingness to do so, but his popularity with blacks generally appeared secure. Liberal Democrats, meanwhile, showed no more inclination to criticize his leadership than they had in 1961.[25]

On February 28 Kennedy sent a civil rights message to Congress. In it he requested legislation to expedite the acquisition of Negro voting and educational rights,* lauded the progress that had been made in the two previous years, and explained, in the boldest language he had used as President, why the country should act on civil rights:

> Race discrimination hampers our economic growth by preventing maximum development and utilization of our manpower. It hampers our world leadership by contradicting at home the message we preach abroad. It mars the atmosphere of a united and classless society in which this Nation rose to greatness. It increases the costs of public welfare, crime, delinquency and disorder. Above all, it is wrong.
>
> Therefore, let it be clear, in our own hearts and minds, that it

---

* Kennedy proposed legislation that would have provided for the following: where voting suits were pending, federal referees could register voters in counties where fewer than 15 percent of the eligible number of persons of any race were registered; voting suits would be given expedited treatment in the courts; tests of voter qualifications would have to be applied uniformly; completion of the sixth grade would constitute a presumption of literacy in federal elections; the Office of Education would be enabled to provide technical and financial assistance to local communities for school desegregation; the life of the Civil Rights Commission would be extended four years and its mandate would be broadened so that it could "serve as a national civil rights clearing house providing information, advice, and technical assistance to any requesting agency, private or public."

is not merely because of the Cold War, and not merely because of the economic waste of discrimination, that we are committed to achieving true equality of opportunity. The basic reason is because it is right.[26]

The documentary and oral record of Kennedy's decision to send the message is thin, but we know that by early February he had made up his mind, apparently without having had extensive consultations with anyone except possibly his brother Robert. Politics undoubtedly played a large role in his decision. By going on record in favor of legislation, Kennedy was at least partially shielding himself from liberal Republican criticism. More important, his description of civil rights as an issue of right and wrong would help mollify black leaders who had of late been voicing dissatisfaction with him. Indeed, that passage was included at the behest of Louis Martin, the top-ranking black at the Democratic National Committee. But Kennedy also certainly believed in the antidiscrimination measures his administration had taken and the new ones he was now proposing, and he had a strong conviction that it was a President's responsibility to exert leadership in identifying and resolving the nation's problems. Two days before the message went to the Hill, Burke Marshall provided a correspondent with some insight into the President's current thinking. Were Kennedy to seek compulsory school desegregation legislation, which appeared to have no chance of passage, "it would be purely for political reasons, in the broadest sense," Marshall wrote. "These reasons would include partisan reasons, but would also include what I suppose you might call an exercise of the moral force of the White House," he expanded.[27]

Kennedy, however, had not decided to make the legislative fight his own. He followed the unsuccessful precedent of the previous year, when the literacy test bill had been left exclusively to the Justice Department. Mindful of its defeat then, and Mansfield's subsequent prediction, the Justice Department procrastinated. Over a month elapsed before it even submitted draft legislation to the House Judiciary Committee. Evidently, public relations considerations directly caused one of the delays. On March 25, Lawrence O'Brien reported to the President that "submission of voting legislation was held up awaiting the end of the New York newspaper strike, so that it would receive full coverage." [28]

Though gratified by the President's new moralistic rhetoric, civil rights supporters were not satisfied with Kennedy's specific legislative proposals. Roy Wilkins called the February 28 message "an admirable document" but wished it had gone much further on school desegregation, housing discrimination, and fair employment. Liberal Republicans, likewise, took note of its omissions while applauding its rhetoric. By the end of March, the President still had not forwarded his drafts to Congress. Consequently, eight Senate Republicans (Jacob Javits, Clifford Case, Kenneth Keating, Hiram Fong, Thomas Kuchel, Hugh Scott, Glenn Beall, and Leverett Saltonstall) introduced their own legislative package. "If the president will not assume the leadership in getting through Congress urgently needed civil rights measures, we in Congress must take the initiative," they asserted. Their bills went well beyond Kennedy's general suggestions in almost all respects. In education, for example, they supported the recommendations of the Civil Rights Commission that local school boards be required to file desegregation plans within 180 days and that the Attorney General be authorized to seek injunctions. Significantly, however, these eight Republicans failed to persuade a single liberal Democrat to co-sponsor any of their bills. Javits attributed this "unhappy" breakdown of bipartisanship to Kennedy's civil rights message. Whether that was the reason is uncertain, but more important was the clear indication that liberal Democrats were remaining steadfastly loyal to Kennedy on civil rights. Clearly a legislative breakthrough in civil rights absolutely required Kennedy's personal backing.[29]

As spring approached, it brought with it some ominous news from Mississippi. A voter registration drive in Greenwood, Mississippi, was meeting resistance from whites. Official harassment, sporadic violence, and arson were impeding the civil rights effort. On February 28, three workers on voter registration were shot at from a passing car and one was seriously wounded. Wiley Branton, head of the Voter Education Project, quickly announced his organization's determination to press on and soon visited Greenwood to encourage the campaign. Violent incidents continued to occur, the registrar remained uncooperative, and the police arrested eight black registration workers. At the end of March, the Justice Department, which had been watching the deteriorating situation, sought a temporary restraining order that would have required local officials to release the jailed activists, refrain from further interference with the campaign, allow Negroes to assemble for peaceful protest, and protect them from violent whites. Several days later, John Doar withdrew the Department's request for the temporary order—while keeping a request for a permanent order pending—when local officials agreed to release the eight workers. Doar accepted this minor victory because he feared the courts would not grant the preliminary injunction to protect the rights of Negroes generally anyway. A lawyer from the Legal Defense Fund, who had come to Greenwood, shared Doar's fear. The drive went on, but though the level of violence receded, the drive for voter registration continued to be frustrated by private and official resistance. "I don't care what Bobbie Kennedy have [sic] told you boys, I don't want you down here," a plantation boss told two registration workers in late April. His comment summed things up quite succinctly. For the time being, white hegemony was successfully resisting the rising aspirations of blacks, even when they had external support from the VEP and the Justice Department.[30]

In the wake of the discouraging events in Greenwood, the Civil Rights Commission decided at its March 29 meeting to issue an unusual interim report which would describe the perilous condition of constitutional rights in Mississippi and make recommendations for safeguarding them. The report listed a number of incidents, among them the shooting of the voter registration worker, the biting of a minister by a police dog, the bombing of the home of the State Advisory Committee's Vice Chairman, and the denial of federal surplus food to impoverished children by local officials in one county. The report pointed out that the federal government was allocating vast sums of money in grants and contracts to Mississippi—in fact $380 million more than it was receiving back from the state in revenue. The Commission recommended that Congress and the President "consider seriously" legislation that would deny federal funds to a state if it persisted in violating the Constitution, and more specifically, that the President "explore" his authority to withhold funds from Mississippi until it demonstrated compliance with the Constitution and federal law. Before issuing the report, however, the Commission dispatched its Chairman and Staff Director to inform the President.[31]

Administration officials had seen the report and briefed the President before he met with Hannah and Bernhard. Burke Marshall and Lee White prepared memoranda which cleared the federal government of responsibility in every incident and case cited by the Commission. They related FBI and Justice Department efforts, sometimes successful, to investigate and prosecute all federal violations. For example, they described the federal legal action in Greenwood which they regarded as successful. On the food distribution case, they told of the Justice Department's investigation and the Agriculture Department's subsequent warning to the county that if local officials did not resume distribution, federal officials would do so themselves, which had the effect of restoring regular distribution. They also contravened the Commission's recommendations. In many programs there was no statutory discretion to withhold funds. Moreover, White asserted, it would be improper for the President to determine on his own authority whether a state was in compliance with the law; that was up to the courts. On top of that, the withdrawal of funds would hurt Mississippi Negroes "as much or more than Whites," as blacks often benefited from federal housing, educational, and welfare contributions. White could not foresee any possible advantages that might accrue from the report's publication. He was given to understand that the Commission believed that "if they, in effect, urge irresponsible action, it will give the administration the opportunity to take a stronger stand." But he feared that the report's release would have only damaging effects, such as to "destroy the Committee's reputation for reasonableness," "permit the uninformed and unsophisticated to urge the administration to do something that simply cannot be done," create the false impression that civil rights problems were confined to Mississippi, "intensify the harshness of feelings in Alabama," where several desegregation crises were looming, and "minimize the efforts and achievements of this administration." [32]

When Hannah and Bernhard presented the report to President Kennedy he tried to dissuade them from making it public. He argued that the report would have been better directed at Congress alone, for he did not have the power they implied he had; he declared that he preferred that it not be published at all because it would only antagonize Southerners in Congress. Although he believed that the report was ill-conceived, Kennedy said he would not try to suppress it. "That would be wrong—couldn't do it anyway. It is independent, has a right to be heard, but I do wish you could get them to reconsider," the President said. [33]

Contrary to the President's wishes, the Commission published the report several days later; as expected, many white Southerners condemned it and some civil rights supporters praised it. But other supporters did not. The Pittsburgh *Courier*, the nation's largest circulating black newspaper, noted that a withdrawal of funds would be vindictive and would hurt Mississippi blacks. The New York *Times* editorialized: "We can think of no suggestion [the cutoff of funds] less calculated to promote civilized race relations or to cool the inflamed passions that erupted in the Civil War." Even the *New Republic*, which had published some highly critical pieces on Kennedy's civil rights record, rejected the Commission's recommendation.[34]

If the Commission's intent had been to publicize the plight of Negroes in Mississippi, it had made a grievous error by including the fund cutoff recommendation, because attention was immediately riveted on that. Both times the press questioned Kennedy about the report, the fund cutoff was the principal issue. Three days after the report appeared, Kennedy was asked at a newspaper editor's luncheon whether he intended "to cut off Federal aid to the State of Mississippi as proposed by your Civil Rights Commission." He responded that he lacked the power to do so, and that it would be unwise to give the President that power. Federal programs, he said, should not encourage or permit discrimination, but the Commission was suggesting "wholesale cutoff . . . as a disciplinary action on the State of Mississippi." That he could not accept. He did point out that Mississippi benefited considerably from federal money, and he hoped "that the people of Mississippi would recognize the assets that come with the Union as well as what they may feel would be the disadvantages of living up to the Constitution." At his next news conference, a newsman again asked him about the cutoff, but this time the question also alluded to the violence described in the Commission's report. Kennedy responded that the government was doing all it could to provide protection, but that it did not have direct jurisdiction over every crime committed. He then reiterated his prior comments on the Commission's proposal to cut off funds.[35]

Thus, attention moved from the actual oppression of blacks in Mississippi to the prospective oppression of Mississippi in the nation. Yet blacks were oppressed there, were beginning to assert themselves, and consequently were encountering white resistance. In the absence of a full Commission inquiry into Mississippi conditions, a central issue was left largely unexamined: where precisely did all three branches of the federal government stand with respect to violence against blacks by white officials and private citizens? Could it and should it do more to protect blacks and civil rights workers? These were the critical questions that lay behind the Commission's charges. Unfortunately, neither the news media, the government, nor the public gave them the careful examination they deserved.

Martin Luther King, meanwhile, was worried that the civil rights movement had lost its momentum. At the end of March, he voiced his anxieties in *The Nation*. The Kennedy administration, he wrote, had succeeded only in moving the nation toward the acceptance of tokenism, which demobilized "the militant spirit which alone drives us forward to real change." He did not question the sincerity of the administration's motives, but implied that they would be subjected to further testing:

Tokenism was the inevitable outgrowth of the Administration's design for dealing with discrimination. The Administration sought to demonstrate to Negroes that it has concern for them, while at the same time it has striven to avoid inflaming the opposition. The most cynical view holds that it wants the votes of both and is paralyzed by the conflicting needs of each. I am not ready to make a judgment condemning the motives of the Administration as hypocritical. I believe that it sincerely wishes to achieve change, but that it has misunderstood the forces at play. Its motives may better be judged when and if it fails to correct mistakes as they are revealed by experience.

The South, King argued, was bifurcated. One part was ready for rapid racial progress; the other adamantly opposed all substantive change. The administration had a duty, he believed, to place its weight behind the dynamic South. If it did so its international reputation would be enhanced, its moral commitment assured, and even its political fortunes improved because its fate in the next election rested with black voters in Northern cities. In this way, King marshalled all the familiar arguments for political support of civil rights. His only concrete recommendation, however, was that Kennedy fight for the legislation he had proposed in his February 28 message to Congress. Rather ironically, within a matter of weeks King had personally injected new life into the movement, and Kennedy, soon after, responded by going considerably further than King's relatively moderate suggestion of March. The civil rights campaign in Birmingham was about to lead to far greater change than had all the discontent of the winter.[36]

NINE

From Alabama to the Second Reconstruction

Two racially motivated crises developed in Alabama in the spring of 1963, one dramatically recorded by news cameras, the other generally removed from public view. In Birmingham Martin Luther King led a civil rights drive by that city's blacks which captured the world's attention while in Montgomery Governor George Wallace hovered near the brink of another Ole Miss-style confrontation. Events in Birmingham and their implications convinced President Kennedy to seek significant new legislation. The climax to the Wallace affair then provided Kennedy with the appropriate opportunity to entreat the Congress and the nation to institute its Second Reconstruction.

BIRMINGHAM had the dubious distinction of being the most thoroughly segregated large city in the country. Local ordinance and custom prevented its approximately 140,000 blacks (out of a population of 350,000) from using "whites only" public facilities such as lunch counters, dressing rooms, and water fountains. In early 1963 only the interstate transportation terminals had been integrated. Although Birmingham was a bustling industrial center, the South's major steel producing city, blacks generally found themselves confined to the most menial and ill-paying jobs. With some difficulty blacks could register to vote, but few did. Consequently blacks had little political power. The city's black and white leaders rarely communicated with one another. Although the city had some black activists they had been unable to effect change in Birmingham.

In the winter of 1962–63, Martin Luther King's Southern

Christian Leadership Conference, in conjunction with its active Birmingham affiliate led by the Rev. Fred Shuttlesworth, laid plans for assaulting the city's structure of segregation with the protest tactics tried out in Albany, Georgia. They raised a considerable sum of bail money, pinpointed targets, and conducted training sessions in churches on the techniques and philosophy of nonviolent protest. The campaign was set to begin in March, immediately after a municipal election to choose a mayor and city council. (Birmingham had voted to switch from the commission form of government the previous fall.) When the election failed to produce a majority for anyone, King decided to postpone the campaign until after the runoff election. Competing in it were two segregationists, T. Eugene ("Bull") Connor, the city's long-time police commissioner and ardent enforcer of segregation and Albert Boutwell, a former lieutenant governor and, by comparison to his opponent, a moderate. Of the two Boutwell was clearly preferable to the city's blacks, and rather than give Connor an easily exploitable issue, King postponed the campaign. On April 2, Boutwell won a narrow victory, and Connor immediately initiated court proceedings to prevent him from assuming control of the city. Until the case was settled, Birmingham actually had two administrations serving simultaneously, a situation which exacerbated the crisis precipitated by King's protest campaign.[1]

Immediately after the runoff election, King launched the protest campaign with a series of relatively small sit-in demonstrations at downtown stores. He declined Burke Marshall's advice to postpone the campaign until the Connor–Boutwell suit had been settled. Marshall had undertaken what he knew to be a futile effort to dissuade King at the request of a Birmingham newspaper editor. It turned out to be useful since Marshall thereby established his own credibility with certain powerful whites in Birmingham—later a valuable asset when he tried to mediate the city's racial crisis.

Marshall subsequently learned that these whites had no doubts that he tried to dissuade King from initiating demonstrations; they had wiretapped King's phone.[2]

The first several days of demonstrations saw a repetition of the Albany experience. The police decorously arrested demonstrators and then obtained an injunction against the demonstrations. King stood at a crossroads. To obey the injunction meant a cessation of the campaign. By this time over four hundred blacks had been arrested for a variety of protest activities, including marches, sit-ins, and pray-ins. In addition the movement was sponsoring daily mass meetings and a boycott of downtown stores. In Albany King had obeyed an injunction, but in that case it had emanated from a federal rather than a state court. Although the movement urgently needed King's assistance in raising bail money, he decided that there were even more compelling reasons for him to make the symbolic act of going to jail. Hence, on Good Friday, April 12, he led a protest march in violation of the court order and was arrested.[3]

At first King was placed in solitary confinement and kept incommunicado. His wife, who had recently given birth to a child, was worried about his safety and, remembering an earlier time when her husband had been jailed, phoned the President from her Atlanta home. Robert Kennedy soon returned her call and promised to do all he could to have her husband's situation improved. Several hours later the President himself called Coretta King and gave his reassurances. Apparently the Kennedys had some influence with King's jailers for the conditions of his imprisonment were soon ameliorated, and he was even allowed to telephone his wife.[4]

From jail King responded to eight white Birmingham clergymen who had been urging that the city's racial problems be resolved by the courts, not in the streets. In his "Letter from Birmingham Jail," King wondered why the clergymen had expressed no concern about the conditions that had provoked the demonstrations. The purpose of his program of direct action, he frankly admitted, was "to create a situation so crisis-packed that it will inevitably open the door to negotiation." As for the movement's disrespect for local law enforcement, he asserted man's "moral responsibility to disobey unjust laws." King expressed disappointment in white moderates who counselled patience but failed to promote racial progress. He also repudiated their contention that he was an outsider or an extremist. Indeed, he stationed himself "in the middle of two opposing forces in the Negro community." On the one side were those Negroes, either drained of their self-respect or members of the comfortable middle class, who urged complacency. On the other stood black nationalist groups such as Elijah Muhammad's Muslim movement, which propagated "bitterness and hatred" and came "perilously close to advocating violence." King warned that, if whites spurned the civil rights movement, millions of blacks would turn in frustration to "black-nationalist ideologies—a development that would inevitably lead to a frightening racial nightmare." [5]

King's dire warning was no scare tactic. Within hours of his jailing, young blacks had gone on a brief rock-and-bottle-throwing rampage following the arrest of another group of nonviolent demonstrators, including King's brother who was a minister in Birmingham. After a week in prison, Martin Luther King accepted release on bond in order to reassume active leadership of the campaign. While demonstrations and arrests continued, secret negotiations were opened between representatives of the black community and members of the Senior Citizens Committee, an organization which leading members of the city's business establishment had set up the previous year to avert the very kind of crisis they were now facing. When the negotiations proved fruitless, King began to consider new tactics to increase the pressure. Up to this point, most of the demonstrators had been adults but, as in

Albany, the jails were proving to be too large to be kept filled even by the great numbers of adult blacks willing to go and stay in jail. King now turned to the city's black children to swell the numbers in his nonviolent army. On May 2, thousands of children marched for the first time and over nine hundred were arrested.

Apparently the children's march enraged Bull Connor, who up to this point had, in the manner of Albany's Laurie Pritchett, exercised restraint. Beginning on May 3 the police concentrated, not on arresting marchers, but on physically repulsing them. Several blacks were bitten by police dogs, many others were injured by nightsticks and by water from high-pressure fire hoses. Connor himself achieved further notoriety from his seeming delight in the treatment his men were meting out to the demonstrators. When informed that Fred Shuttlesworth had been injured by a fire hose and taken away in an ambulance, Connor cracked: "I'm sorry I missed it. I wish they'd carried him away in a hearse." The nonviolent philosophy did not always prevail among the city's blacks, and sporadic incidents of bottle throwing resulted in Governor George Wallace's sending in hundreds of state troopers to supplement the local police. National and international television and newspaper coverage, meanwhile, became heavy and paid particular attention to the fact that police were committing much of the violence against defenseless blacks, many of them women and children. Highly dramatic news photographs and films showed torrents of water pommeling demonstrators, police dogs biting them, and policemen clubbing them.[6]

On May 4, Burke Marshall, accompanied by Joseph F. Dolan, an Assistant Deputy Attorney General, arrived in Birmingham. They came to try to mediate the dispute, not to enforce federal law. The principal goals of the campaign—the elimination of segregated public accommodations and discriminatory employment practices—lay beyond the scope of their authority, since neither were forbidden by any federal statute. Marshall met separately with white and black spokesmen, attempting to get each side to define its position and to negotiate. The administration in Washington also tried to reason with and bring pressure on both sides. Robert Kennedy urged King to stop using children as demonstrators, arguing that they would be injured, but King would not yield. The children, he countered, suffered even greater injury from segregation. The President and members of the Cabinet and outside friends of the administration persuaded business executives whose companies had subsidiaries in Birmingham to bring pressure on their companies' executives in Birmingham to arrive at a settlement. The racial crisis was hurting the city's economy and its businesses.[7]

By May 7 the two sides in Birmingham were meeting together and negotiating seriously. The following day President Kennedy opened his press conference with an optimistic statement that Birmingham's business leaders had pledged to take positive steps to meet "the justifiable needs of the Negro community" and that Negro leaders had agreed to suspend demonstrations. But there was a third major party to the dispute, the old city commission faction which continued to exercise power in the absence of a judicial resolution of the election results. Opposed to any settlement which yielded to desegregation, it tried to scuttle the agreement. King and Ralph Abernathy, his chief aide, were rearrested and convicted on an old charge, and a high bail was set during appeal. Joseph Dolan managed to restrain angry Negro leaders who wanted to resume demonstrations. Bail was quickly raised, King and Abernathy were released, and negotiations continued. The Senior Citizens Committee agreed to desegregate public facilities such as lunch counters within ninety days, to promote some blacks from menial positions and to hire others in private businesses within sixty days, and to establish regular communications with the black community.

The protest movement had achieved real concessions, but it still had not won the outright release of eight hundred demonstrators still in jail. Joseph Rauh, general counsel to the United Automobile Workers, expeditiously arranged for his and other unions to put up the large sum of money required to make bail. With that, the settlement was publicly announced on May 10.[8]

The agreement came under immediate attack. Mayor Hanes, of the old city commission, called it a "capitulation by certain weak-kneed white people under threats of violence by the rabble rousing Negro, King." He warned that the victory would only serve to encourage King, who already had the backing of the Attorney General, to disrupt another city. He vowed to oppose the integration efforts. On radio the next day Connor, too, attacked the settlements and proposed that white people boycott those stores that cooperated in the accord. That night, a Saturday, the Ku Klux Klan held a rally in a local park. Soon after it broke up, the home of the Rev. A. D. King, Martin Luther King's brother, was bombed. He and his family were at home but escaped injury even though the house was wrecked. Somewhat later, the motel that had been the headquarters of the movement was also bombed. Bombings were not new to Birmingham, but coming where and when they did, these two set off serious rioting by Negroes against the police. Despite the efforts of movement leaders to calm the situation, the rioting lasted through the night.[9]

These distressing events drew national attention, including that of President Kennedy who went on television and radio briefly the next night to give his support to the endangered accord which he called a "tribute to the process of peaceful negotiation and to the good faith of both parties." He warned that the federal government would "not permit it to be sabotaged by a few extremists on either side who think they can defy both the law and the wishes of responsible citizens by inciting or inviting violence." As tangible evidence of the government's determination, he announced that he had already taken three steps: he was sending Burke Marshall back to Birmingham "to consult with local citizens" (Joseph Dolan and other Justice Department officials were already there); he had alerted units of the military trained in riot control and dispatched some of them to the Birmingham area; and he had ordered the execution of the necessary preliminary steps for calling the Alabama National Guard into federal service. In conclusion, he hoped that Birmingham's citizens would "maintain standards of responsible conduct that will make outside intervention unnecessary." [10]

Birmingham remained tense. George Wallace questioned the President's constitutional authority to send troops and challenged him to reveal the names of whites who were negotiating with law-violating Negroes. Justice Department officials meanwhile worked assiduously to safeguard the original agreement. Martin Luther King helped to contain the angry feelings of blacks. On May 15, the Senior Citizens Committee publicly endorsed the settlement and made known the names of its members, among whom were many of the city's ranking businessmen. A week later the city's Board of Education ordered the suspension or expulsion of more than a thousand of the student demonstrators. King dissuaded blacks from resuming protests, and Judge Elbert Tuttle immediately countermanded the school board's orders. The very next day Alabama's Supreme Court ruled against the city commission in its bid to stay in office, thus bringing a salutary resolution to that problem. Slowly, then, the situation improved, troops stayed on their bases, and a fragile peace settled upon the beleaguered city. [11]

The Birmingham campaign, which received instant, extensive and dramatic coverage in the media, profoundly affected the nation's blacks. From his vantage point on the Democratic

National Committee where he monitored the black scene,
Louis Martin reported to Robert Kennedy on May 13 of a rapidly changing mood:

> Events in Birmingham in the last few days have seemed to elec-
> trify Negro concern over civil rights all across the country. As
> this is written, demonstrations and marches are underway or
> being planned in a number of major cities, including Chicago.
> The accelerated tempo of Negro restiveness and the rivalry of
> some leaders for top billing coupled with the resistance of seg-
> regationists may soon create the most critical state of race rela-
> tions since the Civil War.

That the campaign actually succeeded in winning key objectives could only further accelerate the pace of social activism.
The message of Birmingham to the nation's blacks was quite
clear: street demonstrations could win tangible gains.[12]

Quite in keeping with his attitude in the past, President
Kennedy had sympathy for the feelings of black people at this
critical juncture. On May 4 he met with a delegation from the
Americans for Democratic Action. That morning many newspapers had printed a picture of a police dog attacking a black
woman in Birmingham. Kennedy explained to these liberals
that there was nothing further he could constitutionally do
about the situation, but he said that the picture had made
him "sick." Although he regretted that King had not postponed the demonstrations until Boutwell had taken office, he
was "not asking for patience." "I can well understand," he
added, "why the Negroes of Birmingham are tired of being
asked to be patient." [13]

Kennedy involved his administration in Birmingham just
as he had involved it in previous crises in the South. His aim
was unchanged—to mediate differences, to promote a peaceful and progressive settlement. But, as in Albany, the administration had relatively little power to effectuate this.
Burke Marshall could reason with the opposing sides, Cabinet members and the President himself could persuade busi-

ness leaders to pressure their local subordinates, but no federal law could guarantee the basic objectives of King's campaign. No federal statute required lunch counters to serve blacks, department stores to hire them, or local officials to talk to them. Even the most egregious actions taken by Bull Connor—the violent acts against demonstrators in the streets—did not violate federal law. When a total breakdown in order occurred and a race riot loomed as a possibility, the President could and did warn that federal troops were available, but the President did not see the military occupation of Southern cities as a proper solution. By May 7, Kennedy began to consider a range of other alternatives—including calling a conference of business, labor and racial leaders, and asking Congress for new legislation to deal with the underlying issues—and he asked his brother Robert to prepare a legal remedy to avert future Birminghams. [14]

The unyielding, at times violent, resistance of some whites made additional Presidential involvement more compelling. If the authorities in Birmingham had acted as reasonably as had many of their counterparts in neighboring states, the situation there would not have become as aggravated as it did. Georgia's state government, for example, was firmly in the hands of moderates who prided themselves on their ability to avoid confrontation and make quiet progress. When President Kennedy met with Georgians privately he was apt to compliment them on their prudent leadership. On the other hand, extremists like Bull Connor so exacerbated racial problems that they invited the very things they wanted to prevent: Blacks became more demanding, not less; and liberal and moderate whites, including the President, became more sympathetic to the cause of oppressed blacks. "The civil rights movement," Kennedy would later sardonically remark, "should thank God for Bull Connor. He's helped it as much as Abraham Lincoln." [15]

Significantly, Kennedy's personal confrontation with white

Southern extremism caused him to revise an historical attitude which had been an important basis for his moderation
in the past. The Ole Miss crisis had set him to wondering
about the validity of his totally negative view of Reconstruction. In the following months he had read some of the works
of C. Vann Woodward, a prominent Southern historian who
had much greater concern for the plight of blacks than the
historians from whom Kennedy had drawn his first impression of Reconstruction. As he observed the harsh behavior of
extremists in the spring, he evidently became ever more
skeptical of his former view of Southern whites as victims of
Radical Republican oppression. Indeed, after meeting with
the family of Medgar Evers, a black Mississippi civil rights
leader who was murdered in June, Kennedy sadly observed
to Arthur Schlesinger, his resident historian: "I don't understand the South. I'm coming to believe that Thaddeus Stevens
was right. I had always been taught to regard him as a man of
vicious bias. But, when I see this sort of thing, I begin to
wonder how else you can treat them." [16]

The Birmingham crisis touched another sensitive Kennedy
nerve when it attracted a great deal of publicity abroad. The
United States Information Agency kept Robert Kennedy
closely apprised of the developing foreign reaction and, on
May 17, sent a summary to the President. On the whole, the
agency found that news coverage had been more balanced
than in previous cases of racial discord. Yet, "many headlines
were sensationalized" and "pictures played up the brutality
of police measures," according to Donald Wilson, Acting
Director of the agency. In several countries, particularly in
Ghana and Nigeria, the media "poured out caustic denunciation of the racial outrage." Radio Moscow, after a hesitant
beginning, was currently devoting a quarter of its output to
Birmingham, much of it beamed to African audiences. Given
Kennedy's expansionist view of his country's role in the

world, the damage Birmingham had done to America's image undoubtedly concerned him.[17]

Most important, however, Birmingham indicated to Kennedy that the civil rights movement had acquired powerful new momentum. The willingness of thousands of people to suffer jail and injury demonstrated a remarkable determination by blacks to acquire equal treatment with whites. After hundreds of years first of slavery, then of segregation and second-class citizenship, black Americans were insistently saying "we shall overcome," in the words of their most famous freedom song. Equally important, it appeared likely that blacks would turn to violence and to extremist ideologies if their drive were frustrated by white resistance. Martin Luther King had made this point in his letter from the Birmingham jail. The sporadic violence by Birmingham blacks gave it graphic illustration. Similarly, the President and Attorney General emphasized it when they met with a group of Alabama editors on May 15. If moderate Negroes failed to get what they wanted, they warned, the doors would be thrown open to extremist groups such as the Black Muslims.[18]

Thus, the specter of violence and extremism loomed, with the Black Muslims seeming particularly threatening. Elijah Muhammad, their founder, implored blacks to purge themselves of what he regarded as the debilitating, degrading, and corrupting influences of Christianity. Where civil rights leaders strove for an integrated society, he desired the complete separation of the races. Whites, he believed, had so victimized blacks that they deserved only enmity in return. Though a relatively small group, the Black Muslims seemed to many to have a great potential for growth, particularly in the black ghettoes of Northern cities. James Baldwin, a brilliant black writer, did the most to call wide public attention to this group. His "Letter from a Region in My Mind," was published in *The New Yorker* in November 1962, and under the

ominous title *The Fire Next Time* it became a best-selling book
in the spring. Baldwin himself rejected Black Muslim tenets,
but he described the horrors of ghetto life and discussed the
philosophy and great appeal to the ghetto masses of Elijah
Muhammad's teachings.[19]

Robert Kennedy, while rejecting black separatism, refused
to write off the Black Muslims as subversives. Publicly he
characterized black extremism as an understandable, though
unjustifiable, reaction to the historic mistreatment of blacks
by whites. He had read and been moved by Baldwin's pro-
vocative work, and when Dick Gregory, the satiric comedian
and civil rights activist, suggested through Burke Marshall
that Robert Kennedy meet with Baldwin, he readily consented. They had an amiable breakfast discussion on May 23
at Kennedy's Virginia home, and Kennedy proposed that
Baldwin assemble a group of people conversant with the
problems of the cities to discuss with him possible actions
the government might take. The Attorney General was going
to New York the next day to try to convince chain store executives to desegregate voluntarily, and so they arranged to
meet there in the Kennedy family apartment during the
day.[20]

Baldwin brought together fourteen people with diverse
backgrounds. Kenneth Clark was a prominent psychologist,
Edwin C. Berry the Director of the Chicago Urban League,
and Clarence B. Jones a principal attorney for Martin Luther
King. Harry Belafonte and Lena Horne were famous entertainers, Lorraine Hansberry a distinguished playwright.
Others were personal associates of Baldwin, including his
brother, a friend of his brother, his secretary, and the pro-
ducer of his television show. Also present were Rip Torn, an
actor, and Robert P. Mills, an agent. Finally, there was former Freedom Rider Jerome Smith, a CORE field worker who
had suffered violence and jail as a result of his civil rights
activities. Most of them were black.[21]

The meeting almost immediately became an angry, emotional confrontation. Jerome Smith set its tone by declaring that he was nauseated by the necessity of having to be in the same room with the Attorney General, of having to plead, in effect, for the rights of Negroes. Kennedy tried to recount the administration's civil rights accomplishments and told of the new legislation that was under consideration. He looked to the older members of the group for support, but found little. Their sympathies clearly lay with the young activist. At one point Baldwin asked Smith if he would take up arms to defend the United States. Smith's unambiguous no shocked Kennedy, but it was understood by the others. "I didn't know whether to laugh or cry or both," Kenneth Clark remarked after the meeting. "We were unable to communicate clearly and skillfully that this was not a group of Negroes begging the white power structure to be nice to Negroes. We were trying to say that this was an emergency for our country, as Americans. This never got over." Five years later, riding on Robert Kennedy's funeral train, Clark vividly recalled the atmosphere that day:

It really was one of the most violent, emotional verbal assaults and attacks that I had ever witnessed. Bobby became more silent and tense, and he sat immobile in the chair. He no longer continued to defend himself. He just sat, and you could see the tension and the pressure building in him. Harry Belafonte, more than anyone else, tried to move in in terms of raising personal contacts, such as swimming in the pool with the Kennedys, and things of that sort. [Belafonte had been a house guest of Robert Kennedy.] He tried to bring a human, social thing into it, but nobody paid any attention to that. It didn't work. The rest of us came right back to the issue. And it went on for hours—about three hours of this kind of searing, emotional interaction and confrontation. The point we were trying to put over was: Look. The Kennedys have a tremendous amount of credit with the American people. This credit must be used by them. You and your brother must use this credit to lead the American people

into an awareness and understanding of the nature of this problem, and what has to be done. . . .

This was the abrasive clash here: our insisting that the crisis
demanded extraordinary acts, and Bobby retreating and saying,
no, and occasionally coming back and saying . . . well, implying
. . . that we were ungrateful; that we were insatiable, et cetera.
It was *the* most dramatic experience I had ever had.[22]

Members of the group did make some specific recommendations to Kennedy. Clarence Jones, for example, suggested
that the President make a series of televised speeches urging
the elimination of discrimination and that to prevent a recurrence of the Oxford situation the President himself escort the
first black students onto the University of Alabama campus.
Robert Kennedy rejected the latter proposal as senseless and
phony. As the meeting broke up, several participants, including Jones and Belafonte, expressed their appreciation to Kennedy privately for his efforts in Birmingham and elsewhere.
Belafonte told Kennedy that he had done more for civil rights
than any other Attorney General. Why, Kennedy asked, had
he not said this to the others? The singer explained that if he
had done so they would have thought he had "gone over to
the other side." [23]

Robert Kennedy left the meeting bitter and angry. He told
Arthur Schlesinger:

They didn't know anything. . . . They don't know what the laws
are—they don't know what the facts are—they don't know what
we've been doing or what we're trying to do. You couldn't talk to
them as you can to Roy Wilkins or Martin Luther King. They
didn't want to talk that way. It was all emotion, hysteria. They
stood up and orated. They cursed. Some of them wept and
walked out of the room.

He was particularly upset with the praise he received—in
private—at the meeting's end. In fact, he had been devoting
the major part of his time to civil rights for the past couple
months. He was in New York that day to urge businessmen

to desegregate; he was organizing similar meetings for the President to participate in; he was working within the administration for a major new civil rights bill; he had been deeply involved in the Birmingham crisis; and he was making the government's preparations for its impending confrontation with Governor George Wallace. Understandably he resented the steady stream of criticism that had been directed at him. Afterward he had Burke Marshall ask Al Rosen, an executive at the FBI, if the Bureau had "anything of interest" on the participants. But after a few days his anger subsided, and he reflected that if he had gone through what Jerome Smith had, perhaps he too might not want to defend the country.[24]

Well before this emotional encounter Robert Kennedy had become the moving force within the administration for a Presidential initiative on behalf of civil rights, but other highly respected counsellors like Theodore Sorensen, Kenneth O'Donnell, and Lawrence O'Brien urged caution in the name of political realism. Civil rights legislation might be impossible to pass, just as Mike Mansfield had said it was the year before. They also raised the argument that had guided Kennedy since his election—that a fight for civil rights might so antagonize Southern Democrats that they would block the rest of his program. In 1963 Kennedy was ardently seeking a Keynesian-type tax cut from a Congress where older economic views still held considerable power. The President thought the tax cut essential to the nation's economic growth and health. Moreover, prosperity was not immaterial to his own reelection prospects. Lyndon Johnson, too, believed that a civil rights fight would be a mistake. In early June, Norbert Schlei elicited his opinions. "The Vice President said that he was a team player and he would be as helpful as he could if the plan went forward as scheduled," Schlei reported to Robert Kennedy. "He said, however, that he thought the legislative proposal would be disastrous for the President's program and would not be enacted if submitted now." Johnson proceeded to reaffirm his own devotion to the cause of Negroes and made some useful practical suggestions on what the President might do to promote his legislation.[25]

President Kennedy undoubtedly recognized the ramifications of a legislative fight, but other concerns prevailed. Unless something were done the events in Birmingham would be duplicated repeatedly, as indeed they began to be almost immediately. Federal law generally did not reach the immediate cause of most such demonstrations —discrimination. Military occupation did not offer a desirable solution. It ran up a high political cost, was distasteful to Kennedy, and could not eliminate discriminatory practices anyway. The army could impose order but not institute justice. Since January 1961 the administration had influenced, though not controlled, the direction of the civil rights movement. The shift in emphasis from Freedom Rides to voter registration work reflected, in part, the administration's sway. But with Birmingham the civil rights movement appeared to pass it by. Street demonstrations became a popular, dramatic, and successful tactic. Black people were showing an unprecedented determination to acquire their rights immediately, and they might resort to extremism should they be thwarted. "The essence of Kennedy's civil rights strategy since inauguration," Sorensen candidly wrote in his memoir, "had been to keep at all times at least one step ahead of the evolving pressures, never to be caught dead in the water, always to have something new." In an unpublished recollection, he elaborated: "The situation was rapidly reaching a boil which the President felt the federal government should not permit if it was to lead and not be swamped." Perhaps most important, it was Kennedy's perception of himself as a decisive leader that affected him. Disturbed by the turbulence, Luther Hodges urged the President to make a television address appealing strictly for the preservation of law and order. Hodges told Kennedy he was being blamed for encouraging Negroes to disobey the law, and warned him of the political risks he ran by supporting civil rights. Kennedy conceded that his legislation might not pass and that his civil rights advocacy might cost him the next election, but believed that he had to proceed. "There comes a time when a man has to take a stand and history will record that he has to meet these tough situations and ultimately make a decision," Hodges vividly recalled the President telling him.[26]

Thus, it would seem, a number of factors caused Kennedy to change his civil rights strategy. Intellectually Kennedy had long believed in the principle of racial equality, but the disturbing events of the spring added an emotional dimension to that belief. Meanwhile, as a result of his frustrating encounters with diehard segregationists, he had thrown out an important historical assumption. Having abandoned the myth of Reconstruction as a "black nightmare," he could much more easily embark the nation on a Second Reconstruction. With Birmingham, American race relations seemed to be entering a period of crisis, yet the federal government lacked the necessary tools to deal with it. Thousands of blacks were taking to the streets to demand their rights—rights no federal law guaranteed. When local authorities proved obdurate and arrested or repulsed the demonstrators, a situation was created that both soiled America's reputation abroad and bred violence and extremism among blacks at home. Most important, in Kennedy's view, it fostered an atmosphere in which he could only weakly respond to events rather than direct and shape them. It cast him in a weak and defensive position when his personality and view of the Presidency called for decisive leadership and a measure of control over events. Kennedy recognized that a reversal of his strategy carried considerable risks, but inertia ran heavier risks still. Consequently he began to lay the groundwork for a major change in direction.

At the President's request, the Justice Department had

begun to consider a legislative solution to the racial crisis in early May. Burke Marshall quickly hit upon the idea of a public accommodations law. Most demonstrations had been directed at eliminating racially discriminatory practices in public facilities, such as lunch counters. By outlawing such practices, the federal government would go a long way toward removing the grievances that had sparked many demonstrations in the first place. In 1875 Congress had passed such a law, assuming it to be constitutional under the Fourteenth Amendment, but the Supreme Court had declared it unconstitutional eight years later; so Marshall proposed that the new law be based on the commerce clause of the Constitution which the court in recent years had interpreted broadly. At the moment seven sit-in cases were pending before the Supreme Court, involving the constitutionality of the arrest of blacks who had sat-in at lunch counters. The Justice Department anticipated that the Court would decide these cases against the Negroes, and believed that passage of a public accommodations law would offset "the wide frustrations and anger which such a decision would create." It took a more cautious approach to legislation protecting the right to demonstrate. Although a bipartisan group of twelve liberal Senators wrote the President in mid-May urging support of the old Title III formula, Robert Kennedy and Burke Marshall had serious reservations about this course. They feared that its enactment would necessarily involve the federal courts in the "business of police protection and the preservation of law and order." When that happened local police might completely abdicate their law enforcement responsibilities which could result in mob action. Inevitably, Title III would also place the federal courts in the position of controlling demonstrations. The Justice Department projected instances where "25 pickets may be reasonable but 100 would not. The Negro leaders nevertheless would want 100, and the fear of jail has largely been eradicated, particularly among young Negroes."

"To some degree," the Department predicted, "this would pit the federal government as well as local authorities against the Negro demonstrators with the result of increasing the division between the races in the United States." The Department also contemplated various kinds of school desegregation legislation, as well as the voting rights provisions and Civil Rights Commission extension proposed in the President's February 28 message. Finally, practically everyone involved in the early discussions, including the President, were sure that stiff Fair Employment Practices legislation would be impossible to pass, although they considered proposing a bill which would give statutory authority to the President's Committee on Equal Employment Opportunity.[27]

In the early stages of the discussions, the architects of the legislation at the Justice Department consulted few outsiders. They did use Louis Martin as a sounding board for the civil rights reaction. He responded very enthusiastically to the public accommodations idea and did not think that the absence of Title III would hurt. In mid-May the President apparently broached the subject with Democratic Congressional leaders, and shortly thereafter he informed the public that legislation was in the offing. At his press conference on May 22, a reporter inquired whether he intended to ask for new legislation. Answering affirmatively, the President indicated that the final decision would be made in a few days. He spoke of the need for developing a "legal outlet" as an alternative to demonstrations, and then noted:

I would hope that we would be able to develop some formulas so that those who feel themselves, or who are, as a matter of fact, denied equal rights, would have a remedy. As it is today, in many cases they do not have a remedy and therefore they take to the streets and we have the kinds of incidents that we have in Birmingham. We hope to see if we can develop a legal remedy.[28]

The administration did not expect civil rights legislation to win quick enactment, and so Robert Kennedy went ahead with his efforts to convince businessmen to desegregate voluntarily. Starting on May 22 he met with executives from variety, drug and department stores, theaters, hotels, and restaurants. Within two weeks, in part because of his work, he could report progress in more than forty cities. He also arranged for the President to meet with over one hundred businessmen in early June, and he helped plan future meetings on the subject of race relations at the White House for groups of lawyers, teachers, clergymen, and labor officials as well. The Kennedys hoped that these meetings, in addition to encouraging voluntary desegregation, would help build a national consensus in favor of the legislation.[29]

The establishment of a consensus, they anticipated, would put pressure on the Republicans in Congress whose cooperation they deemed essential to passage of the legislation. To this end, Robert Kennedy suggested that the administration emphasize that the legislation was needed to get Negro protesters "off the streets and into the courts," a key phrase which he coined. To end the tumultuous street demonstrations with their potential for violence it would be necessary to create a legal alternative or safety valve. Though this fundamentally conservative argument in part reflected the administration's underlying concern, the Kennedys decided very consciously to accentuate it in order to win Republican support.[30]

To build a consensus, the President used the occasion of a western tour to speak out more boldly on civil rights. In a commencement address on education at San Diego State College on June 6, he called for the elimination of segregation, *de jure* in the South and *de facto* in the North. Meeting with the Democratic State Committeewomen of California on June 8, he described the effects of discrimination in education. He pointed out that a basic federal Civil Service exam had been given in the South recently. Of 1,400 Negroes who took it, only 80 passed, an outcome that he attributed to discrimination. The following day in Honolulu, he devoted his entire speech before the United States Conference of Mayors to race relations. He asked the mayors "to be alert, not alarmed" at the demonstrations that were expected around the country over the summer. He requested their support for forthcoming legislation "which would help move these disputes off the streets and into the courts" by establishing uniform national law affecting all equally. In addition, he called on the mayors to accept their responsibilities to fulfill American ideals. He suggested that they establish biracial human relations committees, abolish local discriminatory regulations, hire without discriminating, enact equal opportunity ordinances, and encourage young people to get an education. The President declared that he was not asking them to do anything that the federal government was not doing. Specifically, he cited the antidiscrimination efforts being made in Washington, D.C. "We face a moment of moral and constitutional crisis," he concluded, "and men of generosity and vision must make themselves heard in every section of this country." [31]

Yet, Kennedy's pronouncements failed to capture national attention. In his influential column in the New York *Times* on June 9, James Reston criticized the President's leadership on civil rights. He wrote that Kennedy was not emotional enough about the racial crisis, that he was too cool and statistical. Kennedy, Reston continued, was political rather than philosophical, given to manipulation rather than education. In leadership he was well meaning but ineffective. Roy Wilkins expressed satisfaction with the administration's new moves, but Martin Luther King called Kennedy's approach to civil rights "inadequate" as compared to Eisenhower's "miserable" one. He accused the President of a failure of leadership and urged him not to proceed with a scheduled trip to Europe but to stay and fight for his civil rights legislation. Above all, King asserted, it was time for the President to address civil rights as a moral issue. Robert Kennedy, too, believed that the President should make a fervent speech to the nation. Other advisers again counselled caution, but the President agreed with his brother. He needed only the appropriate moment. George Wallace provided it.[32]

On the night of the Oxford riot, the President had asked his brother if there would be "any more like this one coming up soon." The Attorney General replied that he could expect to lose Alabama's electoral votes in addition to Mississippi's. A lawsuit to desegregate its university was already in the courts and was expected to reach the critical stage of enforcement in the spring of 1963. "Let's be ready," the President urged.[33]

Wallace, elected Governor of Alabama in 1962 on a strict segregationist platform, had promised "to stand in the schoolhouse door" to prevent integration. Senator John Sparkman brought the President some encouraging news in late November when he predicted that the "situation in Alabama is going to be much better than in Mississippi." University officials, according to Sparkman, did not intend to give Wallace the power that their counterparts in Mississippi had surrendered to Barnett. The university's trustees, faculty, and students were all concerned that the school's reputation would suffer as a result of violence. Editorial opinion from around the state shared that sentiment. Furthermore, Sparkman informed him, Wallace had on two separate occasions asked him to say to Robert Kennedy: "Please give Alabama as much breathing time as possible." Wallace also wanted the Attorney General to know that he was under no misapprehension that he could actually succeed in physically barring Negroes. The President pointed out to his brother that he and Sparkman had served with Wallace on the Democratic Platform Committee in 1952 "and this experience, the Senator thinks, can be helpful in some highly confidential talks with him." [34]

The ensuing weeks and months did not find Wallace in a

conciliatory mood however. "I'm gonna make race the basis of politics in this state, and I'm gonna make race the basis of politics in this country," he reportedly told a group of legislators before his swearing-in ceremony. Richmond Flowers, elected Attorney General with Wallace, took exception. Just before Wallace delivered his inaugural address, Flowers issued a statement warning that "to defy the same federal arm that speaks for America to Castro, Khrushchev, and Mao Tse-Tung . . . is only a chance to fight and can bring nothing but disgrace to our state, military law upon our people, and political demagoguery to the leaders responsible." Evoking the spirit of the Southern Confederacy, Wallace's speech breathed fire: "In the name of the greatest people that have ever trod this earth, I draw the line in the dust and toss the gauntlet before the feet of tyranny. And I say, Segregation now! Segregation tomorrow! Segregation forever!" He asserted that Southerners would use their combined electoral power in 1964 to determine the next occupant of the White House and warned federal judges and Washington officials that "we give the word of a race of honor that we will tolerate their boot in our face no longer." The Justice Department later got Flowers to try to talk sense to Wallace, but the Governor swore he would not compromise. "Dammit, send the Justice Department word, I ain't compromising with anybody. I'm gonna *make 'em* bring troops into this state," Flowers recalled Wallace telling him.[35]

At a meeting of the university's trustees on April 8, Wallace continued to talk belligerently. The university's president presented the details of the applications of two Negroes to the school's Huntsville branch. Wallace was adamant, and announced that he intended to call Senators Hill and Sparkman to have them ask that the Negroes be transferred away from Huntsville. Burke Marshall learned that he made these calls. "The Governor also said that he intended to call Werner Von Braun and tell him that an incident in Huntsville would be bad for the space program," Marshall informed Robert Kennedy. The Justice Department was also expecting Wallace to initiate investigations into the backgrounds of the two applicants.[36]

At this point, on April 25, Robert Kennedy went to Montgomery to try to reason with Wallace. The turning spools of a tape recorder made it plain that Wallace had no intention of being led into making any concessions that could be used against him later, in the moment of crisis, as had happened to Barnett. At the outset, Wallace stated that he was taping the conversation for "posterity," but he doggedly tried to extract a vow from the Attorney General that he would use troops, which suggested that Wallace had a more immediate political purpose in mind. It was strictly up to Wallace whether troops were necessary, Kennedy insisted. Much as Barnett had once done, Wallace contested the authority and propriety of the federal government requiring integration, but, in addition, he made explicit references to Presidential politics. He pointed out that John Kennedy had won in 1960 by carrying seven Southern states, many of them narrowly. Even in one where his margin of victory had been substantial, Alabama, Wallace predicted "the outcome would not be the same today." (Wallace also revealed that he had supported Kennedy's Vice Presidential candidacy in 1956, had contributed $250 to his 1960 campaign and had raised $1,000 more in his rural home county.) [37]

Following the meeting, Kennedy called on Grover C. Hall, Jr., editor of the Montgomery *Advertiser* and a confidant of Wallace. Hall said he had told Wallace that it would be foolish to stand in the doorway but that the Governor was committed. Shocked that Wallace could court violence like this so soon after Oxford, Kennedy asked whether there were any pressures, such as business opinion, that could be brought to bear on Wallace. There were none, replied Hall; Wallace would use his own influence with the Klan to prevent violence but would definitely stand in the doorway. That same day Wallace told an Alabama television audience that he had met with the Attorney General, and that he had not gone back on his pledges. He promised to keep his "covenant" with the people. He also noted that Robert Kennedy had not altered his position either. An Alabama ally soon reported to the Attorney General that most Alabamans were saying that he was a "good sport" for meeting Wallace "face to face." [38]

Despite Wallace's intransigence, the President tried to get through to him when he spoke at a Tennessee Valley Authority commemoration at Muscle Shoals on May 18. The TVA, Kennedy asserted, represented the great good that came from people of all sections of the country working together. He acknowledged that "from time to time statements are made labeling the Federal Government an outsider, an intruder, an adversary." Rejecting that view, he extolled the example that had been set by George Norris, the father of TVA, who came from McCook, Nebraska, 1,100 miles away from Muscle Shoals.[39]

With Senator Lister Hill and Congressman Robert Jones listening in, the President talked with Wallace on board a helicopter later in the day. Kennedy thanked Wallace for having seen the Attorney General, and Wallace replied that it was helpful to have such discussions and that he was happy that the President had come to Alabama. Kennedy then inquired about Birmingham. There were sufficient police on the scene to maintain law and order, Wallace answered. The situation would remain tense, the President countered, as long as no progress was made. Kennedy said he failed to understand why people who had Negroes serving tables in their homes could protest their working in downtown stores. The major problem in Birmingham, Wallace offered, was the influence of outside leadership. Most blacks did not support King, he maintained, and "had behaved themselves very well during the recent trouble." Wallace charged that King and Abernathy competed with each other to see "who could go to bed with the most nigger women, and white and red women too. They ride around town in big cadillacs smoking expensive cigars." Kennedy responded that outside leadership would not be necessary if the city made progress and noted that Birmingham's reputation was being ruined throughout the country and the world. He added that unless progress were made industries would leave the city. Again Wallace castigated King and averred that he could keep things under control in Birmingham. The conversation ended with Wallace expressing his admiration for the President and recollecting that he had campaigned for him in 1960. After Kennedy left the state, Wallace called a press conference to say that his conversation with the President had been cordial but that he had given no ground.[40]

Three days later the Justice Department organized a massive effort to exert economic pressure on Wallace. Winton M. Blount, president of a major construction company in Montgomery, President of the State Chamber of Commerce, and Trustee of the University of Alabama, supplied a list of the state's 375 leading executives. Burke Marshall sent it to Cabinet members and agency heads, requesting that they get in touch with anyone they knew personally. Marshall explained that Wallace intended to create a dangerous incident, that he was going to use state police to prevent the Negroes' admission, that he planned to make his own arrest or removal by force necessary as well as require the federal government to use troops. Wallace's behavior could well lead to violence, which would "unquestionably adversely affect the reputation and economy of the state," and damage the university. The Oxford violence had cost Ole Miss a serious loss of faculty and an estimated 50 percent decline in the number of tuition-paying out-of-state students. Wallace, Marshall added, stood alone in his defiance—his Attorney General, Lieutenant Governor, and most of the state's newspapers did not support him. Nearly 80 percent of the executives reached agreed to get in touch with Wallace personally or through subordinates. In this way the Kennedy administration tried to make sure that Wallace knew that the leading businessmen of his state opposed defiance.[41]

Wallace broke off communications with the administration, and as the day of confrontation neared, Robert Kennedy could only guess at what the Governor would do. In mid-May, John Doar learned, two Tuscaloosa police officials talked to Wallace about maintaining law and order. (The main campus of the university was located at Tuscaloosa and it now appeared likely that it, rather than Huntsville, would be integrated first.) The officials reported that Wallace flew into a rage, declaring that "law and order" was a communistic term. On May 31, the FBI reported that it had learned in confidence that Wallace intended to use state police to bar the entry of Negroes, which would necessitate the calling of federal troops. On June 4, Edwin Guthman heard from a Southern newsman that the whole thing was "greased," that Wallace would make a meaningless gesture and then step aside. The next day Frank Rose, the university's president, sent word that he had spoken to Wallace two days before and that Wallace had indicated that he would stand in the doorway, then withdraw gracefully. Claude Sitton of the New York *Times* also told the Department that Wallace had intimated to him that when pushed he would yield, but that he would also at the same time withdraw the state police. (It will be recalled that serious violence had followed the removal of the state police in Oxford.) But on June 5, an FBI informant revealed that Al Lingo, head of the state police, had called the Grand Dragon of the Ku Klux Klan at a Klan meeting. Lingo reportedly warned him that any known Klansmen seen in the Tuscaloosa area during the coming confrontation would be arrested on sight. Thus, the intelligence reports grew more encouraging over time, but public Klan meetings continued to be held in the area after Lingo's alleged warning. Meanwhile, Wallace activated five hundred National Guardsmen—to maintain order, not block the entrance, he said. Like Barnett in Mississippi, Wallace urged Alabamans to remain peaceful while he stood up for them against the encroaching government.[42]

President Kennedy, in the meantime, had decided not to use a large force of federal marshals. If the small number of mashals sent to implement the court's order were unable to do so he would deploy a large force of federalized National Guardsmen and other federal troops. He did not want a repetition of Oxford, where the withdrawal of the state police had left the undermanned marshals at the mercy of a mob. If Wallace's state police kept the mob rule down, there would be no need for the approximately six hundred marshals the government could muster. If they did not, many more federal men than the six hundred marshals would be needed. Of course, Kennedy would have preferred that Wallace not block the students' entrance and that Alabama police maintain order. The President hoped that if Wallace did stand in the doorway, federal officials could avoid arresting or pushing him, as he wanted to deny Wallace the martyrdom he seemed to be seeking.[43]

On the morning of June 11, with television cameras recording the event, Deputy Attorney General Nicholas Katzenbach confronted Wallace, who stood behind a lectern set up at the doorway to the building where students registered in Tuscaloosa. Each read a proclamation. Katzenbach's was from the President and ordered the Governor to stop blocking the implementation of a court order to admit the Negro students. Wallace's was his own, and denounced the purportedly unconstitutional intrusion of the federal government into Alabama's affairs. He went so far as to "forbid" the federal government's action. Katzenbach asked Wallace whether he intended to act on his defiance. After the Governor failed to reply, marshals and Justice Department lawyers accompanied the two Negro students to their dormitories without incident or interference. Simultaneously, the President federalized the National Guard. Later that day, General Henry Graham, commander of the Alabama–Mississippi National Guard, on behalf of the federal government and before the cameras, asked Wallace to step aside so that the students could register. The Governor thanked the citizens of his state for their restraint, asked for its continuance since the Guardsmen were their "brothers," saluted Graham, and moved aside. The two students registered.

Wallace had his moment in the national spotlight, but he carefully kept his defiance symbolic and did not violate a court order. He also fulfilled his responsibility to prevent violence. State and local police maintained security at the campus and all but a small detail of federal officials quickly left the school. University officials had earlier taken steps to prevent a student uprising. Thus, the Oxford disaster was not repeated. Two days later another black student registered at the university's Huntsville branch without Wallace's presence and without any difficulty.[44]

The events of June 11 provided the President with an excellent moment to address the nation on civil rights. Things had gone according to his fondest hopes. The students had been registered without difficulty. The campaign, both public and private, to moderate Wallace's behavior had evidently worked. In a springtime of uncertainty, it seemed a rare moment of unambiguous federal triumph. Although the legislative package was still not ready to go to Congress, Kennedy decided late in the day to request time from the networks for eight that evening. Sorensen did not even have time to complete writing the speech before he went on the air and Kennedy had to extemporize the conclusion.[45]

Kennedy delivered one of the most eloquent, moving and important addresses of his Presidency. It marked the beginning of what can truly be called the Second Reconstruction, a coherent effort by all three branches of the government to secure blacks their full rights. The issue, the President asserted, was primarily moral, "as old as the scriptures and . . . as clear as the American Constitution." Ascending what Theodore Roosevelt called the "bully pulpit," Kennedy preached:

> The heart of the question is whether all Americans are to be afforded equal rights and equal opportunities, whether we are going to treat our fellow Americans as we want to be treated. If an American, because his skin is dark, cannot eat lunch in a restaurant open to the public, if he cannot send his children to the best public school available, if he cannot vote for the public officials who represent him, if, in short, he cannot enjoy the full and free life which all of us want, then who among us would be content to have the color of his skin changed and stand in his place? Who among us would then be content with the counsels of patience and delay?

A principal reason he cited for taking immediate steps to secure Negroes their rights was the threat of violence which accompanied street demonstrations. "The events in Birmingham and elsewhere have so increased the cries for equality that no city or state or legislative body"—and, one could infer, no President—could "prudently choose to ignore them." Nationwide legislation must be passed "if we are to move this problem from the streets to the courts." Thus, Kennedy based his appeal primarily on moral dictates and social necessity.

In its desire to preserve the fabric of society, to provide a legal alternative to street demonstrations, Kennedy's argument could be construed as conservative. And in a sense it was, but it should be pointed out that most conservatives preferred to leave the underlying problems to local prerogatives even if that meant, as it almost necessarily did, strict police control of demonstrations. Kennedy, however, rejected that point of view. America, he argued, faced a "moral crisis" which could not be "met by repressive police action." He therefore wanted Congress, state and local government, as well as private citizens, to resolve the crisis by removing its causes. Hence, Kennedy also manifested a liberal's faith— that government had the duty and the ability to correct a deeply rooted social injustice.

Kennedy reiterated somewhat more familiar justifications for a new civil rights activism as well. In a manner reminiscent of his campaign, he graphically described the economic consequences of discrimination:

> The Negro baby born in America today, regardless of the section of the Nation in which he is born, has about one-half as much chance of completing a high school as a white baby born in the same place on the same day, one-third as much chance of completing college, one-third as much chance of becoming a professional man, twice as much chance of becoming unemployed, about one-seventh as much chance of earning $10,000 a year, a life expectancy which is 7 years shorter, and the prospects of earning only half as much.

The President still worried about the foreign implications of America's racial problem, but he had come to feel that the intrinsic moral issue was more important than what the world thought of America:

> We preach freedom around the world, and we mean it, and we cherish our freedom here at home, but are we to say to the world, and much more importantly, to each other that this is a land of the free except for the Negroes; that we have no second-class citizens except Negroes; that we have no class or cast [sic] system, no ghettoes, no master race except with respect to Negroes?

He also argued, as he and his brother had insisted all along, that the racial problem was national, not sectional, in scope. And he maintained that it was not a partisan issue, adding, it would seem hopefully, that "in a time of domestic crisis men of good will and generosity should be able to unite regardless of party or politics."

Assuredly Kennedy would need bipartisan support because he was asking Congress the following week "to make a commitment it has not fully made in this country to the proposition that race has no place in American life or law." To a considerable extent, the judiciary and executive branches were already committed, he explained, but the time had now arrived for Congress to provide "other necessary measures" which were in its domain alone. First, he wanted "legislation giving all Americans the right to be served in facilities which are open to the public—hotels, restaurants, theaters, retail stores and similar establishments." He noted that in the previous two weeks 75 cities had made progress toward desegregation of public facilities but observed that many were "unwilling to act alone." To accelerate the slow pace of school desegregation, Kennedy was asking Congress to authorize the government "to participate more fully in lawsuits." He also indicated that he would request legislation in other areas, including voting.

The address lacked the details required for legislation, but Kennedy was directing his remarks more to the public than to Congress. At the end he emphasized the moral responsibility that rested upon all Americans to ensure an equal opportunity in life to every child. Extemporaneously he concluded:

> As I have said before, not every child has an equal talent or an equal ability or an equal motivation, but they should have the equal right to develop their talent and their ability and their motivation, to make something of themselves.
>
> We have a right to expect that the Negro community will be responsible, will uphold the law, but they have a right to expect that the law will be fair, that the Constitution will be color blind, as Justice Harlan said at the turn of the century.
>
> This is what we are talking about and this is a matter which concerns this country and what it stands for, and in meeting it I ask the support of all our citizens.[46]

Public reaction to Kennedy's fervent new advocacy was rather mixed. In the three days after his speech, telegrams and letters to the White House ran over four-to-one in favor of the President's stand. On June 16, the Gallup poll asked a sample of the public if it believed that Kennedy was "pushing racial integration too fast or not fast enough," and 36 percent answered "too fast," 18 "not fast enough," 32 "about right," and 14 had no opinion. (The comparable percentages for Southern whites were 62, 4, 21, and 13 and for whites outside the South, 30, 17, 33, and 16.) Moreover, Kennedy's personal popularity plummeted in the South, obviously because of adverse white opinion. In June he attained only a 33 percent approval rating compared to 60 in March and 52 in late May. Unfortunately Gallup did not report on black public opinion in June, but civil rights advocates greeted the President's address enthusiastically. "A hallmark in the annals of American history," Martin Luther King called it. Roy Wilkins was pleased that Kennedy had posed the moral issue, though he observed that the address had failed to emphasize adequately the pressing problem of employment discrimination. Jackie Robinson, a Republican stalwart who had campaigned vigorously against Kennedy in 1960, announced that if the Presidential election were held the next day, he would vote for Kennedy.[47]

The signs from Congress, however, foretold an uphill fight to gain passage for the proposed legislation. The Republican leadership had met with Kennedy several hours before he went on the air. After the meeting, Everett Dirksen announced that Kennedy had asked for no pledges and had received none. He declared his and Charles Halleck's opposition to Fair Employment legislation, and he said he was unsure about the constitutional basis for public accommodations legislation. On June 12, seventeen Southern Democrats and one Republican, John Tower of Texas, caucused for 90 minutes. Afterward, Richard Russell, their leader, angrily denounced what he described as the threat of violence Kennedy had raised. The conservative Georgian vowed that he would be unaffected by such threats. A further omen came from the House on June 12 where a roll call was held on increasing the authorization for the Area Redevelopment Administration (ARA). The Democratic leadership was confident of passage, but it was defeated 209–204, as 18 Southern Democrats and 20 Republicans who had supported ARA in the past reversed themselves. "The [conservative] coalition is functioning again—and I predict it will keep on functioning for the remainder of the session," a leading Republican rejoiced.[48]

One thing did become instantly clear. Kennedy had not exaggerated by speaking of a crisis. This point received tragic confirmation when, several hours after Kennedy went off the air, Medgar Evers, the courageous leader of the NAACP in Mississippi, was murdered in ambush outside his home in Jackson. Evers's murder gave shocking evidence of the hatred that racism could breed and suggested the lengths to which some would go to halt the Second Reconstruction. His assassination touched off an angry response by Jackson's blacks, whose campaign for equal rights had met with powerful resistance and even violence by authorities. At the same time, in Danville, Virginia, in Cambridge, Maryland, in Gadsden, Alabama, in New York City, and in a rapidly growing number of places throughout the country, the pace, the intensity, and turbulence of a civil rights revolution were steadily increasing.[49]

TEN

Kennedy at the Center

Kennedy's speech on June 11 marked a turning point. With it he moved from the periphery to the center of the civil rights controversy. His subsequent campaign to convince the Congress and the nation to follow him into a Second Reconstruction came to dominate the nation's news. His efforts assumed importance not only for their potential impact on race relations, but for their complex political ramifications as well. Meanwhile the unfolding drama was heightened by the continued growth of the civil rights movement and the sometimes irrational resistance of Southern whites to social change.

THE President and his aides had two basic objectives in drafting civil rights bills to place before Congress—to obtain legislation that would deal with substantive problems of racial discrimination and that could be enacted. To a group of liberal Democratic Representatives, Burke Marshall from the Justice Department and Charles Daly of Lawrence O'Brien's staff "emphasized that the civil rights parcel was not being sent up as a political or public relations exercise, but as a serious program designed for passage." As the administration and its Congressional allies well realized, however, passage would not come easily. The cloture rule of the Senate stood as a particularly formidable barrier. "In present circumstances, there is only one practicable way in which this result [passage] can be assured," Mike Mansfield cautioned Kennedy, "by counting 67 votes on cloture for whatever bill is pushed. Any phraseology in the legislation, any parliamentary tactic or political statement which subtracts from the total of votes obtainable for cloture is to be avoided." [1]

Kennedy elicited Congressional opinion before sending up his specific requests. As expected, Congressional leaders were cool toward legislation for enforcing fair employment practices. Surprisingly, however, the administration found strong sentiment in favor of legislation that would require cutting off federal funds from discriminatory programs. Kennedy himself had recently opposed this principle when the Civil Rights Commission recommended it, but Democratic leaders saw it as an opportunity to deter future (Adam Clayton) Powell Amendments which had in the past defeated several pieces of social welfare legislation. By establishing a general rule, they hoped to make obsolete what had often been used as an obstructive ploy. Meanwhile the concept appealed to Republicans who tended to view it as an economy measure: if the government had to cut off funds because of discrimination, it would naturally be spending less money. (Perhaps too they reckoned that a Democratic administration would have to punish Democratic areas.) Initially Kennedy was inclined to request a fairly restricted public accommodations bill, one which he thought Congress would approve. But at the last minute he took the advice of John McCormack, Speaker of the House, that he seek a broad bill and then, if necessary, let Congress whittle it down. [2]

Eight days after addressing the nation on civil rights, the President sent his requests to Congress in writing. He placed even greater emphasis than before on the social necessity for national action and entreated Congress to stay in session until it had enacted an omnibus bill. In February Kennedy had asked for legislation to buttress voting rights, to provide technical and financial assistance to school districts which were desegregating, and to extend and revise the Civil Rights Commission. On top of these requests Kennedy now asked for a number of new measures. He proposed a broad law banning the segregation of public facilities and sought authority for the Attorney General to initiate proceedings against the segregation of schools. He also requested a comprehensive statute that would clarify the authority of federal administrators to use the purse strings to eliminate discrimination in individual programs but would not allow them to cut off all aid to an area "as a means of punishment."

Kennedy also renewed and expanded earlier requests for educational and training programs. These would assist the underprivileged and unemployed of all races but, as Kennedy pointed out, a disproportionate number of Negroes suffered from these conditions. To combat unemployment in particular he called for rapid approval of the tax cut he had proposed. On the economic front, too, he announced a number of executive actions he was taking to eliminate discrimination, specifically in the construction field and in apprenticeship programs. From Congress he sought a permanent statutory base for his Committee on Equal Employment Opportunity. The Justice Department, he asserted, had done "yeoman service" in mediating local racial disputes; "[b]ut the problem has grown beyond the time and energies which a few otherwise burdened officials can make available—and, in some areas, the confidence of all will be greater in an intermediary whose duties are completely separated from departmental functions of investigation or litigation." Consequently, he planned to create, by executive order, a Community Relations Service which he hoped Congress would later authorize by specific legislation.[3]

Two weeks before the delivery of the message, Mike Mansfield opened negotiations with his Republican counterpart, Everett Dirksen. In addition, the President conferred with Dirksen and Charles Halleck several times. On June 13 Dirksen agreed to act with Mansfield as co-sponsor of a bill which would include all of the administration's proposals with the exception of that relating to public accommodations. Dirksen also consented to allow Thomas Kuchel, his party whip and a liberal on civil rights, to join with Hubert Humphrey in sponsoring a bill that also included the administration's proposal to outlaw segregation in public accommodations. Mansfield, Humphrey and their aides, strongly believing "that the crucial factor [in getting the legislation enacted] was a common Mansfield-Dirksen-Republican front," emphasized the necessity of maintaining "complete communication between the two leaders . . . at every step of the proceedings." Mansfield told the President that without Dirksen's cooperation "the whole legislative effort in this field will be reduced to an absurdity," for Dirksen held the key to cloture. It would be up to Dirksen to persuade the crucial half-dozen to a dozen Republicans "who by inclination would not be for cloture" but whom Dirksen might win over on the grounds that it was in the "over-all political interest of the Republican Party in not getting behind the Democrats in this field." Mansfield warned that he had concluded from his conversations with Dirksen that the Republican leader would lose his persuasive power "if the impression develops that the Democratic Party is trying to make political capital." [4]

Thus, the soothing breezes of bipartisanship wafted through the Senate air on June 19, when the President's message arrived. Mike Mansfield introduced the administration's full bill and joined with Everett Dirksen in sponsoring a separate bill with identical language save for the omitted public accommodations title. The Majority Leader had feared that he would alienate Dirksen by sponsoring the whole measure, but the White House evidently believed that greater risks would be run if it seemed that Mansfield did not fully back the administration. These bills were referred to the Judiciary Committee. Simultaneously, Mansfield co-sponsored a separate public accommodations bill with Warren Magnuson, Chairman of the Commerce Committee, to which it was referred. (Since the Commerce Committee would undoubtedly

report a bill and the Judiciary Committee, under James Eastland's chairmanship, might well not, the bill's Democratic
managers anticipated that the full legislation could be offered
as an amendment to the public accommodations title.) Afterward Hubert Humphrey and Thomas Kuchel happily revealed that the administration's omnibus bill would have
eight Democratic and eight Republican principal co-sponsors.
(Altogether, 42 Senators attached their names to the bill.) Liberals of both parties hailed the spirit of cooperation that had
been established.[5]

Republican cooperation with the administration, however,
had distinct limits. Kennedy had called Dwight Eisenhower
to Washington on June 12 to try to enlist him in the cause;
but the former President reportedly told Kennedy, as well as
a group of Republican Congressmen, that passing a "whole
bunch of laws" would not solve the civil rights problem, although he did favor voting rights. Dirksen informed the Senate on June 19 that he could not support the public accommodations title because it was unenforcible and "would
contravene the Constitution and would be an invasion of a
private right." At a meeting of the House Republican Policy
Committee on June 18, Halleck observed that the civil rights
issue had political overtones, expressed pride in the Republican record on it, and attested that he had made "no commitment at all to the President." William McCulloch, the important senior Republican on the House Judiciary Committee,
commented that the Justice Department had not even evaluated the bills previously introduced by Republicans. On
June 27, Robert G. ("Bobby") Baker, who enjoyed a reputation for prescience in judging the mood of the Senate, where
he served as Secretary to the Majority Leader, reported to
Mansfield that the President's bill had only 47 sure votes. He
believed that a Mansfield-Dirksen bill, amended to include a
toned-down public accommodations provision, would command a solid majority but would have only a "50–50 chance

of securing cloture." Its fate, Baker expected, would rest with Republican Senators Aiken, Hickenlooper, and Dirksen. Although Republicans hardly agreed among themselves about civil rights, as members of a minority party they shared a partisan purpose, and on July 1 the Joint Senate-House Republican Leadership, consisting of eleven men of disparate views, issued a statement chiding Kennedy. Quoting the President and Attorney General on the need for Republican cooperation, they rebuked President Kennedy for his lack of leadership over his own party. "Is the Democratic party the true majority party in the United States as Mr. Kennedy contended in his 1960 Presidential campaign," they asked, "or is it, in fact, two minority parties over which he exercised little or no leadership or control?" "Given a Republican in the White House and Republican majorities in the Senate and the House," they concluded, "this country would get the leadership it needs." [6]

While the administration tried to win Republican support for its civil rights bill, it also strove to ameliorate Southern reaction against it. At Mansfield's suggestion, Robert Kennedy briefed Southern Democratic Senators about the bill on June 10. Columnist Jack Anderson reported that Kennedy expressed greater concern about racial tension in the North than the South and that the Senators discussed the issue with him calmly. Afterward, Richard Russell described the meeting as amicable. "We had a complete meeting of the minds," the senior Georgian remarked; "we agreed to disagree." President Kennedy hoped for the emergence of a Southern Vandenberg. That is, he hoped for a Southerner to break with the parochial politics of his region much as Senator Arthur Vandenberg had broken with Midwestern Republican isolationism in the 1940s to help forge a bipartisan foreign policy. Lister Hill and J. William Fulbright were favorite White House candidates for that role, but neither accepted. Kennedy teased his old Senate friend, George Smathers of Florida, about the arrival of the day when he would cast "that really courageous vote." Smathers did not come forward either.

The administration wanted to have its civil rights legislation enacted as quickly as possible. In his June 19 message, Kennedy asked Congress to stay in session until the bill was passed, and Mansfield expressed his willingness to do so. Kennedy only explained part of his reason for this—that the new laws were badly needed. In addition, he feared that as long as racial legislation was pending, Congress would tend to delay its approval of other important bills. After conferring in July with fourteen key Democratic Congressmen, including representatives from the South and border states, an aide to Robert Kennedy reported: "Southerners who will vote against administration [sic] on civil rights cannot, prior to that *agin* vote, put themselves in a position of cooperating with the administration and furnishing the margin of victory on other bills. After the civil rights vote they will be freer, having gotten their *agin* on the record." As this suggests, Kennedy was by no means writing off the Southern wing of his party.[7]

In addition to cooling Southern passions, the administration hoped to restrain the civil rights movement. Although heightened racial tensions had contributed significantly to Kennedy's decision to seek legislation, he feared that too much strife would retard the Congressional process. Congress would resent having a gun held to its head in the form of mob violence. Undoubtedly, too, the administration would, for reasons of its own, like to avoid a recurrence of a trying situation such as the one it had faced in Birmingham. As a practical politician, Kennedy probably also recognized that it would harm neither him nor the legislation if he called publicly for restraint. Hence, at the conclusion to his June 19 message to Congress he included a carefully worded plea to this effect. After granting that the recent demonstrations had focused the nation's attention on racial injustices, the President went on to say:

But, as feelings have risen in recent days, these demonstrations have increasingly endangered lives and property, inflamed emotions and unnecessarily divided communities. They are not the way in which this country should rid itself of racial discrimination. Violence is never justified; and, while peaceful communication, deliberation and petitions of protest continue, I want to caution against demonstrations which can lead to violence.

This problem is now before the Congress. Unruly tactics or pressures will not help and may hinder the effective consideration of these measures. If they are enacted, there will be legal remedies available; and, therefore, while the Congress is completing its work, I urge all community leaders, Negro and white, to do their utmost to lessen tensions and to exercise self-restraint. The Congress should have an opportunity to freely work its will. Meanwhile, I strongly support action by local public officials and merchants to remedy these grievances on their own.[8]

Kennedy amplified these arguments three days later when he met with a delegation of civil rights leaders. He pointed out that they needed the votes of Congressmen from small states who might be alienated by demonstrations, such as the proposed March on Washington the leaders were contemplating. Whitney Young of the Urban League observed that Kennedy's remarks about demonstrations were being interpreted to mean he opposed the march. "We want success in Congress," the President replied, "not just a big show at the Capitol. Some of these people are looking for an excuse to be against us. I don't want to give any of them a chance to say, 'Yes, I'm for the bill, but I'm damned if I'll vote for it at the point of a gun!'" A. Philip Randolph countered that the Negroes were already in the streets. Moreover, they might refuse their leaders' requests to leave the streets, and so the best hope was to lead them in a disciplined, nonviolent way. Kennedy readily agreed that the demonstrations had brought results. Indeed, they had caused him to act faster, he conceded, but now they were imperiling the legislation. Lyndon

Johnson added his voice to the President's. To obtain the critical votes necessary to stop a filibuster, Johnson remarked, "we have to be careful not to do anything which would give those who are privately opposed a public excuse to appear as martyrs."

James Farmer and Martin Luther King argued that they should go ahead with plans for the March in Washington. Farmer acknowledged the administration's difficult legislative problem, but noted that the civil rights leaders had a problem too. If they called off demonstrations and the proposed legislation were defeated, their followers might be so embittered that they would reject their leadership and resort to violence. King observed that every demonstration he had ever led seemed ill-timed, including Birmingham. He defended the March on Washington as a way of dramatizing the issue.

Kennedy shortly thereafter reflected that his own political fortunes were riding on the legislation. He said he had just seen a poll which indicated that public approval of the administration had fallen from 60 to 47 percent. (The origins and whereabouts of this poll remain a mystery. Gallup did not find a precipitous drop in public approval, although he did report significant disagreement with Kennedy's civil rights advocacy.) The President also warned that the controversy over civil rights was not only endangering his political future but was posing a threat to other essential legislation as well. He stressed the importance of their preserving "confidence in the good faith of each other." They all had their problems and would from time to time disagree on tactics, he suggested; "[b]ut the important thing is to keep in touch." As he was leaving the meeting, he added that Negro youths must be encouraged to take advantage of whatever educational opportunities were available to them.[9]

During June and July the President also tried to enhance the legislation's prospects for passage by holding a series of meetings at the White House for separate groups of businessmen, labor officials, clergymen, lawyers, women, and educators. In all, Kennedy met with over 1,600 people in what was a highly ambitious and unusual exercise of Presidential leadership. By these meetings he hoped not only to establish a broad consensus in favor of his legislation but also to encourage a variety of intermediate steps to combat discrimination. In every instance, of course, the President tailored his comments to the particular interests and attitudes of the groups he was seeing. The conferences produced tangible results as well as some affecting moments.[10]

At a meeting with labor leaders on June 13, the President acknowledged the strong support that they had given civil rights in the past. He attributed the high rate of Negro unemployment to three things: the overall job shortage, discrimination, and lack of training. By sustaining his economic measures before Congress and by expurgating discrimination from their own ranks, Kennedy asserted, the unions could combat all three. After describing some of the government's efforts to eliminate discrimination in federally funded employment, he opened the meeting to discussion. Walter Reuther made the most memorable comment, an impassioned plea for unions to admit blacks freely.[11]

The lawyers conference apparently had a more conservative tone. An unsigned background document in Lee White's files noted that many Southern lawyers believed that the administration had "affirmatively 'egged on' the Negroes to defy local laws and court decrees against demonstrations and violence." The document refuted that charge by enumerating instances where the Justice Department had urged Negroes to postpone or stop demonstrations or had successfully mediated an end to racial disputes. The "purpose of legislation and voluntary efforts," according to this document, was "to remove pressure for demonstrations and worse." However, this conference consisted of more than a conservative defense by the administration. The President also listed a number of practical things the legal profession could do to combat discrimination. At his request, Bernard G. Segal and Harrison Tweed, two prominent attorneys, formed the Lawyers' Committee for Civil Rights under Law, which became an influential lobbying group. Both Lyndon Johnson and Robert Kennedy delivered emotional talks on the racial problem. The Attorney General described the plight of one courageous Southern judge who had put the law ahead of racism. His community rewarded him with ostracism. The judge could endure that, but he had greater difficulty bearing the pain when the grave of his son, who had been killed in an automobile accident, was desecrated. [12]

The meeting with religious leaders provided an embarrassing moment but also yielded substantial results. A white Southern minister, who believed that segregation was a "principle of the Old Testament," asked the President if he knew of a way to get around moral and religious convictions against intermarriage. "I think the question of inter-marriage is really a question removed from what we are concerned with. That is a matter for the individuals wholly involved," Kennedy responded. No one's mind was likely to be changed on that subject, the President explained, but he hoped that all could agree on equality in education, jobs, and public accommodations. The conference with clergymen gave a powerful impetus to the creation of legislative lobbying by clerics. The clerical lobby would prove particularly valuable in winning over Congressmen and Senators from districts and states where blacks and labor groups lacked influence. [13]

Not surprisingly, the administration took its most conservative stance with the Business Council. Present at this July 11 meeting were approximately 60 of the Council's 118 members—many of the absentees were vacationing abroad—and about six other executives who did not belong to the Council. "This is, of course, a very sophisticated group in many ways and predominantly Republican," Lee White briefed the President. "It would seem appropriate to emphasize the national and nonpartisan character of the problem. In addition, it may be well to mention the foreign implications inasmuch as almost all of these companies have international activities." [14]

According to a memorandum Council Chairman Frederick Kappel prepared after the meeting, the President began by pointing out that the racial problem "had become critical and must be dealt with directly if the situation is to be kept within bounds." Moreover, the crisis was "being exploited abroad" and had "serious implications in our international relations." Vice President Johnson then spoke about Negro unemployment. If Negroes could be put to work, it would relieve welfare costs, Kappel recorded Johnson as saying, and "at the same time bring about a long range advance in helping society in general to be more self-supporting and self-respecting." Johnson commended the various programs for training workers and encouraging youth to return to school. Outlining the administration's legislation, Robert Kennedy said that the recent demonstrations had been provoked by segregation in public accommodations. Denial of access to public places and businesses was an insult to Negroes which kept "the pot boiling." Kappel wrote that the Attorney General "thought that what had been proposed was the minimum that would be required to overcome the obstacles to getting people off the streets and the situation under control."

After a general discussion, the President made several suggestions. He asked that Council members "take a hard, personal look at the employment situation in their respective companies." A lot had already been accomplished but things had reached a critical stage. "He did not want action that would discriminate against the employment of whites but he felt that in some circumstances business would be justified in going out and finding qualified Negroes in order to get programs started and established," Kappel reported. Kennedy asked Council members to support job-training programs for Negroes and observed that businessmen contemplating establishing operations in the South could be particularly helpful by hiring Negroes. Finally, he urged the businessmen to support the proposed legislation. If they had recommendations for improving the legislation, he would appreciate having them. Yet, Kappel noted, he added a warning:

> But in studying the legislation, we should consider what might happen if Congress failed to enact any legislation. He believed that legislation or some legal solution was going to have to come if not this year, then next or some future year, and that unless the emotion that is now behind the demonstrations is relieved fairly soon any real long-range solution is going to be increasingly difficult and less satisfactory.

At the meeting's conclusion, Kappel assured the President that the individual members would work constructively on their own, and that he would keep the problem before the membership. But, he cautioned, the Council did not assume positions on legislation nor did "it undertake to represent a point of view of its members as such." [15]

The value of lobbying with the Business Council remained to be seen, but the administration's efforts to persuade other businessmen to accept voluntary desegregation (the efforts had begun in earnest on May 22) paid handsome early dividends. By July 9 the Justice Department counted 177 cities in Southern and border states where some public facilities had been desegregated. In addition, another 22 cities reported "some concrete advance such as activities of a civic committee or the issuance of desegregation instructions by management." Altogether, then, some 40 percent of cities with a population over 10,000 in the South and in Border states registered some progress. To Louis Oberdorfer, the Assistant Attorney General who ran this project, these facts proved that the South was "not a monolithic bastion of resistance to desegregation," and showed that a great many people were "ready to make changes." Certainly the administration deserved credit for encouraging these changes, but Southern businessmen were aware of the adverse economic consequences that racial upheaval held for them and faced up to the need for change. "I'm no integrationist," Sidney Smyer, a real estate executive who headed the white negotiating team in Birmingham, told a reporter, "but I'm not a goddam fool, either." [16]

In addition to its behind-the-scenes campaign of persuasion, administration spokesmen paraded before the relevant Congressional committees to educate the public and their representatives. For example, Secretary of State Dean Rusk, whose soft drawl reflected his Georgia upbringing, described to the Senate Committee on Commerce the several ways discrimination damaged the image of the United States abroad. He made clear at the outset, however, that he considered the foreign policy aspects to be secondary. More important than the country's foreign image, he asserted, was its democratic ideal. He described the nature of Communist propaganda about American racial discrimination, and discussed the problems caused by the discriminatory treatment of non-white diplomats and visitors in the United States. A harsh interrogation by South Carolina's Strom Thurmond failed to ruffle the Secretary of State, and at the end of his testimony he received a standing ovation from the audience. Rusk's well publicized performance undoubtedly pleased the President, but the administration did not reveal that the Cabinet's other Southerner, Luther Hodges, refused to testify for the bill. It was a North Carolina newspaper that headlined that story in mid-August. [17]

Robert Kennedy, the administration's most important witness for the civil rights bill, testified repeatedly—always cogently and often passionately. On the opening day of hearings before the Senate Commerce Committee on the public accommodations bill, he proposed three tests for the bill: Was there a need to end discrimination in public accommodations? Did Congress possess the authority to end it? Was action by the federal government necessary? He answered yes to all three questions. Here, in contrast to comments he made before the Business Council, he emphasized the moral issue. The legislation, he argued, was needed, not to stop disorder, but to prove "to millions of our fellow citizens the very premise of American democracy—that equal rights and equal opportunity are inherent by birth in this land." It would be better, the President's brother observed, if the localities and states were to deal with the problem of discrimination, but it was clear that many would not:

> We believe therefore that the Federal Government has no moral choice but to take the initiative. How can we say to a Negro in Jackson:
> "When a war comes you will be an American citizen, but in the meantime you're a citizen of Mississippi and we can't help you."
> How, by any moral standards, can we tell our Negro citizens:
> "Our forefathers brought your forefathers over here against their will, and we are going to make you pay for it."
> Yet isn't that just what the argument boils down to?
> The United States is dominated by white people, politically and economically. The question is whether we, in this position of dominance, are going to have not the charity but the wisdom to stop penalizing our fellow citizens whose only fault or sin is that they are born.

He opened his testimony before the Senate Judiciary Committee in a similar vein with a graphic illustration of the inhumanity of discrimination. He pointed out that according to two current tourist guidebooks, there was only one establishment where a Negro could obtain overnight lodgings in Montgomery, Alabama, and none in Danville, Virginia. Yet, a dog, traveling with a white person, was welcome to stay in five places in Montgomery and four in Danville.[18]

The Attorney General spent a large portion of his time before the Senate Judiciary Committee debating with North
Carolina's Sam Ervin on the merits and constitutionality of
the administration's bills. Ervin did not ground his opposition to civil rights legislation on racial theory or on the argument that the racial problem was best left to the states and
localities to deal with as they saw fit. Rather, he argued that
existing criminal statutes covering official misconduct were
all that the federal government needed to protect the right to
vote. He insisted that most of the proposed legislation, as
well as portions of the 1957 and 1960 Civil Rights Acts the
Supreme Court had already found constitutional were in fact
unconstitutional. Ervin also invoked memories of Reconstruction:

> I do not wish to see Congress repeat the follies of Reconstruction
> days. I cannot forget the fact that under the Reconstruction acts
> we had a federal garrison stationed in my hometown until about
> the year 1874 and that I have been informed by the older men of
> my community that when they went to the polls in 1868, they
> had to march to the polls under the supervision of Federal troops.

Ironically, some of the Justice Department's strongest critics
from the opposite direction to Ervin, such as Howard Zinn,
also believed that the existing criminal statutes provided a
sufficient legal basis for protecting the right to vote. However, they wanted to use these laws precisely to institute the
kind of forceful Reconstruction Ervin abhorred.[19]

Ervin jousted with Kennedy on the field of constitutional
law, but the Attorney General proved an adept combatant,
able frequently to exchange precedent for precedent with the
former judge from North Carolina. Still, Robert Kennedy preferred to deal with substantive social problems rather than
strictly with matters of law. Therefore he repeatedly tried to
engage Ervin in a discussion of discrimination itself. When
Ervin, at one point, stated that he had no personal knowledge
of the existence of discrimination in Mississippi, Kennedy

quickly offered to send him there with Burke Marshall as his guide. The Senator declined the offer, explaining that he could not spare any time from his fight to "preserve constitutional principles and the individual freedoms of all citizens of the United States." [20]

In addition to testifying publicly, the administration continued to lobby key Congressmen privately. The Justice Department's ranking officers assiduously heard out and courted those moderate and conservative Republicans and border and western state Democrats whose votes they deemed critical. Robert Kennedy even held a series of boat parties for these Congressmen. This lobbying process, though absolutely essential, proved slow and sometimes discouraging. For example, on July 22 Burke Marshall reported to Nicholas Katzenbach, who served as chief of operations, of conversations that he and the Attorney General had held in which they heard that two important Republicans, Representative William McCulloch of Ohio and Senator George Aiken of Vermont, believed that Republicans would back the legislation if the public facilities to be covered were more specifically identified. McCulloch dismissed as "superficial" the contention of liberal Republicans on his committee that the public accommodations title had to be based on the Fourteenth Amendment rather than the commerce clause. On the other hand, Senator Bourke Hickenlooper of Iowa, another influential Republican, did not believe that the commerce clause could be the constitutional basis for the public accommodations title. As a matter of fact, Hickenlooper did not even know what the administration's bill contained; he had the false impression that it included the old Title III, which he adamantly opposed. Yet, Marshall wistfully concluded, Hickenlooper had not "crystallized a position against the legislation, and may follow others." Democratic Senator Mike Monroney of Oklahoma, too, had such strong convictions about the limitations of the commerce clause that it did not seem possible to persuade him "to support the public accommodations title in its present form." To make matters worse, Monroney would give no clues as to what changes had to be made before he could vote for this provision. He did find the rest of the bill satisfactory, however.[21]

Lobbyists from civil rights and liberal organizations worked hard to generate support for the legislation. On July 2 Roy Wilkins convened a meeting of national organizations interested in passage of civil rights legislation. These groups recognized that it was essential to win over fence straddlers, but they also wanted the legislation expanded to include an explicit Fair Employment Practices Commission and an across-the-board Title III. In the following weeks, spokesmen for these organizations publicly called for stiffer legislation in the other areas as well. In view of the rather meager results of Congressional struggles in 1957 and 1960 and the build-up in the movement's force in the 1960s, it was understandable that they were now seeking the maximum.[22]

The zeal of these advocates, however, presented a problem for the White House and Justice Department. Liberals dominated the House Judiciary subcommittee, which was handling the bill initially. The administration worried that civil rights lobbyists would succeed in getting these liberals to include provisions that would arouse sufficient opposition, in either the full committee or in the chambers of Congress, to endanger the whole bill. For example, a majority of the subcommittee wanted the bill to use the words "Fair Employment Practices." The administration found nothing objectionable in those words, but it beseeched those liberals who wanted to include them to demonstrate that they commanded the necessary Republican votes for passage. The problem of civil rights zealotry was compounded by the pledge William McCulloch had extracted from the Justice Department that whatever was passed by the House, which was to act first, would not be traded away in the Senate. Previously the

House had approved broad civil rights legislation only to see it eviscerated by the Senate. The administration had expected that provisions of the House bill would again be compromised in the Senate, but McCulloch would have none of it. His determination was probably no more and no less than an expression of pride in the work of the House and of its Judiciary Committee. Nonetheless, the administration's commitment to McCulloch meant that the House bill had to be kept within reasonable bounds, which the administration endeavored to do.[23]

The administration proceeded cautiously, uncertain how a majority of Congress would react not only to the contents of its civil rights bill but also to the antidiscrimination measures emanating from the executive branch. The administration did, however, continue to pursue a vigorous program of executive action. At meetings of the President's Committee on Equal Employment Opportunity, Robert Kennedy several times sharply reproached its staff director, and indirectly its chairman, Lyndon Johnson, for failing to follow through on enforcement. The White House also continued to appoint blacks to executive positions in government. Still, the President several times manifested a fear of offending members of Congress with executive fiats. He realized that his advocacy of civil rights legislation was already straining his relations with Southern Democrats, whose votes he needed for other priority legislation such as the tax cut.[24]

An episode involving the military illustrated the President's heightened concern about offending Southern Democrats. In the spring, Adam Yarmolinsky, an aide to Secretary of Defense Robert McNamara, had asked Lee White about the requests of airmen in South Dakota who were seeking permission to participate in antidiscrimination demonstrations while out of uniform and off-duty. White could see nothing wrong with the requests, and the Air Force quietly granted them. The permissions did receive some publicity, however, and Governor George Wallace lashed out at them when he testified against the civil rights bill before the Senate Commerce Committee in July. "Perhaps," the Governor remarked, "we will now see Purple Hearts awarded for street brawling." McNamara quickly disallowed the practice. In the meantime, the President upbraided White for having authorized it in the first place. He ordered White to warn every department and agency official who might wish to duplicate the Air Force's action to clear it with the White House first.[25]

When the administration's efforts to combat discrimination in federal employment evoked an angry reaction, the President responded in a manner calculated to placate. Over the summer, the Dallas *Morning News*, an extremely conservative newspaper, and Congressman Bruce Alger, a right-wing Texas Republican, charged that the Post Office and Civil Service had given preferential treatment in appointments and promotions to blacks. In response, Congressman Joe Pool of Dallas, a fairly senior Democrat, succeeded in having an investigation of "discrimination in reverse" begun by a subcommittee of the House Post Office and Civil Service Committee. John W. Macy, Jr., Chairman of the Civil Service Commission, assured the White House that the allegations lacked substance. Taking no chances, the President seized an early opportunity to present his views on preferential treatment. At a press conference on August 20, a reporter asked him to comment on the suggestion by some Negro leaders that blacks were entitled to "special dispensation for the pain of second-class citizenship over these many decades and generations." He also sought the President's opinion specifically on the subject of job quotas based on race. Kennedy responded that most Negroes did not want special treatment, only equal treatment, particularly in education. The past, the President reflected, could not be undone. "We have to do the best we can now," he explained, but quotas would cause "a good deal of trouble."

Our whole view of ourselves is a sort of one society. That has not been true. At least, that is where we are trying to go. I think that we ought not to begin the quota system. On the other hand, I do think that we ought to make an effort to give a fair chance to everyone who is qualified—not through a quota, but just look over our employment rolls, look over our areas where we are hiring people and at least make sure we are giving everyone a fair chance. But not hard and fast quotas. We are too mixed, this society of ours, to begin to divide ourselves on the basis of race or color. [26]

Another incident demonstrated Kennedy's reluctance to use executive action during the debate over the administration's civil rights bill. In June he had extended his executive order on equal employment opportunity to construction contracts financed wholly or in part by the federal government. As a consequence, a contract provision was developed requiring state highway departments that were receiving funds to assume the burden of enforcement. When Louisiana highway officials learned of the provision they balked, but the federal highway administrator refused to waive the regulations. A state official therefore complained to Senator Russell Long and Congressman Hale Boggs, warning that the administration was trying to embarrass them. Long phoned Kennedy, who prevailed upon the highway administrator to waive the regulations for contracts being let in August. After a similar situation occurred before the September lettings, the President's Committee on Equal Employment Opportunity adopted revised regulations eliminating the stiff requirement. In a memorandum Lee White prepared for the President as background for his meeting with Louisana's Governor, he recapitulated the tangled series of events and observed: "The Governor might be interested to know that the question raised by Louisiana was considered, found to be valid, and corrective action taken. Of course, the less that is said about this in the newspapers, the better off everyone will be." [27]

A highly sensitive matter involving Martin Luther King also reflected Kennedy's wariness of Congress. A number of segregationists (including George Wallace) who testified against the civil rights bill charged that Communists were behind the recent demonstrations and behind King. One of their favorite pieces of evidence was a picture of King in the company of alleged Communists at the Highlander Folk School in Tennessee. Neither the public nor Congress gave much credence to these charges, but Senator Mike Monroney of Oklahoma, one of those whose support for the civil rights bill the administration considered essential, apparently was concerned about them. In a letter dated July 23, which Robert Kennedy made public, the Attorney General assured Monroney that civil rights groups had successfully resisted Communist efforts to infiltrate them. Privately Burke Marshall informed Monroney about "the most serious efforts" that they knew of "by Communists to infiltrate the Southern Christian Leadership Conference." Marshall told Monroney that, at the direction of the President, he had informed King of the probable Communist Party affiliation of two associates, Hunter Pitts O'Dell, a staff member of SCLC, and Stanley Levison, a New York lawyer and long-time friend, advisor, and contributor to King. Subsequently, King fired O'Dell and "discontinued all open connection with Levison." [28]

In his letter terminating O'Dell's services on July 3, 1963, King did not mention any involvement of the White House. Rather, he reiterated facts already familiar to O'Dell. Several months before, O'Dell had submitted his temporary resignation pending an investigation by SCLC into charges brought by newspapers in Birmingham and New Orleans that he was a Communist. It was, King wrote, "SCLC's firm policy that no Communist nor Communist sympathizer" be allowed on its staff or in its membership. Although SCLC had not been able to find any connection between him and the Communist Party, King wrote him, it had decided to make his resignation permanent. "In these critical times we cannot afford to risk" even the impression of Communist infiltration, King explained. He thanked O'Dell for the "years of unselfish service" and compared his sacrifice to "the sufferings in jail and through loss of jobs under racist intimidation." [29]

King continued to communicate with Levison privately. He maintained the utmost confidence in his friend's integrity and accepted his word that he was not a Communist. Indeed, before long their relationship was as close as ever. J. Edgar Hoover learned of this fact either from a source within the FBI or from information supplied by a local police department. (Apparently several police departments had King under surveillance—possibly illegal electronic surveillance.) Hoover had held King in the lowest regard at least since the time King criticized FBI performance in 1962, and perhaps since the day he first heard of the civil rights leader's friendship with people whom he regarded as Communists. When he was informed that King had resumed his friendship with Levison after he had agreed to terminate it, Hoover saw confirmation of his worst suspicions about the minister. The FBI began to circulate memoranda first to the Justice Department and then to other agencies and the White House to the effect that Levison was a continuing evil influence upon King. In order to lay Hoover's suspicions to rest and to eliminate the possibility that FBI data would leak to members of Congress, which could damage the prospects of the civil rights bill, Robert Kennedy authorized a tap on King's telephone in the fall. While of questionable ethical propriety, the tap was legal. In any case, it was another instance of the Kennedy administration's unusual sensitivity to the possibility of any adverse reaction in Congress that might hurt the chances for passage of the civil rights bill.[30]

This sensitivity had in part prompted Kennedy to urge restraint with respect to street demonstrations, but the eruption of social unrest which had started in the spring continued unabated. According to Justice Department records, there were 978 demonstrations in 209 cities in the period from May 20 to August 8. Protests against segregation in public accommodations accounted for the largest number, 453, of these demonstrations. In July, *Newsweek* published a survey by Louis Harris which indicated that forty percent of the 1,257 Negroes interviewed had "taken part in a sit-in, marched in a mass protest, or picketed a store." The Justice Department tried to act as mediator in some of the more explosive situations. Robert Kennedy personally intervened in crisis-racked Cambridge, Maryland, to work out a short-lived truce. In Danville, Virginia, the Department filed an unprecedented brief to remove criminal cases growing out of a protest campaign from an unfair local court to a federal court, but the federal judge hearing the dispute was unmoved by it. In Gadsden, Alabama, Joseph E. Nolan, a Justice Department executive, served in a capacity similar to that of Burke Marshall in Birmingham. The Justice Department, however, had neither sufficient personnel available nor the necessary legal resources to do the job of mediation on much more than an ad hoc basis. Understandably the Department eagerly anticipated the funding by Congress of the Community Relations Service.[31]

An increase in the number of complaints about police brutality accompanied the rising tide of demonstrations. On July 18, Hyman Bookbinder of the Eleanor Roosevelt Foundation, formerly an administration official with civil rights responsibilities, reported to Lee White that in the two previous days four civil rights leaders had raised the problem of police brutality with him. They believed, he related, that the administration was "not particularly concerned about the recent indignities and cruelties which have been visited upon civil rights prisoners, especially women." Bookbinder proposed that the President appoint a special committee of inquiry, headed by someone like Ralph McGill, to look into the matter. White passed on the recommendation to Burke Marshall.

Preoccupied with the legislative struggle and doubtful about finding any solutions to this problem, Marshall suggested instead a meeting of law enforcement officials. Perhaps the appearance of another and even more brutal Bull Connor would have sparked public, Congressional, and Presidential interest in police brutality, but in his absence the problem received relatively little attention.[32]

A federal prosecution of civil rights activists in Albany, Georgia, angered some people in the movement but failed to arouse national concern. On August 9, a federal grand jury, after months of investigation, indicted eleven persons, primarily blacks, and including five leaders of that city's racial protests. They were charged with obstruction of justice and perjury. The government claimed the defendants had picketed the store of a white juror in retaliation for his having voted for the acquittal of a sheriff charged with brutality against a Negro prisoner. The local U.S. Attorney, unsympathetic to the Albany Movement, according to Burke Marshall, brought the case, but despite his sympathies, Robert Kennedy would not quash it. It was particularly galling to members of the Albany Movement that the indictments followed an investigation by a large number of FBI agents. The FBI had never been much help to Albany's blacks when they were the victims of brutality. "It seems to be a great disparity when my pregnant wife is kicked to the ground and beaten by a police in Camilla, Georgia. She later loses the baby and yet the Federal Government says that there is nothing that they can do," [sic] Slater King, President of the Albany Movement and one of those indicted, wrote Constance Baker Motley. Several months later Slater King lamented to Joni Rabinowitz, a co-defendant, that there had been "little or no publicity concerning our cases." He was particularly "disgusted" that SCLC had let them down by failing to publicize their plight. (The Albany defendants were found guilty, but their convictions were overturned on appeal.) [33]

One act of protest did capture national attention—the March on Washington. On August 28, more than 200,000 people, perhaps a quarter white, marched in the nation's capital. Bayard Rustin, a socialist who had conceived the demonstration in December 1962, originally thought it would have chiefly an economic orientation, that its primary purpose would be to demand jobs, a higher minimum wage, and a guaranteed income. But by the summer the March on Washington Movement comprised a great number of organizations sympathetic to civil rights. The inclusion of so many groups shifted the focus to support for the passage of the civil rights legislation. To maintain a consensus, militant tactics, such as a sit-in at the Capitol, were rejected. Similarly, March organizers prevailed upon John Lewis, chairman of SNCC, to tone down his speech. Angered by the Albany prosecutions and by what he considered the federal government's poor record in the area of police protection, Lewis had planned what came close to being a denunciation of the civil rights bill. The milder but still powerful speech Lewis delivered did point out that the administration's bill contained nothing to protect Negroes from violence and brutality—no Title III—and that the voting rights section would not succeed in getting Negroes registered. Roy Wilkins, too, endorsed a strengthening of the President's proposals. Martin Luther King, however, climaxed the day with a magnificent oration. Rather than dwell on government policy, King described the grim realities of racial discrimination, then raised hopes for a new day. The massive assembly responded tumultuously as King pictured in richly poetic and Biblical language his dreams for America. With millions more watching on television or listening on the radio, this most charismatic of all civil rights leaders concluded his unforgettable celebration of freedom:

When we let freedom ring, when we let it ring from every village and every hamlet, from every state and every city, we will be able to speed up that day when all God's children, black men and white men, Jews and Gentiles, Protestants and Catholics, will be able to join hands and sing in the words of that old Negro spiritual, "Free at last! Free at last! Thank God almighty, we are free at last!" [34]

Worried about the possible effects on Congress, the President had initially cautioned civil rights leaders against the march, but when they proceeded anyway he gave the demonstration his imprimatur. At a press conference on July 17, Kennedy characterized the march as "a peaceful assembly calling for a redress of grievances, . . . in the great tradition." Some civil rights supporters, in Congress and out, believed the march would be a tactical error. Emanuel Celler and House Majority Leader Carl Albert feared it would create opposition to the bill. A number of border state Democrats in the House told Joseph Dolan that a march would not bother them but were worried that their constituents at home would think they had been pressured by it if they then voted for the bill. Therefore, it would make it harder for them to back the bill. Similarly, though a number of labor unions participated in the march independently, the AFL-CIO Executive Council refused to endorse it. The administration, meanwhile, had accepted the march's inevitability and undertook to see that everything went smoothly. Members of the Justice Department, employees of the Democratic National Committee, as well as Stephen Smith, the President's brother-in-law, worked behind the scenes with the committee supervising the march and with District of Columbia officials to arrange an orderly and peaceful demonstration. [35]

Political caution dictated that Kennedy keep some distance between himself and the demonstration. He did not address the march, according to Sorensen, because he knew that he would have to fashion his comments for a national audience and the huge crowd might react unfavorably to his speech. Likewise, he did not confer with its leaders immediately before the march because if they should present him with a list

of demands he would not or could not meet, the march might
become a demonstration against him. He did, however, see
its ten principal leaders, including Lewis, after its conclusion.
Kennedy was delighted with the way the march had been
conducted and, like most of those who had heard it, was
deeply impressed with King's stirring address. Indeed, he
greeted the leaders late in the afternoon with the refrain from
King's peroration, "I have a dream." Kennedy thanked them
for the kind of demonstration they had conducted, and
quickly moved the discussion to the Congressional situation.
He called upon them to devote their energies to securing the
passage of the civil rights bill.[36]

The march probably had no significant effect on the legislative process itself, but it did create a favorable impression of
the civil rights movement among the public. The impressive
demonstration had graphically depicted the commitment of
masses of people, black and white, to the goal of racial equality. Never before in American history had there been a gathering of this size. Although civil rights leaders and organizations had sometimes been at odds with each other over
tactics, in this important instance they had worked effectively
together. Moreover, the numerous prayers, hymns, and Biblical references which emanated from the podium repeatedly
emphasized the central place that religion held in the movement. Above all, the march illustrated that when Negroes and
their supporters were treated decently, they would act re-
sponsibly and peacefully. "Many had been fearful of disor-
ders; I among them," Emanuel Celler offered. But "[t]here
was no bitterness where bitterness could have been expected.
There was no racism in reverse," he went on. The President
observed in a statement that was made public:

One cannot help but be impressed with the deep fervor and the
quiet dignity that characterized the thousands who have gathered in the Nation's Capital from across the country to demonstrate their faith and confidence in our democratic form of gov-

ernment. . . . The leaders of the organizations sponsoring the March and all who have participated in it deserve our appreciation for the detailed preparations that made it possible and for the orderly manner in which it has been conducted.[37]

Soon after the March on Washington had dramatically shown the nation one kind of commitment, George Wallace demonstrated another kind. On September 2 the Alabama Governor issued an executive order to prevent the opening of Tuskegee High School, which was to be desegregated. Proclaiming that he was trying to preserve peace, Wallace surrounded the tranquil school with state troopers. The next day black students entered formerly all-white schools in a number of Southern cities, including Charleston, Baton Rouge and Memphis, but in Alabama the Governor stood fast against change in the four cities that were slated to initiate desegregation in his state. Local officials resented Wallace's interference, however. "The very thing that Governor Wallace decries in Federal intervention he would himself impose upon Birmingham if state troopers were sent in for Wednesday's opening," George Seibels, a Birmingham City Councilman, said. On September 4 two black children registered at a white elementary school in that city without incident. But later in the day a bomb destroyed the home of Arthur D. Shores, a Negro lawyer. A riot by angry blacks erupted. Despite the efforts of civil rights leaders to stop it, before it ended a number of persons were injured and a young black man was killed by gunfire, reportedly from the police. Subsequently, the Birmingham school board closed three white schools that were supposed to desegregate. In Washington, meanwhile, a spokesman for Robert Kennedy voiced the suspicion "that Wallace is trying to provoke us into opening the school by force. We would rather not accommodate him if it can be avoided." Court orders, he asserted, would be enforced. In addition, it was reported that the Attorney General had ordered the FBI to investigate the bombing.[38]

Wallace persevered in his resistance, but opposition to his tactics built up within Alabama as he dispatched state troopers to four more schools that were scheduled to desegregate. In Huntsville, one of the affected cities, the police chief characterized the Governor's action as a "tyrannical use of power." The state police were neither invited nor required, he explained. The Mayor and City Council wired Wallace to remove his forces. Even the Montgomery *Advertiser*, a staunch supporter of Wallace in the past, found the Governor's behavior repugnant. "The Advertiser must sorrowfully conclude that, in this instance, its friend has gone wild. Alabama is not a banana republic. It is in no need of an adventurer to ride down upon local authority," it editorialized.[39]

Wallace began to relent. While he promised an audience of ardent segregationists that he would "go the last mile," he reportedly assured school boards in Mobile and Huntsville that he would not interfere. In a statewide television address on September 8, Wallace announced that he would permit schools to open in the four affected cities, and the next day Wallace did nothing to stop four black youngsters from attending previously all-white Huntsville schools. Several hours later all five federal district court judges in Alabama, acting at the request of the Justice Department, enjoined Wallace from halting desegregation. With that, the Governor called out the National Guard. In a statement from the White House, the President pointed out that desegregation had been carried out peacefully in 144 school districts. "In the State of Alabama, however," Kennedy went on, "where local authorities repeatedly stated they were prepared to carry out court directives and maintain public peace, Governor Wallace has refused to respect either the law or the authority of local officials. For his own personal and political reasons—so that he may later charge Federal interference—he is desperately anxious to have the Federal Government intervene in a situation in which we have no desire to intervene." [40]

Early the next morning the President federalized those

units of the Alabama National Guard that had taken up positions around schools in the four cities. In Birmingham, segregationist protestors demonstrated, but police, rather than
troops, maintained order. Meanwhile, in Mobile, Tuskegee,
and Huntsville calm prevailed. In this way, public school
desegregation made its entrance into Alabama. Local authorities and citizens accepted their responsibility to abide by federal law. Wallace had only succeeded in delaying the inevitable by a few days, and in garnering more notoriety for
himself—which was probably all he wanted in the first
place.[41]

After a respite of only a few days, Alabama leaped back
into the news. On September 15, a bomb exploded at a black
church. Four little girls were killed as they sat in their sab-
bath finery in Sunday school class. Fourteen other persons
were injured. The explosion caused extensive damage to the
church and surrounding property. Enraged at this dastardly
act, young blacks rioted sporadically throughout the day, setting fires, and hurling rocks at the police, who responded
with greater force and shot and killed two blacks. Martin
Luther King immediately demanded federal intervention and
the next day joined with 150 Negro business and professional
people in proposing that the Army take over the city. President Kennedy, the same day, issued a statement "on behalf
of all Americans. . . . expressing a deep sense of outrage and
grief over the killings of the children." He implicated Governor Wallace in the atrocity: "It is regrettable that public dis-
paragement of law and order has encouraged violence which
has fallen on the innocent." At the same time, he praised
Negro leaders for counselling restraint and announced that
Burke Marshall and bomb specialists from the FBI had arrived
in Birmingham. However, an administration spokesman also
indicated to the press that the Army was not the answer. Birmingham's problems, he suggested, could only be resolved
from within.[42]

Three days later Kennedy implemented a recommendation

that friends of the administration had put forward during the Albany crisis the summer before. He named two prominent citizens, Kenneth Royall, former Secretary of the Army, and Earl ("Red") Blaik, former West Point football coach, as his personal mediators. At the same time, he met with King and other Negro leaders, who afterward praised his action, declaring that mediation had to be given a chance. The President tried to get the negotiations off to a good start four days later when he participated in conferences at the White House between his mediators and two separate groups of white representatives from Birmingham. At one point, Kennedy was alone with five Birmingham whites and experienced the difficult task of reasoning with someone whose attitude seemed essentially irrational. One of the Alabamans criticized the public accommodations bill for interfering with property rights. Kennedy "just stared at him and said, 'Well, that's nothing, nothing,' " Burke Marshall recalled. The President "couldn't see why that was a big issue. He couldn't understand why anyone would want to refuse service to a Negro," Marshall elaborated.[43]

The mediators' arrival in Birmingham the next day coincided with another bombing directed at Negroes. Fortunately, this time only property suffered, and the bombings ceased as state police arrested the two men who were their likely perpetrators. Floyd Mann, former director of the state police, reported to Burke Marshall on the bizarre circumstances behind the arrests, which he had learned of from high ranking police officials. Al Lingo, head of the state police, it seemed, had received a tip originating with a Klansman that the federal government was about to nab the bombers. Although the state had absolutely no evidence incriminating them, Lingo ordered their arrests with the hope of preventing their prosecution by federal or Birmingham authorities. Marshall informed the Attorney General that Mann believed it was the arrested men themselves who "gave the state enough information to warrant the charges on illegal possession of dynamite," which had been filed. The story bespoke the sorry condition of law and order in the Wallace administration.[44]

Although not so cynical as the state's police director, Birmingham's white leaders proved resistant to further changes in racial practices; and since King soon began leading demonstrations demanding that the city hire Negro policemen and firemen, Birmingham remained a powder keg. The President's mediators, meanwhile, proved far less effective than Burke Marshall had been in the earlier crisis. Their task was difficult enough as it was, but they did not help matters by their inclinations to regard demonstrators as extremists and King as an outsider. Before long, an aide to King publicly criticized the envoys and demanded that the Kennedys lay down the law to white Southern politicians. Articles unfavorable to Royall and Blaik appeared in the black press. When they left the city in the second week of October with no wish to return, the situation was suspended in delicate balance.[45]

At one point before he departed, Blaik gave the President a progress report. During their conversation, he inquired about Kennedy's sense of humor. Kennedy responded that it was still in good shape. Testing it, Blaik recalled that he had seen an automobile in Birmingham with a sign on it that read: "Kennedy for King—Goldwater for President." After a moment's pause, Kennedy laughed heartily at the double entendre. What lay behind it, however, could not have been totally amusing to him, for it was becoming clear through the summer and fall that on balance the civil rights issue was costing him popularity.[46]

On the positive side, Kennedy's civil rights advocacy was winning him an unprecedented level of support among blacks. In July *Newsweek* published a Harris poll that showed Kennedy enjoyed overwhelming popularity among blacks. Asked how they would vote in a Kennedy–Rockefeller election, the blacks surveyed chose Kennedy 89 percent to 3 percent, with the remainder undecided. Against Goldwater, the breakdown was 91 to 2. Harris estimated that Kennedy would pick up an additional 580,000 Negro votes in 1964 over what he had captured in 1960. In early September, Gallup reported that 89 percent of blacks approved the way Kennedy was handling the Presidency and only 5 percent disapproved. In a Presidential trial heat that Gallup conducted in late September, nonwhites favored Kennedy by 95 percent over Goldwater. Because of Kennedy's popularity among blacks, the Democratic National Committee began to lay plans for a large-scale voter registration drive in Northern cities, to which it hoped to attract the assistance of civil rights organizations. As in the past, the Democrats had a more effective propaganda apparatus for holding black support than did the Republicans. Frederick Sontag, who was organizing a project to improve the Republican image on civil rights, relayed to Congressman Thomas Curtis in late August the dismaying information "that 24 of 25 Negro Republicans interviewed in the South (all leaders) had never *heard* of the Republican National Committee Minorities Division, that none had had any contact with it, and that *every one* of them gets *weekly* mailing from Louis Martin at the Democratic National Committee." [47]

While Kennedy was attaining new popularity among blacks, he was fast losing ground among white Southerners. In July, John Bailey, Chairman of the Democratic National Committee, learned that former Democrats in Northern Florida were working in the Goldwater movement. Richard Russell observed on television's *Meet the Press* in August that Goldwater would defeat Kennedy in Georgia if the election were held that day. (He also said that it would be "very difficult" for him to support Kennedy actively.) Gallup found that well over 70 percent of Southern whites believed that Kennedy was pushing racial integration too fast. His overall approval rating in the South averaged in the low forties in the summer and fall, though it rose to 51 percent in November. In Presidential trial heats, Gallup reported that Goldwater had substantially outdistanced Kennedy in the South. Louis Harris published similar findings in October and noted that Goldwater was the principal beneficiary of the President's declining popularity in the South. He supplemented his data with graphic quotations from some of those surveyed. "He's stirred up all the colored people to get their vote. It's terrible; he encouraged them to break state laws," a Raleigh, North Carolina, housewife said of the President. A South Carolina pipe fitter denigrated the President as a "perfect ass." Of Robert Kennedy, a Tennessee carpenter offered: "He's a 'nigger' man." Obviously Kennedy had aroused not only opposition but anger. Indeed, Congressman Hale Boggs of New Orleans later recalled that he had never seen anything to compare to the virulent and violent feeling aimed at the President and therefore decided to speak out against it. The speech he delivered, which Boggs regarded as quite pedestrian, was treated as if it were highly controversial.[48]

Kennedy, however, would not concede the South to anyone. Indeed, he hoped that Goldwater would be his opponent in 1964. Not only would a Kennedy–Goldwater race permit a clear ideological division, but he expected that he could defeat the Arizonan easily. In May, when Kennedy learned from Benjamin Bradlee, a close friend and journalist, that Goldwater would be the subject of an upcoming *Newsweek* cover story, he ruminated about a possible Goldwater nomination. "I can't believe we will be that lucky," he said. "I can't believe Barry will be that lucky either. The trouble is that if he's the nominee, people will start asking him questions, and he's so damn quick on the trigger he will answer them. And when he does, it will be all over." Six months later Kennedy expressed his incredulity to Bradlee that Goldwater had written a Tennessee Democrat that if he were president he would sell the Tennessee Valley Authority to private enterprise. It was the kind of political blunder Kennedy had predicted the conservative Senator would commit.[49]

The South could not be regarded as homogenous politically. Following the confrontations with federal authority in two states, Alabama and Mississippi were irretrievably lost to Kennedy. Robert Kennedy sent the President a full-page political advertisement from a Jackson newspaper which indicated the strident tone of that state's politics. The ad supported the candidacy of former Governor J. P. Coleman, supposedly the moderate in the upcoming primary. It had a large photograph of Coleman's opponent, Lieutenant Governor Paul Johnson, shaking hands with Chief U.S. Marshal James McShane at Ole Miss. The caption read: "When the fist came down, the hand went out, and Meredith went in." (Johnson won the election.) Elsewhere, however, the politics of resistance did not dominate. In Georgia, for example, voters had rejected the extremist candidacy of a former governor in 1962. Indeed, Louis Harris suggested to the President in September that the outstanding development in the South did not relate to the racial issue, but to the region's rapid economic growth. "You can well go into the South throughout 1964 not to lay down the gauntlet on civil rights," Harris advised, "but rather to describe and encourage the new industrial and educational explosion in the region." He recommended that Kennedy identify himself with the new South while leaving the Republicans and renegade Democrats to the old South. "Such a tack will not only help you in the rest of the country, but will also pay handsomely in the South itself," the pollster concluded.[50]

Kennedy apparently agreed with Harris, but he did not wait for 1964 to launch his campaign for the South. In two talks he gave in early October in Arkansas, Kennedy emphasized the South's recent economic growth. At the state fairgrounds in Little Rock, he paid generous tribute to Arkansas's powerful Congressional delegation, noting the important legislation its members affected, and declared:

These are forward-looking measures and they are forward-looking men, and their contribution to the welfare of this country may come as a surprise to those whose view of the South may be distorted by headlines and headline-seekers. The old South has its problems and they are not yet over, nor are they over in the rest of the country. But there is rising every day, I believe, a new South, a new South of which Henry Grady spoke about 80 years ago, and I have seen it in your universities, in your cities, in your industries. The new South I saw this morning on the Little Red River, the dams and reservoirs through the White River and the Arkansas River Basin in a sense symbolize the new South, for they mean navigation for your commerce, protection for your cities, opportunity for your people.

Kennedy's warm reception in the state prompted the *Arkansas Gazette* to observe editorially "that the Republicans may be counting prematurely in adding up all those electoral votes for 1964 from a Solid Republican South." Several weeks later, when Benjamin Bradlee asked him whether he was planning to drop Lyndon Johnson from the ticket in 1964, Kennedy emphatically responded: "That's preposterous on the face of it. We've got to carry Texas in '64, and maybe Georgia." At a strategy meeting with Robert Kennedy, Stephen Smith, John Bailey and others on November 13, he spoke of his plans to open the campaign that month with trips to Florida and Texas. He gave five speeches in Tampa and Miami on November 18. It was in the midst of a hectic swing through Texas four days later that he was assassinated. The November strategy session also considered ways, including punitive measures, to discourage independent electors from running under the party banner in 1964. Clearly, Kennedy was not planning to concede the South to the GOP.[51]

The political ramifications of the civil rights upheaval were not confined to the South. In the fall, news reports began to

mention a new phenomenon, called "white backlash." Northern white hostility to civil rights played an important part in
several elections. In Boston, Louise Day Hicks received heavy
support from white voters in winning reelection to the committee which controlled that city's schools. She vehemently
opposed the NAACP's efforts to end *de facto* segregation. A
Democrat narrowly won the governorship in Kentucky, but it
was believed that he would have triumphed easily had it not
been for white hostility to civil rights. When Kennedy campaigned in racially troubled Philadelphia in late October, he
received one of the chilliest receptions since taking office.
Moreover, George Wallace had begun to ruminate publicly
about entering Presidential primaries in Northern and border
states in order to demonstrate the level of national opposition
to civil rights.[52]

The emergence of Northern backlash, however, seems more
significant in retrospect than it appeared at the time. Eventually it would help elect a conservative President, but in 1963
Kennedy believed that its influence would be largely confined to local politics. Since he continued to score well in
public opinion polls, he had little reason to think otherwise.
According to a Gallup survey in September, he led Richard
Nixon by 58 to 37 percent. In two trial heats conducted in October he outdistanced Goldwater 55 to 39 percent. On November 10, Kennedy enjoyed a 59 percent approval rating,
with only 28 percent disapproving his handling of the Presidency. Nationally, 55 percent of whites approved, with 32
percent disapproving. Although a poll conducted on November 20 indicated that whites generally believed that Kennedy was pushing civil rights too fast, evidently other issues
outweighed this one in the minds of some of them. A
number of Northern Democratic Congressmen, meanwhile,
were becoming nervous about backlash, but not to the point
where they would oppose the President's legislation. A Chicago Representative told Charles Daly of Lawrence O'Brien's

staff that he had conducted a poll in his highly ethnic district which showed that his constituents were three-to-one against the civil rights bill. But, Daly recalled, the Congressman went on to say: "I sent out a newsletter and told those sons of bitches they were three to one for it." In Daly's view, the Congressman had been motivated by a sense of morality as well as loyalty to the President.[53]

In late October, a number of important Southern Senators met quietly and concluded that their best strategy was to delay consideration of the legislation as long as possible since they detected a steadily growing disenchantment with civil rights across the country. An aide to J. William Fulbright, acting with the Senator's full knowledge, discreetly informed the White House about the meeting and its conclusion. That Southern opponents were engaging in delay surely came as no surprise to Kennedy, for he was well aware that the Senate Judiciary Committee had recessed in mid-September, subject to the call of the chair, occupied by James Eastland. Furthermore, O'Brien and Sorensen on October 22 had briefed the President, prior to a meeting with Democratic Congressional leaders, that Harry Byrd, Chairman of the Senate Finance Committee, was summoning an excessively large number of witnesses on the tax cut. It appeared to them that Byrd was using a slowdown on this important fiscal measure as a weapon against civil rights.[54]

Kennedy had wanted to win House approval first anyway, but the danger there was that its Judiciary Committee would report out a bill containing provisions that would prove unacceptable to the House or Senate or that the administration would not want to enforce. Since the administration had a commitment to McCulloch that the House version would not be eviscerated by the Senate, the House bill would have to be a relatively limited piece of legislation. Celler and the other liberal Democrats who dominated the House subcommittee considering the legislation were reluctant to accept the Mc-

Culloch strategy. On the contrary, they responded to the friendly pressure of civil rights lobbyists to draft a far-reaching bill. By late September, Arnold Aronson, Secretary of the Leadership Conference on Civil Rights, reported to the cooperating organizations that "the civil rights bill coming out of subcommittee is so comprehensive that in spite of the pitfalls ahead, it is hard not to feel a jubilant sense of victory." According to Aronson, the bill would include an FEPC provision, an across-the-board Title III allowing the Attorney General to initiate suits to defend the rights of individuals, and coverage of all public accommodations save "owner-occupied boarding houses of five rooms or less." [55]

The subcommittee bill went well beyond what key Republicans were prepared to accept. McCulloch opposed a sweeping Fair Employment law and favored a more circumscribed public accommodations title. While the subcommittee wanted to cover federal and state elections, McCulloch preferred to include the former only. Even liberal Republicans had difficulty with the subcommittee's bill. John Lindsay told an ADA lobbyist on October 8 that the bill was poorly drafted. Title III was so loosely worded, he said, that it would give a farmer the right to have the Attorney General sue in his behalf against the Secretary of Agriculture. Lindsay also noted that the public accommodations provision was subject to conflicting interpretations.[56]

The administration set out to convince liberal Democrats to relent and to firm up Republican confidence in its sincerity about bipartisanship. Accordingly, Robert Kennedy met on October 15 with the full committee in executive session to urge modification of the bill and afterward reiterated some of his arguments at a press conference. His cause was assisted by sympathetic reports in the press, including the New York *Times* and the *New Republic*. In his column on October 18, William S. White, widely known as an ally of Lyndon Johnson, forcefully described the administration's dilemma.

"Robert Kennedy's main problem no longer is to fight off Southern and other conservative opposition simply to any kind of substantive civil rights measure," he wrote. "It is now to fight off Northern Democratic ultra-liberals pushing a violently punitive bill." [57]

Concern about prospective Republican support prompted many of Robert Kennedy's specific recommendations for modification, but he objected to Title III more on philosophical grounds. Intended to protect protestors from violence, Title III authorized the Attorney General to bring suit whenever there was official deprivation of a federally protected right. Hence, every time a state violated an individual's right—in school prayer cases, for example—the Attorney General would have to decide whether to seek vindication of his right. Before the Judiciary Committee, Robert Kennedy vehemently objected to Title III. He argued that Title III would not be effective because it could not "prevent or punish sporadic acts" of violence since injunctions could not "prevent crimes by unknown persons." Before a judge could grant an injunction, he believed, the government would have to prove that a federally protected right had been or was about to be violated, which might often be difficult. Moreover, he pointed out that not all demonstrations were protected by the First and Fourteenth Amendments and that limitations upon time, place, size, and duration were constitutionally permissible. Robert Kennedy did not like what these limitations implied:

> These factors would necessarily involve the Federal courts in determinations, historically made by local officials, as to how many people should be allowed to protest, in what manner, and at what time of day. This use of the courts to control demonstrations might well be as unsatisfactory to the demonstrators as to the police. In addition, a Federal court would have considerable difficulty anticipating what police action might or might not be justified in the fast changing conditions which frequently accompany demonstrations and counter-demonstrations.

These difficulties point to the basic danger of relying on injunctions to control in advance the actions of local police. One result might be that State and local authorities would abdicate their law enforcement responsibilities, thereby creating a vacuum which could be filled only by Federal force. This in turn—if it is to be faced squarely, Mr. Chairman, would require creation of a national police force. This is a step which is historically, and with good reason, abhorrent to our Federal system. I am sure all members of the committee would be opposed to such a drastic development unless all means of dealing with the underlying injustices fail.

Clearly, Title III went against the grain of what had been the administration's enforcement policy from the beginning: to get local authorities to exercise their responsibilities to uphold law and order and to minimize federal interference with local prerogatives. Title III had the potential for upsetting long-standing relationships between the state and federal governments. As Burke Marshall had pointed out in the spring, its enactment could also place the civil rights movement on a collision course with the federal courts. In its place, Robert Kennedy proposed that the Attorney General merely be allowed to sue to enjoin racial discrimination in state and municipal facilities such as parks and libraries.[58]

The administration's attempts to have the subcommittee bill modified incensed some civil rights leaders. A "sell-out," Clarence Mitchell declared. He also strongly objected to the closed session at which Robert Kennedy had delivered his important testimony. "Everybody in there is a white man, and what they are doing affects 10 percent of the population that is black. I don't know if the Negroes are being protected." "This kind of political expedience brought me to the point of nausea," James Farmer wrote Harry Golden, a white liberal living in North Carolina. The civil rights lobby meanwhile struggled to preserve the subcommittee version by attempting to bring public pressure to bear on the White House and members of the Judiciary Committee in the form of editorials, telegrams, letters, and personal visits.[59]

As the Committee moved toward completion of its work in late October, the administration worked feverishly to obtain a satisfactory bill, with the President himself taking a direct hand in the negotiations. Its position was enhanced by its willingness to adopt many Republican proposals. The administration accepted McCulloch's preferences to limit the voting provision to federal elections and to restrict public accommodations coverage to commercial establishments rather than to include all licensed offices as the subcommittee had proposed. Meanwhile, the employment section, the most bitter pill for some Republicans to swallow, was sugar-coated for them. The version the administration selected was written by liberal Republicans on the House Education and Labor Committee, in particular, Robert Griffin. In his conversations with Charles Halleck, Kennedy repeatedly reminded him that it was "the Republican FEPC bill." The administration also went along with Republican wishes that went beyond its original requests: to make the Civil Rights Commission permanent and to gather registration and voting statistics. The President's tone with the Republicans was not, however, entirely conciliatory. Norbert Schlei later recalled that at a critical juncture in the discussions Kennedy warned Halleck that if the Republicans killed the bill, he was not going to let them escape with impunity. In the next election, Kennedy threatened, he would pin the blame for the bill's demise squarely on them. To liberal Democrats meantime, the administration presented a simple choice: either accept a compromise or get no bill at all. When it became known that Southerners planned to vote for the subcommittee version because they perceived it as an easier target, the President's hand was greatly strengthened among liberals of both parties. The revelation supported his basic contention.[60]

By October 29, the administration had commitments from McCulloch and Halleck, and from Celler and enough other liberal Democrats to proceed confidently with the full Judiciary vote. Things went according to plan as the subcommittee bill was defeated 19–15, the minority consisting largely of Southerners and die-hard liberals. The Committee then approved the bipartisan compromise bill. The final vote was a comfortable 23–11, with 9 Republicans joining 14 Democrats against 3 Republicans and 8 Southern Democrats. The President and Attorney General hailed the bipartisan effort. Two days later, Robert Kennedy again saluted the Republicans at a luncheon of Democratic women in Washington. The civil rights issue, he also suggested, "should disappear in the 1964 campaign." Civil rights leaders were somewhat disappointed at the outcome, but they recognized that by winning substantial Republican support a major hurdle had been passed. They also still hoped to strengthen the legislation on the floor of the House.[61]

Four days after the breakthrough in the House, the administration achieved a comparable gain in the Senate, though not one known to the public. On November 2 Nicholas Katzenbach accompanied Everett Dirksen to the Army–Air Force football game in Chicago and during most of the trip they discussed civil rights. Both Army and civil rights registered victories. Dirksen would not commit himself about specifics in the bill, but he assured the Deputy Attorney General that the legislation would come to a vote in the Senate. Since Dirksen was a man of his word and was highly influential with his Republican colleagues, President Kennedy was very pleased to hear Katzenbach's report of the conversation.[62]

Congressional cooperation with the administration disturbed some Republicans. Within days of the Judiciary Committee's action, 40 percent of the House GOP membership attended a meeting to protest Halleck's leadership. Some were annoyed that Halleck had extricated the administration from its dilemma; others were upset at Halleck's failure to consult adequately with them before making commitments. In response to internal dissatisfaction, McCulloch wrote a lengthy letter to his Republican colleagues spelling out how GOP demands and suggestions had been incorporated into the final product. He pointed out, for example, that after the subcommittee had added a broad FEPC, "[u]pon *Republican* demand, the Commission was limited to investigatory and conciliatory functions. If the Commission wishes to compel action it must institute a civil suit in a Federal district court where the businessman or labor union will be entitled to a trial *de novo* and in which he can only be found liable if the charges against him are supported by a preponderance of the evidence." Apparently the letter soothed feelings somewhat, but the most conservative Republicans remained unmoved. Several of them placed a furled umbrella on Halleck's desk as a symbol of his "appeasement." In a letter to Halleck, the chairman of the Southern Association of Republican State Chairmen referred to Halleck's cooperation with the White House as a "grandstand act." "It is hard to hide one's bitter disappointment in the performance of those from whom something better is expected," the Southerner concluded.[63]

The Republican leaders soon showed that they had no intention of giving Kennedy the quick, final victory that he would have liked. In a joint press conference, on November 21, Dirksen began by excoriating Kennedy for his weak legislative leadership on taxes and civil rights. He observed that the President had failed to fulfill his promise for civil rights legislation in 1961; and after Kennedy's hand was forced by "the crisis of demonstrations and violence . . . he expected Congress to act in a few months on a program he had delayed for two and one half years." He went on to say:

Historically, the passage of the civil rights legislation is a long, drawn-out affair. This is because many members of Mr. Kennedy's own political party are opposed to civil rights legislation. Had the President kept his campaign pledge and sent his program to Congress in 1961, new civil rights statutes would have been on the books before demonstrations and violence were ever precipitated.

Halleck spoke in a similar vein. Asked when the House might act on the bill, he answered that his "best guess" was sometime after the Christmas recess.[64]

At his last press conference on November 14, President Kennedy acknowledged that his key pieces of legislation were proceeding slowly, but voiced optimism about the longer haul. "My judgment is that by the time this Congress goes home, in the sense of next summer, that in the fields of education, mental health, taxes, civil rights, this is going to be a record that is going to be—however dark it looks now, I think that 'westward, look, the land is bright,' and I think that by next summer it may be," he predicted. He proved to be correct. Seven months after Kennedy's death, Congress enacted civil rights legislation much as Kennedy had proposed and then fought for. What might have happened had Kennedy not been assassinated is of course impossible to establish; but many of those closest to the legislative process later reflected that essentially the same goal would have been reached.[65]

Conclusion: John F. Kennedy and the Second Reconstruction

PRESIDENT Kennedy's murder stunned the nation. There are probably few adults today who cannot recall the exact circumstances of their hearing the news on November 22, 1963. Across the country people wept openly in the streets, and millions attended hurriedly called memorial services. Normal activities slowed and even ceased as a vast audience sat mesmerized in front of their television sets which broadcast little for three days other than films of Kennedy's career, eulogies, news about the assassination, and then, finally, his deeply moving funeral. Outside the United States the reaction to Kennedy's death often reached equal intensity.

The enormous impact of his death can be explained by a number of factors. Assassinations had become rare in American life; the last murder of a President (McKinley) had occurred sixty-two years before. Yet, even had Kennedy died suddenly of natural causes, the public reaction would have been great. Kennedy had been the picture of youth and vitality. He had two small children and a glamorous young wife. He belonged to a large, wealthy, and closely knit family, many of whose members could be individually identified by the public. Indeed, the Kennedy family had a special aura, almost royal in aspect, which captivated the popular imagination. Over and above all this, Kennedy had become identified with hopes for peace and social and economic progress. In an age when humanity's very survival appeared to be at stake,

the unexpected, violent death of the person who seemed to
represent its best chances for the future shocked and frightened many millions of people.[1]

White Southerners, many of whom had come to resent
Kennedy's civil rights advocacy, nevertheless generally
grieved his death. It was true that in a number of segregated
school rooms in the South white children applauded word of
Kennedy's death, but authorities went to great lengths to
hide these displays of passion, which they considered shame-
ful. White Southerners, segregationist or not, for the most
part mourned the President's passing along with the rest of
the country. "I thought it was terrible, I didn't think a thing
like this could happen in this country," Bull Connor said.
James Gray of Albany called the assassination "a stunning
shock." "Our politics were miles apart, and getting further all
the time. But we remained good friends," he went on. The
day of the funeral many Southern government offices,
schools, and businesses closed down just as in the rest of the
country. Over 1,200 people attended a memorial service at
Ole Miss. More than 2,000, including the Governor-elect and
many state officials, crowded into an interfaith service in the
cathedral in Jackson, Mississippi. It became one of the most
integrated gatherings in Mississippi history to that time.
George Wallace described his attendance at Kennedy's funeral as "one of the saddest tasks I have ever performed." [2]

Two public opinion studies completed soon after the assassination suggest that black Americans were particularly troubled by Kennedy's death. A national survey asked people to
compare their own reactions with those of other people.
Overall, 30 percent believed that they were more upset than
"most people," but 49 percent of blacks thought they were
more upset. Two-thirds of blacks, as compared to 38 percent
of all respondents, agreed with the statement that they were
"so confused and upset, they didn't know what to feel." Furthermore, half of the blacks surveyed, compared with one-

fifth of the total sample, "worried how this might affect my own life, job and future." A study of 1,348 Detroit schoolchildren, 1,006 white and 342 black, produced complementary findings. Its director reported that Negro children were considerably more distraught and anxious. Many of them expressed concern about "how my folks will now get along," and 81 percent of black children, compared to 69 percent of white, said that they "felt the loss of someone very close and dear." Seventy percent of the black youngsters and 55 percent of the white "worried about how the U.S. would get along without its leader." [3]

Kennedy's death hit many civil rights activists especially hard. "Nothing had ever affected me as deeply as President Kennedy's death, not even the news that Martin had been stabbed in Harlem," Coretta King wrote in 1969. The assassination confirmed her husband's private fears that America was a "sick society." Anne Moody, a courageous black activist who had virtually been run out of her native Mississippi, was working in a New Orleans restaurant on the day Kennedy was killed. In her poignant memoir, *Coming of Age in Mississippi*, she recalled losing consciousness momentarily when she heard the news. She and the other black employees were afraid to contemplate what Kennedy's death might mean to Negroes. After entering the dining room, her shock and fear turned to anger. "When I turned around and looked at all those white faces—all of those Southern white faces— fire was in my eyes. I felt like racing up and down the tables, smashing food into their faces, breaking dishes over their heads, and all the time I would shout and yell MURDERERS! MURDERERS! MURDERERS!" Later, on the streetcar, she looked to see the expressions on the faces of blacks. "I knew they must feel as though they had lost their best friend—one who was in a position to help determine their destiny. To most Negroes, especially to me, the President had made 'Real Freedom' a hope." Addressing a dinner in New York on No-

vember 26, Fred Shuttlesworth, the black leader from Birmingham, began by paying tribute to Kennedy. "It would be
impossible to think or speak of the Negro revolt—which has
become in truth an American Revolution—and its impact
upon our American Society at this time or even in the future,
without saluting our martyred President, John Fitzgerald
Kennedy, whose understanding, skill and determination of
purpose helped in a positive way, to lay the groundwork for a
better system of democracy than that which we now know,"
he said. "The dedication to freedom and desire for justice
found in Negro leadership and the passionate yearnings of
the oppressed masses in this country were matched by his
own courage of convictions, grasp of the needs of the hour,
and his devotion to making the U.S. Constitution become
meaningful to all its citizens." [4]

Kennedy's death probably frightened blacks, in part because his successor, Lyndon B. Johnson, came from Texas and
bore the identity—indeed stigma—of a white Southerner.
Johnson, however, took pride in having gotten the 1957 Civil
Rights Act through Congress. As Vice President, he had endeavored to erase his image as the candidate of the white
South and had actively cultivated Negro support. Within ten
days of assuming the Presidency, moreover, he publicly committed himself to fulfilling Kennedy's civil rights program.
"We have talked long enough in this country about equal
rights. We have talked for 100 years or more. It is time now to
write the next chapter and to write it in books of law," the
new President told a joint session of Congress on November
27. Early passage of the pending civil rights legislation, he
declared, would be the most fitting memorial to President
Kennedy. After a prolonged struggle, which included the successful invoking of cloture, Congress heeded Johnson's plea
in June. Before Johnson left the White House in January 1969,
he had guided additional pieces of important civil rights legislation through Congress, had secured enactment of a variety

of other pieces of social and economic legislation which had a bearing on the lives of many blacks, and had established his own substantial record of executive action and moral leadership in the field of civil rights. In concrete accomplishments, Johnson eventually outstripped his predecessor's civil rights record. It is clear, however, that the foundations for Johnson's record—in Congress, through executive action, and through Presidential leadership—were laid by Kennedy.[5]

In the quarter century before Kennedy became President, his predecessors initiated a number of measures to advance civil rights, but Kennedy's activism in this regard far surpassed any of theirs. Franklin D. Roosevelt tolerated civil rights advocacy among his lieutenants, although he cautiously refrained from using the Presidency or his own enormous personal prestige to promote equal treatment of blacks. Under considerable pressure from militant blacks on the eve of American entrance into World War II, Roosevelt created the Fair Employment Practices Commission, but invested it with meager enforcement powers. Harry S Truman pioneered in the employment of Presidential power on behalf of racial progress, ordering the desegregation of the military, speaking out against the ill-treatment of blacks, and creating a blue-ribbon committee on civil rights. Overall, however, civil rights played a relatively minor role in his administration, with issues of foreign policy, the economy, and internal security predominating. An uncooperative Congress, meanwhile, blocked his legislative recommendations on civil rights. Dwight D. Eisenhower proceeded down the trails of executive action Truman had blazed, but displayed little enthusiasm for the task. His heart never belonged to the civil rights cause, and Eisenhower generally played a passive role in the gains that did occur during his Presidency, including the *Brown* decision and its follow-up, and the enactment of civil rights legislation in 1957 and 1960. Kennedy, by contrast, turned Truman's trails into wide avenues. He used his executive powers broadly, promoting an end to racial discrimination in voting, schools, the federal government, jobs, public facilities, and housing. He committed the moral authority of the President to racial justice in the most clear-cut terms ever. And he proposed and made significant progress toward securing the most important piece of civil rights legislation in a century. Under Kennedy civil rights became a focal point of public policy and political debate. Moreover, so unambiguous had Kennedy's commitment to civil rights been that it is hard to imagine any Vice President who succeeded him in November 1963, reversing it.

Kennedy's motives for proceeding as he did on the civil rights issue were complex, but for the sake of understanding may be divided into three types: political, attitudinal or intellectual, and personal. Naturally his actions at different times derived from different combinations of these and to different degrees. For example, politics dominated during the 1960 campaign, but when the Birmingham crisis erupted, factors of attitude and personality were most important. In addition, each kind of motive changed intrinsically over time; his political needs as a newly elected President, for instance, differed somewhat from the requirements of candidacy. Likewise his view of Reconstruction underwent a significant change. Looking briefly at each of these motives in isolation helps clarify Kennedy's actions and effects.

Kennedy was a consummate politician. As a Senator ambitious for the Presidency, he curried the favor of civil rights proponents and opponents. In the end he succeeded in winning critical support from both sides without trading away basic principle. He promised new Presidential leadership but assured the white South that he would not be vindictive. Once elected, he had to contend with a Congress in which the Southern wing of his party possessed disproportionate power. Consequently, he did not immediately carry through on his promise of civil rights legislation and compromised on his executive action program. Nevertheless, that program marked a significant break with the past, achieved some meaningful results, and, perhaps most important, raised the hopes of black people. Indeed, higher black expectations led ultimately to Kennedy's changing his approach in June 1963. The task of getting his proposed legislation enacted in turn presented a challenge to his political leadership, which he rose to meet. He rallied important segments of the public to his cause, and in time won several key Congressional skirmishes. Simultaneously, as a candidate for reelection, he began to mend his Southern fences preparatory to his next and expectedly last campaign. To the end, he neither abandoned nor excoriated the white South. Black voters, it appeared, had meanwhile given him nearly complete allegiance.

Certain ideas guided Kennedy. As an American nationalist, he was troubled by the damage racial intolerance was inflicting upon his country's image abroad, particularly in the Third World where he hoped to expand American influence. As a student of American history, on the other hand, he for a long time accepted a simplistic though widely held view of Reconstruction as a vindictive reign of terror and corruption which the North had visited upon the South. This perspective helped smooth his relations with Southern officeholders. Eventually, confrontations with ardent segregationists led him to question his former assumptions about the first Reconstruction and eased the way toward his launching a second, though he never advocated punishing the region. In addition, Kennedy worried about the damaging effects racial discrimination had on the nation's economy and on the health and education of its citizens. He shared the modern liberal's faith that the central government, led by an active President, could and should solve pressing social problems, of which racial discrimination was a leading one. Finally, Kennedy believed that all citizens should receive the same treatment regardless of race. Racial discrimination offended him intellectually. Hence, he shared with the civil rights movement a fundamental belief.

Personal factors also shaped Kennedy's handling of civil rights. His grace and style charmed black delegates in personal meetings. Sensitivity and empathy contributed to his making symbolic gestures of significance, such as calling Coretta King, and permitted him to comprehend, on more than an intellectual level, the struggle for equal rights. Finally, Kennedy needed to feel that he was leading rather than being swept along by events. As President, he was uncomfortable playing a passive role. Therefore, when in the spring of 1963 he perceived that he was losing the reins of leadership, he boldly reached out to grasp them once again.[6]

Kennedy's exercise of leadership probably helped instill in many potential civil rights activists a confidence and daring that they would not otherwise have had. In this regard it might be recalled that James Meredith applied to Ole Miss the day Kennedy was inaugurated and that for Anne Moody, Kennedy had made " 'Real Freedom' a hope." Indeed, the spirit Kennedy conveyed may well have made possible the eruption of social protest to which he in turn responded. Certainly Kennedy did not create the civil rights movement, but he did affect its course. Some of the things that occurred during his years as President probably would have occurred in any case. Most definitely the Freedom Rides would have taken place and undoubtedly there would have been some other direct challenges to segregation. But what would have happened had Richard Nixon been elected President? Would he have sent marshals to Montgomery, would a Voter Education Project have been created, would the Justice Department have dramatically stepped up enforcement under the guidance of someone like Robert Kennedy, would thousands of blacks have demonstrated in Birmingham, and, most important, if they had, would Nixon have responded by proposing and working for enactment of sweeping civil rights legislation?

Those conservative critics who in 1963 charged Kennedy

with encouraging massive law-breaking were in a sense not so wide of the mark. Kennedy, of course, never urged blacks to march in the streets, but he did foster an atmosphere where protests against the status quo could occur. He created that atmosphere through symbolic acts such as phoning Coretta King, appointing Thurgood Marshall to the federal bench, and opening the White House to blacks, and through more substantive deeds such as establishing a close working relationship between the Justice Department and the civil rights movement, sending marshals to Montgomery and Oxford, and using the executive powers of his office to combat discrimination. He also contributed to it in a general way, for in his campaign and in office, he represented change, not continuity; the future, not the past.

One could well draw up a balance sheet of Kennedy's civil rights record. On the minus side, one might list the appointment of segregationist judges in the South, the delay in the housing order followed by the promulgation of the narrowest possible one, as well as numerous instances of executive cautiousness. Kennedy could be faulted for not making even more high-level appointments of blacks than he did, especially to the White House staff, and for failing to remove barriers to effective criminal enforcement that existed within the federal government, specifically within the FBI. One might also want to add the fact that Kennedy did not win enactment of his proposed legislation. Yet, to blame the murdered Kennedy for that implies a certain callousness.

The plus side of the ledger would be considerably longer. It would include a large number of executive actions, such as the appointment of blacks to high offices and the gains in federal employment generally. In the upper civil service ranks, black employment increased 88 percent from June 1961 to June 1963, as compared to an overall increase at these levels of under 23 percent. High on the list would belong the many accomplishments relating to law enforcement, including the use of marshals to prevent mob rule in Montgomery, the application of legal pressure to bring about desegregation of transportation terminals, and the persistent implementation of court orders to effect desegregation at the universities of Mississippi and Alabama. Between Robert Kennedy's swearing in and his resignation in the summer of 1964, the number of voting rights suits increased from ten to sixty-nine, including statewide cases in Mississippi and Louisiana. The administration also scored some gains by promoting voluntary action. For example, partly as a result of Justice Department efforts, between May and December 1963, some voluntary desegregation of public accommodations took place in 356 out of 566 cities in the South and border states; biracial committees were established in at least 185 of these cities. Because the administration played a role in the creation of the Voter Education Project, it might be afforded partial credit for its accomplishments. By April 1964, the VEP had registered nearly 580,000 new voters in the South. President Kennedy's proposal of a broad civil rights bill in 1963 and his preliminary successes in getting that bill through Congress would also deserve places on the plus side of the ledger. Finally, Kennedy's exercise of moral leadership, through rhetorical advocacy and through personal example, would certainly merit inclusion in the positive column.[7]

A balance sheet does not convey Kennedy's full importance, however. Kennedy was significant not only for what he did, but for what he started. His Presidency marked a profound change from the inertia that had generally characterized the past. In a tragically foreshortened term of less than three years, he instituted a vigorous and far-reaching effort to eliminate racial discrimination in American life. Operating within the bounds of a democratic political system, Kennedy both encouraged and responded to black aspirations and led the nation into its Second Reconstruction.

Notes

ABBREVIATIONS USED IN NOTES

ADA	Americans for Democratic Action MSS
BM	Burke Marshall Papers
CORE	Congress of Racial Equality MSS.
DNC	Democratic National Committee Papers
KLOHP	Kennedy Library Oral History Program
LBJ	Lyndon Baines Johnson Papers
NAACP	National Association for the Advancement of Colored People Files
NYT	New York Times
POF	President's Office Files of John F. Kennedy
PreP	Pre-Presidential Files of John F. Kennedy
RFK	Robert F. Kennedy Papers
SRC	Southern Regional Council Files
TCS	Theodore C. Sorensen Papers
VEP	Voter Education Project Files
WHSF	White House Subject Files of John F. Kennedy

ONE
A Moderate in a Moderate Time

1. Among the best accounts of the South's response to *Brown* are: Numan V. Bartley, *The Rise of Massive Resistance: Race and Politics in the South During the 1950's;* Neil R. McMillen, *The Citizens' Council: Organized Resistance*

Many of the manuscript collections I examined were still being processed by archivists. I have indicated box numbers only in those instances where I thought the document had come to its permanent resting place and in those instances where I thought the temporary location would help researchers find the documents in the future.

to the Second Reconstruction, 1954–64; Reed Sarratt, *The Ordeal of Desegregation: The First Decade;* Benjamin Muse, *Ten Years of Prelude: The Story of Integration Since the Supreme Court's 1954 Decision.*

2. Luther H. Hodges, *Businessman in the Statehouse,* pp. 88–89.

3. J. W. Peltason, *Fifty-Eight Lonely Men: Southern Federal Judges and School Desegregation,* pp. 135–46; Bartley, *Rise of Massive Resistance,* pp. 146–47; Muse, *Ten Years of Prelude,* pp. 53–55, 87–92.

4. Burke Marshall, Assistant Attorney General for Civil Rights, 1961–1964, later learned from a university official that the Justice Department had declined this request. Marshall wanted to examine the Justice Department file on this case but found that it was empty. See: Burke Marshall, interviewed by Anthony Lewis, June 14, 1964, KLOHP 86–87.

5. Eisenhower quoted by Emmet John Hughes, *The Ordeal of Power: A Political Memoir of the Eisenhower Years,* p. 201. See also: Dwight D. Eisenhower, *The White House Years: Waging Peace, 1956–1961,* p. 150; Simeon Booker, *Black Man's America,* pp. 208–9; E. Frederic Morrow, *Black Man in the White House;* Arthur Larson, *Eisenhower: The President Nobody Knew,* pp. 124–33.

6. No complete account of the Little Rock crisis has been published. This account drew on the following: Sherman Adams, *Firsthand Report: The Story of the Eisenhower Administration,* pp. 343–59; Eisenhower, *Waging Peace,* pp. 162–75; Bartley, *Rise of Massive Resistance,* pp. 251–69; Peltason, *Fifty-Eight Lonely Men,* pp. 162–220; Muse, *Ten Years of Prelude,* pp. 122–45; Brooks Hays, *A Southern Moderate Speaks,* pp. 130–94; Daisy Bates, *The Long Shadow of Little Rock;* Virgil T. Blossom, *It Has Happened Here;* Wiley Branton, personal interview.

7. Letter from Stewart Udall, *New Republic,* Nov. 11, 1957, pp. 3, 25; *The Nation,* Nov. 2, 1957, 293; Charles Morgan, Jr., *A Time to Speak,* p. 67; Unsigned mimeo, "How President Eisenhower's Evasions Have Created the Climate in which Governor Orval Faubus Has Felt Free to Defy United States Law," PreP, 555a.

8. Edward D. Hollander to Julius C. C. Edelstein, May 9, 1958, ADA, Series 5, Box 9; John T. Eliff, "Aspects of Federal Civil Rights Enforcement: The Justice Department and the FBI, 1939–1964," *Perspectives in American History,* 5 (1971), 652–58; Foster Rhea Dulles, *The Civil Rights Commission, 1957–1965,* pp. 16–25 and *passim.*

9. Mark deW. Howe to John F. Kennedy, July 23, 1957, TCS, 9; Walter F. Murphy, "The South Counter-attacks: The Anti-NAACP Laws," *Western Political Quarterly,* 12 (June 1959), 371–90; Paul L. Murphy, *The Constitution in Crisis Times, 1918–1969,* pp. 337–38.

10. Contemporaneous writings on the Democratic Party in the 1950s are voluminous. Historians have recently begun to treat it, as in Barton J. Bernstein, "Election of 1952," in Arthur M. Schlesinger, Jr., ed. *History of Ameri-*

can Presidential Elections, 1789–1968, IV, 3215–66; Joseph Bruce Gorman, *Kefauver: A Political Biography;* Herbert S. Parmet, *The Democrats: The Years After FDR.*

11. On this trend, see: Bayard [Rustin] and Stanley [Levison] to Martin Luther King, Jr., n.d., Martin Luther King MSS, Boston University; Boston University; Minutes, Board of Directors Meeting, Sept. 12, 1960, NAACP; George Belknap, "Political Behavior Report: The Northern Negro Voter," May 1960, RFK, 1960 Campaign and Transition; "Negro Voters in Northern Cities," May 15, 1960, RFK, 1960 Campaign and Transition; Richard Scammon, "How Will Negroes Vote?" *New Republic,* Sept. 16, 1957, pp. 11–14; Henry Lee Moon, "The Negro Vote in the Presidential Election of 1956," *Journal of Negro Education,* 26 (Summer 1957), 219–30; Harold E. Gosnell and Robert Martin, "The Negro as Voter and Officeholder," *ibid.,* 32 (Fall 1963), 415–25.

12. Bernard Cosman, "Presidential Republicanism in the South, 1960," *Journal of Politics,* 24 (May 1962), 303–22; Philip E. Converse, "On the Possibility of Major Political Realignment in the South," in Angus Campbell, et al., eds., *Elections and the Political Order,* pp. 212–42.

13. Ed E. Reid to Theodore Sorensen, Nov. 22, 1958, TCS, 21.

14. *Congressional Record,* Aug. 30, 1957, p. 16661 (Russell quotation); Harry McPherson, *A Political Education,* pp. 142–48; Rowland Evans and Robert Novak, *Lyndon Johnson: The Exercise of Power,* pp. 125–40; J. W. Anderson, *Eisenhower, Brownell, and the Congress: The Tangled Origins of the Civil Rights Bill of 1956–1957;* Howard E. Shuman, "Senate Rules and the Civil Rights Bill," *American Political Science Review,* 51 (1957), 955–75.

15. Paul Douglas, "The 1960 Voting Rights Bill: The Struggle, the Final Results, and the Reasons," *Journal of Intergroup Relations,* I (Summer 1960), 82; Daniel M. Berman, *A Bill Becomes a Law: Congress Enacts Civil Rights Legislation,* 2nd ed.; James L. Sundquist, *Politics and Policy: The Eisenhower, Kennedy, and Johnson Years,* pp. 238–50.

16. Theodore C. Sorensen, *Kennedy,* p. 471.

17. On Kennedy's ancestors and father, see: Rose Fitzgerald Kennedy, *Times to Remember;* Richard J. Whalen, *The Founding Father: The Story of Joseph P. Kennedy;* David E. Koskoff, *Joseph P. Kennedy: A Life and Times;* Joseph F. Dinneen, *The Kennedy Family.*

18. Most informative on Kennedy's upbringing is the book *Times to Remember* by his mother, Rose. Kennedy's recollection about his visit to his relatives in 1947 is recorded in Kenneth P. O'Donnell and David F. Powers, with Joe McCarthy, *"Johnny, We Hardly Knew Ye": Memories of John Fitzgerald Kennedy.* On Kennedy's encounter with prejudice and his associations with blacks, I relied on Belford V. Lawson, interviewed by Ronald J. Grele, Jan. 11, 1966, KLOHP; Marjorie M. Lawson, interviewed by Ronald J. Grele, Oct. 25, 1965, KLOHP; Marjorie Lawson, personal interview.

19. Robert J. Donovan, *PT 109; John F. Kennedy in World War II;* Sorensen *Kennedy,* pp. 17–18; John F. Kennedy, ed. *As We Remember Joe.*

20. On Kennedy's decision to enter politics and his early political career, see: Rose Kennedy, *Times to Remember,* pp. 305–27; O'Donnell and Powers, "*Johnny, We Hardly Knew Ye,*" pp. 43–93; Sorensen, *Kennedy,* pp. 11–92; James MacGregor Burns, *John Kennedy: A Political Profile.*

21. John F. Kennedy, *Profiles in Courage,* pp. 131, 152–53, 161. For an historiographical survey published three years after Kennedy's book, see: Bernard A. Weisberger, "The Dark and Bloody Ground of Reconstruction Historiography," *Journal of Southern History,* 25 (1959), 427–47.

22. Sorensen, *Kennedy,* pp. 80–87; O'Donnell and Powers, "*Johnny, We Hardly Knew Ye,*" pp. 117–20; Gorman, *Kefauver,* pp. 249–52; G. Fred Switzer to Harry F. Byrd, May 3, 1956, G. Fred Switzer MSS; John F. Kennedy to Joseph P. Kennedy, June 29, 1956, TCS, 9; Transcript, *Face the Nation,* July 1, 1956, TCS, 12.

23. Gorman, *Kefauver,* pp. 252–65; Sorensen, *Kennedy,* pp. 88–91; Ralph McGill, interviewed by Charles T. Morrissey, Jan. 6, 1966, KLOHP, 16.

24. J. P. Coleman to John F. Kennedy, Nov. 5, 1956; Marvin Griffin to John F. Kennedy, Oct. 11, 1956; William Colmer to John F. Kennedy, Oct. 26, 1956; A. Willis Robertson to John F. Kennedy, Oct. 8, 1956, all in: POF, Special Events, 1; Paul Dever to Stephen A. Mitchell, Aug. 20, 1956, TCS, 9; Sorensen to J. P. Coleman, March 16, 1959, TCS, 23.

25. O'Donnell and Powers, "*Johnny, We Hardly Knew Ye,*" pp. 126–28; Sorensen, *Kennedy,* pp. 91–102.

26. Herbert Tucker to John F. Kennedy, June 21, 1957; Kennedy to Tucker, June 24, 1957; Ruth Batson to Kennedy, June 24, 1957; Kennedy to Batson, June 29, 1956, PreP, 458.

27. John F. Kennedy to Ruth Batson, Aug. 1, 1957, PreP, 458; Kennedy to Samuel H. Beer, Aug. 3, 1957, TCS, 9; Clarence Mitchell, interviewed by John Stewart, Feb. 9, 1967, KLOHP, 1; *Congressional Record,* Aug. 1, 1957, pp. 13306–7; Luther Hodges to John F. Kennedy, July 28, 1957; Kennedy to J. P. Coleman, Aug. 1, 1957; Kennedy to Luther Hodges, Aug. 1, 1957; Kennedy to Marvin Griffin, Aug. 1, 1957, all in PreP, 458; Theodore Sorensen to Robert F. Kennedy, Dec. 14, 1959, TCS, 25.

28. Commencement Address by John F. Kennedy, University of Georgia, June 10, 1957, PreP, 6; Speech by John F. Kennedy, Mississippi Economic Council, April 16, 1958, PreP, 8; Kennedy's statement on Little Rock, Sept. 27, 1957, PreP, 555; Lloyd D. Bell to John F. Kennedy, Sept 29, 1957; Kennedy to Bell, Oct. 14, 1957, TCS, 9; Clippings on Mississippi incident, PreP, 555 and TCS, 9.

29. James H. Gray to Theodore Sorensen, Nov. 25, 1958 and attached clipping from Albany *Herald,* Nov. 24, 1958, TCS, 22; Theodore Sorensen to J. P.

Coleman, March 16, 1959; Coleman to Sorensen, March 19, 1959, TCS, 23; John Patterson, interviewed by John Stewart, May 26, 1967, KLOHP, 5–9.

30. Memo to files from Robert F. Kennedy, Nov. 16, 1959, TCS, 22; G. Fred Switzer to Harry Byrd, May 27, 1959, G. Fred Switzer MSS; Price Daniel to Harry Byrd, Oct. 26, 1959, Harry F. Byrd MSS, 243.

31. John F. Kennedy to Clarence Mitchell, July 10, 1957, TCS, 9; Roy Wilkins to Peter Arlos, May 16, 1958, PreP, 476; John F. Kennedy to Roy Wilkins, May 6, 1958; Wilkins to Kennedy, May 29, 1958, TCS, 9.

32. O. Phillip Snowden to John F. Kennedy, July 21, 1958, PreP, 476; John F. Kennedy to Roy Wilkins, July 18, 1959, PreP, 555; John F. Kennedy to Phil David Fine, Aug. 14, 1958; Kennedy to Lewis Weinstein, Aug. 14, 1958, TCS, 13; Memo, n.d., attached to letter from W. Montague Cobb to John F. Kennedy, Sept. 4, 1958, TCS, 13; Marjorie M. Lawson to John F. Kennedy, Nov. 26, 1958, TCS, 9.

33. News release from Kennedy headquarters, Oct. 19, 1958, PreP, 497; Pittsburgh *Courier*, Nov. 1, 1958, in TCS, 19; Marjorie Lawson to John F. Kennedy, Nov. 26, 1958, TCS, 9; Roy Wilkins to John F. Kennedy, Dec. 9, 1958, TCS, 9; Marjorie Lawson to John F. Kennedy, July 29, 1959, TCS, 23.

34. Belford V. Lawson, interviewed by Ronald J. Grele, Jan. 11, 1966, KLOHP, 1–10; Marjorie Lawson, personal interview; Undated memo by Belford and Marjorie Lawson, TCS, 19; Marjorie Lawson to John F. Kennedy, Nov. 26, 1958 (two memoranda) TCS, 9; Marjorie Lawson to John F. Kennedy, Dec. 2, 1958, TCS, 13; Marjorie Lawson to John F. Kennedy et al., July 29, 1959, TCS, 23.

35. Marjorie Lawson, personal interview; Virginia Tabb Battle to P. L. Prattis, Aug. 20, 1958, TCS, 19; Marjorie Lawson to Steve Smith, May 19, 1959, PreP, 500.

36. Belford Lawson, interview, KLOHP, 9–10; Sorensen, *Kennedy*, p. 471; Speech by Kennedy before United Negro College Fund, April 12, 1959, PreP, Speeches, 6.

37. Paul H. Douglas, *In the Fullness of Time*, pp. 255–56; Paul H. Douglas, interviewed by John Newhouse, June 6, 1964, KLOHP, 11; Frank McCulloch to Paul Douglas, Oct. 16, 1958, Paul H. Douglas MSS; Burns, *John Kennedy*, pp. 201–6.

38. John F. Kennedy to George Gallup, Feb. 14, 1958; Gallup to Kennedy, March 14, 1958, TCS, 9; Report from Edward L. Greenfield & Co., April 14, 1958, TCS, 17; "An Analysis of a Trial Pairing of Vice President Richard M. Nixon vs. Senator John F. Kennedy" by Louis Harris and Associates, Oct. 1957, PreP, Polls of Political Opinion, 1954–1960, p. 598; "A Study of the Election for United States Senator in Massachusetts," by Louis Harris and Associates, June 1958, PreP, 594; "A Study of Wisconsin's Second, Tenth, and Fifth Congressional Districts in the 1960 Democratic Primary," by Louis Harris and Associates, March 21, 1960, PreP, 598.

TWO
The 1960 Campaign: Promises and Comprises

1. Marjorie M. Lawson, interviewed by Ronald J. Grele, Oct. 25, 1965, KLOHP, 10–17.

2. Price Daniel to Harry Byrd, Oct. 26, 1959; Harry Byrd to Price Daniel, Nov. 13, 1959; Walter Sillers to Harry Byrd, June 1, 1960; Byrd to Sillers, May 26, 1960; Gessner T. McCorvey to Harry Byrd, June 9, 1960, all in Harry F. Byrd MSS, 243; J. Lindsay Almond, Jr., interviewed by T. H. Baker, Feb. 5, 1969, Lyndon Baines Johnson Library, 10; Harry F. Byrd to Robert G. Baker, July 5, 1960, LBJ, Senate Files.

3. Pittsburgh *Courier*, Jan. 30, 1960; Notes on Senator Johnson's remarks to Legislative Conference, Jan. 13–14, 1960, LBJ, Senate Files; Harris Wofford, interviewed by Larry Hackman, May 22, 1968, KLOHP, 71; Hobart Taylor, Jr., interviewed by Stephen Goodell, Jan. 6, 1969, Lyndon Baines Johnson Library, 9; Remarks by Adam Clayton Powell at rally, June, 25, 1960, LBJ, Senate Files; Alice Allison Dunnigan, *A Black Woman's Experience—From Schoolhouse to White House*, pp. 563–66.

4. "An Important Message to All Liberals," from James M. Burns et al., June 17, 1960, ADA, Series 6, Box 17.

5. *NYT*, June 24 and 25, 1960; Pittsburgh *Courier*, June 25, 1960.

6. Bob Kennedy to Steve Smith, May 31, 1960, RFK, 1960 Campaign and Transition, 7; "The South's Choice After Johnson," n.d., TCS, 25; John Patterson, interviewed by John Stewart, May 26, 1967, KLOHP, 13; Marjorie Lawson to John Kennedy, June 20, 1960, RFK, 1960 Campaign and Transition, 7.

7. Robert F. Kennedy to John F. Kennedy, June 24, 1960, RFK, 1960 Campaign and Transition, 7; Ted Sorensen to Bob Kennedy, June 27, 1960, TCS, 25; John F. Kennedy to Harry Byrd, June 27, 1960 (and press release), Harry F. Byrd MSS, 245; A. Willis Robertson to G. Fred Switzer, June 25, 1960; Switzer to Robertson, June 27, 1960, G. Fred Switzer MSS.

8. *NYT*, July 10 and 11, 1960; Remarks of Kennedy at NAACP rally, July 10, 1960, PreP, 1960 Campaign Files, 2.

9. Wofford's comments in *American Journey: The Times of Robert Kennedy*, Interviews by Jean Stein, p. 40; *Current History*, Oct. 1960, pp. 237–40; Pittsburgh *Courier*, July 23, 1960; Harris Wofford, interviewed by Berl Bernhard, Nov. 29, 1965, KLOHP, 29; Memo to cooperating agencies from Arnold Aronson, Aug. 5, 1960, CORE, Series 5, Box 25; Sorensen, *Kennedy*, 157; Chester Bowles to Adlai Stevenson, July 23, 1960, Chester Bowles MSS, 301; Roy Wilkins to Chester Bowles, Chester Bowles MSS, 218.

10. Richard Taylor, "Pressure Groups and the Democratic Platform: Kennedy in Control," in Paul Tillett, ed., *Inside Politics: The National Conven-*

tions, 1960, pp. 84–96; W. L. Prieur to Harry Byrd, July 21, 1960, Harry F. Byrd MSS, 249.

11. Sorenson, *Kennedy,* 159; J. Lindsay Almond, interviewed by Larry J. Hackman, Feb. 7, 1968, KLOHP, 11–12; Marjorie Lawson, interview, KLOHP, 21.

12. Sorensen, *Kennedy,* pp. 162–65; O'Donnell and Powers, *"Johnny, We Hardly Knew Ye,"* pp. 189–98, Arthur M. Schlesinger, *A Thousand Days: John F. Kennedy in the White House,* pp. 50–57; Myer Feldman, interviewed by Charles T. Morrissey, April 10, 1966, KLOHP, 268–77; Theodore Sorensen to John F. Kennedy and Robert F. Kennedy, June 29, 1960, TCS, 21; "A Study of the Presidential Election of 1960 in South Carolina," by Louis Harris and Associates, June, 1960, PreP, 597; J. Lindsay Almond, interview, KLOHP, 2–3.

13. Remarks of Senators Johnson and Kennedy at Congressman Dawson's Meeting, July 15, 1960, LBJ, Senate Files; O'Donnell and Powers, *"Johnny, We Hardly Knew Ye,"* pp. 189–200; Schlesinger, *A Thousand Days,* pp. 57–58; *NYT,* July 16, 1960.

14. Karl A. Lamb, "Civil Rights and the Republican Platform: Nixon Achieves Control," in Tillett, *Inside Politics,* pp. 55–84; *Current History,* Oct. 1960, pp. 237–40; Joseph L. Rauh to Roy Wilkins, July 23, 1960, Paul H. Douglas MSS; Theodore H. White, *The Making of the President, 1960,* p. 204.

15. Richard M. Nixon, *Six Crises,* pp. 313–18; White, *The Making of the President,* pp. 206–7.

16. U. S. Congress, Senate, Committee on Commerce, *Freedom of Communications,* Report 994, 87th Cong., 1st sess., Pt. 1, 68–72; LEM[Louis E. Martin] to Civil Rights Section, Aug. 11, 1960, DNC, 144; Arthur Schlesinger, Jr. to Archibald Cox, Aug. 16, 1960, DNC, 203; Arthur Schlesinger, Jr. to John F. Kennedy, Aug. 30, 1960, POF, Special Correspondence, 6.

17. *Freedom of Communications,* Pt. 2, 1–8, 39–52; Nixon, *Six Crises,* p. 325; *Time,* Oct. 17, 1960, p. 23; Ithiel de Sola Pool, Robert P. Abelson, Samuel L. Popkin, *Candidates, Issues, and Strategies: A Computer Simulation of the 1960 Presidential Election,* pp. 152–56.

18. E. Frederic Morrow, *Black Man in the White House,* pp. 295–96; Simeon Booker, interviewed by John F. Stewart, April 24, 1967, KLOHP, 14; *NYT,* Oct. 13 and 14, 1960; Pittsburgh *Courier,* Oct. 22, 1960; Nixon, *Six Crises,* pp. 350–51; John Kenneth Galbraith, *Ambassador's Journal: A Personal Account of the Kennedy Years,* pp. 6–7.

19. Memorandum for Speechwriters, July 23, 1960, TCS, 26; *Freedom of Communications,* Pt. 3, 74; Roy Wilkins, interviewed by Berl Bernhard, Aug. 13, 1964, KLOHP, 4; Harris Wofford to John F. Kennedy, Sept. 23, 1960, RFK, 1960 Campaign and Transition, 2.

20. *Freedom of Communications,* Pt. 1, 12–13, 961; Harris Wofford, interviewed by Larry Hackman, May 22, 1968, KLOHP, 47; *Freedom of Communications,* Pt. 1, 189–93, 428, 432, 575–78, 580–83; Pt. 3, 149–52.

21. I learned a great deal about the Civil Rights Section from personal interviews with Marjorie Lawson and Louis Martin, and from Harris Wofford's interviews at the Kennedy Library.

22. Unsigned, undated memo to Bobby Kennedy et al., RFK, 1960 Campaign and Transition, 2; Marjorie Lawson to John F. Kennedy et al., June 6, 1960, RFK, 1960 Campaign and Transition, 7; "Negro Voters in Northern Cities," Simulmatics, Report No. 1, May 15, 1960, RFK, 1960 Campaign and Transition, 16; "Political Behavior Report: The Northern Negro Voter," George Belknap, May 1960, RFK, 1960 Campaign and Transition, 7.

23. See, for example: *Ebony,* Nov. 1960, pp. 8–9, 14–15; *Jet,* Oct. 27, 1960, pp. 12–15; Nov. 10, 1960, 22–23; *Afro-American* (Baltimore), Oct. 8, 1960, Magazine Section; Pittsburgh *Courier,* Aug. 8, Oct. 1, Oct. 8, Oct. 29, Nov. 5, 1960.

24. Undated, unsigned memorandum to Bobby Kennedy et al., RFK, 1960 Campaign and Transition, 2; Simeon Booker, interview, KLOHP, 10–16; Pierre Salinger, *With Kennedy,* p. 38; Transcript of Conference on Constitutional Rights, Oct. 11, 1960 and related materials, DNC, 144; Minutes, Board of Directors Meeting, Oct. 10, 1960, NAACP.

25. The account of the phone call episode relies on the following: Comments by Harris Wofford, Andrew Young, John Seigenthaler in *American Journey,* pp. 90–94; Harris Wofford, interviewed by Bernhard, KLOHP, 16–27; Louis Martin, personal interview; Ralph McGill, interviewed by Charles T. Morrissey, Jan. 6, 1966, KLOHP, 11–13; William B. Hartsfield, interviewed by Charles T. Morrissey, Jan. 6, 1966, KLOHP, 1–6 and attached letter.

26. Sorensen, *Kennedy,* p. 216; *Freedom of Communications,* Pt. 4, 895, 961; Montgomery *Advertiser,* Oct. 26, 1960.

27. Simeon Booker, interview, KLOHP, 16; Pittsburgh *Courier,* Nov. 5, 1960; *Jet,* Nov. 10, 1960; " 'No Comment' Nixon versus a Candidate with a Heart, Senator Kennedy: The Case of Martin Luther King," DNC, 140; Harris Wofford to John F. Kennedy, June 9, 1960, Chester Bowles MSS, 218.

28. Earl Brown to Louis Martin, Sept. 3, 1960, DNC, 144; Statements by Rev. J. H. Jackson (in favor of religious toleration), DNC, 145; Henry Lee Moon, "The Negro Voter," *The Nation,* Sept. 17, 1960, p. 157; Roy Wilkins, personal interview.

29. *NYT,* Dec. 14, 1960; Morrow, *Black Man in the White House,* p. 296; Anthony Lewis, *Portrait of a Decade: The Second American Revolution,* p. 115; White, *The Making of the President,* p. 315; Nixon, *Six Crises,* pp. 362–63; Galbraith, *Ambassador's Journal,* p. 6; Alice [Dunnigan] to Louie [Martin], n.d., DNC, 144.

30. Unsigned, undated memo to Bobby Kennedy et al., RFK, 1960 Campaign and Transition, 2; Wofford, interviewed by Hackman, KLOHP, 47–48; Wofford, interviewed by Berhard, KLOHP, 28ff.

31. *Freedom of Communications*, Pt. 3, 149–52; J. Lindsay Almond, interview, KLOHP, 20.

32. Harry Byrd to James F. Byrnes, Aug. 25, 1960, Harry F. Byrd MSS, 242; Bob Kennedy to Sarge Shriver, Aug. 4, 1960, RFK, 1960 Campaign and Transition, 1; Press release, Aug. 18, 1960, RFK, 1960 Campaign and Transition, 1.

33. GER [George E. Reedy] to Senator [Johnson], Aug. 23, 1960, LBJ, Senate Files; Clipping, New York *Herald Tribune*, Sept. 26, 1960, DNC; Confidential source; Richard Russell to Rufus Harris (for immediate release), Oct. 14, 1960, LBJ, Senate Files; Excerpts of Remarks of Senator Herman E. Talmadge, Oct. 14, 1960, LBJ, Senate Files; Transcript of Remarks of Richard Russell to press, Nov. 7, 1960, LBJ, Senate Files, Orville Freeman, personal diary, July 14, 1962, microfilm, Kennedy Library.

34. *New Republic*, Oct. 24, 1960, p. 4; *Newsweek*, Oct. 24, 1960, pp. 42–44; *Time*, Oct. 24, 1960, pp. 25–26; Itinerary of Lyndon Johnson's trip, Oct. 10–14, 1960, Howard W. Smith MSS, 204.

35. Joseph L. Rauh, Jr. to Myer Feldman, Sept. 16, 1960, ADA, Series 6, Box 18; Frank W. McCulloch to Paul Douglas, Oct. 3, 1960, Paul H. Douglas MSS; Roy Wilkins to Lyndon Johnson, Oct. 17, 1960; Johnson to Wilkins, Oct. 22, 1960, LBJ, Senate Files.

36. Joint statement by Senators James O. Eastland and John Stennis, Aug. 19, 1960, John W. McCormack MSS, 102; *Time,* Oct. 26, 1960, p. 26; Charles Morgan, Jr. *A Time to Speak*, p. 67; Olin Johnston to Lyndon Johnson, Aug. 25, 1960 and Press Release, Aug. 25, 1960, LBJ, Senate Files.

37. Robert F. Kennedy to Harry Byrd, n.d., Harry F. Byrd MSS, 245; File of John Kennedy's campaign speeches; Transcript of Barry Gray Show, Robert Kennedy, guest, Aug. 24, 1960; Clippings relating to AFL-CIO support of Kennedy, all in Harry F. Byrd MSS, 245; Howard W. Smith to Harry Byrd, Sept. 21, 1960, Harry F. Byrd MSS, 260; J. Lindsay Almond, interview, Johnson Library, 16–20; J. Lindsay Almond, interview, KLOHP, 5–8; Collins Denny, Jr. to Watkins Abbitt and William Tuck, Sept. 30, 1960, Harry F. Byrd MSS, 241; Harry F. Byrd to Wilton B. Persons, Oct. 28, 1960, Harry F. Byrd MSS, 249.

38. Harry Byrd to James F. Byrnes, Oct. 19, 1960, Harry F. Byrd MSS, 242. Basic election returns are conveniently located in: Richard Scammon, compiler and editor, *America at the Polls: A Handbook of American Presidential Election Statistics, 1920–1964*.

39. Bernard Cosman, "Presidential Republicanism in the South, 1960," *Journal of Politics*, 24 (May 1962), 303–22.

40. Polls done by Louis Harris in North Carolina, Tennessee, Maryland,

Sept., 1960, PreP, Polls of Political Opinion, 1954–1960; Hazel Gaudet Erskine, "The Polls: Race Relations," *Public Opinion Quarterly*, 26 (Spring 1962), 148; Russell Middleton, "The Civil Rights Issue and Presidential Voting Among Southern Negroes and Whites," *Social Forces*, 40 (March 1962), 209–15; Ithiel de Sola Pool et al., *Candidates, Issues and Strategies*, p. 100; Philip E. Converse et al., "Stability and Change in 1960: A Reinstating Election," *American Political Science Review*, 55 (June 1961), 280.

41. Harold E. Gosnell and Robert E. Martin, "The Negro as Voter and Officeholder," *Journal of Negro Education*, 32 (Fall 1963), 419; Roberta S. Sigel, "Race and Religion as Factors in the Kennedy Victory in Detroit, 1960," *Journal of Negro Education*, 31 (Fall 1962), pp. 436–47, Middleton, "The Civil Rights Issue"; Ithiel de Sola Pool et al., *Candidates, Strategies, and Issues*, p. 100.

42. Atlanta *Daily World*, Nov. 10, 1960; Marjorie Lawson, personal interview. Ironically, Martin Luther King, Jr., himself could not vote because he had failed to pay his $1.50 poll tax in Alabama. See: Pittsburgh *Courier*, Nov. 12, 1960.

43. *The Crisis*, Dec. 1960, p. 658.

THREE
Leadership and Caution in the White House

1. *Congressional Quarterly Almanac*, 1961, pp. 40–60; Sorensen, *Kennedy*, pp. 475–76.

2. Tom Wicker, *JFK and LBJ: The Influence of Personality Upon Politics*, pp. 28–82; Joseph S. Clark to John F. Kennedy, Dec. 15, 1960, POF, Legislative Files, 1; Joseph L. Rauh to Frank McCulloch, Nov. 11, 1960, Paul H. Douglas MSS: Paul H. Douglas to John F. Kennedy, Nov. 14, 1960 and attached note, Paul H. Douglas MSS; Unsigned analysis [probably by Joseph Rauh and John Silard], Nov. 22, 1960, Harris Wofford Files, 9; *Congressional Record*, Jan. 10, 1961, p. 520; Monthly Report of the Washington Bureau, Feb. 10, 1961, NAACP; Mike Mansfield, interviewed by Seth P. Tillman, June 23, 1964, KLOHP, 42; Clinton P. Anderson, interviewed by John F. Stewart, April 14, 1967, KLOHP, 45–46.

3. Unsigned memo to Mike Feldman, Feb. 16, 1961, POF, Staff Memoranda, 2; Harris Wofford to John F. Kennedy, Dec. 30, 1960, RFK, 1960 Campaign and Transition, 21.

4. Roy Wilkins to Harris Wofford, April 5, 1961, Harris Wofford Files, 11; John F. Kennedy, *Public Papers of the Presidents*, 1961, p. 157; Wofford speech before National Civil Liberties Clearing House, March 23, 1961, Harris Wofford Files, 16; *Afro-American* (Baltimore), April 1, 1961.

5. *Afro-American* (Baltimore), March 11, 1961, April 1, 1961; Roy Wilkins to Harris Wofford, April 5, 1961, Harris Wofford Files, 11; *The Crisis*, Feb., 1961, 105; *NYT*, Jan. 7, 1961.

6. Lee C. White to Larry O'Brien, Feb. 23, 1961, POF, Legislative Files, 1; *Afro-American* (Baltimore), Feb. 25, 1961, July 8, 1961; Adam Clayton Powell, Jr., *Adam by Adam*, 202–3; Report of the Washington Bureau, May 4, 1961, NAACP.

7. Hubert Humphrey to Larry O'Brien, March 24, 1961, and attached memo from Mike Mannatos to O'Brien, March 29, 1961, WHSF, 482; Unsigned memo for Senator Hubert Humphrey, March 27, 1961, POF, Legislative File, 1; NYT, May 9–10, 1961; Harris Wofford to the President, May 22, 1961, WHSF, 359; Louis Martin to Ted Sorensen, May 10, 1961, WHSF, 492; Statement of Roy Wilkins, May 10, 1961 and attached memo to All Participating Organizations from Wilkins, May 12, 1961, ADA, series 5, Box 12.

8. *NYT*, Jan. 18, Feb. 13, May 11, Nov. 19, 1961; *Congressional Record*, May 4, 1961, 7340; Roy Wilkins to Paul Douglas, Jan. 16, 1961, Paul H. Douglas MSS: Joint Statement by Rep. Thomas B. Curtis et al., Jan. 2, 1961, Charles Halleck MSS: Thomas B. Curtis to Charles A. Halleck, Jan. 2, 1961, Charles Halleck MSS: Transcript, GOP Leaders Press Conference, March 9, 1961, Charles Halleck MSS.

9. "November, 1960, Tour," Nov. 30, 1960, Benjamin Muse Field Reports, SRC; "Visit to Washington *Post*, Nov. 30, 1960," Dec. 1, 1960, Benjamin Muse Field Reports, SRC; "Press Coverage of *The Federal Executive and Civil Rights*, n.d. SRC, 78.

10. Martin Luther King, Jr., "Equality Now," *The Nation*, Feb. 4, 1961, 91–95; John Hannah to Myer Feldman, Feb. 7, 1961, Myer Feldman Files, 1532; Harris Wofford to Kenneth O'Donnell, July 11, 1961, WHSF, 358; "Proposals for Executive Action to End Federally Supported Segregation and Other Forms of Racial Discrimination," submitted, Aug. 29, 1961, by Roy Wilkins and Arnold Aronson, WHSF, 360; Press release from Leadership Conference on Civil Rights, Aug. 29, 1961, CORE, Series 5, Box 25.

11. Minutes, Board of Directors Meeting, Jan. 3, 1961, NAACP; *The Crisis*, Feb. 1961, p. 105; *Afro-American* (Baltimore), Feb. 18, 1961; Pittsburgh *Courier*, Jan. 7, 1961.

12. Roy Wilkins, interviewed by Berl Bernhard, Aug. 13, 1964, KLOHP, 6; Simeon Booker, *Black Man's America*, 204; *Ebony*, March 1961, pp. 33–41.

13. "Appointment of Negroes to High Government Posts," n.d., WHSF, 370; Louis Martin, personal interview; *Afro-American* (Baltimore), Oct. 7, 1961, Juy 21, 1962; Pittsburgh *Courier*, Sept. 2, 1961; Lee White, interviewed by Milton Gwirtzman, May 26, 1964, KLOHP, 73. On Thurgood Marshall, see: Richard Kluger, *Simple Justice, passim.*

14. *Afro-American* (Baltimore), July 8, 1961, July 15, 1961; Pittsburgh *Courier*, July 8, 1961, July 15, 1961; Marjorie Lawson, personal interview.

15. Simeon Booker, interviewed by John Stewart, April 24, 1967, KLOHP, 28; Media list, n.d., Harris Wofford Files, 5; Telegram, C. Sumner Stone, Jr. to President Kennedy, April 28, 1961, WHSF, 370.

16. *NYT*, April 30, 1961; Clipping, New York *Herald Tribune*, Sept. 21, 1961, DNC; Schlesinger, *A Thousand Days*, p. 932; *Sorenen, Kennedy*, p. 477; Pedro Sanjuan, interviewed by Dennis O'Brien, Aug. 6, 1969, KLOHP, 47–49; "Visit to Washington *Post*, Nov. 30, 1960," Dec. 1, 1960, Benjamin Muse Field Reports, SRC; Booker, *Black Man's America*, p. 201–2; Robert F. Kennedy to Board of Governors, Metropolitan Club, April 11, 1961, Howard W. Smith MSS, 204; Carl Rowan to Robert F. Kennedy, Sept. 23, 1961, RFK, Attorney General, General 12; Rafer Johnson to Robert F. Kennedy, June 27, 1963, RFK, Attorney General, General, 31.

17. Pittsburgh *Courier*, Sept. 2, 1961; Clarence Mitchell, personal interview; Arthur A. Chapin, Jr., interviewed by John Stewart, Feb. 24, 1967, KLOHP, 46; Sanjuan, interview, KLOHP, 57, 65–67; Roy Wilkins to Andrew Hatcher, March 21, 1961, WHSF, 359; Monthly Report of the Washington Bureau, Aug. 25, 1961, NAACP.

18. Harris Wofford, interviewed by Berl Bernhard, Nov. 29, 1965 and by Larry Hackman, May 22, 1968, KLOHP, 34–35, 62–63, 102–3, 128; Harris Wofford to Kenneth O'Donnell, June 12, 1961, WHSF, 358; Lee White, interview, KLOHP, 55–57.

19. Agenda for Cabinet Meeting, March 2, 1961, Timothy J. Reardon Files, 1453; Draft of notes of Subcabinet meeting, July 21, 1961, Harris Wofford Files, 14; Frederick G. Dutton to the President, May 26, 1961, POF, Staff Memoranda, 2; Roy Wilkins, interview, KLOHP, 7.

20. John Hannah to Myer Feldman, Feb. 7, 1961, Myer Feldman Files, 1532; Myer Feldman to the President, Feb. 6, 1961, POF, Subject Files, 2, Dulles, *The Civil Rights Commission*, p. 100 and *passim*.

21. Statement by Bishop Stephen G. Spottswood, Harris Wofford Files, 5; Report of Executive Secretary to Board, Sept. 11, 1961, NAACP; Roy Wilkins, interview, KLOHP, 11; Clarence Mitchell, interview, KLOHP, 11–12.

22. Booker, *Black Man's America*, p. 25; Harris Wofford, interviewed by Larry Hackman, KLOHP, 66; Kennedy, *Public Papers of the Presidents*, 1961, p. 517; Joseph L. Rauh, Jr., interviewed by Charles T. Morrissey, Dec. 23, 1965, KLOHP, 100–103.

23. Kennedy, *Public Papers*, 1961, pp. 69, 124–25, 150, 218, 304, 396, 504, 572, 591, 644–45; *NYT*, July 22, 1961; *Rights for Americans: The Speeches of Robert F. Kennedy*, Edited, with a commentary, by Thomas A. Hopkins, pp. 26–28.

24. Kennedy, *Public Papers*, 1961, pp. 22, 124–25; Speech by Harris Wofford before National Civil Liberties Clearing House, March 23, 1961, Harris Wofford Files, 16; *Rights for Americans*, p. 22.

25. Roy Wilkins to President Kennedy, Aug. 16, 1961, Harris Wofford Files, 11; Louis Martin to Theodore Sorensen, Dec. 6, 1961, Lee White Files, 20; *The Crisis*, Oct. 1961, p. 499; Simeon Booker, "Mr. Civil Rights Goes to Africa," *Ebony*, Oct., 1961, pp. 88–94; Kennedy, *Public Papers*, 1961, pp.

1–3, 19–28; Sorensen, *Kennedy*, pp. 240–45; Frederick G. Dutton, interviewed by Charles T. Morrissey, May 3, 1965, KLOHP, 54.

26. Minutes, first meeting of the President's Committee on Equal Employment Opportunity, April 11, 1961, Harris Wofford Files, 8; *Rights for Americans*, p. 84; Notes on first meeting of the Civil Rights Subcabinet Group, April 14, 1961, WHSF, 358.

27. Schlesinger, *A Thousand Days*, pp. 139–40; Chester Bowles, interviewed by Robert R. R. Brooks, Feb. 2, 1965, KLOHP, 13.

28. Dean Rusk to Robert Kennedy, Jan. 31, 1961, WHSF, 365; Memo by Pedro Sanjuan, May 17, 1961, WHSF, 365; Pedro Sanjuan, interviewed by Dennis O'Brien, Aug. 6, 1969, KLOHP, 27–56; *Department of State Bulletin*, Oct. 2, 1961, pp. 551–52; Oct. 23, 1961, pp. 671–73; Fred Dutton to Pierre Salinger, Aug. 10, 1961, WHSF, 365; *Afro-American* (Baltimore), Sept. 3, 1961; *NYT*, Jan. 21, April 28, July 12, Sept. 26, 1961.

29. Sanjuan, interview, KLOHP, *passim;* Pogress Reports, Special Protocol Services, Office of the Chief of Protocol, June 16, 1963, BM, 6.

30. Kennedy, *Public Papers*, 1961, p. 150; Hobart Taylor, Jr., interviewed by Stephen Goodell, Jan. 6, 1969, Johnson Library, 14–15; Johnson's remarks, transcript of meeting of PCEEO, Nov. 15, 1962, George Reedy Files, 10.

31. GER [George E. Reedy] to Lyndon Johnson, n.d., LBJ, Vice Presidential, Civil Rights; Johnson's remarks, transcript of meeting of PCEEO, Nov. 15, 1962, George Reedy Files, 10; Hobart Taylor, Jr., interviewed by John F. Stewart, Jan. 11, 1967, KLOHP, 9–11.

32. Hobart Taylor, interview, Johnson Library, 17–18; Robert Troutman, Jr. to Lyndon Johnson et al., Dec. 5, 1961, LBJ, Vice Presidential, Civil Rights; Statement by Lyndon Johnson, May 2, 1961, LBJ, Vice Presidential, Civil Rights; GER [George E. Reedy] to the Vice President, July 24, 1961, George Reedy Files, 6; President's Committee on Equal Employment Opportunity, *The First Nine Months*, esp. pp. 47, 61–62; Harris Wofford, interviewed by Hackman, KLOHP, 134.

33. Arthur Goldberg to John F. Kennedy, July 5, 1962, Lee White Files, 20; *Wall Street Journal*, March 7, 1961; Michael I. Sovern, *Legal Restraints on Racial Discrimination in Employment*, pp. 106–13; Hobart Taylor, Jr., interview, Johnson Library, 20–21.

34. Chester Bowles to John F. Kennedy, Jan. 31, 1961, POF, Subjects, 2; John Seigenthaler to Frederick Dutton, April 11, 1961, WHSF, 370.

35. Unissued press release, PCEEO, July 20, 1961, WHSF, 370; Frederick Dutton to John F. Kennedy, June 22, 1961, WHSF, 370; Survey results, Harris Wofford Files, 10, 15; President's Committee on Equal Employment Opportunity, *Report to the President*, (1963), pp. 38–103.

36. *Afro-American* (Baltimore), Dec. 8, 1962; President's Committee, *The First Nine Months*, pp. 7–8, 16–17; Roy Wilkins, interview, KLOHP, 7; Thurgood Marshall, interviewed by Berl Bernhard, April 7, 1964, KLOHP,

14; John W. Macy, Jr., interviewed by Fred Holborn, May 23, 1964, KLOHP, 67; John Seigenthaler to Frederick J. Dutton, April 11, 1961, WHSF, 370.

37. Frederick G. Dutton to Harris Wofford, Andrew Hatcher and Louis Martin, July 8, 1961, WHSF, 358.

38. NYT, Jan. 6, 1961; Sorensen, Kennedy, pp. 480–81; Harris Wofford to John F. Kennedy, Oct. 10, 1961, Harris Wofford Files, 8; Berl Bernhard to Frederick Dutton et al., Nov. 17, 1961, Harris Wofford Files, 1; Weekly reports to Frederick Dutton, Oct. 17 and Nov. 28, 1961, Housing and Home Finance Agency, Microfilm, 6; Lee White to John F. Kennedy, Nov. 13, 1961, WHSF, 358; Robert C. Weaver, interviewed by Daniel Patrick Moynihan, May and Oct., 1964, KLOHP, 158–60; John Sparkman to John F. Kennedy, Oct. 6, 1961, WHSF, 371; Albert Rains to John F. Kennedy, Oct. 7, 1961, WHSF, 371; William Hartsfield to John F. Kennedy, Oct. 19, 1961, WHSF, 371. On Kennedy's housing bill, see; Mark I. Gelfand, A Nation of Cities: The Federal Government and Urban America, 1933–1965.

39. Sorensen, Kennedy, p. 473; Frederick Dutton to C. Douglas Dillon, March 15, 1961, WHSF, 359; Speech by C. Douglas Dillon, Oct. 17, 1962, RFK, Attorney General, General, 17; Robert McNamara to John F. Kennedy, March 16, 1961, WHSF, 359; Robert F. Kennedy, Just Friends and Brave Enemies, p. 111.

40. Fred Dutton to Frank Reeves, April 12, 1961, WHSF, 370; Ralph Horton to Theodore Sorensen, Oct. 5, 1961, WHSF, 370; Carlisle P. Runge to Lee White, Oct. 26, 1961, Lee White Files, 24; Lee White to John F. Kennedy, Nov. 13, 1961, WHSF, 358; NYT, June 24, 1962.

41. Luther Hodges to John F. Kennedy, June 1, 1961, WHSF, 373; Afro-American (Baltimore), March 11, 1961; Monthly report of the Washington Bureau, March 10, 1961, NAACP; Allen J. Ellender to John F. Kennedy, Dec. 29, 1960; Kennedy to Ellender, Jan. 2, 1961, POF, General Correspondence, 2; Frank B. Ellis to John F. Kennedy, Jan. 13, 1961, POF, General Correspondence, 2; Sorensen, Kennedy, pp. 613–14; Allen J. Ellender, interviewed by Larry J. Hackman, Aug. 29, 1967, KLOHP, 22–23; Joseph F. Dolan, interviewed by Charles T. Morrissey, Dec. 4, 1964, KLOHP, 71.

42. James L. Sundquist, Politics nd Policy: The Eisenhower, Kennedy and Johnson Years, passim; Lawrence O'Brien to John F. Kennedy, July 30, 1962, attached to memo from Henry H. Wilson, Jr. to O'Brien, July 18, 1962, POF, Staff Memoranda, 2; Henry H. Wilson, Jr., to Lawrence O'Brien, July 18, 1962, JFK, POF, Staff Memoranda, 64.

FOUR
Southern Law Enforcement Policy

1. Robert F. Kennedy, The Enemy Within, pp. 324–25; Jack Newfield, Robert Kennedy: A Memoir, p. 40.

2. On Robert Kennedy's upbringing, early career and personality, see: *American Journey;* Newfield, *Robert Kennedy;* Rose Kennedy, *Times to Remember;* Edwin Guthman, *We Band of Brothers.*

3. Schlesinger, *A Thousand Days,* pp. 141–43, 292, 702; Alexander M. Bickel, "Robert Kennedy: The Case Against Him for Attorney General," *New Republic,* Jan. 9, 1961, pp. 15–19; *NYT,* Dec. 17, 1960, Jan. 15, 1961; Burke Marshall, personal interview.

4. Guthman, *We Band of Brothers,* 89; Hearing before the Senate Judiciary Committee on Robert Kennedy, Attorney General Designate, 87th Cong., 1st sess., 37.

5. Guthman, *We Band of Brothers,* pp. 86–107; Victor S. Navasky, *Kennedy Justice, passim.* In addition, John Seigenthaler, a special assistant to Robert Kennedy, later became editor of the Nashville *Tennesseean* and Edwin Guthman, who handled press relations, became national editor of the Los Angeles *Times.* Moreover, several of Kennedy's Justice Department attorneys, Herbert Miller, formerly head of the Criminal Division, Nobert Schlei, Katzenbach's successor as Legal Counsel, and William G. Hundley, who worked in the special organized crime unit, served as lawyers to Watergate defendants.

6. Navasky, *Kennedy Justice,* p. 162; Guthman, *We Band of Brothers,* pp. 95–96; Harris Wofford, interviewed by Hackman, KLOHP, 122–25; Monthly Report of the Washington Bureau, Feb. 10, 1961, NAACP; Burke Marshall, personal interview; Burke Marshall, interviewed by Larry J. Hackman, Jan. 19–20, 1970, KLOHP, 1–2; Hearings before the Senate Judiciary Committee on the nomination of Burke Marshall to be an Assistant Attorney General, 87th Cong., 1st sess.; *NYT,* March 16, 1961; Clarence Mitchell, personal interview; John Lewis, personal interview.

7. *Wall Street Journal,* March 6, 1961; Clipping, article by Don Oberdorfer, Washington *Post,* March 5, 1961, DNC: Peter Maas, "Robert Kennedy Speaks Out," *Look,* March 28, 1961, pp. 24–26; Robert Manning, "Someone the President Can Talk To," *New York Times Magazine,* May 28, 1961, pp. 22ff.

8. Ernest F. Hollings to Robert F. Kennedy, March 14, 1961, RFK, Attorney General, General, 27; Guthman, *We Band of Brothers,* pp. 158–61; Burke Marshall, personal interview; Marvin Caplan, "Attorney General Kennedy's New Move to Enforce Integrated Education," *I. F. Stone's Bi-Weekly,* May 8, 1961; Atlanta *Constitution,* May 10, 1961; *NYT,* May 7, 1961.

9. Atlanta *Constitution,* May 3 and May 8, 1961; Guthman, *We Band of Brothers,* pp. 164–65; *Rights for Americans,* pp. 13–16.

10. *Rights for Americans,* pp. 17–26.

11. Atlanta *Constitution,* May 8, 1961; *Rights for Americans,* 16; Guthman, *We Band of Brothers,* pp. 164–65; Pittsburgh *Courier,* May 20, 1961; *Afro-American* (Baltimore), May 20, 1961; Montgomery *Advertiser,* May 7, 1961.

12. August Meier and Elliot Rudwick, *CORE: A Study in the Civil Rights Movement, 1942–1968*, pp. 135–38; James Peck, *Freedom Ride;* Montgomery *Advertiser*, May 16, 1961; Jimmy McDonald, "A Freedom Rider Speaks His Mind," *Freedomways*, 1 (Summer 1961), 158–62.

13. Clipping, Washington *Star*, May 28, 1961, DNC; Burke Marshall, interviewed by Louis Oberdorfer, May 29, 1964, KLOHP, *passim*.

14. John Seigenthaler to anon., Nov. 14, 1961, RFK, Attorney General, General, 58; Montgomery *Advertiser*, May 18 and May 19, 1961; John Patterson, interviewed by John Stewart, May 26, 1967, KLOHP; Report from Benjamin Muse, July 13, 1961, SRC.

15. Montgomery *Advertiser*, May 20 and May 21, 1961; *NYT*, May 21, 1961; Clippings, New York *Herald Tribune*, May 21 and May 22, 1961, White House Scrap Books; Clippings, Washington *Star*, May 28, 1961, DNC; John Seigenthaler to anon., Nov. 14, 1961, RFK, Attorney General, General 58.

16. Burke Marshall, *Federalism and Civil Rights*, pp. 65–66; Montgomery *Advertiser*, May 22, 1961; Memorandum of conversation between John Patterson and Robert Kennedy, May 20, 1961, RFK, Attorney General.

17. Montgomery *Advertiser*, May 21, 1961; Burke Marshall, interviewed by Louis Oberdorfer, KLOHP, 23, 35; *Business Week*, June 3, 1961, p. 22.

18. Montgomery *Advertiser*, May 22 and 23, 1961; Clipping, New York *Herald Tribune*, May 22, 1961, White House Scrap Books; *NYT*, May 22 and 23, 1961.

19. Clipping, Washington *Evening Star*, May 22, 1961, White House Scrap Books; Montgomery *Advertiser*, May 22 and 23, 1961; *Wall Street Journal*, May 22, 1961.

20. Memorandum of phone conversation with Jim Folsom, signed "nb," May 22 [1961], RFK, Attorney General; Montgomery *Advertiser*, May 22, 1961; *Wall Street Journal*, May 24 and 26, 1961; Clippings, Washington *Post*, May 22 and 23, 1961, White House Scrap Books.

21. Montgomery *Advertiser*, May 22 and 23, 1961; Clipping, Washington *Post*, May 24, 1961, White House Scrap Books; Burke Marshall, interviewed by Louis Oberdorfer, KLOHP, 34–35; Kennedy, *Public Papers*, 1961, 391.

22. Transcript of telephone conversation between Burke Marshall and Attorney General Patterson, May 22, 1961, RFK, Attorney General.

23. Burke Marshall, interviewed by Louis Oberdorfer, KLOHP, 37–38; Telephone conversation between Robert F. Kennedy and Governor Ross Barnett, May 23, 1961, RFK, Attorney General; Comments by Burke Marshall in *American Journey*, pp. 95–96; "Telephone Calls," list, May 25, 1961, RFK, Attorney General.

24. Meier and Rudwick, *CORE*, 138–39; Montgomery *Advertiser*, May 25, 1961; *NYT*, May 25, 1961; Unsigned memo, 1:45 A.M., May 24, 1961, RFK, Attorney General. Several days later a USIA report assessed the damaging

impact of the Alabama incident on the American image abroad. See: USIA, "Worldwide Reactions to Racial Incidents in Alabama," May 29, 1961, RFK, Attorney General, General, 69.

25. Guthman, *We Band of Brothers*, pp. 177–78.

26. David L. Lewis, *King: A Critical Biography*, pp. 132–36; Meier and Rudwick, *CORE* 139–58; James Farmer to Roy Wilkins, Sept. 18, 1961, CORE, Series 1, Box 7.

27. *NYT*, May 30, June 2, Sept. 25, 1961; Alan S. Boyd, William L. Cary, Newton N. Minow, Joseph C. Swidler, William H. Tucker, interviewed by Dan Fenn, Jr., Aug. 18, 1964, KLOHP, 75–88; Clipping, Washington *Post*, Nov. 3, 1961, DNC.

28. Burke Marshall to Robert F. Kennedy, Jan. 16, 1962, BM, 16; Burke Marshall to Robert F. Kennedy, Feb. 19, 1962, BM, 16; James Farmer, interviewed by John Stewart, March 10, 1967, KLOHP, 7; Meier and Rudwick, *CORE*, 144.

29. Clipping, Washington *Star*, May 28, 1961, DNC; Burke Marshall, interviewed by Anthony Lewis, June 13, 1964, KLOHP, 48–50; *NYT*, June 22, 1961.

30. Burke Marshall, personal interview; Marshall, *Federalism and Civil Rights*, pp. 71–75. (This book is based on the Gino Speranza Lectures, given at Columbia University in March and April, 1964.)

31. *NYT*, June 7, 1961; Clipping, Washington *Post*, May 22, 1961, White House Scrap Books; Montgomery *Advertiser*, May 24, 1961; Hazel Gaudet Erskine, "The Polls: Race Relations," *Public Opinion Quarterly*, 26 (Spring 1962), 145; Hazel Gaudet Erskine, "The Polls: Kennedy as President," *Public Opinion Quarterly*, 28 (Summer 1964), 336. Of the 63 percent of the people surveyed on June 21, 1961 who had a general idea of the Freedom Riders' activities, 24 percent approved, 64 percent disapproved, and 12 percent had no opinion.

32. Nicholas deB. Katzenbach, interviewed by Anthony Lewis, Nov. 16, 1964, KLOHP, 17–21; Burke Marshall, interviewed by Louis Oberdorfer, May 29, 1964, KLOHP, 18–34; Harris Wofford to President-elect Kennedy, Dec. 30, 1961, RFK, 1960 Campaign and Transition, 21; *NYT*, June 20, 1961.

33. Donald R. Matthews and James W. Prothro, *Negroes and the New Southern Politics*, 17–18 and *passim*; Pat Watters and Reese Cleghorn, *Climbing Jacob's Ladder: The Arrival of Negroes in Southern Politics*, p. 49; United States Commission on Civil Rights, *Voting* (1961), pp. 104–12, 252–307.

34. Correspondence between Stephen Currier and Martin Luther King, 1961, Martin Luther King MSS, Boston University; Confidential source (on Currier's attitude toward the Kennedys); Harold Fleming to author, May 16, 1972; Louis Lomax, "The Kennedys Move In on Dixie," *Harper's Magazine*, May 1962, pp. 27–33; Leslie Dunbar to Members of the Executive Committee, July 31, 1961, VEP, 98; Leslie Dunbar to Members of the Execu-

tive Committee, Sept. 13, 1961, VEP, 98; Minutes of National Action Committee of CORE, Oct. 27, 1961, CORE, Series 4, Box 1; Draft notes on Subcabinet group on Civil Rights, Sept. 15, 1961, Harris Wofford Files, 14.

35. Lewis, *King*, pp. 135–37; Howard Zinn, *SNCC: The New Abolitionists*, 58–59; John Lewis, personal interview; Memo on SNCC meeting, June 14, 1961, SRC, 137; Minutes, Board of Directors Meeting, Oct. 9, 1961, NAACP; Report to the Board of Directors, Nov. 13, 1961, NAACP; Roy Wilkins to Leslie W. Dunbar, Oct. 17, 1961; Dunbar to Wilkins, Nov. 10, 1961, VEP, 94.

36. News release, Southern Regional Council, Jan., 1962, VEP, 98; John S. Littleton to Southern Regional Council, March 22, 1962, Benjamin Muse Field Reports, SRC; Watters and Cleghorn, *Climbing Jacob's Ladder*, p. 49; Financial Summary, Jan. 7, 1964, VEP. As of January, 1964, the NAACP received $75,830; CORE, $51,425; National Urban League, $15,961; SCLC, $32,700; SNCC, $23,884. Local grants ranged in size from $200 for a project in Lafayette Parish, Louisiana, to $40,400 for a statewide project in Texas.

37. Wiley A. Branton to David Hunter, Feb. 4, 1964, Stern Family Fund, New York; Wiley Branton, personal interview; Emily Schottenfeld Stoper, "The Student Nonviolent Co-ordinating Committee: The Growth of Radicalism in a Civil Rights Organization," (Ph.D. diss., Harvard University, 1968), p. 58.

38. *NYT*, June 20, 1961; John Lewis, personal interview.

39. *Report of the Attorney General* (1961), pp. 167–68; John Thomas Elliff, "The United States Department of Justice and Individual Rights, 1937–1962," (Ph.D diss., Harvard University, 1967), pp. 650–51. When the White House sought nineteen additional lawyers for the Civil Rights Division in 1963, Congress authorized eight. See: *NYT*, Dec. 9 and Dec. 13, 1963.

40. John Doar and Dorothy Landsberg, *The Performance of the FBI in Investigating Violations of Federal Law Protecting the Right to Vote—1960–1967* (Photocopy, Copyright 1971), 7–8, 15a; Marshall, *Federalism and Civil Rights*, 18–20.

Doar and Landsberg also note that in early 1964 Marshall informally requested the FBI to do the records analysis. The FBI declined, citing manpower limitations. Marshall, "perhaps aware of the other struggles the Department was having with the Bureau on other types of investigations, decided not to press the point. . . . Mr. Marshall's decision ratified a treaty which the Division had already worked out with the Bureau. The Bureau would not have to analyze the records, but it would conduct all the interviews we requested, do it thoroughly, and if, in our judgment, necessary, on an expedited basis. For its parts, the Division would analyze the records and would operate in parallel as an investigative agency in voting matters across the South." (In Doar and Landsberg, *The Performance of the FBI*, pp. 17–17a.)

41. Doar and Landsberg, *The Performance of the FBI,* pp. 11–13.

42. *Ibid.,* pp. 17–17a; *Report of the Attorney General* (1962), p. 162; "The Law and Civil Rights: The Justice Department in the South; an Interview with Thelton Henderson," *New University Thought,* 3, no. 4 (1963), 41–43; Case Documents, BM, 22–26.

43. Burke Marshall to Attorney General, Aug. 14, 1961, BM, 1; Burke Marshall to Attorney General, Aug. 13, 1962, BM, 16; Burke Marshall to Robert Kennedy, June 26, 1961, BM, 1; Burke Marshall to Robert Kennedy, Oct. 22, 1961, BM, 3; Burke Marshall to Robert Kennedy, Jan. 16, 1961, BM, 16; Gerald M. Stern, "Judge William Harold Cox and the Right to Vote in Clarke County, Mississippi," in Leon Friedman, ed. *Southern Justice,* pp. 165–86; Donald S. Strong, *Negroes, Ballots, and Judges: National Voting Rights Legislation in the Federal Courts; Rights for Americans,* 92; Marshall, *Federalism and Civil Rights,* 23–24.

In all of Mississippi there were only two counties which agreed voluntarily to allow photographing of their records. See: Burke Marshall to Robert Kennedy, March 27, 1962, BM, 16.

44. Barbara Carter, "The Fifteenth Amendment Comes to Mississippi," *The Reporter,* Jan. 17, 1963, p. 24; Marshall, *Federalism and Civil Rights,* pp. 25–27.

45. Marshall, *Federalism and Civil Rights,* pp. 25–29; Charles V. Hamilton, "Southern Judges and Negro Voting Rights: The Judicial Approach to the Solution of Controversial Social Problems," *Wisconsin Law Review* (Winter 1965), pp. 72–102.

46. Carl Rachlin to Mrs. Franklin D. Roosevelt, April 16, 1962, CORE, Series 5, Box 5; Alexander M. Bickel, "Civil Rights: The Kennedy Record," *New Republic,* Dec. 15, 1962, pp. 11–16; *New Republic,* Oct. 26, 1963, p. 5; Zinn, *SNCC,* 204–5; Louis Lusky, "Justice With a Southern Accent," *Harper's Magazine,* March 1964, p. 73; Friedman, ed., *Southern Justice, passim;* Alexander M. Bickel, *Politics and the Warren Court,* pp. 56–74.

47. Joseph F. Dolan, interviewed by Charles T. Morrissey, Dec. 4, 1964, KLOHP, 71.

48. Lee White to Larry O'Brien, March 16, 1961, POF, Legislative Files, 1.

49. Burke Marshall, interviewed by Hackman, KLOHP, 14; *NYT,* June 1, 1961; *New Republic,* Oct. 9, 1961, pp. 6–7; William C. Battle to Harry F. Byrd, Jan. 14, 1962, Harry F. Byrd MSS, 242.

50. Joseph Dolan, interview, KLOHP, p. 89; Marshall, *Federalism and Civil Rights,* p. 31; Peltason, *Fifty-Eight Lonely Men;* Marshall Frady, *Wallace,* pp. 131–35. In *Simple Justice,* Richard Kluger described what happened to Judge J. Waties Waring after he broke with his background and community over civil rights in the 1940s.

51. Burke Marshall, interviewed by Hackman, KLOHP, 19–20; Navasky, *Kennedy Justice,* p. 257; Nicholas Katzenbach, interviewed by Anthony

Lewis, KLOHP, 5; Roy Wilkins to President Kennedy, June 22, 1961, Harris Wofford Files, 11; Comment by Marion Wright Edelman in *American Journey*, p. 112.

52. Mary Hannah Curzan, "A Case Study in the Selection of Federal Judges: The Fifth Circuit, 1953–1963," (Ph.D. diss., Yale University, 1968), esp. pp. 36–45. (Because Curzan based part of her research on interviews, only a summary of her work was available, which is what is cited here.) Unfortunately, the quantification of judicial decisions for the purpose of deciding which judges are "segregationists" and which "integrationists" can yield odd and somewhat misleading classifications. By her system of analysis, Frank Johnson comes out a "segregationist."

53. Comment by Marion Wright Edelman in *American Journey*, p. 112; Burke Marshall, interviewed by Anthony Lewis, KLOHP, 93–94; Robert Kennedy to Eleanor Roosevelt, Mary 22, 1962, BM, 3; Marshall, *Federalism and Civil Rights*, p. 31.

54. Joseph Dolan, interviewed by Morrissey, KLOHP, 89.

FIVE
A Harder Road

1. Clipping, William S. White column, Nashville *Tennesseean*, Jan. 2, 1962, *Facts on Film*; Hearings before a Subcommittee of the House Appropriations Committee, 87th Cong., 2nd sess. (Robert Kennedy testified on Jan. 22, 1962.)

2. Memo of visits to Virginia, North Carolina, South Carolina, Mississippi and Tennessee, March 6, 1961, Benjamin Muse Reports, SRC; *Congressional Record*, Aug. 21, 1961, pp. 16478–79.

3. Lee White to the President, Aug. 21, 1961, Lee White Files, 18.

4. *NYT*, Jan. 22, 1961; *Congressional Quarterly Almanac*, 1962, p. 381.

5. John F. Kennedy, *Public Papers of the Presidents*, 1962, pp. 63, 77, 97; *Congressional Quarterly Almanac*, 1962, p. 383.

6. Sorensen, *Kennedy*, p. 481; *Congressional Quarterly Almanac*, 1962, p. 383; Roy Wilkins to Thomas B. Curtis, Feb. 19, 1962, Thomas B. Curtis MSS; Clarence Mitchell to Thomas B. Curtis, Feb. 16, 1962, Thomas B. Curtis MSS, 481.

7. Transcript, Republican National Committee Press Conference, Senator Dirksen and Rep. Halleck, Jan. 30, 1962, Charles Halleck MSS; Thomas B. Curtis to Clarence Mitchell, March 5, 1962, Thomas B. Curtis MSS, 481; *Congressional Record*, Feb. 15, 1962, pp. 2348–50; *Afro-American* (Baltimore), March 3, 1962.

8. *Congressional Quarterly Almanac*, 1962, p. 383; *Congressional Record*, 87th Cong., 2nd sess., 2527–44, 2630–80; Mike Mansfield, interviewed by Seth P. Tillman, June 23, 1964, KLOHP, 37–38; Robert C. Weaver, interviewed by

Moynihan, KLOHP, 114–22. For a discussion of this battle in the context of the long controversy over federal urban policy, see: Gelfand, *A Nation of Cities.*

9. Burke Marshall to Lee White, Feb. 19, 1962, BM, 1; Henry H. Wilson, Jr. to Lawrence F. O'Brien, Feb. 28, 1962, TCS, 58; Correspondence between President Kennedy and Spessard Holland, Feb. 14, March 6, March 7, 1962, WHSF, 374; Monthly Report of the Washington Bureau, April 4, 1962, NAACP; *Congressional Quarterly Almanac,* 1962, pp. 404–6; Sorensen, *Kennedy,* p. 475.

10. Kennedy, *Public Papers,* 1962, p. 8; Remarks by Burke Marshall at the annual conference of the National Civil Liberties Clearing House, March 29, 1962, BM, 13.

11. Burke Marshall, interviewed by Anthony Lewis, June 13, 1964, KLOHP, 64; Burke Marshall, personal interview; Lee White, interviewed by Milton Gwirtzman, May 26, 1964, KLOHP, 75–76.

12. *Congressional Record,* Jan. 30, 1962, pp. 1213–24.

13. Hearings before the Subcommittee on Constitutional Rights of the Senate Judiciary Committee, 87th Cong., 2nd sess., "Literacy Tests and Voter Requirements in Federal and State Elections," pp. 261–94, 490–91.

14. *Congressional Record,* May 1, 1962, 7365.

15. Report by Herman Edelsberg and David A. Brody, "Civil Rights in the 87th Congress Second Session," Jan. 1, 1963, Myer Feldman Files; *NYT,* May 10, 1962; *Congressional Record,* May 8, 1962, pp. 4941–42, 8058; *Congressional Quarterly Almanac,* 1962, p. 377.

16. Kennedy, *Public Papers,* 1962, pp. 381–82; *Congressional Record,* May 14, 1962, pp. 8294ff.

17. *Congressional Record,* May 15, 1962, p. 8416; *Afro-American* (Baltimore), June 2, 1962.

18. Joseph L. Rauh to Paul Douglas, May 18, 1962, Paul Douglas MSS; Monthly report of the Washington Bureau, May 10, 1962, NAACP; Burke Marshall, interviewed by Anthony Lewis, KLOHP, 64–65; Burke Marshall, personal interview.

19. *Congressional Quarterly Almanac,* 1962, pp. 65, 273; Sundquist, *Politics and Policy,* pp. 201–5, 308–14.

20. Larry O'Brien to the President, July 30, 1962, and attached memo to O'Brien from Henry H. Wilson, Jr., July 18, 1962, POF, Staff Memoranda.

21. Erskine, "The Polls: Kennedy as President," p. 336.

22. Frank E. Smith, *Congressman from Mississippi,* pp. 284–86, 295; Burke Marshall to the Attorney General, March 27, 1962, BM, 16. That was not the only time that the Justice Department delayed an action to help a political friend of the administration in the South. About an hour before Justice Department lawyers were to file impacted-area suits in Alabama, Robert

Kennedy stopped them as a favor to Senator Lister Hill who faced a strong challenge from a right-wing Republican. The suits were filed about a month later. See: Burke Marshall, interviewed by Hackman, KLOHP, 15.

23. Smith, *Congressman from Mississippi*, pp. 233–34; *NYT*, June 25, 1962.

24. Report from Benjamin Muse, Jan. 11, 1962, Benjamin Muse Reports, SRC; Report from Benjamin Muse, Feb. 6, 1964, Benjamin Muse Reports, SRC; Report from Benjamin Muse, July 13, 1961, Benjamin Muse Reports, SRC.

25. *Newsweek*, May 14, 1962, p. 29; *Time*, June 8, 1962, p. 25; *Wall Street Journal*, May 28, 1962; Frady, *Wallace*, pp. 131–35.

26. Speech by Burke Marshall at the annual dinner of the Howard Law School, n.d., BM, 13.

27. Joseph L. Bernd, "Georgia: Static and Dynamic," in William C. Havard, ed., *The Changing Politics of the South*, pp. 301–2; Navasky, *Kennedy Justice*, 277–79 (the case was *Gray v. Sanders*); Robert G. Dixon, Jr. *Democratic Representation: Reapportionment in Law and Politics*, pp. 172–82; Numan V. Bartley, *From Thurmond to Wallace: Political Tendencies in Georgia, 1948–1968*, esp. 35–56; *NYT*, Sept. 14, 1962; Atlanta *Constitution*, Sept. 14, 1962.

28. Kennedy, *Public Papers*, 1962, pp. 404, 572.

29. Burke Marshall to Edwin Guthman, July 16, 1962, BM, 2; *Rights for Americans*, pp. 85–90; Burke Marshall to Robert Kennedy, June 14, 1962, BM, 1; Daniel Knapp and Kenneth Polk, *Scouting the War on Poverty: Social Reform Politics in the Kennedy Administration*.

30. Hearings before the Subcommittee on Integration in Federally Assisted Public Education Programs of the House Committee on Education and Labor, 87th Cong., 2nd sess., April 16, 1962, p. 601.

31. Harris Wofford to the President, Jan. 23, 1962, POF, Staff Memoranda; Monthly Report of the Washington Bureau, April 14, 1962, NAACP; Gary Orfield, *The Reconstruction of Southern Education: The Schools and the 1964 Civil Rights Act*, pp. 29–30.

32. *NYT*, Sept. 18, 1962; Burke Marshall to the Attorney General, Jan. 29, 1963, BM, 3.

33. Burke Marshall to the Attorney General, July 31, 1962, BM, 1.

34. *Rights for Americans*, pp. 83 and *passim*.

35. C. Sumner Stone, Jr. to Lyndon Johnson, March 9, 1962, George Reedy Files, 7; *NYT*, June 18 and 20, 1962.

36. Pittsburgh *Courier*, April 14 and July 14, 1962; *Afro-American* (Baltimore), Aug. 4, 1962; William Taylor to Harris Wofford, Dec. 8, 1961, Harris Wofford Files, 10; "The National Association for the Advancement of Colored People Appraises the First Year of the President's Committee on Equal Employment Opportunity," [probably written by Herbert Hill] April

6, 1962, George Reedy Files, 17; Harris Wofford, interviewed by Hackman, KLOHP, 137; Hobart Taylor, Jr., interviewed by Stewart, KLOHP, 18.

37. Robert Troutman, Jr. to President Kennedy, June 30, 1962, POF, Staff Memoranda; Robert Troutman, Jr. to Lyndon Johnson, June 29, 1962, LBJ, Vice President, Civil Rights; Reports of the Executive Secretary to the Board of Directors, June, July, August, 1962, NAACP.

38. John F. Kennedy to the Vice President, Aug. 22, 1962, WHSF, 370.

39. Table attached to letter from Troutman to President, June 30, 1962, POF, Staff Memoranda [I cite these statistics because they were more likely the ones Troutman had available when the controversy was raging. Troutman's final report is in Lee White Files, 20]; Hobart Taylor, Jr., interviewed by Goodell, Johnson Library.

40. GER [George E. Reedy] to Vice President, Aug. 2, 1962, and attached Kheel recommendations, George Reedy Files, 5; Adam C. Powell to Hobart Taylor, Aug. 13, 1962, LBJ, Vice President, Congress; Hobart Taylor, Jr., interviewed by Stewart, KLOHP, 14–18. John Feild resigned from the staff the following March.

SIX
The Problem of Federal Protection

1. Marshall, *Federalism and Civil Rights,* pp. 10–15; Burke Marshall, personal interview; John Doar, personal interview.

2. David Herbert Donald to Mrs. J. G. Randall, March 6, 1962. Mr. Donald kindly provided me with a copy of this letter.

3. "SNCC in Albany," n.d. VEP, 113; Lewis, *King,* pp. 140–59; Pat Watters, *Down to Now: Reflections on the Southern Civil Rights Movement, passim;* James Forman, *The Making of Black Revolutionaries,* pp. 247–62; Zinn, *SNCC,* pp. 122–34.

4. *NYT,* March 14, 18, 26, 1962; *Afro-American* (Baltimore), March 24, 1962; Burke Marshall to Robert Kennedy, March 12, 1962, BM, 16.

5. Transcript, Commission of Inquiry into the Administration of Justice in the Freedom Struggle, May 25, 26, 1962, CORE, Series 5, Box 5; Letters to Eleanor Roosevelt from Richard Salant (President of CBS News), July 27, 1962; from Frank J. Starzel (General Manager of the Associated Press), July 18, 1962; from James C. Hagerty (Vice President of ABC), July 15, 1962; from Julian Goodman (Vice President of NBC), July 20, 1962; from Turner Catledge (Managing Editor of the New York *Times*), July 23, 1962, all in CORE, Series 5, Box 5; among the politicians declining invitations were Sam J. Ervin, Edwin Willis, John V. Lindsay, Harold C. Donahue, William T. Cahill, Robert Kastenmeier and Clark MacGregor, in CORE, Series 2, Box 4; Meier and Rudwick, *CORE,* 168–69.

6. Burke Marshall to Robert Kennedy, March 12, 1962, BM, 16; Burke Marshall to James Farmer, May 10, 1962, CORE, Series 1, Box 4; "Suggested Recommendations of the Committee of Inquiry," Sept. 10, 1962, CORE, Series 1, Box 2; Monthly Report of the Washington Bureau, June 7, 1962, NAACP.

7. U.S. Commission on Civil Rights, *Justice* (1961), esp. pp. 45–54, 69–77, 269; Hearings before the Senate Judiciary Committee, 89th Cong., 1st sess., "Voting Rights," testimony of Attorney General Nicholas Katzenbach, pp. 108–09.

8. Burke Marshall to Robert Kennedy, March 27, 1962, BM, 16; H. R. 10849, March 22, 1962, Emanuel Celler MSS; Burke Marshall, personal interview.

9. U.S. Commission on Civil Rights, *Justice* (1961), 102; Hearings before Subcommittee No. 5 of the House Judiciary Committee, 88th Cong., 1st sess., p. 1231 (John Pemberton of the American Civil Liberties Union observed that there was little chance of obtaining convictions in police brutality cases "regardless of which standard [for prosecution] was used."); Forman, *The Making of Black Revolutionaries*, pp. 223–31; Statements of SNCC workers on trial of D. E. Short, Jan. 25, 1963, Americus, Georgia, VEP, 97; Charles Sherrod to Wiley Branton, Feb. 8, 1963, VEP, 97.

10. Elliff, "Aspects of Federal Civil Rights Enforcement," pp. 658–60; Barbara Carter, "The Role of the Civil Rights Commission," *The Reporter*, July 4, 1963, pp. 12–13; Hearings before Subcommittee No. 5 of the House Judiciary Committee, 88th Cong., 1st sess, pp. 12–13 (Nicholas Katzenbach's comment); Barbara Carter, "The Fifteenth Amendment Comes to Mississippi," *The Reporter*, Jan. 17, 1963, p. 23 (John Doar's comment).

11. U.S. Commission on Civil Rights, *Voting* (1961), 91–97; Doar and Landsberg, *The Performance of the FBI*, pp. 42–57.

12. List of voter intimidation cases under investigation by Justice Department in Mississippi, Sept. 1, 1962, VEP, 94; Robin Higham, ed., *Bayonets in the Streets: The Use of Troops in Civil Disturbances, passim.*

13. Elliff, "Aspects of Federal Civil Rights Enforcement," pp. 605–73; Doar and Landsberg, *The Performance of the FBI*, p. 20; Jack Levine to Bill Turner, Aug. 31, 1962, and other materials, including Pacifica radio interview and Civil Rights Commission interview of Levine, CORE, Series 5, Box 47. Levine and Turner were dissident FBI agents.

    The FBI often received sympathetic treatment in the black press in the early 1960s. See, for example: Simeon Booker, "The Negro in the FBI," *Ebony*, Sept., 1962, pp. 29–34; *Afro-American* (Baltimore), July 13, 1963 (a pro-Hoover piece by Chuck Stone).

14. See: Pat Watters and Stephen Gillers, eds. *Investigating the FBI*; Column by Marquis Childs, Baltimore *Sun*, Feb. 12, 1975; *NYT*, Feb. 28, 1975; *Newsweek*, Dec. 29, 1975, pp. 14–15; Benjamin C. Bradlee, *Conversations with Kennedy*, p. 228.

15. Memorandum by Richard Neustadt, Oct. 30, 1960, TCS, 18; J. Edgar Hoover to John F. Kennedy, Nov. 10, 1960, POF, Special Correspondence, 4; Bradlee, *Conversations with Kennedy*, pp. 33–34; Guthman, *We Band of Brothers*, p. 261.

16. Guthman, *We Band of Brothers*, pp. 260–61; Navasky, *Kennedy Justice*, pp. 11–14 and *passim;* Watters and Gillers, eds. *Investigating the FBI*, pp. 58, 96–97, 156–57; John Doar, personal interview; Burke Marshall, personal interview; Elliff, "Aspects of Federal Civil Rights Enforcement," pp. 643–47.

17. Elliff, "Aspects of Federal Civil Rights Enforcement," pp. 652–70; Doar and Landsberg, *The Performance of the FBI, passim;* "The Law and Civil Rights," *New University Thought*, 3, no. 4, pp. 41–42.

18. Attorney General to the President, Jan. 9, 1962, POF, Departments and Agencies, 13; Kennedy, *Public Papers*, 1962, p. 7; John F. Kennedy to J. Edgar Hoover, Oct. 31, 1962, POF, Special Correspondence, 4; J. Edgar Hoover to Robert F. Kennedy, Nov. 20, 1961, Oct. 31, Nov. 20, 29, 30, 1962, July 5, 1963, RFK, Attorney General, General, 27.

19. "Non Violence," by Charles Sherrod for SNCC, n.d., Charles Sherrod MSS; Leslie Dunbar, personal interview.

20. Report to Voter Education Project from Bob Moses, Dec. 5, 1962, VEP, 94; Statements of SNCC workers on trial of D. E. Short, Jan. 25, 1963, VEP, 97. For further examples, see: Jack Minnis, memorandum on Mississippi Field Trip, Jan. 9–11, 1963, VEP, 94; Jack Minnis to Wiley A. Branton, Aug. 30, 1963, VEP, 98; Charles Sherrod to Wiley Branton, Feb. 8, 1963, VEP, 97.

21. Jack Chatfield to Wiley A. Branton, Dec. 11, 1962, VEP, 97.

22. Statement of Charles Sherrod, Jan. 25, 1963, VEP, 97; "Non Violence," by Charles Sherrod for SNCC, n.d. Charles Sherrod MSS.

23. Pat Watters, *Down to Now*, pp. 172–73; Atlanta *Constitution*, July 11, 1962; *NYT*, July 11, 1962.

24. Atlanta *Constitution*, July 11 and 12, 1962; *NYT*, July 11 and 12, 1962; Watters, *Down to Now*, pp. 204–6.

25. Atlanta *Constitution*, July 13, 1962; *NYT*, July 13, 1962; *Afro-American* (Baltimore), July 21, 1962; Howard Zinn, *The Southern Mystique*, p. 173; Burke Marshall, personal interview; Carl Sanders, interviewed by John F. Stewart, May 22, 1967, KLOHP, 14–15. Sanders recalled urging the Justice Department to inform the leaders of the Albany Movement that their activities were crucifying the real moderates like him. Marshall told me that he still did not know the identity of the man who paid the fines or whom he represented.

26. Atlanta *Constitution*, July 16–20, 1962; "SNCC in Albany," n.d. VEP, 113.

27. *NYT*, July 15 and 20, 1962; Atlanta *Constitution*, July 20, 1962.

28. *NYT*, July 22–25, 1962; Atlanta *Constitution*, July 23–25, 1962; William M.

Kunstler, *Deep in My Heart,* pp. 101–13; Lewis, *King,* pp. 161–62; Navasky, *Kennedy Justice,* p. 257. Although King obeyed Elliot's injunctions, at least 160 Albany blacks did not. They marched and were arrested.

29. Atlanta *Constitution,* July 24–27, 1962; *NYT,* July 25–29, 1962; Lewis, *King,* p. 164; Zinn, *Southern Mystique,* pp. 175–79; Kunstler, *Deep in My Heart,* pp. 114–18; Watters, *Down to Now,* p. 19.

30. Atlanta *Constitution,* July 27 and 28, 1962; *NYT,* July 28, 1962.

31. Clipping, St. Louis *Post Dispatch,* July 30, 1962, SRC, 146; *NYT,* July 30, 1962.

32. Kennedy, *Public Papers,* 1962, pp. 592–93.

33. Martin Luther King, Jr. to John F. Kennedy, Aug. 2, 1962, WHSF, 366; Atlanta *Constitution,* Aug. 2–4, 1962; *NYT,* Aug. 2–4, 1962.

34. Atlanta *Constitution,* Aug. 1, 1962; Memo to Robert F. Kennedy, Aug. 2, 1962, letter to Paul Douglas, Aug. 3, 1962, from Clarence Mitchell, Paul Douglas MSS; *NYT,* Aug. 4, 7, 1962.

35. *Congressional Record,* Aug. 1, 1962, p. 14218; Atlanta *Constitution,* Aug. 3, 1962; Leonard H. Carter to Thomas B. Curtis, Aug. 6, 1962; Curtis to Carter, Aug. 14, 1962, Thomas B. Curtis MSS.

36. Atlanta *Constitution,* Aug. 9, 1962; *NYT,* Aug. 9, 1962.

37. Atlanta *Constitution,* Aug. 11, 15, 16, 20, 29, 1962; Lewis, *King,* pp. 167–70; Zinn, *Southern Mystique,* pp. 181–84; Kunstler, *Deep in My Heart,* pp. 121–24.

38. Wyatt Tee Walker, "Albany: Failure or First Step?" *New South,* 18 (June 1963), 3–8; Vincent Harding and Staughton Lynd, "Albany, Georgia," *The Crisis,* Feb., 1963, pp. 69–78; Pat Watters, *Down to Now, passim.*

39. *NYT,* Nov. 15, 1962; Howard Zinn, "Kennedy: The Reluctant Emancipator," *The Nation,* Dec. 1, 1962; Zinn, *Southern Mystique,* pp. 147–213; Walker, "Albany: Failure or First Step?"; Harding and Lynd, "Albany, Georgia"; Lewis, *King,* pp. 169–70; Martin Luther King, Jr., *Strength to Love,* esp. pp. 135–42; Clipping, *Christian Science Monitor,* Nov. 16, 1962, SRC, 146; Clipping, Murray Kempton column, New York *Post,* Nov. 27, 1962, SRC, 146.

40. William Taylor to Lee White, Aug. 15, 1962, Lee White Files, 21.

SEVEN
The Battle of Ole Miss

1. James Meredith, *Three Years in Mississippi,* esp. pp. 50–59; Walter Lord, *The Past That Would Not Die,* pp. 98–112; Burke Marshall to Constance Baker Motley, June 5, 1961, BM, 1. Meredith recalled in his memoir that until the Ole Miss ordeal he was known by his initials, J. H., rather than by his first name, James. Like some other Southern blacks, he had preferred to be

called by his initials so that whites would have to address him somewhat more formally. It was customary for whites to address blacks by their first names, not as "Mr." or "Miss."

2. Lord, *The Past That Would Not Die*, esp. pp. 139–40; Michael Dorman, *We Shall Overcome*, pp. 9–14; James W. Silver, *Mississippi: The Closed Society;* McMillen, *The Citizens' Council.*

3. Chronology of Mississippi events, BM, 19; Comment by Burke Marshall in *American Journey*, p. 104; Nicholas deB. Katzenbach, interviewed by Lewis, Nov. 29, 1964, KLOHP, 12–13; Lee White, interviewed by Gwirtzman, May 26, 1964, KLOHP, 77–78.

4. Chronology of Mississippi events, BM, 19; *Wall Street Journal,* Sept. 26, 1962.

5. Telephone transcripts, Sept. 15, 17, 18, 19, 20, 1962, BM, 20; Chronology of Mississippi events, BM, 19; Meredith, *Three Years in Mississippi*, pp. 182–89; Lord, *The Past That Would Not Die*, pp. 150–56.

6. Lord, *The Past That Would Not Die*, pp. 156–59; Telephone transcript, Sept. 24, 1962, BM, 20.

7. *NYT*, Sept. 26, 1962; Lord, *The Past That Would Not Die*, pp. 157–62; Meredith, *Three Years in Mississippi*, pp. 189–99; Dorman, *We Shall Overcome*, pp. 18–19.

8. Telephone transcript, Sept. 25, 1962, BM, 20; Guthman, *We Band of Brothers*, p. 192.

9. *NYT*, Sept. 26 and 27, 1962; Lord, *The Past That Would Not Die*, pp. 164–66; Meredith, *Three Years in Mississippi*, pp. 201–3.

10. Telephone transcripts, Sept. 27, 1962; Lord, *The Past That Would Not Die*, pp. 167–71; Guthman, *We Band of Brothers*, p. 194; *NYT*, Sept. 27, 1962.

11. *NYT*, Sept. 28, 1962; Telephone transcript, Sept. 27, 1962, BM, 20; Lord, *The Past That Would Not Die*, pp. 171–75.

12. *NYT*, Sept. 28 and 29, 1962; Clipping, New York *Herald Tribune*, Sept. 28, 1962, DNC.

13. *NYT*, Sept. 29, 1962.

14. Chronology of Mississippi events, BM, 19; Telephone transcripts, Sept. 29, 1962, POF, Subjects; Schlesinger, *A Thousand Days*, p. 944.

15. *NYT*, Sept. 29, 1962; Lord, *The Past That Would Not Die*, pp. 174–91; George B. Leonard, T. George Harris and Christopher S. Wren, "How a Secret Deal Prevented a Massacre at Ole Miss," *Look*, Dec. 31, 1962, pp. 19–36.

16. Telephone transcripts, Sept. 29, 1962, BM, 20; Lord, *The Past That Would Not Die*, pp. 190–91.

17. Norbert A. Schlei, interviewed by John F. Stewart, Feb. 20–21, 1968, KLOHP, 13–15. On the mood in Mississippi, see: Lord, *The Past That Would*

Not Die, pp. 173–91; Silver, *Mississippi: The Closed Society,* esp. 118–19; Mc-Millen, *The Citizens' Council,* pp. 342–46.

18. Telephone transcripts, Sept. 30, 1962, BM, 20 and POF, Subjects.

19. Lord, *The Past That Would Not Die,* pp. 196–203; Silver, *Mississippi: The Closed Society,* pp. 162–63; Guthman, *We Band of Brothers,* p. 201.

20. Russell H. Barrett, *Integration at Ole Miss,* p. 146; Guthman, *We Band of Brothers,* pp. 201–2; Silver, *Mississippi: The Closed Society,* pp. 163–64; 175–76; Dorman, *We Shall Overcome,* pp. 54–68.

21. Kennedy, *Public Papers,* 1962, pp. 726–28.

22. Lord, *The Past That Would Not Die,* pp. 203–23; Guthman, *We Band of Brothers,* pp. 201–3; Dorman, *We Shall Overcome,* pp. 54–68.

23. Lord, *The Past That Would Not Die,* pp. 180–84 and *passim;* James J. Kilpatrick to Joe W. Matthews, Jan. 2, 1963, James J. Kilpatrick MSS.

24. Telephone transcripts, Sept. 30, 1962, POF, Subjects; Sorensen, *Kennedy,* pp. 486–88; Guthman, *We Band of Brothers,* pp. 204–5; Lord, *The Past That Would Not Die,* pp. 220–30.

25. *NYT,* Oct. 1–3, 1962, Guthman, *We Band of Brothers,* pp. 206–7.

26. Director of FBI to Attorney General, Jan. 30, 1963, BM, 19; Meredith, *Three Years in Mississippi,* pp. 215–38; Barrett, *Integration at Ole Miss,* pp. 163–256; Silver, *Mississippi: The Closed Society,* pp. 168–243.

27. Burke Marshall to Robert Kennedy, Nov. 19, 1962, BM, 16; Burke Marshall to Robert Kennedy, Dec. 2, 1963, BM, 3; Theodore Sorensen, interviewed by Carl Kaysen, May 3, 1964, KLOHP, 128; *Afro-American* (Baltimore), Oct. 20, 1963; Navasky, *Kennedy Justice,* pp. 235–40; Barrett, *Integration at Ole Miss,* pp. 250–51; Sheldon Tefft, "United States v. Barnett: 'Twas a Famous Victory,' " *Supreme Court Review* (1964), pp. 123–36.

28. *NYT,* Oct. 2, 1962; Clipping, Jackson *Daily News,* Oct. 1, 1962, SRC; Lord, *The Past That Would Not Die,* pp. 234–48; McMillen, *The Citizens' Council,* pp. 346–54; Silver, *Mississippi: The Closed Society,* pp. 122–23; Charles S. Fortenberry and F. Glenn Abney, "Mississippi: Unreconstructed and Unredeemed," in William C. Havard, ed. *The Changing Politics of the South,* 508–9.

29. *NYT,* Oct. 1 and 3, 1962; Clipping, David Lawrence column, Atlanta *Journal,* Oct. 3, 1962, SRC; William Buckley in *National Review,* Oct. 23, 1962; Telegram to the President from Senators Hill and Sparkman and Congressmen Boykin, Grant, Andrews, Rains, Jones, Elliott, Roberts, Selden, Huddleston, Oct. 2, 1962, POF, Subjects; Clipping, Charlotte, N. C. *Observer,* Oct. 1, 1962, SRC; Clipping, Montgomery *Advertiser,* Oct. 2, 1962, SRC.

30. Theodore Sorensen to the President, Sept. 28, 1962, TCS, 30; Paul Duke in *Wall Street Journal,* Oct. 4, 1962; Clipping, James Reston column, Atlanta *Constitution,* Oct. 16, 1962, SRC.

31. Erskine, "The Polls: Kennedy as President," p. 336.

32. *NYT*, Nov. 8, 1962; Donald S. Strong, "Alabama: Transition and Alienation," in William C. Havard, ed., *The Changing Politics of the South*, pp. 438–39; *Congressional Quarterly Almanac*, 1962, 1031; William E. Miller to Charles Halleck, Nov. 9, 1962, Charles Halleck MSS; *The Republican Southern Challenge*, Dec., 1962, SRC; Louis Harris to the President, Nov. 19, 1962, POF, Special Correspondence.

33. Lou Harris to the President, Oct. 4, 1962, POF, Subjects; Pittsburgh *Courier*, Oct. 6, 13, 20, 1962; *I. F. Stone's Weekly*, Oct. 8, 1962; *Liberation*, Nov., 1962, pp. 9–12.

34. *NYT*, Nov. 8, 1962; Louis Harris to the President, Nov. 19, 1962, POF, Special Correspondence. Harris estimated that the slippage among Negroes was .4 percent compared to 2.7 percent for urban voters, 3.1 percent for Jewish voters, 4.0 percent for both Catholic and Polish voters, 4.5 percent for Irish voters, and 5.6 percent for Italian voters.

35. Donald M. Wilson to the President, Oct. 19, 1962, POF, Subjects. The New York *Times* on October 14, 1962 reported that Algerian Premier Ahmed Ben Bella had met with Martin Luther King and had praised Kennedy's support of Meredith at Ole Miss.

36. Sorensen, interviewed by Kaysen, KLOHP, 125–29; Sorensen, *Kennedy*, p. 487.

37. Sorensen, interviewed by Kaysen, KLOHP, 129.

EIGHT

Winter of Discontent

1. John V. Lindsay to the President, Jan. 12, 1962, WHSF, 371; Charles Abrams, President of the National Committee Against Discrimination in Housing, to the President, Dec. 14, 1961 and March 26, 1962, WHSF, 371; "Stroke of the Pen: Dimensions of a Presidential Decision," a film for the John F. Kennedy Library produced by Envision Corporation; Kennedy, *Public Papers*, 1962, pp. 21, 544; Lee White, interview, KLOHP, 83–85; Minutes of the Steering Committee of the National Action Committee of CORE, Sept. 7, 1962, CORE, Series 4, Box 1.

2. Bill Welsh to Lee White, Oct. 4, 1962; Larry O'Brien to Lee White, Sept. 11 and 15, 1962; Martha Griffiths to Lawrence O'Brien, Sept. 18, 1962, all in Lee White Files, 21.

3. Lee White to the President, July 17, 1962, WHSF, 371; HHFA study of NAHB survey, July 16, 1962; Urban League study, July 21, 1962, Lee White Files, 21; Weekly reports from Administrator of HHFA to White House, July 10, 17, 24, 31, 1962, HHFA, Microfilm 6; *Wall Street Journal*, July 9, Nov. 2, 1962.

4. Lee White to the President, Aug. 28, 1962; Norbert Schlei to Lee White,

Sept. 10, 1962; Milton Semer to Lee White, Aug. 17, 1962, all in Lee White Files, 21; Lee White to the President, Nov. 6, 1962, POF, Subjects; Lee White, interview, KLOHP, 85–90; Burke Marshall, interviewed by Oberdorfer, KLOHP, 53–60; Norbert A. Schlei, interview, KLOHP, 29–34; William L. Taylor, *Hanging Together: Equality in an Urban Nation*, p. 91.

5. Kennedy, *Public Papers*, 1962, pp. 831–32; Burke Marshall, interviewed by Oberdorfer, KLOHP, 58; Sorensen, *Kennedy*, p. 482; Lee White, interview, KLOHP, 94.

6. Robert Weaver to Timothy Reardon, Nov. 27, Dec. 4, Dec. 11, Dec. 18, 1962, HHFA, Microfilm 6; *NYT*, Nov. 21 and 22, 1962; *Business Week*, Dec. 1, 1962, p. 30.

7. Dennis Clark, "The Housing Order: Prejudice and Property," *Commonweal*, Dec. 21, 1962, p. 33 ("first use"); *NYT*, Nov. 21 and 22, 1962; "Trends in Housing," Sept.–Oct., 1962 [*sic*], published by National Committee Against Discrimination in Housing, Lee White Files, 21; *Afro-American* (Baltimore), Dec. 1, 1962; *The Crisis*, Dec., 1962, pp. 606–7; Pittsburgh *Courier*, Dec. 1, 15, 22, 1962.

8. Kennedy, *Public Papers*, 1963, p. 126; Robert Weaver to Timothy Reardon, April 30, 1963; Milton Semer to Timothy Reardon, May 21, 1963, HHFA, Microfilm 6; Martin E. Sloane, "One Year's Experience: Current and Potential Impact of the Housing Order," *George Washington Law Review*, 32 (March 1964), 457–88. The order, it should be noted, had no adverse effect on the housing industry.

9. William L. Taylor, "Federal Civil Rights Laws: Can They Be Made to Work," *George Washington Law Review*, 39 (July 1971), esp. p. 982; Sloane, "One Year's Experience," pp. 457–88; Ruth P. Morgan, *The President and Civil Rights: Policy Making by Executive Order*, esp. p. 75; Sundquist, *Politics and Policy*, pp. 278–82.

10. Roger W. Wilkins to Ralph A. Dungan, Nov. 19, 1962, WHSF, 358.

11. Booker, *Black Man's America*, pp. 29–32. The leaders who met with Kennedy were Martin Luther King, Jr., Roy Wilkins, James Farmer, A. Philip Randolph, Whitney Young, and Dorothy Height.
    The administration had encouraged the convening of this conference which it hoped would foster Negro support for American aid to Africa similar to Jewish backing for Israel. The conference produced a number of resolutions including calls for a Marshall plan for Africa, greater participation by Negro Americans in the foreign service, both in Africa and around the world, and U. S. support for sanctions against the Union of South Africa. The State Department came in for sharp criticism at the conference for its failures to use blacks in Africa or elsewhere. Before the President met with the delegation, Lee White reported to him that Dean Rusk had not given equal opportunity the "vigorous attention" it required. See: Lee White to the President, Dec. 17, 1962; Conference resolutions, Lee White Files, 20;

Louis Martin to the Attorney General, Dec. 4, 1962, and attached documents, BM, 5; Relevant documents in CORE, Series 1, Box 1; Pedro Sanjuan, interview, KLOHP, 57–67; *NYT*, Nov. 24, 1962; *Afro-American* (Baltimore), Dec. 1, 1962.

12. Hubert Humphrey, Philip Hart, Joseph Clark, Harrison Williams, Paul Douglas, and Clair Engle to John F. Kennedy, Jan. 8, 1963, WHSF, 363. They also requested and apparently received a conference with Kennedy to discuss these matters.

13. Bradlee, *Conversations with Kennedy*, p. 121; Henry H. Wilson to Ken O'Donnell, Nov. 19, 1962, POF, Staff Memoranda; Theodore Sorensen to the President, Nov. 9, 1962, TCS, 59; Burke Marshall, personal interview.

14. Kennedy, *Public Papers*, 1963, pp. 11–15; *NYT*, Feb. 1, 1963; Monthly Reports of the Washington Bureau, Nov. 9, 1962, Feb. 5, 1963, NAACP; Notes of a conversation between Johnson and Roy Wilkins, Clarence Mitchell, *et al.*, Jan. 24, 1963; George Reedy to Lyndon Johnson, Dec. 13, 1962, Jan. 28, Jan. 31, Feb. 1, Feb. 14, 1963; Harry McPherson to the Vice President, Jan. 24, 1963; Booth Mooney to Lyndon Johnson, Feb. 15, 1963, all in LBJ, Vice Presidential, Congress; Materials on revision of Rule XXII, Paul H. Douglas MSS.

15. Thomas B. Curtis to Grant Reynolds, Jan. 9, 1963; Press release, by Reps. McCulloch, Lindsay, Cahill, MacGregor, Mathias, Martin, Jan. 31, 1963; Grant Reynolds to Thomas Curtis, April 29, 1963, all in Thomas B. Curtis MSS; *NYT*, Feb. 1, 1963; *Afro-American* (Baltimore), Feb. 2, 1963; *Wall Street Journal*, Jan. 8, 1963 (article by Robert D. Novak); Neil MacNeil, *Dirksen: Portrait of a Public Man*, p. 209; William F. Buckley, Jr. to James J. Kilpatrick, Jan. 21, 1963; Kilpatrick to Buckley, Jan. 23, 1963, James J. Kilpatrick MSS.

16. Southern Regional Council, "Plans for Progress: Atlanta Survey," Jan., 1963, BM, 34; *Newsweek*, Feb. 25, 1963, p. 27.

17. John F. Kennedy to Lyndon Johnson, Feb. 21, 1963, WHSF, 370.

18. John F. Kennedy to Lyndon Johnson, May 7, 1963, WHSF, 370; Burke Marshall to the Attorney General, March 1, 1963, BM, 1.

19. Summary, "Meeting of the Vice President's Study Group," March 7, 1963, Lee White Files, 20; Lyndon B. Johnson, *Public Papers of the Presidents*, 1963–1964, I, 47–49. For a favorable evaluation of the Plans for Progress, see: Sovern, *Legal Restraints on Racial Discrimination in Employment*, pp. 140–41.

20. Robert F. Kennedy to John A. Hannah, Dec. 15, 1962, BM, 1.

21. John A. Hannah to Robert F. Kennedy, Jan. 2, 1963, BM, 30; Dulles, *The Civil Rights Commission*, pp. 176–81; Mississippi Advisory Committee to the United States Commission on Civil Rights, *Administration of Justice in Mississippi* (Jan. 1963), esp. pp. 24–25, 27; Robert F. Kennedy to John A. Hannah, March 26, 1963, BM, 1.

22. Lee White to the President, Feb. 12, 1963; U. S. Commission on Civil Rights to President, Feb. 12, 1963, POF, Subjects; Burke Marshall, interviewed by Hackman, KLOHP, 27; Barbara Carter, "The Role of the Civil Rights Commission," *The Reporter*, July 4, 1963, pp. 10–14; Berl I. Bernhard and William L. Taylor to Lee White, Feb. 21, 1963, TCS, 30; Harry McPherson to the Vice President, Feb. 18, 1963, LBJ, Vice Presidential, Civil Rights.

23. Kunstler, *Deep in My Heart*, pp. 148–51; *Moses et al. v. Kennedy, Hoover*, 219 F Supp 762 (1963).

24. Wilkins sent a copy of his remarks to Robert Kennedy on Jan. 8, 1963, RFK, Attorney General, General; Joseph L. Rauh, Jr., interview, KLOHP, 110; Lee White, interview, KLOHP, 104–5; Simeon Booker, interview, KLOHP, 24; *Ebony*, May, 1963, pp. 89–94; *Afro-American* (Baltimore), Feb. 16, 23, 1963.

When President Kennedy learned that Sammy Davis, Jr., a black entertainer, and his wife, Mai Britt, who was white, had been invited, he feared for the racist reaction to their presence. Consequently news photographers were barred from the reception and the White House itself later released its own pictures; Davis and Britt were not in them.

25. Joseph L. Rauh, Jr., interview, KLOHP, 11–13, for Wilkins's story; (there is a slightly different version of it in Schlesinger, *A Thousand Days*, p. 950); Roy Wilkins, personal interview; Clipping, article by Fletcher Knebel in Des Moines *Sunday Register*, March 17, 1963, DNC.

26. Kennedy, *Public Papers*, 1963, pp. 221–30.

27. Theodore Sorensen to Mike Feldman et al., Feb. 5, 1963, TCS, 59; Lee White, interview, KLOHP, 100–102; Burke Marshall, personal inverview; Burke Marshall to Leslie Dunbar, Feb. 26, 1963, BM, 1.

28. Burke Marshall, personal interview; Lawrence O'Brien to the President, Feb. 18, March 4, 11, 12, 18, 25, April 1, 1963, POF, Legislative Files.

29. *Afro-American* (Baltimore), March 9, 1963; *Congressional Record*, Feb. 28, 1963, 3161; March 28, 1963, 5096–5129 (Joint statement, 5096; Javits's evaluation, 5118); *NYT*, March 29, 1963.

30. Reports from Greenwood, spring, 1963 and clippings, VEP, 97; Interview with Willy Peacock, James Jones, Charles McLaurin, VEP, 87; Dictated report of Wiley A. Branton on visit to Mississippi, VEP, 93; Chronology of events following shooting of James Travis, VEP, 93; Report of Charles Ray McLaurin, April 29, 1963, VEP, 94 (for quotation from plantation boss); Burke Marshall to the Attorney General, March 29, 1963, BM, 1; Burke Marshall to Norbert Schlei, April 11, 1963, BM, 1; Forman, *The Making of Black Revolutionaries*, pp. 294–307; Watters and Cleghorn, *Climbing Jacob's Ladder*, pp. 59–63.

31. Dulles, *The Civil Rights Commission*, pp. 182–83; United States Commission on Civil Rights, *Interim Report* (mimeo, April 16, 1963).

32. Burke Marshall to the President, April 8, 1963, BM, 2; Lee White to the President, April 10, 1963, Lee White Files, 23; Milton P. Semer to Lee White, April 9, 1963, POF, Departments and Agencies.

33. Quoted in: Schlesinger, *A Thousand Days*, p. 953.

34. Dulles, *The Civil Rights Commission*, pp. 183–85; Pittsburgh *Courier*, May 4, 1963; *NYT*, April 19, 1963; *New Republic*, April 27, 1963, pp. 3–5.

35. Kennedy, *Public Papers*, 1963, pp. 333, 347–48. On April 30, 1963, the *Wall Street Journal* praised Kennedy's response in an editorial.

36. Martin Luther King, Jr., "Bold Design for a New South," *The Nation*, March 30, 1963, pp. 259–62.

NINE
From Alabama to the Second Reconstruction

1. Michael Cooper Nichols, " 'Cities Are What Men Make Them': Birmingham, Alabama Faces the Civil Rights Movement, 1963" (senior thesis, Brown University, 1974); Martin Luther King, Jr., *Why We Can't Wait*, pp. 39–65; Lewis, *King*, pp. 171–81; Dorman, *We Shall Overcome*, pp. 143–45; Vincent Harding, "A Beginning in Birmingham," *The Reporter*, June 6, 1963, p. 14; *Newsweek*, April 15, 1963, pp. 29–30, April 29, 1963, pp. 26, 29.

2. Burke Marshall, interviewed by Lewis, KLOHP, 95–96; Comment by Burke Marshall in *American Journey*, p. 116.

3. Lewis, *King*, pp. 181–83; King, *Why We Can't Wait*, pp. 73–74; *NYT*, April 4–13, 1963; *Newsweek*, April 22, 1963, pp. 28, 33; Vincent Harding, "A Beginning in Birmingham," *The Reporter*, June 6, 1963, pp. 14–15.

4. Coretta Scott King, *My Life With Martin Luthr King, Jr.*, pp. 224–28; King, *Why We Can't Wait*, pp. 73–74.

5. The letter is reprinted in King, *Why We Can't Wait*, pp. 77–100.

6. *NYT*, May 3–8, 1963; *Life*, May 17, 1963, pp. 26–36; *Time*, May 10, 1963, p. 19; King, *Why We Can't Wait*, pp. 101–8; Dorman, *We Shall Overcome*, pp. 148–54; Lewis, *King*, pp. 192–97; Forman, *The Making of Black Revolutionaries*, pp. 311–16.

7. Burke Marshall, interviewed by Lewis, KLOHP, 96–101; *Afro-American* (Baltimore), May 11, 1963; Comments by Vincent Harding, Roger Wilkins and Andrew Young in *American Journey*, pp. 116–18; King, *Why We Can't Wait*, pp. 110–12; Dorman, *We Shall Overcome*, pp. 154–57; William V. Shannon, "The Crisis in Birmingham," *Commonweal*, May 24, 1963, pp. 238–39.

8. Kennedy, *Public Papers*, 1963, p. 372; *NYT*, May 8–11, 1963; King, *Why We Can't Wait*, pp. 110–13; Dorman, *We Shall Overcome*, pp. 157–65; Lewis, *King*, pp. 198–200; Vincent Harding, "A Beginning in Birmingham," *The Reporter*, June 6, 1963, pp. 16–19.

9. Wire service stories and photographs about Birmingham, POF, Subjects; *Newsweek,* May 20, 1963, pp. 25–27; Clipping, Birmingham *News,* May 12, 1963, RFK, Attorney General; *NYT,* May 12 and 13, 1963; *Life,* May 24, 1963, pp. 34–35; Dorman, *We Shall Overcome,* pp. 171–86; *Wall Street Journal,* May 23, 1963, p. 18.

10. Kennedy, *Public Papers,* 1963, pp. 397–98; *NYT,* May 13, 1963.

11. George Wallace to John F. Kennedy, May 13, 1963, POF, Subjects; *NYT,* May 13 and 14, 1963; King, *Why We Can't Wait,* pp. 114–17; Dorman, *We Shall Overcome,* pp. 171–86; *Wall Street Journal,* May 23, 1963, p. 18.

12. Louis Martin to the Attorney General, May 13, 1963, WHSF, 365a; *Newsweek,* May 27, 1963, pp. 27–28; *Wall Street Journal,* May 17, 1963.

13. Schlesinger, *A Thousand Days,* p. 959 (for Kennedy's comment to ADA); Burke Marshall, personal interview; Roy Wilkins, interviewed by Berl Bernhard, Aug. 3, 1964, KLOHP, 23.

14. William V. Shannon, The Crisis in Birmingham," *Commonweal,* May 24, 1963, pp. 238–39; Theodore C. Sorensen to the President, May 7, 1963, POF, Staff Memoranda; Burke Marshall, interviewed by Lewis, KLOHP, 102; Burke Marshall, personal interview.

15. Lee C. White to the President, Feb. 7, 1963, POF, Subjects; Lawrence F. O'Brien to the President, May 17, 1963, POF, Legislative Files; Sorensen, *Kennedy,* p. 489 (for Kennedy quotation); Schlesinger, *A Thousand Days,* p. 971.

16. Burke Marshall, personal interview (for the fact that Kennedy was reading Woodward and the importance of Kennedy's change of mind); Schlesinger, *A Thousand Days,* p. 966 (for Kennedy quotation).

17. Donald Wilson to Robert F. Kennedy, May 9, 10, 14, 15, 1963, RFK, Attorney General, Civil Rights; Donald Wilson to the President, May 17, 1963, POF, Subjects.

18. *Newsweek,* May 6, 1963, pp. 27–28; May 27, 1963, pp. 26–27; *Wall Street Journal,* May 10, 1963; *NYT,* May 15, 1963; Louis Martin to the Attorney General, May 13, 1963, WHSF, 365a (Martin also stressed the rising importance of the Black Muslims).

When Malcolm X, the Muslims' controversial and eloquent minister, heard about the Kennedys' comments to the Alabama editors, he charged that the President had only alerted troops after Negroes had started to defend themselves. He also questioned Kennedy's motives for even meeting with this particular group, and he noted that instead of censuring the Klan and Citizens' Council, the President had attacked Islam. See: *NYT,* May 17, 1963.

19. James Baldwin, "Letter from a Region in My Mind," *The New Yorker,* Nov. 17, 1962, pp. 59–144; James Baldwin, *The Fire Next Time; Time,* May 17, 1963, pp. 26–27; C. Eric Lincoln, *The Black Muslims in America.*

20. *Afro-American* (Baltimore), May 4, 1963; *NYT*, May 11, 1963; Guthman, *We Band of Brothers*, pp. 219–20; Comment by Burke Marshall in *American Journey*, pp. 118–19.

21. Robert P. Mills to Burke Marshall, June 7, 1963, BM, 8 (lists participants). On Jerome Smith, see: Meier and Rudwick, *CORE*, 115–16, 143 and *passim*.

22. Clipping, New York *Herald Tribune*, May 26, 1963, DNC (for first comment by Kenneth Clark); Comment by Kenneth Clark in *American Journey*, pp. 120–21.

23. Schlesinger, *A Thousand Days*, p. 963 (for Belafonte explanation). In addition to accounts of this meeting in Schlesinger, Guthman and *American Journey*, see: *Newsweek*, June 3, 1963, p. 19; "Louisiana Story" (interview with Jerome Smith), *Freedomways*, 4 (Spring 1964), esp. 247–49; Clarence B. Jones to Editor, New York *Times*, June 7, 1963 in BM, 8; *NYT*, May 25, May 27, June 7, 1963; *I. F. Stone's Bi-Weekly*, June 10, 1963; Clipping, *Village Voice*, June 6, 1963, RFK, Attorney General, General.

24. Schlesinger, *A Thousand Days*, 963; Burke Marshall, personal interview; Burke Marshall to Al Rosen, n.d., attached to list of participants sent by Mills, June 7, 1963, BM, 8; Guthman, *We Band of Brothers*, p. 221.

25. Burke Marshall, interviewed by Lewis, KLOHP, 105–12; Burke Marshall, personal interview; Sorensen, *Kennedy*, pp. 491–94; Norbert Schlei to the Attorney General, June 4, 1963, RFK, Attorney General, Civil Rights.

26. Burke Marshall, interviewed by Lewis, KLOHP, pp. 102–6; Nicholas Katzenbach, interviewd by Lewis, KLOHP, 44; Burke Marshall, personal interview; Sorensen, *Kennedy*, p. 494; Theodore Sorensen, interviewed by Kaysen, p. 131; Luther H. Hodges, interviewed by Dan B. Jacobs, May 18, 1964, KLOHP, 92.

27. Nicholas Katzenbach, interviewed by Lewis, KLOHP, 43–47; Burke Marshall, interviewed by Lewis, KLOHP, 106; Norbert A. Schlei, interviewed by Stewart, KLOHP, 44–45; Comments by Nicholas deB. Katzenbach at conference on "The 1964 Civil Rights Act," at Yale University, Law School, April 7, 1973; "Legislative Possibilities," probably by Burke Marshall, May 20, 1963, TCS, 30 (for Justice Department views); TCS [Sorensen] Agenda for Civil Rights Meeting, May 31, 1963, TCS, 30; Hubert Humphrey, et al. to John F. Kennedy, May 15, 1963, WHSF.

On May 20, 1963 the Supreme Court did rule in a series of cases in favor of Negroes who had been arrested during sit-ins. However, as Thomas P. Lewis has written, it rested "its decisions on a variety of grounds concerned with the peculiar facts of the various cases, all of which are too narrow to support conclusions about the larger issue." See: Thomas P. Lewis, "The Sit-In Cases: Great Expectations," *Supreme Court Review* (1963), 102.

28. Nicholas Katzenbach, interviewed by Lewis, KLOHP, 43; Louis Martin, personal interview; Lawrence F. O'Brien and Theodore Sorensen to the

President, May 14 and May 21, 1963, POF, Legislative Files; Kennedy, *Public Papers*, 1963, p. 423.

29. Robert F. Kennedy to the President, June 4, 1963, TCS, 73; Lee White to the President, June 4, 1963, WHSF, 365b; *Wall Street Journal*, June 5, 1963; Burke Marshall, interviewed by Lewis, KLOHP, 102–3; Kennedy, *Public Papers*, 1963, p. 432; *Time*, June 14, 1963, pp. 23–24; Clipping, Washington *Star*, June 16, 1963, DNC.

30. *NYT*, June 3, 1963 and June 9, 1963 (Sec. IV, 3); Burke Marshall, personal interview; *Wall Street Journal*, May 23, 1963.

31. Kennedy, *Public Papers*, 1963, 446–47, 452–59.

32. *NYT*, June 9, 10, 1963; Burke Marshall, interviewed by Lewis, KLOHP, 109–10; Martin Luther King, Jr. to President Kennedy, May 30, 1963, WHSF, 363.

33. Sorensen, *Kennedy*, p. 491.

34. President Kennedy to Attorney General, Nov. 30, 1962, BM, 18.

35. Frady, *Wallace*, pp. 140–42 (for Wallace's comment to legislators, for Flowers's quotation and for first inaugural quotation); Clipping, Alanta *Journal*, Jan. 14, 1963, SRC (for second inaugural quotation).

36. Burke Marshall to the Attorney General, April 9, 1963, BM, 1.

37. Transcript of conversation between Attorney General Robert F. Kennedy and Governor George Wallace, Montgomery, April 25, 1963, WHSF, 366.

38. Guthman, *We Band of Brothers*, pp. 210–11; "FBI Reports," Tape of Gov. Wallace's TV program following the meeting with Robert Kennedy, April 25, 1963, BM, 18; Ed Reid to Robert F. Kennedy, May 1, 1963, RFK, Attorney General, General.

39. Kennedy, *Public Papers*, 1963, pp. 409–11; *NYT*, May 19 and 20, 1963. The President received a warm welcome in the South.

40. Pierre Salinger, Memorandum of conversation between President Kennedy and Governor George Wallace, May 18, 1963, POF, Subjects (the memorandum was shown to Senator Lister Hill and Congressman Robert Jones; it had Wallace's crude remark deleted; they both agreed that the memorandum was an accurate representation of the conversation); Guthman, *We Band of Brothers*, pp. 211–12; Sorensen, *Kennedy*, p. 492. The President's counsel advised that if an Alabama court officer served him a summons and it was awkward for the Secret Service to defer it, he should accept it "in a humorous vein since the suit will ultimately be quashed." See: Norbert A. Schlei to Lee C. White, May 17, 1963, POF, Subjects.

41. Burke Marshall to members of the Cabinet, May 21, 1963, BM, 3; "Alabama Notebook" and related materials, BM, 17; Wiliam H. Orrick to Attorney General, May 29, 1963, RFK, Attorney General, Civil Rights.

42. D. Robert Owen to Burke Marshall, June 6, 1963, BM, 17; Dorman, *We*

Shall Overcome, pp. 275–95; *Newsweek,* June 3, 1963, pp. 20–21; Burke Marshall, interviewed by Lewis, pp. 107–8.

43. Dorman, *We Shall Overcome,* pp. 301–21; *NYT,* June 12, 1963; *Time,* June 14, 1963, pp. 80, 83 and June 21, 1963, pp. 13–14; *Newsweek,* June 24, 1963, pp. 29–30.

45. Sorensen, *Kennedy,* pp. 494–95; Theodore Sorensen, interviewed by Kaysen, KLOHP, 131; Burke Marshall, interviewed by Lewis, KLOHP, pp. 109–10; Lee White, interviewed by Gwirtzman, KLOHP, 110–13; TCS, second draft of Kennedy's speech, June 11, 1963, TCS, 73. It appears from this draft that Kennedy extemporized the last seven paragraphs. Robert Kennedy also submitted a draft, much of which was adapted by Sorensen; in TCS, 73.

46. Kennedy, *Public Papers,* 1963, pp. 468–71. The press regarded it as one of Kennedy's best and most important speeches. See accounts in: *Time,* June 21, 1963, pp. 13–17; *Newsweek,* June 24, 1963, p. 27; *NYT,* June 12, 1963. For conservatives' views of racial problem, see: Clarence B. Henson, Jr. (publisher of Birmingham *News*) to John F. Kennedy, May 7, 1963, TCS, 30; *Time,* June 14, 1963, p. 29; Editorials, *Wall Street Journal,* May 9, May 14, June 11, June 13, 1963.

47. "wjh" to Andrew Hatcher, June 14, 1963, WHSF, 367 ("Pro": Telegrams, 1381; letters, 661; "Con": Telegrams, 417, letters, 59); Erskine, "The Polls: Kennedy as President," pp. 335–36, 339; George H. Gallup, *The Gallup Poll: Public Opinion 1935–1971,* III, 1823, 1827 (it should be noted that there are several inconsistencies between the data presented in the preceding two works); *NYT,* June 12, 1963; *Afro-American* (Baltimore), June 22, 1963; Press release from office of Jackie Robinson, June 13, 1963, POF, Subjects; G. Mennen Williams to Theodore Sorensen, June 15, 1963, TCS, 30.

48. *NYT,* June 12 and 13, 1963; Sundquist, *Politics and Policy,* pp. 106–7; *Wall Street Journal,* June 14, 1963 (for quotation from Republican leader); William L. Batt, interviewed by Larry J. Hackman, Nov. 16, 1966, KLOHP, 109–12; *Newsweek,* June 24, 1963, pp. 34, 39; Clipping, Joseph Alsop column, Houston *Post,* June 19, 1963, Charles Halleck MSS.

49. *NYT,* June 12–18, 1963; *Afro-American* (Baltimore), June 22, 1963; Dorman, *We Shall Overcome,* pp. 203–33; *Newsweek,* June 24, 1963, pp. 33–34; *Time,* June 28, 1963, pp. 15–17; "Demonstrations—Chronology June 63–Sept. 63," BM, 32.

Byron dela Beckwith was quickly arrested for Evers's murder. He was tried twice but the Mississippi jury could not reach a verdict.

TEN
Kennedy at the Center

1. Comments by Nicholas Katzenbach at conference on "The 1964 Civil Rights Act," Yale University, Law School, April 7, 1973; Chuck Daly to

Lawrence F. O'Brien, June 14, 1963, TCS, 30; Mike Mansfield to the President, June 18, 1963, TCS, 30.

2. Nicholas Katzenbach, interviewed by Lewis, KLOHP, 45–49; Norbert A. Schlei, interview, KLOHP, 44–45, 50–51; Charles Halleck, interview, KLOHP, 11–12; Sorensen, *Kennedy*, p. 497; *NYT*, June 21, 1963.

3. Kennedy, *Public Papers*, 1963, pp. 493–94. For background on the message, see: TCS, 30; Lee White Files, 19; WHSF, 360; Theodore Sorensen, interview, KLOHP, 134–35; Sorensen, *Kennedy*, pp. 496–98. Lyndon Johnson encouraged the President to include dicussion of economic matters and the Community Relations Service proposal.

4. John G. Stewart, "Independence and Control: The Challenge of Senatorial Party Leadership" (Ph. D. diss., University of Chicago, 1968), pp. 171–74 (Stewart was legislative assistant to Hubert Humphrey); Unsigned memorandum, June 18, 1963; Mike Mansfield to the President, June 18, 1963; Memorandum by Senator Mansfield on conference with Senator Dirksen, June 13, 1963, all in TCS, 30; Theodore Sorensen, interview, KLOHP, 136; Transcript, Press Conference, Joint Senate–House Republican Leaders, June 13, 1963, Charles Halleck MSS.

5. *Congressional Record*, June 19, 1963, pp. 11075–173 and memoranda in preceding note.

6. John F. Kennedy to Dwight D. Eisenhower, June 10, 1963, TCS, 30; *NYT*, June 13, 1963; *Time*, June 21, 1963, p. 16; *Congressional Record*, June 19, 1963, p. 11076; Minutes of House Republican Policy Committee Meeting, June 18, 1963, Charles Halleck MSS; Robert G. Baker to Senator Mansfield, June 27, 1963, POF, Legislative Files; Press release, Joint Senate–House Republican Leadership, July 1, 1963, Charles Halleck MSS.

7. Stewart, "Independence and Control," pp. 177–79; Mike Mannatos to Robert F. Kennedy, June 10, 1963, RFK, Attorney General, General, 73; Clipping, Jack Anderson column, Washington *Post*, June 14, 1963, DNC; Clipping, Atlanta *Constitution*, June 11, 1963, SRC (Richard Russell quotation); Sorensen, *Kennedy*, p. 501; Hale Boggs, interview, KLOHP, 19 (for Kennedy's teasing of Smathers); Arthur Schlesinger, Jr. to Robert Kennedy, July 1, 1963, POF, Departments and Agencies; Robert G. Baker to Senator Mansfield, June 27, 1963, POF, Legislative Files; *Congressional Record*, June 27, 1963, pp. 11880–82 for an important speech by Abraham Ribicoff on the need to have a reasoned debate; Joseph F. Dolan to Attorney General, July 17, 1963, RFK, Attorney General, Civil Rights; *U. S. News & World Report*, Aug. 12, 1963, pp. 36–40.

8. Kennedy, *Public Papers*, 1963, p. 493; Theodore Sorensen, interview, KLOHP, 141–42; Sorensen, *Kennedy*, pp. 498–99; G. Mennen Williams to Theodore Sorensen, June 15, 1963, TCS, 30; George E. Reedy to the Vice President, July 3, 1963, LBJ, Vice Presidential, Civil Rights; News release from Emanuel Celler, July 7, 1963, Emanuel Celler MSS; Joseph F. Dolan to

the Attorney General, July 17, 1963, RFK, Attorney General, Civil Rights; Lee White to the President, June 22, 1963, WHSF.

9. Schlesinger, *A Thousand Days,* pp. 968–70 (Schlesinger attended this meeting). See also: Joseph L. Rauh, interview, KLOHP, 103–4, 109. The next day on *Meet the Press* Robert Kennedy warned repeatedly against creating an "aura of pressure" on Congress. See: Clipping, Washington *Post,* June 24, 1963, DNC.

10. Burke Marshall, interviewed by Lewis, KLOHP, 110–11; POF, Subjects; WHSF, 365, 365a; Lee White Files, 19, 22.

11. Lee White, interview, KLOHP, 137–38; Willard Wirtz to the President, for meeting on June 13, 1963, WHSF, 365.

12. Note, undated and unsigned in the lawyers' meeting file, Lee White Files, 22; Lee White to the President, June 21, 1963, WHSF, 365a; Burke Marshall, interviewed by Lewis, KLOHP, 11; Lee White, interview, KLOHP, 142–43; Bernard G. Segal and Harrison Tweed to lawyers, July 1, 1963, Lee White Files, 22.

13. Burke Marshall, interviewed by Lewis, KLOHP, 111; Transcript, meeting with religious leaders, June 17, 1963, POF, Subjects (the President did not want the meeting recorded so that the participants would be at their ease, but this conference seems to have been an exception); Harry and Ruth Klingman to Dean E. McHenry, April 13, 1964, BM, 28 (the Klingmans were lobbyists for civil rights. Here they described the unique contribution of the clerical lobby).

14. Lee White to the President, July 11, 1963, WHSF, 365a.

15. Memorandum, July 17, 1963, attached to covering letter from Frederick Kappel to members of the Business Council, July 17, 1963, Lee White Files, 19. White received these documents from Louis Oberdorfer of the Justice Department on July 19, 1963. Oberdorfer advised that they be handled "very securely."

16. Louis F. Oberdorfer to Robert F. Kennedy, July 9, 1963, POF, Subjects; Several memoes by Oberdorfer to Robert Kennedy, esp. Nov. 13, 1963, and Dec. 27, 1963, RFK, Attorney General, Civil Rights; Smyer quoted in Charles E. Silberman, "The Businessman and the Negro," *Fortune,* Sept., 1963, p. 99.

17. Hearings before Senate Commerce Committee, 88th Cong., 1st sess., "Civil Rights—Public Accommodations," pp. 281–319; *NYT,* July 11, 1963; *Afro-American* (Baltimore), July 20, 1963; Theodore Sorensen, interview, KLOHP, 135; Luther Hodges, interview, KLOHP, 93; Robert F. Kennedy to the President, Aug. 16, 1963, and attached clippings from Winston-Salem *Journal,* Aug. 14, 16, 1963, POF, Subjects. The first clipping indicated that the Justice Department was investigating a proposed highway relocation near Rockingham to see if any federal laws had been violated. The second clipping notes that Hodges was from Rockingham. The significance of these stories remains a mystery to me.

18. Hearings before Senate Commerce Committee, 88th Cong., 1st sess., "Civil Rights—Public Accommodations" (July 1, 1963), p. 25; Hearings before the Senate Judiciary Committee, 88th Cong., 1st sess., "Civil Rights—The President's Program" (July 16, 1963), p. 94.

19. Hearings before the Senate Judiciary Committee, 88th Cong., 1st sess., "Civil Rights—The President's Program," p. 170; Howard Zinn, "Kennedy: The Reluctant Emancipator," *The Nation*, Dec. 1, 1962, pp. 373–76; Zinn, *SNCC*, 192–211; *New Republic*, Oct. 26, 1963, pp. 3–4.

20. Hearings before the Senate Judiciary Committee, 88th Cong., 1st sess., "Civil Rights—The President's Program" (Sept. 11, 1963), pp. 417–18.

21. Nicholas Katzenbach to the Attorney General, June 29, 1963, RFK, Attorney General, Civil Rights; Joseph F. Dolan to Deputy Attorney General, July 8, 1963, RFK, Attorney General, Civil Rights; Notes on Boat parties, RFK, Attorney General, General; Burke Marshall to Nicholas Katzenbach, July 22, 1963, BM, 1.

22. David Cohen to John P. Roche, July 3, 1963, ADA, Series 5, Box 11; David Cohen to Joe Rauh, June 24, 1963, ADA, Series 5, Box 11; Hearings before Subcommittee No. 5 of the House Judiciary Committee, 88th Cong., 1st sess., "Civil Rights," for testimony by civil rights lobbyists; *NYT*, July 23, 1963.

23. Nicholas Katzenbach to the Attorney General, Aug. 19, 1963, RFK, Attorney General, Civil Rights; Nicholas Katzenbach to Emanuel Celler, Aug. 13, 1963, RFK, Attorney General, Civil Rights; Nicholas Katzenbach, interview, KLOHP, 50–52.

24. Lee White, interview, KLOHP, 157–58; Transcript of meeting of President's Committee on Equal Employment Opportunity, May 29, 1963, George Reedy Files, 18; Transcript of meeting of PCEEO, July 18, 1963, LBJ, Vice President, Civil Rights; Dan H. Fenn, Jr. to Ralph Dungan, Aug. 12, 1963, POF, Subjects.

25. Lee White, interview, KLOHP, 157–58; *Newsweek*, July 29, 1963, p. 36. Another military-related incident occurred around the same time. The Committee on Equal Opportunity in the Armed Forces, chaired by Gerhard A. Gesell, reported in June of a serious discrimination problem in towns near military bases. When the President signed the official letter accepting the report, he probably did not realize that the committee had recommended that, in the absence of improvement, offending towns be declared off-limits to servicemen. Secretary McNamara would not repudiate this recommendation, abhorrent to Southern whites, but he announced his hope that it would never have to be implemented. Similarly, he issued a directive ordering all base commanders to establish voluntary programs to end discrimination in off-base housing. Upon reviewing these voluntary programs four years later, he discovered that they had failed miserably. See: Lee White, interview, KLOHP, 156; WHSF, 360 and Lee White Files, 23;

Robert S. McNamara, *The Essence of Security: Reflections in Office*, pp. 123–24.

26. John W. Macy, Jr. to Lawrence F. O'Brien, Aug. 13, 1963, Lee White Files, 20; John W. Macy, Jr., interview, KLOHP, 73; Lee White, interview, KLOHP, 159; Kennedy, *Public Papers*, 1963, pp. 633–34.

27. Lee White, interview, KLOHP, 163–64; Lee White to the President, Aug. 22, 1963, POF, Subjects.

28. The available documentation for this matter is scanty, but see: Note by Burke Marshall for the file, Dec. 20, 1963, BM, 8; *Afro-American* (Baltimore), Aug. 3, 1963; Clipping, Atlanta *Constitution*, July 25, 1963, VEP.

29. Copy of letter from Martin Luther King, Jr. to Jack O'Dell, July 3, 1963, sent to Marshall the same day, BM, 8.

30. This argument is based on: Navasky, *Kennedy Justice*, pp. 135–55; Comments by Burke Marshall and Roger Wilkins in *American Journey*, pp. 84–86; Burke Marshall, interviewed by Hackman, KLOHP, 36–45; Burke Marshall, personal interview.

Navasky offers several hypotheses on this episode and concludes that Robert Kennedy authorized the wiretap "because there would have been no living with the Bureau if he didn't." Although I do not find this conclusion convincing, I am indebted to Navasky for presenting valuable evidence to support a conflicting interpretation.

31. Edwin Guthman to the Attorney General, Aug. 13, 1963, POF, Subjects; "Demonstrations—Chronology June 63–Sept. 63," BM, 32; *Newsweek*, July 29, 1963, esp. pp. 26–27; "J.E.N." [Joseph E. Nolan] Report, July 2, 1963, RFK, Attorney General, Civil Rights; Memo by Burke Marshall on Cambridge, Maryland, n.d., RFK, Attorney General, Civil Rights; Report by Cambridge Non-Violent Action Committee, Sept., 1963, State Historical Society of Wisconsin; James W. Ely, Jr., "Negro Demonstrations and the Law: Danville as a Test Case," *Vanderbilt Law Review*, 27 (October 1974), 927–68; Meier and Rudwick, *CORE*, 225–51; *Afro-American* (Baltimore), June–Sept., 1963; Benjamin Muse, *The American Negro Revolution*, pp. 30–38; Burke Marshall to the Attorney General, July 23, 1963, POF, Subjects.

32. Hyman Bookbinder to Lee White, July 18, 1963; Lee White to Burke Marshall, July 22, 1963; Burke Marshall to Lee White, July 25, 1963, all in BM, 31. The four "civil rights leaders" were Kenneth Clark, Dorothy Height, Whitney Young, and Justine Polier.

33. "Background of Cases of 9 Negroes Indicted by Federal Grand Jury," Aug. 9, 1963, VEP, 94; Howard Zinn, *The Politics of History*, pp. 192–93; Navasky, *Kennedy Justice*, pp. 121–22; Burke Marshall, personal interview; Slater H. King to Constance Baker Motley, Aug. 13, 1963, Slater H. King MSS; Slater H. King to Joni Rabinowitz, Dec. 20, 1963, Slater H. King MSS.

34. Jervis Anderson, *A. Philip Randolph: A Biographical Portrait*, pp. 323–25; Forman, *The Making of Black Revolutionaries*, pp. 331–37; Zinn, *SNCC*,

190–215; Archie E. Allen, "John Lewis—Keeper of the Dream," *New South*, 26 (Spring 1971), 20–21; *NYT*, Aug. 29, 1963; Murray Kempton, "The March on Washington," *New Republic*, Sept. 14, 1963, pp. 19–20; Lewis, *King*, pp. 218–30 (for quotations from King's speech).

35. Kennedy, *Public Papers*, 1963, p. 572; Lee White, interview, KLOHP, 148–51; Hearings before Subcommittee No. 5 of the House Judiciary Committee, 88th Cong., 1st sess., "Civil Rights," p. 1767; Joseph F. Dolan to Attorney General, July 17, 1963, RFK, Attorney General, Civil Rights; News release from Emanuel Celler, July 7, 1963, Emanuel Celler, MSS; Anderson, *A. Philip Randolph*, p. 327; Transcript of conversation between representatives of civil rights groups and Washington police, July 11, 1963, George Reedy Files, 18; Louis Martin to John Bailey, Aug. 1, 1963, POF, Subjects; Jerry Bruno to the Chairman, Aug. 22, 1963, POF, Subjects; Jerry Bruno to John Bailey, Aug. 15, 1963, POF, General Correspondence.

36. Theodore Sorensen, interview, KLOHP, 141–43; Sorensen, *Kennedy*, 504–5; A. Philip Randolph to John F. Kennedy, Aug. 13, 1963, WHSF, 365; Kenneth O'Donnell to A. Philip Randolph, Aug. 22, 1963, WHSF, 365; Transcript of "March on Washington . . . Report by the Leaders," Aug. 28, 1963, WHSF, 365.

37. Clarence Mitchell, interview, KLOHP, 41; Hobart Taylor to Lyndon Johnson, Aug. 29, 1963, George Reedy Files, 9; News release, Sept. 1, 1963, Emanuel Celler MSS; Kennedy, *Public Papers*, 1963, p. 645.

38. *NYT*, Sept. 3, 1963; Sept 4, 1963 (comment by George Seibels); Sept. 5, 1963; Sept. 6, 1963 (comment by Justice Department spokesman).

39. *NYT*, Sept. 7, 1963 (both quotations.)

40. *NYT*, Sept. 8, 1963 ("last mile"); Sept 9 and 10, 1963; Kennedy, *Public Papers*, 1963, pp. 661–62.

41. *NYT*, Sept. 11, 1963.

42. *NYT*, Sept. 16–18, 1963; Kennedy, *Public Papers*, 1963, pp. 681–82.

43. Kennedy, *Public Papers, 1963*, pp. 692–93, 702–3; *NYT*, Sept. 20, 24, 1963; Burke Marshall, interviewed by Lewis, KLOHP, 69.

44. *NYT*, Sept. 25, 1963; Burke Marshall to the Attorney General, Oct. 4, 1963, BM, 3.

45. Burke Marshall to Pierre Salinger, Oct. 9, 1963, BM, 1; Report of Royall and Blaik, Oct. 10, 1963, sent to President, Dec. 16, 1963, BM, 18; *Afro-American* (Baltimore), Oct. 5, 1963; Pittsburgh *Courier*, Oct. 5, 1963.

46. Earl H. Blaik, interviewed by Charles T. Morrissey, Dec. 2, 1964, KLOHP, 10.

47. *Newsweek*, July 29, 1963, pp. 28–29; Gallup, *The Gallup Poll*, III, 1838, 1841; Louis Martin to John Bailey, July 25, 1963; Matt Reese to Bailey, Aug. 15, 1963; Louis Martin to Bailey, Aug. 15, 1963; Louis Martin to Bailey, Oct. 3, 1963; Matt Reese to Bailey, Nov. 15, 1963, all in POF, Subjects; Frederick Sontag to Thomas Curtis, Aug. 21, 1963, Thomas Curtis MSS.

48. Bill Brawley to John Bailey, July 31, 1963, POF, Subjects; Transcript, *Meet the Press,* Aug. 11, 1963, Southern Christian Leadership Conference MSS; Gallup, *The Gallup Poll,* III, 1828–51; Clipping, New York *Herald Tribune,* Aug. 18, 1963, Charles Halleck MSS: Erskine, "The Polls: Kennedy as President," pp. 336, 339; *Newsweek,* Oct. 21, 1963, p. 55; Hale Boggs, interview, KLOHP, 32.

49. Sorensen, *Kennedy,* p. 754; O'Donnell and Powers, "*Johnny, We Hardly Knew Ye,*" pp. 384–85; Bradlee, *Conversations with Kennedy,* pp. 190, 232.

50. Robert Kennedy to John Kennedy, Aug. 20, 1963, attached to clipping from Jackson *Clarion-Ledger,* Aug. 17, 1963; Louis Harris to the President, unsigned, Sept. 3, 1963, POF, Special Correspondence.

51. Kennedy, *Public Papers,* 1963, pp. 760–65, 860–77, 882–98 (quotation, 763); Clipping, Arkansas *Gazette,* Oct. 6, 1963, sent to President by Brooks Hays, Oct. 20, 1963, POF, Staff Memoranda; Bradlee, *Conversations with Kennedy,* pp. 218–19; O'Donnell and Powers, "*Johnny, We Hardly Knew Ye,*" 386; Stephen Smith to the President et al., Nov. 13, 1963, RFK, Attorney General, General.

52. *Newsweek,* Oct. 21, 1963, p. 56; *New Republic,* Oct. 26, 1963, p. 2; *Wall Street Journal,* Oct. 11, 1963; *NYT,* Oct. 31, Nov. 6, 1963; Clipping, Atlanta *Journal–Constitution,* Aug. 18, 1963, SRC.

53. Sorensen, *Kennedy,* pp. 501, 505–6; Theodore Sorensen, interview, KLOHP, 144; Gallup, *The Gallup Poll,* III, 1840–52; Charles U. Daly, interview, KLOHP, 65–66.

54. Lee White to Lawrence O'Brien, Oct. 30, 1963, Lee White Files, 22; Theodore Sorensen and Lawrence O'Brien to the President, Sept. 10, 17, Oct. 22, 1963, TCS, 59.

55. Nicholas Katzenbach, interview, KLOHP, 59–60; Clarence Mitchell to Emanuel Celler, Sept. 25, 1963, Emanuel Celler MSS: Arnold Aronson to Cooperating Organizations, Sept. 20, 27, 1963, ADA, Series 5, Box 12.

56. Attorney General to the President, Oct. 23, 1963, BM, 8; David Cohen to Joseph L. Rauh, Jr. Oct. 8, 1963, ADA, Series 5, Box 11.

57. *NYT,* Oct. 6, 16, 1963; *New Republic,* Oct. 26, 1963, 3–4; David Cohen to Beryl Radin, Oct. 30, 1963, ADA, Series 5, Box 11; Clipping, William S. White column, Washington *Star,* Oct. 18, 1963, DNC; Transcript, Press conference of Robert Kennedy, Oct. 15, 1963, TCS, 30.

58. Hearings before the House Judiciary Committee, 88th Cong., 1st sess., "Civil Rights," executive session, Oct. 15, 1963, esp. Robert Kennedy's opening statement, pp. 2652–62.

59. *NYT,* Oct. 17, 1963 (Mitchell quotation); *Afro-American* (Baltimore), Nov. 2, 9, 1963; Pittsburgh *Courier,* Nov. 2, 1963; Clarence Mitchell to Emanuel Celler, Oct. 18, 1963, Emanuel Celler MSS: James Farmer to Harry Golden, Oct. 24, 1963, CORE, Series 1, Box 5; Arnold Aronson to cooperating organizations, Oct. 18, 1963, CORE, Series 5, Box 25.

60. Attorney General to the President, Oct. 23, 1963, BM, 8; Nicholas Katzenbach, interviewed by Lewis, KLOHP, 65–73; Charles Halleck, interview, KLOHP, 12–13; Norbert Schlei, interview, KLOHP, 54; David Cohen to Beryl Radin, Oct. 30, 1963, ADA, Series 5, Box 11; Monthly report of the Washington Bureau, Nov. 8, 1963, NAACP; Robert W. Kastenmeier, interviewed by Ronald Grele, Oct. 25, 1965, KLOHP, 14–15.

61. Charles Halleck, interview, KLOHP, 13; *NYT*, Oct. 30, 1963; Kennedy, *Public Papers*, 1963, p. 820; Clipping, Washington *Star*, Nov. 1, 1963, DNC; Richard Haley to CORE Group Leaders, n.d., CORE, Series 5, Box 23; David Cohen to Beryl Radin, Oct. 30, 1963, ADA, Series 5, Box 11.

62. Nicholas Katzenbach, interview, KLOHP, 75–76; *NYT*, Nov. 3, 1963.

63. *NYT*, Nov. 2, 1963; Report of the Washington Bureau, Nov. 8, 1963, NAACP; Henry Scheele, *Charlie Halleck: A Political Biography*, pp. 225–27; Sorensen, *Kennedy*, p. 501; William McCulloch to colleagues, Nov. 6, 1963, Thomas B. Curtis MSS; Wirt A. Yerger, Jr., (chairman) to Charles Halleck, Nov. 14, 1963, Charles Halleck MSS.

64. Transcript, Press conference, Joint Senate–House Republican Leadership, Nov. 21, 1963, Charles Halleck MSS.

65. Kennedy, *Public Papers*, 1963, p. 849; Nicholas Katzenbach, interviewed by Lewis, KLOHP, 74–75; Comments by Burke Marshall, "The 1964 Civil Rights Act," Yale University, Law School, April 7, 1973; Richard Bolling, interviewed by Ronald J. Grele, Nov. 1, 1965, KLOHP, 49; Charles Halleck, interview, KLOHP, 26–27; Clarence Mitchell, interview, KLOHP, 46.

Conclusion: John F. Kennedy
and the Second Reconstruction

1. On reaction to the assassination, see: William Manchester, *The Death of a President*.

2. Manchester, *Death of a President*, p. 250; Birmingham *Post Herald*, Nov. 23, 25, 26, 1963 (Connor's comment in Nov. 23); Atlanta *Constitution*, Nov. 23, 25, 26, 1963 (Gray's comment in Nov. 23); Montgomery *Advertiser*, Nov. 23–27, 1963 (Wallace's comment in Nov. 26); Benjamin Muse, Field Report, Feb. 6, 1964, SRC.

3. Paul B. Sheatsley and Jacob J. Feldman, "The Assassination of President Kennedy: A Preliminary Report on Public Reactions and Behavior," *Public Opinion Quarterly*, 28 (Summer 1964), 189–215; Roberta S. Sigel, "An Exploration of Political Socialization: School Children's Reactions to the Death of a President," in Martha Wolfenstein and Gilbert Kleiman, eds. *Children and the Death of a President*, pp. 51–52.

4. Coretta King, *My Life With Martin Luther King, Jr.*, 243–45; Anne Moody, *Coming of Age in Mississippi*, pp. 318–20; Speech by Fred Shuttlesworth, National Guardian Dinner, Nov. 26, 1963, Fred L. Shuttlesworth MSS.

5. Lyndon B. Johnson, *Public Papers of the Presidents*, 1963–64, I, 8–10; *NYT*, Nov. 28, 30, 1963; Hobart Taylor, Jr. to George Reedy, Jan. 28, 1963, George Reedy Files, 2; Hobart Taylor, Jr. to Lyndon Johnson, Aug. 29, 1963, George Reedy Files, 9.

6. For an interesting evaluation of Kennedy's personality, see: James David Barber, *The Presidential Character: Predicting Performance in the White House*, pp. 293–343.

7. President's Committee on Equal Employment Opportunity, *Report to the President*, (Nov. 26, 1963), p. 39; "The Ten Principal Achievements of the Department of Justice in the Field of Civil Rights, 1961–1964," n.d., BM, 1; Louis Oberdorfer to Robert Kennedy, Dec. 27, 1963, RFK, Attorney General, Civil Rights; Results of VEP Programs, April 1, 1962 to March 31, 1964, VEP, 87.

Bibliography

I. Manuscript Collections

Americans for Democratic Action. State Historical Society of Wisconsin.

Anderson, Trezzvant W. Atlanta University.

Bowles, Chester. Yale University.

Byrd, Harry F. University of Virginia.

Celler, Emanuel. Library of Congress.

Civil Rights Commission. John F. Kennedy Library.

Congress of Racial Equality. State Historical Society of Wisconsin.

Curtis, Thomas B. University of Missouri, Columbia.

Dabney, Virginius. University of Virginia.

Democratic National Committee. John F. Kennedy Library.

Douglas, Paul H. Chicago Historical Society.

Feldman, Myer. John F. Kennedy Library.

Freeman, Orville. Personal diary. John F. Kennedy Library.

General Services Administration. John F. Kennedy Library.

Halleck, Charles A. Indiana University.

Horsky, Charles. John F. Kennedy Library.

Housing and Home Finance Agency. John F. Kennedy Library.

Johnson, Lyndon Baines. Lyndon B. Johnson Library.

Kennedy, John F. Pre-Presidential, President's Office Files, White House
Subject Files. John F. Kennedy Library.

Kennedy, Robert F. John F. Kennedy Library.

Kilpatrick, James J. University of Virginia.

King, Martin Luther, Jr. Boston University.

King, Slater. State Historical Society of Wisconsin.

McCormack, John W. Boston University.

McShane, James. John F. Kennedy Library.

Marshall, Burke. John F. Kennedy Library.

Miller, Francis Pickens. University of Virginia.

National Association for the Advancement of Colored People. New York,
New York.

Reardon, Timothy. John F. Kennedy Library.

Reedy, George E. Lyndon B. Johnson Library.

Schlesinger, Arthur M., Jr. John F. Kennedy Library.

Sherrod, Charles. Martin Luther King, Jr. Center for Social Change, Atlanta.

Hearings before a Subcommittee of the Committee on Appropriations. House. 87th Cong., 2nd sess. On Justice Department appropriation.

Hearings before the Subcommittee on Integration in Federally Assisted Public Education Programs of the Committee on Education and Labor. House. 87th Cong., 2nd sess.

Hearings before a Subcommittee of the Committee on Appropriations. House. 88th Cong., 1st sess. On Justice Department appropriation.

Hearings before the Committee on Commerce. Senate. 88th Cong., 1st sess. "Civil Rights—Public Accommodations."

Hearings before the Committee on the Judiciary. Senate. 88th Cong., 1st sess. "Civil Rights—The President's Program, 1963."

Hearings before Subcommittee No. 5 of the Committee on the Judiciary. House. 88th Cong., 1st sess. "Civil Rights."

Hearings before the Committee on the Judiciary. House. 88th Cong., 1st sess. "Civil Rights."

Hearings before the Committee on the Judiciary. Senate. 89th Cong., 1st sess. "Voting Rights."

John F. Kennedy. *Public Papers of the Presidents.* 1961, 1962, 1963.

Lyndon B. Johnson. *Public Papers of the Presidents.* 1963–1964, I.

Mississippi Advisory Committee to the United States Commission on Civil Rights. *Administration of Justice in Mississippi.* January 1963.

President's Committee on Equal Employment Opportunity. *The First Nine Months.* 1962.

—— *Report to the President.* 1963.

Report of the Attorney General. 1961, 1962, 1963.

U. S. Commission on Civil Rights. *Employment.* 1961.

—— *Federal Civil Rights Enforcement.* 1970.

—— *Federal Civil Rights Enforcement.* 1971.

—— *Interim Report.* April 16, 1963.

—— *Justice.* 1961.

—— *Voting.* 1961.

U. S. Congress. Senate. Committee on Commerce. *Freedom of Communications.* Report 994. 87th Cong., 1st sess.

IV. Books and Articles

Adams, Sherman. *Firsthand Report: The Story of the Eisenhower Administration.* New York: Harper, 1961.

Allen, Archie E. "John Lewis—Keeper of the Dream." *New South,* 26 (Spring 1971).

American Journey: The Times of Robert Kennedy. Interviews by Jean Stein, Edited by George Plimpton. New York: Harcourt Brace Jovanovich, 1970.

Anderson, Clinton P. with Milton Viorst. *Outsider in the Senate: Senator Anderson's Memoirs.* New York: World, 1970.

Anderson, J. W. *Eisenhower, Brownell, and the Congress: The Tangled Origins of the Civil Rights Bill of 1956–1957.* University, Alabama: University of Alabama Press, 1964.

Anderson, Jervis. *A. Philip Randolph: A Biographical Portrait.* New York: Harcourt Brace Jovanovich, 1973.

Baldwin, James. *The Fire Next Time.* New York: Dial, 1963.

——— "Letter from a Region in My Mind." *The New Yorker* (Nov. 17, 1962).

Barber, James David. *The Presidential Character: Predicting Performance in the White House.* Englewood Cliffs, N.J.: Prentice-Hall, 1972.

Barrett, Russell H. *Integration at Ole Miss.* Chicago: Quadrangle, 1965.

Bartley, Numan V. *From Thurmond to Wallace: Political Tendencies in Georgia, 1948–1968.* Baltimore: Johns Hopkins, 1973.

——— *The Rise of Massive Resistance: Race and Politics in the South During the 1950's.* Baton Rouge: Louisiana State University Press, 1969.

Bates, Daisy. *The Long Shadow of Little Rock.* New York: David McKay, 1962.

Berman, Daniel M. *A Bill Becomes a Law: Congress Enacts Civil Rights Legislation.* Second Edition. New York: Macmillan, 1966.

Berman, William J. *The Politics of Civil Rights in the Truman Administration.* Columbus: Ohio State University Press, 1970.

Bernstein, Barton J. "The Ambiguous Legacy: The Truman Administration and Civil Rights." *Politics and Policies of the Truman Administration.* Edited by Barton J. Bernstein. Chicago: Quadrangle, 1972.

——— "Election of 1952." *History of American Presidential Elections, 1789–1968,* IV. Edited by Arthur M. Schlesinger, Jr. New York: Chelsea House, 1971.

Bickel, Alexander M. *Politics and the Warren Court.* New York: Harper & Row, 1965.

Blossom, Virgil T. *It Has Happened Here.* New York: Harper & Row, 1959.

Booker, Simeon. *Black Man's America.* Englewood Cliffs, N.J.: Prentice-Hall, 1964.

Bowles, Chester. *Promises to Keep: My Years in Public Life, 1941–1969.* New York: Harper & Row, 1971.

Bradlee, Benjamin C. *Conversations with Kennedy.* New York: Norton, 1975.

Burns, James MacGregor. *John Kennedy: A Political Profile.* New York: Harcourt, Brace, 1959.

Campbell, Angus, Philip E. Converse, Warren E. Miller, Donald E. Stokes. *Elections and the Political Order.* New York: Wiley, 1966.

Chase, Harold W. *Federal Judges: The Appointing Process.* Minneapolis: University of Minnesota Press, 1972.

Converse, Philip E., Angus Campbell, Warren E. Miller, Donald E. Stokes. "Stability and Change in 1960: A Reinstating Election." *American Political Science Review,* 55 (June 1961).

Cosman, Bernard. "Presidential Republicanism in the South, 1960." *Journal of Politics*, 24 (May 1962).

Dalfiume, Richard M. *Desegregation of the U.S. Armed Forces: Fighting on Two Fronts, 1939–1953*. Columbia, Mo.: University of Missouri Press, 1969.

David, Paul T., ed. *The Presidential Election and Transition, 1960–1961*. Washington: Brookings Institution, 1961.

Dinneen, Joseph F. *The Kennedy Family*. Boston: Little, Brown, 1959.

Dixon, Robert G., Jr. *Democratic Representation: Reapportionment in Law and Politics*. New York: Oxford University Press, 1968.

Doar, John, and Dorothy Landsberg. *The Performance of the FBI in Investigating Violations of Federal Laws Protecting the Right to Vote—1960–1967*. n.p.: photocopy, 1971.

Donald, Aida DiPace, ed. *John F. Kennedy and the New Frontier*. New York: Hill & Wang, 1966.

Donovan, Robert J. *PT 109: John F. Kennedy in World War II*. New York: McGraw-Hill, 1961.

Dorman, Michael. *We Shall Overcome*. New York: Dial, 1964.

Douglas, Paul H. *In the Fullness of Time*. New York: Harcourt Brace Jovanovich, 1972.

——— "The 1960 Voting Rights Bill: The Struggle, the Final Results, and the Reasons." *Journal of Intergroup Relations*, I (Summer 1960).

Dulles, Foster Rhea. *The Civil Rights Commission, 1957–1965*. East Lansing, Mich.: Michigan State University Press, 1968.

Dunnigan, Alice Allison. *A Black Woman's Experience—From Schoolhouse to White House*. Philadelphia: Dorrance, 1973.

Eisenhower, Dwight D. *The White House Years: Mandate for Change, 1953–1956*. Garden City, N.Y.: Doubleday, 1963.

——— *The White House Years: Waging Peace, 1956–1961*. Garden City, N.Y.: Doubleday, 1965.

Elliff, John T. "Aspects of Federal Civil Rights Enforcement: The Justice Department and the FBI, 1939–1964." *Perspectives in American History*, 5 (1971).

Ely, James W., Jr. "Negro Demonstrations and the Law: Danville as a Test Case." *Vanderbilt Law Review*, 27 (October 1974).

Erskine, Hazel Gaudet. "The Polls: Kennedy as President." *Public Opinion Quarterly*, 28 (Summer 1964).

——— "The Polls: Race Relations." *Public Opinion Quarterly*, 26 (Spring 1962).

Evans, Rowland, and Robert Novak. *Lyndon Johnson: The Exercise of Power*. New York: New American Library, 1966.

Forman, James. *The Making of Black Revolutionaries*. New York: Macmillan, 1972.

Frady, Marshall. *Wallace*. New York: World, 1968.

Freund, Paul A. *On Law and Justice*. Cambridge: Harvard University Press, 1968.

Friedman, Leon, ed. *Southern Justice*. New York: Pantheon, 1965.

Galbraith, John Kenneth. *Ambassador's Journal: A Personal Account of the Kennedy Years*. Boston: Houghton Mifflin, 1969.

Gallup, George H. *The Gallup Poll: Public Opinion, 1935–1971*. New York: Random House, 1972.

Gelfand, Mark I. *A Nation of Cities: The Federal Government and Urban America, 1933–1965*. New York: Oxford University Press, 1975.

Golden, Harry. *Mr. Kennedy and the Negroes*. Cleveland: World, 1964.

Goldwater, Barry. *The Conscience of a Conservative*. New York: Hillman, 1960.

Gorman, Joseph Bruce. *Kefauver: A Political Biography*. New York: Oxford University Press, 1971.

Gosnell, Harold E., and Robert Martin. "The Negro as Voter and Officeholder." *Journal of Negro Education*, 32 (Fall 1963).

Greenberg, Jack. *Race Relations and American Law*. New York: Columbia University Press, 1959.

Guthman, Edwin. *We Band of Brothers*. New York: Harper & Row, 1971.

Hamilton, Charles V. *The Bench and the Ballot: Southern Federal Judges and Black Voters*. New York: Oxford University Press, 1973.

—— "Southern Judges and Negro Voting Rights: The Judicial Approach to the Solution of Controversial Social Problems." *Wisconsin Law Review* (Winter 1965).

Handlin, Oscar. "Party Maneuvers and Civil Rights Restrictions." *Commentary*, September, 1952.

Harvey, James C. *Civil Rights During the Kennedy Administration*. Hattiesburg, Miss.: University & College Press of Mississippi, 1971.

Havard, William C., ed. *The Changing Politics of the South*. Baton Rouge: Louisiana State University Press, 1972.

Hays, Brooks. *A Southern Moderate Speaks*. Chapel Hill: University of North Carolina Press, 1959.

Higham, Robin, ed. *Bayonets in the Streets: The Use of Troops in Civil Disturbances*. Lawrence, Kansas: University Press of Kansas, 1969.

Hodges, Luther H. *Businessman in the State House*. Chapel Hill: University of North Carolina Press, 1962.

Hughes, Emmet John. *The Ordeal of Power: A Political Memoir of the Eisenhower Years*. New York: Atheneum, 1963.

Kennedy, John F., ed. *As We Remember Joe*. Privately printed. Cambridge, Mass.: University Press, 1945.

—— *Profiles in Courage*. New York: Harper & Row, 1956.

—— *Why England Slept*. New York: Wilfred Funk, 1940.

Kennedy, Robert F. *The Enemy Within*. New York: Harper & Row, 1960.

—— *Just Friends and Brave Enemies*. New York: Harper & Row, 1962.

Kennedy, Rose Fitzgerald. *Times to Remember*. New York: Doubleday, 1974.

King, Coretta Scott. *My Life With Martin Luther King, Jr*. New York: Holt, Rinehart and Winston, 1969.

King, Martin Luther, Jr. *Strength to Love*. New York: Harper & Row, 1963.

——— *Stride Toward Freedom: The Montgomery Story*. New York: Harper & Row, 1958.

——— *Why We Can't Wait*. New York: Harper & Row, 1964.

Kluger, Richard. *Simple Justice: The History of Brown v. Board of Education and Black America's Struggle for Equality*. New York: Knopf, 1976.

Knapp, Daniel and Kenneth Polk. *Scouting the War on Poverty: Social Reform Politics in the Kennedy Administration*. Lexington, Mass.: Heath Lexington Books, 1971.

Koskoff, David E. *Joseph P. Kennedy: A Life and Times*. Englewood Cliffs, N.J.: Prentice-Hall, 1974.

Kunstler, William M. *Deep in My Heart*. New York: Morrow, 1966.

Larson, Arthur. *Eisenhower: The President Nobody Knew*. New York: Scribner, 1968.

"The Law and Civil Rights: The Justice Department in the South; An Interview with Thelton Henderson." *New University Thought*, 3, no. 4 (1963).

Lewis, Anthony. *Portrait of a Decade: The Second American Revolution*. New York: Random House, 1964.

Lewis, David L. *King: A Critical Biography*. New York: Praeger, 1970.

Lewis, Thomas P. "The Sit-In Cases: Great Expectations." *Supreme Court Review* (1963).

Lincoln, C. Eric. *The Black Muslims in America*. Boston: Beacon Press, 1961.

Lomax, Louis E. *The Negro Revolt*. New York: Harper, 1962.

Lord, Walter. *The Past That Would Not Die*. New York: Harper & Row, 1965.

McCoy, Donald R. and Richard Reutten. *Quest and Response: Minority Rights and the Truman Administration*. Lawrence, Kansas: University Press of Kansas, 1973.

McMillen, Neil R. *The Citizens' Council: Organized Resistance to the Second Reconstruction, 1954–64*. Urbana, Ill.: University of Illinois Press, 1971.

McNamara, Robert S. *The Essence of Security: Reflections in Office*. New York: Harper & Row, 1968.

MacNeil, Neil. *Dirksen: Portrait of a Public Man*. New York: World, 1970.

McPherson, Harry. *A Political Education*. Boston: Little, Brown, 1972.

Manchester, William. *The Death of a President*. New York: Harper & Row, 1967.

Marshall, Burke. *Federalism and Civil Rights*. New York: Columbia University Press, 1964.

——— "Federal Protection of Negro Voting Rights." *Law and Contemporary Problems*, 27 (Summer 1962).

——— "The Protest Movement and the Law." *Virginia Law Review*, 51 (June 1965).

——— "A Recollection of Robert Kennedy as a Lawyer." *Georgetown Law Journal*, 57 (October 1968).

——— Review of *Mississippi: The Closed Society* by James W. Silver. *Georgetown Law Journal*, 52 (Fall 1964).

Matthews, Donald R., and James W. Prothro. *Negroes and the New Southern Politics*. New York: Harcourt Brace Jovanovich, 1965.

Matusow, Allen J. "From Civil Rights to Black Power: The Case of SNCC, 1960–1966." *Twentieth Century America: Recent Interpretations*. Edited by Barton J. Bernstein and Allen J. Matusow. New York: Harcourt Brace Jovanovich, 1969.

Meier, August, and Elliot Rudwick. *CORE: A Study in the Civil Rights Movement, 1942–1968*. New York: Oxford University Press, 1973.

Meredith, James. *Three Years in Mississippi*. Bloomington, Ind.: Indiana University Press, 1966.

Middleton, Russell. "The Civil Rights Issue and Presidential Voting among Southern Negroes and Whites." *Social Forces*, 40 (March 1962).

Moody, Anne. *Coming of Age in Mississippi*. New York: Dial, 1968.

Moon, Henry Lee. *Balance of Power: The Negro Vote*. New York: Doubleday, 1948.

——— "The Negro Vote in the Presidential Election of 1956," *Journal of Negro Education*, 26 (Summer 1957).

Morgan, Charles, Jr. *A Time to Speak*. New York: Harper & Row, 1964.

Morgan, Ruth P. *The President and Civil Rights: Policy Making by Executive Order*. New York: St. Martin's, 1970.

Morrow, E. Frederic. *Black Man in the White House*. New York: Coward-McCann, 1963.

Munger, Frank J., and Richard F. Fenno, Jr. *National Politics and Federal Aid to Education*. Syracuse: Syracuse University Press, 1962.

Murphy, Paul L. *The Constitution in Crisis Times, 1918–1969*. New York: Harper & Row, 1972.

Murphy, Walter F. "The South Counter-attacks: The Anti-NAACP Laws." *Western Political Quarterly*, 12 (June 1959).

Muse, Benjamin. *The American Negro Revolution: From Nonviolence to Black Power, 1963–1967*. Bloomington, Ind.: Indiana University Press, 1968.

——— *Ten Years of Prelude: The Story of Integration Since the Supreme Court's 1954 Decision*. New York: Viking, 1964.

——— *Virginia's Massive Resistance*. Bloomington, Ind.: Indiana University Press, 1961.

Navasky, Victor S. *Kennedy Justice*. New York: Atheneum, 1971.

Newfield, Jack. *Robert Kennedy: A Memoir*. New York: Dutton, 1969.

Nixon, Richard M. *Six Crises*. Garden City, N.Y.: Doubleday, 1962.

O'Brien, Lawrence F. *No Final Victories: A Life in Politics from John F. Kennedy to Watergate*. Garden City, N.Y.: Doubleday, 1974.

O'Donnell, Kenneth P. and David F. Powers with Joe McCarthy. *"Johnny,*

We Hardly Knew Ye": *Memories of John Fitzgerald Kennedy*. Boston: Little, Brown, 1972.

Orfield, Gary. *The Reconstruction of Southern Education: The Schools and the 1964 Civil Rights Act*. New York: Wiley, 1969.

Parmet, Herbert S. *The Democrats: The Years After FDR*. New York: Macmillan, 1976.

―――― *Eisenhower and the American Crusades*. New York: Macmillan, 1972.

Patterson, James T. *Congressional Conservatism and the New Deal: The Growth of the Conservative Coalition in Congress, 1933–1939*. Lexington, Ky.: University Press of Kentucky, 1967.

Peck, James. *Freedom Ride*. New York: Simon & Schuster, 1962.

Peltason, J. W. *Fifty-Eight Lonely Men: Southern Federal Judges and School Desegregation*. New York: Harcourt. Brace & World, 1961.

Pool, Ithiel de Sola, Robert P. Abelson, Samuel L. Popkin. *Candidates, Issues and Strategies: A Computer Simulation of the 1960 Presidential Election*. Cambridge: Massachusetts Institute of Technology Press, 1964.

Powell, Adam Clayton, Jr. *Adam by Adam*. New York: Dial, 1971.

Rankin, Robert S., and Winfried R. Dallmayr. *Freedom and Emergency Powers in the Cold War*. New York: Appleton-Century-Crofts, 1964.

Rights for Americans: The Speeches of Robert F. Kennedy. Edited and with a commentary by Thomas A. Hopkins. Indianapolis: Bobbs-Merrill, 1964.

Rosenthal, Alan. *Toward Majority Rule in the United States Senate*. New York: McGraw-Hill, 1962.

Salinger, Pierre. *With Kennedy*. Garden City, N.Y.: Doubleday, 1966.

Sarratt, Reed. *The Ordeal of Desegregation: The First Decade*. New York: Harper & Row, 1966.

Scammon, Richard, compiler and editor. *America at the Polls: A Handbook of American Presidential Election Statistics, 1920–1964*. Pittsburgh: University of Pittsburgh Press, 1965.

Scheele, Henry Z. *Charlie Halleck: A Political Biography*. New York: Exposition Press, 1966.

Schlesinger, Arthur M., Jr. *A Thousand Days: John F. Kennedy in the White House*. Boston: Houghton Mifflin, 1965.

Sheatsley, Paul B., and Jacob J. Feldman. "The Assassination of President Kennedy: A Preliminary Report on Public Reactions and Behavior." *Public Opinion Quarterly*, 28 (Summer 1964).

Shuman, Howard E. "Senate Rules and the Civil Rights Bill." *American Political Science Review*, 51 (1957).

Sigel, Roberta S. "Race and Religion as Factors in the Kennedy Victory in Detroit, 1960." *Journal of Negro Education*, 31 (Fall 1962).

Silberman, Charles E. "The Businessman and the Negro." *Fortune*, September 1963.

Silver, James W. *Mississippi: The Closed Society*. New York: Harcourt, Brace & World, 1964.

Sindler, Allan P. "The Unsolid South: A Challenge to the Democratic Party." *The Uses of Power: 7 Cases in American Politics.* Edited by Alan F. Westin. New York: Harcourt, Brace & World, 1962.

Sitkoff, Harvard. "Harry Truman and the Election of 1948: The Coming of Age of Civil Rights in American Politics." *Journal of Southern History,* 37 (November 1971).

Sloane, Martin E. "One Year's Experience: Current and Potential Impact of the Housing Order." *George Washington Law Review,* 32 (March 1964).

—— and Monroe H. Freedman. "The Executive Order on Housing: The Constitutional Basis for What It Fails to Do." *Howard Law Journal,* 9 (Winter 1963).

Smith, Frank B. *Congressman from Mississippi.* New York: Pantheon, 1964.

Sobel, Lester A., ed. *Civil Rights, 1960–1966.* New York: Facts on File, 1967.

Sorensen, Theodore C. *Kennedy.* New York: Harper & Row, 1965.

Southern Regional Council. *The Federal Executive and Civil Rights.* Atlanta: Southern Regional Council, 1961.

—— *Law Enforcement in Mississippi.* Atlanta: Southern Regional Council, 1964.

Sovern, Michael I. *Legal Restraints on Racial Discrimination in Employment.* New York: Twentieth Century Fund, 1966.

Stampp, Kenneth M. *The Era of Reconstruction, 1865–1877.* New York: Knopf, 1965.

Strong, Donald S. *Negroes, Ballots and Judges: National Voting Rights Legislation in the Federal Courts.* University, Alabama: University of Alabama Press, 1968.

Sundquist, James L. *Politics and Policy: The Eisenhower, Kennedy and Johnson Years.* Washington, Brookings Institution, 1968.

Taylor, William L. "Federal Civil Rights Laws: Can They Be Made to Work." *George Washington Law Review,* 39 (July 1971).

—— *Hanging Together: Equality in an Urban Nation.* New York: Simon & Schuster, 1971.

Tefft, Sheldon. "United States v. Barnett: 'Twas a Famous Victory.' " *Supreme Court Review* (1964).

"Theories of Federalism and Civil Rights." *Yale Law Journal,* 75 (May 1966).

Tillett, Paul, ed. *Inside Politics: The National Conventions, 1960.* Dobbs Ferry, N.Y.: Oceana Publications, 1962.

Wasserstrom, Richard. Review of *Federalism and Civil Rights* by Burke Marshall. *University of Chicago Law Review,* 33 (Winter 1966).

Watters, Pat. *Dow to Now: Reflections on the Southern Civil Rights Movement.* New York: Pantheon, 1971.

—— and Reese Cleghorn. *Climbing Jacob's Ladder: The Arrival of Negroes in Southern Politics.* New York: Harcourt, Brace & World, 1967.

—— and Stephen Gillers, eds. *Investigating the FBI.* New York: Doubleday, 1973.

Weisberger, Bernard A. "The Dark and Bloody Ground of Reconstruction Historiography." *Journal of Southern History,* 25 (1959).

Whalen, Richard J. *The Founding Father: The Story of Joseph P. Kennedy.* New York: New American Library, 1964.

White, Theodore H. *The Making of the President, 1960.* New York: Atheneum, 1961.

Wicker, Tom. *JFK and LBJ: The Influence of Personality Upon Politics.* New York: Morrow, 1968.

Wofford, Harris. "The Law and Civil Disobedience." *Presbyterian Outlook,* September 26, 1960.

———— "Non-Violence and the Law: The Law Needs Help." *Journal of Religious Thought,* 15 (Autumn–Winter 1957–1958).

Wolfenstein, Martha and Gilbert Kleiman, eds. *Children and the Death of a President.* Garden City, N.Y.: Doubleday, 1965.

Zinn, Howard. *The Politics of History.* Boston: Beacon Press, 1970.

———— *SNCC: The New Abolitionists.* Boston: Beacon Press, 1965.

———— *The Southern Mystique.* New York: Knopf, 1964.

V. Dissertations and Theses

Curzan, Mary Hannah. "A Case Study in the Selection of Federal Judges: The Fifth Circuit, 1953–1963." Ph.D. diss., Yale University, 1968.

Elliff, John Thomas. "The United States Department of Justice and Individual Rights, 1937–1962." Ph.D. diss., Harvard University, 1967.

Nichols, Michael Cooper. " 'Cities Are What Men Make Them': Birmingham, Alabama Faces the Civil Rights Movement." Senior thesis, Brown University, 1974.

Stewart, John G. "Independence and Control: The Challenge of Senatorial Party Leadership." Ph.D. diss., University of Chicago, 1968.

Stoper, Emily Schottenfeld. "The Student Nonviolent Coordinating Committee: The Growth of Radicalism in a Civil Rights Organization." Ph.D. diss., Harvard University, 1968.

Sullivan, Donald Francis. "The Civil Rights Program of the Kennedy Administration: A Political Analysis." Ph.D. diss., University of Oklahoma, 1965.

Young, Roy Earl. "Presidential Leadership and Civil Rights Legislation, 1963–1964." Ph.D. diss., University of Texas at Austin, 1969.

VI. Newspapers

Afro-American (Baltimore), 1960–1963.   Montgomery *Advertiser,* 1960–1963.

Atlanta *Constitution,* 1961–1963.   New York *Times,* 1957–1963.

Atlanta *Daily World,* 1960.   Pittsburgh *Courier,* 1960–1963.

Birmingham *Post Herald,* Nov., 1963.   *Wall Street Journal,* 1960–1963.

VII. Periodicals

Business Week, 1961–1963.
Commonweal, 1961–1963.
Congressional Quarterly Almanac, 1957–1964.
The Crisis, 1960–1963.
Current History, 1960–1963.
Department of State Bulletin, 1961.
Ebony, 1960–1963.
Freedomways, 1961–1964.
Harper's Magazine, 1961–1964.
Jet, 1960.
Liberation, 1961–1963.
Life, 1960–1963.
Look, 1961–1963.

The Nation, 1957–1963.
National Review, 1961–1963.
Negro History Bulletin, 1961–1963.
New Republic, 1957–1963.
New South, 1961–1964.
Newsweek, 1960–1963.
The Reporter, 1961–1963.
Saturday Evening Post, 1961–1963.
Saturday Review, 1961–1963.
I. F. Stone's Bi-Weekly, 1963.
I. F. Stone's Weekly, 1961–1963.
Time, 1960–1963.
US News and World Report, 1961–1963.
Vital Speeches, 1961–1963.

VIII. Personal Interviews

Branton, Wiley A.
Confidential sources.
Doar, John.
Dunbar, Leslie.
Freund, Paul.
Jordan, William H., Jr.

Lawson, Marjorie M.
Lewis, John.
Marshall, Burke.
Martin, Louis.
Mitchell, Clarence.
Wilkins, Roy.

IX. Miscellaneous

Facts on Film. Southern Education Reporting Service. 1960–1963.

Letter. David Herbert Donald to Mrs. J. G. Randall, March 6, 1962. Copy given to author by David Herbert Donald.

Letter. Harold C. Fleming to author, Mary 16, 1972.

Moses et al. v. Kennedy, Hoover. 219 F Supp 762 (1963).

"The 1964 Civil Rights Act." Conference at Yale University Law School. April 7, 1973. Panelists: William McCulloch, Nicholas Katzenbach, Burke Marshall, Emanuel Celler, Clarence Mitchell, John G. Stewart.

"A Stroke of the Pen: Dimensions of a Presidential Decision." Film for the John F. Kennedy Library. Produced by Envision Corporation, 1975.

Index